D0741939

Rebel and Saint

Comparative Studies on Muslim Societies
General Editor, Barbara D. Metcalf

Rebel and Saint

Muslim Notables, Populist Protest, Colonial Encounters (Algeria and Tunisia, 1800–1904)

JULIA A. CLANCY-SMITH

University of California Press

BERKELEY   LOS ANGELES   LONDON

University of California Press
Berkeley and Los Angeles, California

University of California Press, Ltd.
London, England

Chapter 7 includes material that appeared in three essays previously
published by the author: "The Shaykh and His Daughter: Coping in
Colonial Algeria," in *Struggle and Survival in the Modern Middle
East*, ed. Edmund Burke, III (Berkeley: University of California Press,
1993); "The House of Zainab: Female Authority and Saintly
Succession in Colonial Algeria," in *Women and Gender in Middle
Eastern History: Shifting Boundaries in Sex and Gender*, ed. Nikki R.
Keddie and Beth Baron (New Haven: Yale University Press, 1992);
and "The 'Passionate Nomad' Reconsidered: A European Woman in
L'Algérie Française (Isabelle Eberhardt, 1877–1904)," in *Western
Women and Imperialism: Complicity and Resistance*, ed. Nupur
Chaudhuri and Margaret Strobel (Bloomington: Indiana University
Press, 1992). Reprinted by permission of the publishers.

Library of Congress Cataloging-in-Publication Data

Clancy-Smith, Julia A.
    Rebel and saint : Muslim notables, populist protest, colonial
encounters : Algeria and Tunisia, 1800–1904 / Julia A. Clancy-Smith.
        p.   cm. — (Comparative studies on Muslim societies ; 18)
    Includes bibliographical references and index.
    ISBN 0-520-08242-7
    1. Algeria—History—1516–1830.   2. Algeria—History—1830–
1962.   3. Tunisia—History—1516–1881.   4. Tunisia—History—
1881–1956.   5. Islam and politics—Algeria.   6. Islam and politics—
Tunisia.   7. Sufis—Algeria—Political activity.   8. Sufis—Tunisia—
Political activity.   I. Title.   II. Series.
DT294.C56   1994
965—dc20   93-17223
                                                                   CIP

Printed in the United States of America
9   8   7   6   5   4   3   2   1

The paper used in this publication meets the minimum requirements
of American National Standard for Information Sciences—Permanence
of Paper for Printed Library Materials, ANSI Z39.48-1984. ⊚

*To Elisabeth Anna Smith and Charles D. Smith
and the late Dr. Martin Joseph Clancy II*

Contents

Maps

Preface

Al-mashakil jayya min al-Jaza'ir.

There is a popular saying in the Jarid (Djerid), the oasis region adjoining the borders with Algeria, regarding Tunisia's historically more powerful neighbor: "Al-mashakil jayya min al-Jaza'ir" ("problems come from Algeria"). This proverb, which repeatedly came up in conversations with the Jarid's people, assumed a new significance after the Algerian FIS's (Islamic Salvation Front) triumph in the first round of legislative elections held on 26 December 1991. While many Tunisians of different classes, educations, or backgrounds believe that the Tunisian Islamic party (al-Nahda) could never score an electoral victory similar in scale to that of the FIS, still people fret about the possible across-the-border effects from the Algerian elections. Aside from the renewed vigor, or at least hope, that events in Algeria might instill in Tunisia's Islamic parties, the average inhabitant of the Jarid worries about the repercussions on tourism, which now forms the basis of the area's fragile economy. Concerns about the tourist industry, which fluctuates in accordance with global political and economic changes, are shared widely in a Tunisia dependent upon the income generated by foreign visitors, mainly from Europe.

Deep social discontents now beset the three Maghribi nations. Islamist parties and platforms serve more as powerful stimuli for larger and as yet uncharted movements whose complex origins lie in both the colonial and independence eras. After religiously based populist protest was ground under the heel of modern European armies and bureaucracies by the early part of this century, religious figures retreated into ostensibly nonpolitical attempts at cultural salvation. This was true both in Algeria during the interwar period, where the Reformed Ulama of Shaykh 'Abd al-Hamid b. Badis (died 1940) wielded cultural weapons to redeem and renew Muslim society, and in Tunisia, where the Khalduniyya and other reform groups sought to regenerate quietly from within. In this same period, the political torch passed to more or less secular nationalists who, while deploying Islamic symbols and discourse, made use of Western ideologies and institutions to expel, with great violence in Algeria's case, France from North Africa. These political arrangements fought for, worked out, and negotiated over from the 1930s on are now being contested in city streets, campuses, mosques, and other forums, old and new. After a hiatus of many decades, religious notables cum political actors are once again on center stage—or at least trying to reach that stage—in the Maghrib's capitals as well as in many places in the Islamic world. Yet the question remains of how religious militants of the late twentieth century, like Abbasi Madani, for example, relate to the Bu Ziyans or 'Abd al-Qadirs of the century past, the age of early, heroic resistance. And can this heroic age, however imagined, be recovered or redeployed to meet the moral and social challenges of the present and future?

Numerous Tunisians voiced another worry stemming from Algeria's painful, fledgling experiment in democracy, one that relates directly to a second, related theme of this study—the potential mass movement into Tunisia of Algerians unwilling to live under an Islamic regime which has announced its intent to impose substantial modifications in dress, food, and living habits upon its citizens. With the doors to Europe closed ever more firmly to North Africans, and with growing uncertainty about Algeria's political future, many Algerians with financial and family connections in Tunisia are openly talking about emigration.

In the nineteenth century, subjects of the fallen Turkish regime fled eastward as individuals or groups to Tunisia soon after France's 1830 occupation of Algeria. Even after 1881, when Tunisia unwillingly became a French protectorate, this current of emigration persisted, although on a somewhat reduced scale. While there is a certain parallelism in the movements of people between the two countries in the nineteenth century and the final decade of the twentieth, a fundamental difference also exists. Those Algerians who took flight from the French army came to Tunisia principally to escape life under a Christian power which regarded Islam, its beliefs, practices, and institutions, as the single greatest obstacle to France's imperial agenda—to make Algeria French. Due to the centuries-old ties between the two Ottoman regencies, the advent of the Europeans with their imposing armies, weapons, technologies, and land-hungry settlers had a prodigious impact upon Tunisia. Conversely, that Tunisia welcomed the emigrants from next door, affording a refuge for dissidents, had an enormous influence upon the evolution of politics in Algeria and the political behavior of Algerian dissidents.

The Tunisian beylik provided assistance to beleaguered fellow Muslims from Algeria in numerous ways. Being respected Muslim princes, the rulers (*beys*) of the Husaynid dynasty (c. 1715–1957) were looked to for deliverance—as potential rescuers from the humiliations and travails of foreign occupation. The Tunisian provinces along the borders with Algeria and their towns, such as Nafta (Nefta), Tala (Thala), and al-Kaf (el-Kef), served as temporary or permanent havens for migrants or bases of militant action for rebels. Military supplies and basic necessities from Tunisia, designated as "contraband" by French officials, flowed across the frontiers despite concerted colonial efforts to halt exchanges of goods and peoples between the two countries. Rumors, news, and information about events in Europe or the Ottoman Empire also reached Algeria through the Tunisian beylik. Finally, Tunisia represented a pole of religious attraction for Algerians, particularly those from the Constantine (Algeria's eastern province) and from the upper Sahara. As Islamic education progressively deteriorated under the willed neglect or active hostility of the French regime in Algeria, Tunisia's *madrasas* (religious colleges), sufi *zawaya* (plural of *zawiya*, a sufi center), and its great mosque-university, the Zaytuna, located in the capital, offered religious and other kinds of instruction to students and scholars from France's colony. In the past century, Algerian students might first have come here to the Jarid, especially to the oasis of Nafta regarded as a provincial holy city, second only to al-Qayrawan (Kairouan), to seek Islamic instruction in its numerous sufi centers and madrasas. The most gifted and ambitious would then pursue advanced learning in the capital at the feet of the Zaytuna's erudite masters.

In large measure, Tunisia's attraction for Algerian religious and other figures explains the political trajectory of both countries in the past century. If sufi orders have traditionally crisscrossed various kinds of borders and frontiers—political as well as spiritual and social—protest movements in nineteenth-century North Africa did likewise. Indeed it can be argued that the physical and moral displacement of Algerian sufi leaders from the Rahmaniyya, Tijaniyya, and Qadiriyya orders into southwestern Tunisia brought the French colonial encounter into Tunisia's backyard.

When Arabic printing presses became widely available in Tunis by the close of the nineteenth century, the city functioned as a publishing center for Algerian scholars seeking to have religious works printed which the European-controlled publishing establishment in Algeria declined to handle. This development explains why the biography of the great Algerian Rahmaniyya shaykh, Sidi Muhammad b. Abi al-Qasim (c. 1823–1897), who lived and died in al-Hamil (el-Hamel), a small oasis not far from Bu Sa'ada (Bou Saada), was only printed in Tunis (c. 1890).

And the fact that I had to travel to Rabat to consult the writings of Muhammad ibn 'Abd al-Rahman al-Jurjuri, the Algerian founder of the Rahmaniyya brotherhood *(tariqa)* whose spiritual lessons are currently housed in Morocco's al-Khizana al-'Amma collection, is significant. It provides evidence not only for Sidi 'Abd al-Rahman's own journeys and spiritual itinerary but also for the geographic range of his reputation as well as the movements of his disciples, ideas, and imitators during the years following the master's death in the last decade of the eighteenth century.

Tuzar, the Jarid
6 January 1992

Acknowledgments

My own peregrinations to gather information on the religious notables and other dramatis personae who figure in this study took me far and wide—to some ten archival collections and libraries on three continents. These journeys, a form of research nomadism, and the wealth of documentation amassed would not have been possible without the beneficent support, financial and otherwise, of a large number of institutions and individuals. While I can never hope to repay the debt which stretches back more years than I care to recall, I can at least acknowledge the extent of my liabilities.

My deep respect for, and abiding interest in, the Maghrib and its gracious people began with the Peace Corps in Tunisia in 1973, where we, the volunteers, had the good fortune to learn about all things Tunisian from Laurence O. Michalak, then the summer training director. Larry's enthusiasm for the country was infectious and has remained with me until this day. Subsequently, I studied North African history with John Ruedy at Georgetown University, who proved to be a formidable intellectual mentor then as he still is now. Other Georgetown faculty, former and present, to whom I owe a debt of gratitude are Thomas Ricks, Barbara Stowasser, and Michael Hudson, to name only a few. In 1977 while still at Georgetown, I had the uncommon privilege of serving as Jacques Berque's teaching assistant, the start of a long intellectual friendship which later continued in France as well as in California. From 1978 on the G. E. von Grunebaum Center for Near Eastern Studies and the History Department of the University of California, Los Angeles, offered extensive financial assistance and intellectual inspiration. The UCLA faculty also deserve special mention: Claude Audebert, Edward Berenson, Nikki R. Keddie, the late Malcolm Kerr, Afaf Lutfi al-Sayyid Marsot, who kindly served as a mentor, friend, and as the chair of my dissertation committee, Georges Sabagh, and many others. Over the past decade, Edmund Burke III, of the University of California, Santa Cruz, has acted as an invaluable intellectual preceptor as I delved into the thicket of popular protest. Ross E. Dunn of San Diego State University also has provided much encouragement. In addition, L. Carl Brown, Dale F. Eickelman, R. Stephen Humpfreys, and John Voll have offered greatly appreciated suggestions for improving portions of the manuscript.

My years at Georgetown University and the University of California, Los Angeles, were punctuated by extended periods of study in France. While in Paris at the École des Hautes Études en Sciences Sociales in 1976–1977, I had the opportunity to study with Mme. Germaine Tillion. Subsequently, the French government provided me with the financial wherewithal to study with Jacques Berque at the Collège de France, Paris, in 1980, a richly rewarding experience. I also had the opportunity to attend Lucette Valensi's stimulating seminars in Paris that year and again in 1982. Numerous research trips to the Maghrib and Europe from 1981 until the present were funded by the following institutions and organizations: the Social Science Research Council; Fulbright-Hays International Doctoral Dissertation Program; Council for International Exchange of Scholars/ Fulbright Islamic Civilization Program; American Philosophical Society; and the American Institute for Maghrebi Studies. The University of Virginia provided summer faculty research grants and a year of leave from teaching responsibilities to write.

On the other side of the Atlantic and on the southern shores of the Mediterranean, the staffs of numerous archives and libraries in Tunisia, Morocco, France, Great Britain, and Malta have greatly facilitated my research forays, particularly Monsieur Moncef Fakhfakh of the Dar el-Bey, Tunis, and Mme. Jeanne Mrad of the Centre d'Études Maghrébines à Tunis. Special thanks are also due to the very efficient staff of the Bibliothèque Générale in Rabat and its director, Mohamed Ben Sherifa. Beyond institutional support, Tunisian colleagues and friends have provided all manner of sustenance to me and my family over the years: Alya Baffoun, Samya El Mechat, Khalid Mrad, Pat and Dick Payne, Noura and Mohamed Rostom, Fredj Stambouli, Abdeljelil Temimi, and countless others who have overwhelmed us with their hospitality. Closer to home, colleagues and graduate students at the University of Virginia have also contributed in one way or another to the present endeavor: Richard Barnett, Timothy Faulkner, Robert Fuller, Patrick Gibbons, R. Carey Goodman, Ann Lane, Melvyn Leffler, Cynthia Metcalf, Farzaneh Milani, and Joseph Miller.

Still closer to home, my greatest debt is to my husband, Charles ("Carl") D. Smith, who has, with unfailing good humor, read many drafts of this manuscript, both in early incarnations as a dissertation and in later versions, and has suffered for years from the effects of the distracted spouse syndrome. My daughter, Elisabeth, "helped" in her own inimitable way by inquiring cheerfully, if a bit impatiently, after school every day: "Have you finished your book today, Mommy?" Elisabeth is happy to know that I will now be spending much less time with strangers like Bu Ziyan and more with her.

Note on Transliteration

Anyone who has traveled across North Africa's beautiful landscapes is acquainted with the intractable problems posed by the transliteration of proper names, geographical places, concepts, and institutions. These have their origins in classical Arabic, vernacular Arabic, Berber dialects, Ottoman Turkish, and, in many cases, have come down to English speakers from French. To complicate matters, during the colonial era in the Maghrib, Arabic and Berber terms were frequently rendered from colloquial forms into the French language. While total consistency is impossible, I have attempted to stay as close to the written Arabic in rendering proper names and places as is feasible without unduly confusing the reader who may be more familiar with another system of transliteration. Thus, for example, Nefta becomes Nafta, but the western province of Algeria remains Oran instead of Wahran. For the names of geographical regions, I have mainly relied upon Jamil M. Abun-Nasr's *A History of the Maghrib in the Islamic Period*, which strikes me as achieving a reasonable compromise between the correct Arabic rendition and differing usage. As for proper names and institutions, only the ayn (') and hamza (') are employed in the text and notes. Full diacritics are provided for the glossary. Moreover, words more widely used in English, for example, *ulama*, appear without diacritics. The system of transliteration is that employed by the *International Journal of Middle East Studies*.

Chronology

1525
Algeria incorporated into Ottoman Empire

1574
Tunisia incorporated into Ottoman Empire

1668–present
'Alawi dynasty in power in Morocco

c. 1715–c. 1793
Life of Sidi Muhammad b. 'Abd al-Rahman, founder of the Rahmaniyya sufi order

1715
Husaynid dynasty established in Tunisia; abolished in 1957

1792
Spanish evacuation of Oran in western Algeria

1808–1839
Reign of Ottoman sultan, Mahmud II

1822–1859
Reign of Sultan 'Abd al-Rahman of Morocco

April 1827
The dey of Algiers, Husayn, has an altercation with the French consul, Pierre Deval

June 1827
French naval squadron imposes blockade of Algiers

14 June 1830
French landing at Sidi Ferruch

5 July 1830
Husayn Dey signs convention with France; French flag raised over qasba in Algiers

July 1830
  Charles X Restoration government falls; Louis Philippe comes to power
1830–1847
  Ahmad, last bey of the Constantine, attempts to establish an independent state in eastern Algeria
1832–1847
  Amir 'Abd al-Qadir leads resistance movement, mainly centered in the Oran
1837–1855
  Ahmad Bey comes to power in Tunisia; initiates modernization and reform program
1840
  Thomas Bugeaud appointed governor-general of Algeria; institutes the policy of total occupation of the country
1844
  French army under the Duc d'Aumale lays siege twice to the oasis of Biskra
1844
  Bureaux Arabes officially created
1844
  Mustafa b. 'Azzuz emigrates from Algeria to the Tunisian Jarid; begins constructing a Rahmaniyya zawiya in the oasis of Nafta
1844
  Defeat of Moroccan army by France at battle of Isly convinces Sultan 'Abd al-Rahman to withdraw support for 'Abd al-Qadir's jihad
1848
  Second Republic declared; Algeria formally made French territory divided into three *départements*
1849
  Bu Ziyan launches a millenarian rebellion centered in Za'atsha
1849
  French army lays siege to Za'atsha and pre-Sahara for 52 days during October and November
1850–1855
  Jihad led by the Sharif of Warqala, Muhammad b. 'Abd Allah, in Algerian and Tunisian pre-Sahara
1851
  European settlers in Algeria number 131,283; over 115,000 hectares of land expropriated
1852
  Fall of al-Aghwat to French army

1854
Fall of Tuqqurt to French army
1857
Marshal Louis Randon takes the Kabylia
1871–1872
Muqrani rebellion in eastern Algeria
1823–1897
Life of Shaykh Muhammad b. Abi al-Qasim, founder of the Rah-
maniyya center of al-Hamil
c. 1850–1904
Life of Zaynab, daughter of the shaykh of al-Hamil; directs Rahmaniyya
zawiya of al-Hamil, 1897–1904
1864
Revolt of the Awlad Sidi al-Shaykh in western Algeria
March 1881
French troops invade Tunisia from Algeria
1883
Convention of al-Marsa makes Tunisia a French protectorate

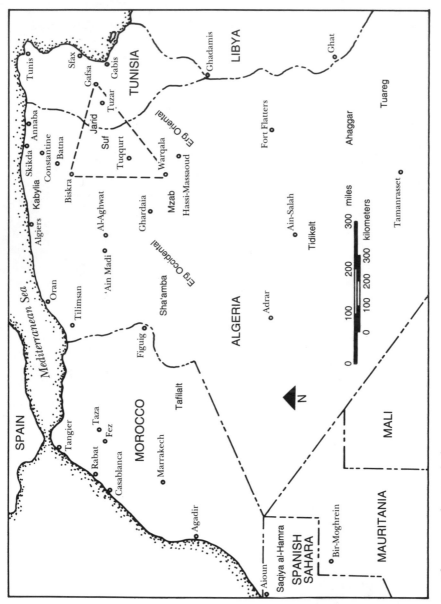

1. The present-day Maghrib

Introduction

As the nineteenth century drew to a close, an Algerian female saint and sufi, residing in a small oasis on the Sahara's upper rim, composed a letter containing gentle rebukes to local French military officials: "I beg you to display solicitude and friendship by keeping away from me people who are unjust and disturb the peace and to examine attentively my case from the legal viewpoint since you are just and equitable."[1] Why was an Algerian woman, Lalla Zaynab, reminding colonial authorities of their duties while simultaneously characterizing France's rule as "just" and "equitable"? Are Zaynab's words and the fact that she corresponded with Algeria's foreign masters to be interpreted as evidence of collaboration or of accommodation? Were her actions unusual or was Zaynab, a Muslim woman revered for her piety and erudition, merely acting as other religious notables did in the past century? And what do letters appealing to those ostensibly monopolizing certain kinds of power betray about the nature of relations between colonizer and colonized, about the cultures of colonialism?

The present study seeks to change the way we think about North African history during the turbulent nineteenth century.[2] This perhaps immodest objective results from a decade of painstaking inquiry into the political behavior of a group of provincial, yet regionally powerful, Muslim notables and their clienteles. The complex responses of these notables, both individual and collective, to the imposition of the French colonial regime upon Algeria after 1830 shaped, indeed altered, the course of Maghribi history. That history and that century were fashioned by a succession of encounters between the peoples of North Africa on the one hand and the twin forces of European imperialism and the larger world economy on the other. In these multiple confrontations, inconclusive skirmishes, bet hedging, implicit pacts, and prudent retreats were as important to historical process as

1

violent clashes or heroic last stands. But first these encounters, involving religious notables and ordinary people alike, must be examined on three levels, all of them intertwined.

The first is the local level—the world of Saharan religious figures and the tribal or village folk who constituted their followers. Seemingly remote due to geographical location from the century's prevailing currents of historical change, these peoples were in fact caught up in much wider, relentless processes. To varying degrees, they were painfully aware of the larger, often menacing forces around them. Their collective *mentalité* was in part constructed through a ceaseless filtering of information and news received from "outside." And that "outside" was itself continuously shifting. At times it could mean no more than the next oasis or a regional pilgrimage center; at others, the world beyond was comprised of a North African capital or the cities of the *Mashriq* (eastern Arab world) and Hijaz. As colonialism gained momentum in the Maghrib, the outside came to include places, people, and events in Europe.

The next level was that of the Islamic ecumene, which for North Africans stretched from the shores of the Atlantic and Mediterranean deep into the Sahara and eastward to the Mashriq-Hijaz complex, while also encompassing Istanbul, the imperial core for both Algeria and Tunisia. More or less direct and continuous links between the local community and *Dar al-Islam* (the Islamic world) nurtured socioreligious aspirations and political programs, while sharpening, particularly for the Algerians under French rule, the sense of moral loss and outrage. In the Islamic world, local communities often looked to local religious notables to explain, manage, or broker events and changes unleashed by triumphant European imperialism. From this perspective, the reactions of Saharan peoples to the deepening crises of the nineteenth century have a resonance with collective responses elsewhere in Africa or Asia.

Finally, the last tier relates to world history. World-system theory has tended to ignore peoples located on the margins of non-Western states.[3] As will be argued, the inhabitants of the North African hinterland were neither the silent victims of imperial thrusts into their lands nor the passive subjects of Muslim rulers seeking to counter those thrusts through modernization programs. Not only did the provincial Muslim notables and common folk studied here confront—and perhaps comprehend, if somewhat dimly—the outside forces intervening in society but they also sought to manipulate them to their advantage, sometimes successfully, at other times less so. For the purposes of this study, *notables* refers to holy persons regarded by their communities as legitimately and simultaneously claiming the status of saint (*waliy*), sufi, and scholar (*'alim*).[4] The collective biographies of these saints, sufis, and *'ulama'* (ulama) span not only the supple frontiers between eastern Algeria (the Constantine) and Tunisia but also bridge several generations of holy persons, male and female. For the most part, these holy persons resided within a specific ecological environment, the pre-Sahara, in both Algeria and Tunisia, although the adjacent mountains of the Awras (Aurès) also participated in the political and religious rhythms of the region. Their followings were tribespeople, villagers, and oasis peasants as well as "secular" elites—tribal big men, desert princes, or the great families, allied first with the Turks and subsequently the colonial regime. The struggles of these elites, local and otherwise, to snatch the remnants of the partially toppled Turkish state after 1830, and thereby turn adversity to personal advantage, molded the political world in which the Muslim notables lived. Finally, while most of the notables studied here were members of one branch of the Rahmaniyya tariqa—the Saharan Rahmaniyya—other sufi orders and other types of religious leaders, principally rebellious *mahdi*s (Muslim redeemers), also figure in the historical narrative.

The common folk, too, play a not insignificant role as clients and disciples of privileged saintly lineages and sufi masters; on more than one occasion, ordinary people worked as pressure groups for or against specific kinds of political action. In several instances, they obliged reticent religious patrons to plunge into the uncertainties of populist protest.[5] And it was the colonial regime's abiding fear of collective unrest which compelled French authorities to seek compromises with religious notables. In addition to acting as both followers and advocates, people of modest substance actively contributed to politics as bearers of news, information, and rumors. These rumors articulated a language of power which boldly defied France's divinely ordained civilizing mission. Thus, these rumors had an ideological dimension, and as such they constituted a form of implicit political discourse in a society of restricted literacy. Finally, due to the turmoil of the conquest era in North Africa, followers or disciples might be transformed into leaders.

Bu Ziyan (Abu Ziyan), the self-styled messianic leader of the 1849 Za'atsha (Zaatcha) revolt, originally came from the ranks of the humble. The mahdi of Warqala (Ouargla), Muhammad b. 'Abd Allah, who led a sequel rebellion between 1851 and 1855, was also of modest origins. Like Bu Ziyan, his uncommon acts of piety propelled him from the margins of the rural religious establishment onto the center stage of anticolonial resistance. Of course, for ordinary people, active participation even in religiously sanctioned jihad was not an "unalloyed impulse" for it offered the opportunity to best local rivals or settle outstanding scores.[6]

But this is more than an investigation of the most dramatic manifestation of collective action and protest—armed revolt. For it seeks to dredge up the subterranean sociocultural universe which made rebellion possible and imaginable or conversely impeded such. Thus the "how" of rebellion is as important as its causation; revolt serves as a vehicle for exploring other relationships, particularly how events from "outside" were experienced by those caught in their wake. Many of these forces have been buried under the debris of the upheavals associated with France's lengthy pacification of her unsubmissive African *département*. Moreover, all of the options available to religious notables, tribal elites, and ordinary people are explored as they strove to oppose and challenge, or merely cope and come to terms with, the devastating reality of foreign conquest.

The underlying assumption here is that various kinds of sociopolitical action—bet hedging, revolt, shifting trade strategies, migration, withdrawal, or avoidance protest—were in the aggregate the main motors of historical change during much of the past century rather than alternative forces, such as novel technologies, new economic systems, or new classes. Nevertheless, the narrative is perhaps unduly prejudiced toward the more flamboyant expressions of collective grievances—movements led by mahdist rebels—since these are the best documented for the nineteenth century.[7]

What follows is an investigation of the political behavior of religious notables and other figures, or more accurately, of the implicit cultural norms governing that behavior. For just as there existed a moral economy of peasant rebellion, the political behavior of Muslim notables was dictated by shared and commonly accepted norms.[8] In addition, it is argued that even as jihad was proclaimed or the millennium predicted, implicit pacts were being tentatively worked out between some religious notables and representatives of the colonial order. These unstated agreements were crucial to modern Algerian history since they permitted the survival of her cultural patrimony in a society literally and figuratively under siege.

Political action thus is broadly defined to include not only participation in jihads or mahdist movements but also such things as moral persuasion, propaganda, *hijra* (emigration), evasion, withdrawal, and accommodation with the colonial regime. Indeed, many of these strategies were continually merged—employed together or alternatively—as North Africans, whether of notable status or humble station, sought to create a space where the impact of asymmetrical power could be attenuated. In this most failed, a few succeeded, and some achieved success in failure.

To the extent that the sources permit, the story—or rather collection of stories—is told from the perspective of the North African population. To the indigenous inhabitants of the desert or mountains, the worlds of military and civilian authorities as well as of the European *colons* (settlers) appeared as distant, strange, and hostile; this was true for much of the nineteenth century. The brutal suppression of uprisings aside, the colonial regime's authority was remote, experienced unevenly, and in some cases mediated through familiar intermediaries, among them, sufi *shaykhs* (masters). Nevertheless, information and rumors about the curious, if repellent, foreigners reached the village and tribe, contributing to a local worldview of a social order overturned. Therefore, I have attempted to portray events, transformations, and the daily flow of life from the peculiar vantage point of those concerned. And most of these stories have not been told or have enjoyed only a partial hearing.

Until now two constructs, one colonial and the other indigenous, regarding the political behavior of religious leaders, particularly sufi shaykhs, during the conquest era have prevailed. Moreover, the periodization of modern North African history has been informed in large measure by these two competing models of the political behavior of Muslim notables. The colonial model held that certain sufi orders, especially the Rahmaniyya and its leaders, were inherently political, thus resolutely opposed to Algeria's French masters throughout the past century: "Everywhere, the leaders of the Rahmaniyya order exhort their followers to revolt against French domination."[9] However, embedded within the colonial canon and in colonial sources and largely adopted uncritically by postcolonial authors, is another, more ambiguous, nuanced account of how religious notables reacted to and contended with foreign domination. Many were in fact risk avoiders more than last-ditch resisters.

Rather than enthusiastically enlisting in militant programs to expel the intruding Europeans, local Muslim notables found to their dismay that politics intruded, cruelly at times, more subtly at others, into their spiritual bailiwicks or mundane affairs. For many saints and sufis, had politics not come to find them the preferred mode of coping would have surely been to ignore the presence of the infidels—and thereby come to terms with it.[10] This risk avoidance on the part of religious figures is seen in both the uprisings studied here, the 1849 Za'atsha revolt and the rebellion inspired by the self-proclaimed mahdi Muhammad b. 'Abd Allah. Simply stated, I have employed a biographical case study approach to debunk the myth that Muslim notables, especially the Rahmaniyya, were invariably the causative agents in anticolonial resistance in the rebellious half century stretching from 1830 to 1871—only to subsequently become compliant collaborators in the French imperial experiment.

Moreover, some of the Rahmaniyya erudites of the pre-Sahara challenge characterizations of the North African holy man as a "warrior saint" or "martial marabout" who fused "strong-man politics with holy-man piety."[11] In fact many of the most puissant saints were reluctant to take up the cudgels of violent protest even when participation in revolt held forth the promise of deliverance from infidel rule. This diffidence had many causes—the personality of the religious notable in question, the spiritual politics then in force between sufi-saintly lineages and their holy rivals, the demands and needs of followers, and how different events were perceived and lived. It was rather the mahdi, and the collective will of popular followings, that together forced some hesitant religious leaders into the tumult of the political arena, often with disastrous consequences.

The second paradigm of saintly behavior—the indigenous—is found in the writings of the Algerian scholar, Muhammad al-Hafnawi, and to a lesser extent, in those of the Tunisian chronicler, Ahmad ibn Abi al-Diyaf.[12] Both of these writers' works offer invaluable biographical sketches of sufis, saints, ulama, and other notables residing both in the cities and countryside. If the colonial literature portrayed sufi activists, such as Shaykh Mustafa b. 'Azzuz (c. 1800–1866), as scheming behind-the-scenes foes of France's grand design for North Africa, indigenous accounts from the period usually omit any mention of overtly political acts by religious figures. Thus was the nature and social uses of hagiography in this period.[13] But the silence of traditional sources should not be construed as some sort of subterfuge. Rather the silence itself speaks loudly about hidden cultural norms defining the supple boundaries between the realms of the political and the religious.

One thesis is that an underground yet momentous transformation unfolded quietly sometime during the tumultuous era of Algeria's conquest (1830–1871) and the century's close. This transformation involved the establishment of unstated, although compelling, pacts between prominent religious figures, such as Muhammad b. Abi al-Qasim (c. 1823–1897) and his daughter, Lalla Zaynab (c. 1850–1904), and colonial officials. The elaboration of these unwritten contracts and their observance by both parties meant that Algerian Muslim culture survived and in some cases was able to flourish modestly under the less than favorable circumstances of the period. Moreover, by taking the historical narrative down to 1904, the date of Lalla Zaynab's death, I suggest the existence of unsuspected continuities between the early conquest epoch and later periods; some of the transformations normally associated with the Third Republic were already incipient or well under way prior to the Muqrani (Mokrani) revolt of 1871.

Movement and Movements

This is also a story about various kinds of movement—physical displacements such as travel, migration, pilgrimage, flight—and social or spiritual journeys from one status to another. And movement of whatever sort implies borders and boundaries, implicating those who either bridged frontiers or conversely kept them in place. By adhering to the nascent Rahmaniyya movement of the late eighteenth and early nineteenth centuries, clans of somewhat parochial saints in the Kabylia, Awras, and pre-Sahara achieved a remarkable degree of social mobility. Tariqa membership, along with popular cults celebrating the special piety of living and deceased holy persons, represented a lever for sociospiritual advancement.

If local saints served as the hinges of daily life between the natural and supernatural, saintly-sufi lineages also served as mediators between Islam as locally received and the wider Islamic ecumene. This mediation in turn was related to the kinds of movement associated with *hajj*, or pilgrimage, which is both physical and interior or spiritual. For Shaykh Muhammad b. 'Abd al-Rahman (c. 1715–1793/1794), founder of the Rahmaniyya order, the hajj to Mecca in 1740 brought an altered sense of Islamic community and, upon his return to Algeria, an utterly changed social standing vis-à-vis his own people. Sidi 'Abd al-Rahman's labors to effect reform and renewal in the Algerian Kabylia, his native land, ultimately gave birth to a new sufi order which by 1850 had expanded outward from its original nucleus to encompass followers in the Constantine, the Sahara, and neighboring Tunisia. After 1830 in Algeria, hajj to the East and permanent migration out of French-held lands were frequently combined as strategies for personal salvation or collective redemption. As significant as hijra, or migration, from the colony was *inkimash*, a form of inward religiospiritual movement or withdrawal employed by those Muslims who lacked the will or the means to depart from their homeland.

The movements of political or religious émigrés from Algeria to adjacent Islamic states—a form of self-imposed exile—were also critical to the construction of wider historical processes. I have deliberately chosen to cross back and forth between the shifting political limits separating Algeria from adjacent states because of their immense importance. In the course of the nineteenth century, the frontiers between the North African states were transformed into zones of exchange, compromise, and contest. Sufi shaykhs and their followers, merchants, recalcitrant tribes, and rebels ignored those borders, manipulating them to advantage as long as possible. In doing so, they inadvertently caused the borders to be ever more rigidly defined and carefully policed as frantic colonial officials sought to close Algeria off from external influences.

Paradoxically, the geospiritual hinterlands of some activist sufis, such as the Rahmaniyya Shaykh Mustafa b. 'Azzuz, may have been initially extended by the French inroads into the Algerian pre-Sahara. Driven into southwestern Tunisia in 1844, 'Azzuz's relocation in the Jarid brought the turbulent frontier up to the beylik's borders. From the safety of his large, prosperous zawiya in Nafta, Sidi 'Azzuz sent out spiritual runners far and wide. By the eve of his death in 1866, he had become the focal point of a smaller movement, within the larger Rahmaniyya idiom, whose members referred to themselves as " 'Azzuziyya." Functioning as a political haven and cultural redoubt for Algerians during much of the century, Tunisia (and Morocco) continued to serve as a religious and intellectual sanctuary for fellow Muslims even after 1881. Tunisia's open-door policy toward Algerian émigrés was one element, among several, that eventually brought its forced incorporation into France's expanding African empire.

Over-the-border migrations were intimately connected to the movement of information conveyed from place to place by myriad bearers and go-betweens. Access to news and rumors conferred a certain degree of mastery over events and their interpretation, even if those rumors deepened the collective sense of a topsy-turvy world. The endless cycle of rumors about revolt and imminent deliverance from the degradation of foreign rule may have contributed to outbursts of rebellious behavior in nineteenth-century North Africa. Yet they also betrayed a sense of injustice and moral uncertainty as North Africans strove to comprehend the incomprehensible.

Moreover, if improvised news and hearsay circulated far and wide among the humble and mighty alike, the information circuits came to include the doings of the French masters of Algeria or even events in Europe. 'Abd al-Qadir, the leader of initial Algerian Muslim resistance from 1832 to 1847, not only had an elaborate network of informants but also perused French newspapers to keep abreast of parliamentary debates in Paris. And Shaykh Mustafa b. 'Azzuz pressed the French explorer, Henri Duveyrier, during their 1860 meeting in the Tunisian Jarid to provide him with details about Western technology. The point is that information—like spiritual authority or political legitimacy—became, as will be argued, a commodity to be fought over and negotiated for. And in an age of intense uncertainty for both colonizer and colonized, access to news and information represented a contested arena for the powerless and empowered alike.

The biographies collected here demonstrate how people participated either willingly or unwittingly in, were buffeted by, or in some cases forged larger social processes. Indigenous political elites, religious notables, and simple folk were ensnared in translocal forces which at times gradually filtered down to the village, town, or tribe and at others burst precipitously upon them. Conversely, defiant groups on the margins of the state or just beyond the colonial state's grasp lured France into campaigns and conquests which did not figure in imperial agendas haphazardly constructed in Paris. Thus, the European conquerors were frequently ensnared as well in regions and struggles for which they were ill prepared and for which they hastily devised solutions.

If policies and decisions made in the Métropole suffered endless permutations before reaching Algiers, grand schemes hammered out by governors-general in the capital of *Algérie Française* were deformed by the time they reached communities situated on the edges of the turbulent frontiers. And small-scale actions and hidden as well as explicit forms of contention contributed as much to the configurations of the colonial enterprise in the Maghrib as did large-scale movements or the decrees of those at the pinnacle of the imperial hierarchy.

My conclusions point to the need for rethinking or reimagining the constantly fluctuating dialogue between the local and the translocal; new borders and markers for recasting North African history during the past century are needed. For certain questions and certain periods, the nation-state as a unit of analysis does not suffice. Rather it camouflages or overlooks many of the significant forces and transformations occurring at the perimeters of the state or just beyond its unforeseen limits.

A Word on Sources

This study does not pretend to be a full-blown "history from below." The relative dearth of evidence from the past written by ordinary people whose extraordinary deeds catapulted them momentarily into history's mainstream precludes such. The protagonists did not keep diaries or daily accounts of their endeavors. Nor would rebels like Bu Ziyan—had he survived—set about writing memoirs or autobiographies, genres largely unknown to that society in that age. In large part, documentation for rebellious activity is drawn from colonial observers and actors—military leaders, Bureaux Arabes officers, explorers, adventurers, and travelers—many of whom, although not all, had a stake in narrating events and conditions as accurately as possible. The richest source by far are the archives of the Bureaux Arabes, whose meticulous accounts from "on the scene" resemble "whodunit" detective tales or police reports. The principal aim of the literature of surveillance was to ascertain the causes and motives underlying insurrection as well as to identify prime movers. In addition, there was a prophylactic dimension to these minute investigative inquiries; the ultimate intent was to learn from the past to better control the still unpredictable political future.

Moreover, some of the sources are akin to court records or legal transcripts. While the accused were often absent from the proceedings, having perished during revolts or fled the country, they were no less indicted, put on trial, and usually condemned. If the record of the 1849 rebellion led by Bu Ziyan reads like a novel—with a beginning, climax, and dramatic end—it also represents the text of a trial. Those who wrote about Bu Ziyan and his followers were not only judging him and North African society but also the colonial regime itself, its potential flaws and political soft spots. An element of the inquisitorial undergirds the documents in their assessment of what went "wrong" and thus why events transpired as they did. Zaynab's story also reads like a court case, although she was not on trial for classic insurrectionary behavior. Zaynab stood accused of being a "fille insoumise" (a "disobedient woman"). Her indocility toward those in authority—male military officers and their indigenous Muslim allies—provoked panic in Algiers in an era celebrated as the apogee of French Algeria. Letters and gentle rebukes were perceived as threatening the fragile edifice of colonial control. Ironically—or perhaps tragically—these stories, or fragments of such, are about people who altered unintentionally the direction of North African history even as they struggled against changes deemed undesirable to their vision of a desirable social order.

1   A Desert Civilization

The Pre-Sahara of Algeria and Tunisia, c. 1800–1830

> Many of the people of the Jarid are richer than the people of Ifriqiya because they possess remarkable and diverse varieties of dates.[1]

Traveling south from the city of Constantine, one reaches the small oasis of al-Qantara, located in a narrow gorge at the western edge of the Awras mountains. Named for the Roman bridge still in existence near the village, al-Qantara spanned several ecological and sociopolitical zones. It was a transitional point between Tell and Sahara, extensive agriculture and intensive arboriculture, and—as the painter Eugène Fromentin described it in 1848—between winter and summer.[2] Below al-Qantara sprawls the startling greenness of Biskra, the gateway to the Sahara. From Biskra going due east to the Gulf of Gabis (Gabès) in southern Tunisia stretches a vast and more or less unified geological subregion. Low and flat, it is composed of chains of *sabkhas* (salt marshes, often referred to incorrectly as *shatts*, or chotts), interspersed by oases devoted primarily to date-palm cultivation. The alternating pattern of dun-shaded sand and meager scrub, abruptly broken by the vivid color of the oases, inspired medieval Arab geographers to describe this part of the Sahara as "the skin of the leopard." Nevertheless, the region's other appellation—*balad al-'atash*, or "country of thirst"—was deemed equally appropriate.[3]

Until beset by the grave socioeconomic crises of the present century, the North African oases represented a "civilisation du désert." This civilization elicited the admiration of travelers, geographers, and writers, both Arab and later European, who were struck by the ingenious irrigation networks, flourishing handicrafts, and complex web of commercial exchanges linking the Mediterranean with the desert and the Maghrib with sub-Saharan Africa.[4]

Biskra has always been the political, administrative, and economic center of the Ziban (singular, Zab), an archipelago of oases that stretches as far east as the region of the Suf (Souf) adjacent to the Tunisian border. Biskra's

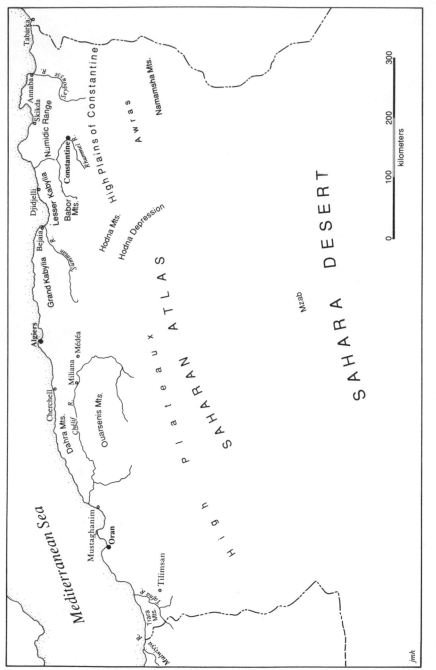

2. Northern Algeria, physical features. Reproduced from John Ruedy, *Modern Algeria* (Bloomington: Indiana University Press, 1992), by permission of Indiana University Press.

counterpart in Tunisia is the Jarid complex, with the villages of the Nafzawa (Nefzaoua) as an appendage. Conventional studies of the pre-Sahara in Algeria and Tunisia have, for the most part, treated these areas and their populations purely within the boundaries of the nation-state.[5] It is contended here that the oases from Biskra to the Jarid formed not only a relatively uniform geographical entity but a unified economic and sociocultural domain as well.[6] This remained true until the middle of the nineteenth century, when a series of dramatic political changes linked to anticolonial protest in Algeria, and to state-directed reforms in Tunisia, compromised that unity. Nevertheless, the activities of religious notables, pilgrims, and merchants, who moved constantly across the borders, served as a cultural bridge between the Tunisian and Algerian pre-Sahara until the early decades of the present century.

Biskra is located at the mouth of a large depression, the Wadi Biskra, which extends from the western edge of the Saharan Atlas range to the Awras. One of the most historically important passes in this part of the Sahara was the oasis of al-Qantara, where the high plateaus of the southern Constantine abruptly give way to the desert. Known as *fumm al-Sahra'* (mouth of the Sahara), al-Qantara was the shortest, most practicable route for caravans, missionaries, or military contingents moving between the Tell and the Ziban, Tuqqurt (Touggourt), and Warqala.[7] Thus, the gorge, and others like it, have historically marked the shifting limits of central government authority in this part of North Africa.

In eastern Algeria, the Ziban historically represented a march or frontier zone, due to its location at the point of confluence between central government rule from the north and that of powerful nomadic chieftains or Saharan dynasties in the south.[8] Theoretically, the authority of the bey of the Constantine extended as far as Tuqqurt; in reality, the territory of the Namamsha confederacy and the Awras mountains constituted the terminus of effective Turkish rule. Containing some of Algeria's highest peaks, the wild massifs of the Awras formed a barrier between the northern Constantine and the desert. Because of this, the inhabitants of the southern Awras were more deeply involved in the economic and religious rhythms of the Ziban and pre-Sahara and its political life than with the north.[9] Indeed the Awras remained a haven for rebels and dissidents for most of the colonial period; it was no accident that the Algerian revolution first broke out there. Likewise the Bu Sa'ada region to the southwest of the Hodna chain enjoyed easy access to the Ziban's oases with which both the market town of Bu Sa'ada and the small nearby oasis of al-Hamil maintained intense spiritual, commercial, and other kinds of ties.[10] These ties also influenced the pattern of Rahmaniyya implantation from the late eighteenth century into the next.

By holding the post of *shaykh al-'arab*, who was confirmed to office by the bey of the Constantine, tribal strongmen mediated relations between central governments and local populations, whether sedentary oasis cultivators or pastoral nomads; a few Saharan dynasties, such as the Banu Jallab of Tuqqurt and the Wadi Righ (Oued Rir), succeeded in maintaining a jealously guarded semi-independence from Algiers until the nineteenth century. By controlling the passageways into Ifriqiya, the deep Sahara, or the Algerian Tell, elites such as the Banu 'Ukkaz or the Banu Jallab exerted considerable political and economic clout. This was true to a lesser extent of southwestern Tunisia. There the Jarid's leading oases, Nafta and Tuzar (Tozeur), located in a narrow corridor between the shatt al-Gharsa and the shatt al-Jarid, dominated east-west exchanges between the two countries. In contrast to the situation in the southern Constantine, the beys of Tunis exerted relatively more influence upon the peoples of the Jarid through the mechanism of the annual *mahalla* (tax-collecting expedition). Nevertheless, the mahalla constituted more an exercise in ritualized political negotiation than an unambiguous statement about sovereign relations between the Jarid and Tunis.[11]

The prosperity and location of a particular group of oases determined the degree of interest in—or indifference to—them by central governments seeking to maximize tributary relations with an economy of means. For pre-Saharan peoples, who sought to minimize outside fiscal interference, the relative advantage that distance from the political center conferred was partially offset by the absolute necessity of trading with cities and entrepôts in the north, particularly to obtain grains. The oases in this part of the pre-Sahara ranged in size and function from modest villages or hamlets, like Za'atsha, to regional market towns, such as Bu Sa'ada, to large, bustling caravan centers, such as Biskra, Warqala, Tuzar, or Nafta. Propinquity to trade routes was the single most important factor shaping the degree of involvement in various types of exchanges—local, regional, interregional (Tell to desert), and international (either trans-Saharan or Mediterranean). These exchange networks, however, were not necessarily discrete but fed into one another. Moreover, the presence of prominent Islamic religious and cultural institutions—madrasas, zawaya, and shrine centers—enhanced the commercial attraction of oases like Biskra, Sidi 'Uqba, or Nafta.[12] Ethnicity combined with membership in a lineage, the product of trade, migrations, and the historically fluid interchange between sedentary life and pastoralism, fashioned both collective loyalties and social cleavages.

The inhabitants of the Ziban, the Suf, and the Jarid were predominantly Arabic speakers; a good portion of the Wadi Righ (Warqala and Tuqqurt) were Berbers or Arabized Berbers. Due to the trans-Saharan trade in slaves and other commodities, blacks inhabited some oases in relatively large numbers; for example in southern Tunisia they formed as much as one-quarter of the total sedentary population.[13] The vast majority of the pre-Sahara's populace was Sunni Muslim of the Maliki rite, although religious minorities existed. Both the Jews and *Ibadiyya* (Islamic schismatics) formed religiocommercial communities distinct from their neighbors. While the Ibadites were mainly concentrated in the Mzab's seven oasis cities, small diaspora communities were found in the Wadi Righ and the Ziban. Permanent settlements of Mzabis were not permitted in the Suf since the Suwafa (inhabitants of the Suf) rightfully feared them as formidable commercial competitors. Jewish communities were scattered about in the larger oasis towns and cities—in Biskra, Warqala, Tuqqurt, Tuzar, etc.—and even in some parts of the Mzab. Jewish traders often enjoyed ties of patronage with Muslim associates and were indispensable for economic and other sorts of exchanges. The same was true of the ubiquitous Kabyle colporteurs, who also traded extensively in the Sahara as far south as Tuqqurt.[14]

Peasant Cultivators of the Pre-Sahara

The transition from desert to oasis signifies an abrupt socioecological change from extremely low to very high population densities, and from extensive to intensive modes of resource extraction.[15] Thus, the oases represented "mediating centers" for different groups vying for control over resources, over other human groups, and over nature itself. Here animal husbandry, commerce, industrial activities, and agriculture were juxtaposed in a remarkably intricate system seeking to utilize the meager resources of an inhospitable environment through risk avoidance. From a material standpoint, risk avoidance meant that producers, whether sedentary or pastoral, attempted to diversify production, however minimally, and to construct patron-client networks to offset natural or man-made calamities and thus assure subsistence. Yet risk avoidance was a goal pursued in the realm of politics as well and was intimately related to the narrow range of options available in the pre-Saharan economy.

Since desert rainfall is infrequent and negligible, only irrigated agriculture can support large populations. The waters that flow from the mountains above Biskra have been organized into elaborate hydraulic systems for millennia. From Roman times, the region has been populated and farmed without interruption by peasant cultivators. Like the oases of the Jarid, Biskra was composed of more or less contiguous palm groves covering some 1,300 hectares and enclosing 150,000 date palms as well as thousands of other fruit-bearing trees. An oft-cited proverb from the Sahara holds that the date palm "likes its head in the sun and its roots in the water." Certainly the *Phoenix dactylifera* was the most perfectly suited to climatic conditions in the oases. And the totality of oasis economy, society, and civilization was tied in one way or another to the date-palm gardens.[16]

The more prosperous oases combined both cash-crop, market-oriented agriculture with subsistence farming, although in relative mixes that varied from place to place. This system brought integration into larger networks of exchange which worked against social and political closure. The two principal centers for the production and marketing of dates were the Ziban, which in the last century boasted some three million productive date palms, and the Jarid-Nafzawa complex, which counted almost two million trees. These were the only regions in North Africa that produced the *daqala al-nur* date in quantities large enough to stimulate a considerable export sector. This type of "luxury" date was mainly a cash crop produced for sale (or barter) in local, regional, or international markets; it was also collected as a tax in kind by traditional central authorities. Many of the more common varieties of dates—and they were legion until the twentieth century—belonged both to the subsistence and to the "barter" sectors; some were mainly for home consumption while others were sought by consumers outside of the oases.[17]

Particularly in the Jarid and the Ziban, the peasants cultivated citrus and other types of fruit trees which flourished under the shade "umbrella" provided by the date palms. Underneath this second layer of vegetation grew yet another stratum of flora—vines, vegetables, and fodder; much of this was consumed by the garden owner or cultivator and represented a short-term insurance policy against natural or political disasters. If heavy autumn rains spoiled the date crop or tribal warfare disrupted the caravan traffic bringing grains from the north, then the garden could provide adequate nourishment. A few of the oases, notably Biskra, were able to produce grains (barley and wheat), although never in quantities to achieve self-sufficiency. The demand for grains grown elsewhere in North Africa and consumed by pastoral nomads and peasants in the Sahara was the flywheel of interregional commerce between Tell and the desert. And the need to procure grains from the outside also shaped the array of political choices available to desert rebels. Apart from dates, some cash or "industrial" crops were produced in the traditional oasis economy. The Suf has long cultivated an excellent tobacco, which was highly prized among North

Africans and mainly sent to Tunisia through the contraband trade.[18] Attempts to grow Egyptian cotton in the Ziban in the middle of the past century failed, however, to yield satisfactory results. Henna, so important for ritual-ceremonial and medicinal purposes, could be grown only in limited quantities, and imported Egyptian henna met the remainder of local needs. In the nineteenth century, these industrial plants—henna, tobacco, and *wars* (a plant used in dying textiles)—were raised in small quantities and used by the peasant cultivators to pay taxes or to acquire a limited range of products not produced by the local economy, particularly raw or finished silk and cotton thread needed for weaving.[19] Since these items appeared insignificant to the overall structure of production and exchange in the oases, they were frequently overlooked in colonial economic studies. Yet their importance to the precarious peasant household economy was considerable, above all in relation to textiles made on looms in the domestic compound.

As in Asia or preindustrial Europe, textile manufacture was the single most important handicraft activity until factory-made European commodities began to compete with indigenous products in the past century. Oasis cottage industries produced a wide variety of woven articles designed to meet domestic needs and to effect various kinds of exchanges.[20] Weaving, whether in the village or tribe, was mainly a female activity organized along a gender-based division of labor (although there were some exceptions to this general rule). After meeting household demand, family looms turned out a surplus intended for exchange in local or even regional markets. While textile production did not give rise to an artisan "class" as such, it was relatively specialized since certain types of textiles were made by specific groups. The finished products were normally not marketed by female producers but reached consumers through a series of intermediaries formed by kinship or patron-client relations or both. Local or regional specialization as well as the distribution of cottage industry fabrics created extensive trade networks.[21]

For example, Tuzar produced an especially fine woolen *burnus* (a hooded cloak), while Nafta was famous for its *safsari* (cloak) of silk mixed with high-grade wool. Both of these were exported not only to other parts of the Maghrib but also to the Mashriq and commanded hefty prices. Their consumers were mainly urban, oasis, and tribal elites or Tunisian court notables who collected these luxury garments annually as a tax in kind from Jaridi producers.[22] Thus, in addition to the demand for cereals and dates, the marketing of finished textiles was an important component in regional and transregional commerce and linked the southern Constantine and Tunisian Jarid with northern cities and Mediterranean ports. Taken together these three commodities—dates, textiles, and grains—created a triangular system of exchange involving merchants, peasant cultivator-weavers, and pastoral nomads. Nevertheless, the most crucial item for the Sahara in that triangular trade was grain. The incessant demand for cereals grown in the Tell would place limits upon sustained political action by desert peoples, particularly during the revolt of 1851–1854.

Beside the peasantry, other social groups participated in the political economy of the Sahara—merchants or traders, privileged saintly lineages, and pastoralists. However, rigid distinctions did not necessarily exist between either pastoral nomads and oasis cultivators or between merchants and nomads. In times of crisis, sedentary oasis dwellers have abandoned their gardens for herding or stock breeding; throughout the centuries pastoral-nomadic peoples have settled to engage in agriculture, frequently in combination with animal husbandry. During certain moments in the date cultivation cycle, pastoralists gathered in large numbers in the oases to barter their products for dates, provide transportation and guides for caravans, or offer their labor for the harvest.

Yet the pastoral nomads were both friend and foe. While they supplied indispensable goods and services, tribal groups often exacted tribute from traders and oasis inhabitants. In years of drought or insufficient pasturage, nomads raided caravans and travelers, rendered trade routes insecure, or swarmed into the oases, much to the dismay of sedentary populations. Intertribal quarrels, one main source of political unrest in the Sahara, spilled over into the social life of desert towns and villages; the reverse was also true as oasis vendettas and struggles found a resonance among allied pastoral-nomadic groups. Thus, one of the most significant elements in the Sahara's political economy was sedentary-nomad mutualism which juxtaposed complementary modes of production, resulting in both cooperation and conflict.

Pastoral Nomads of the Pre-Sahara

The Desert is Our Father, Our Mother is the Tell.[23]

Anthropologists have observed that the phenomenon of "vertical nomadism"—a fixed, annual migratory regime linking several different ecological niches—was more characteristic of Morocco and Algeria than Tunisia. Comparing North Africa with Southwest Asia, Donald Johnson also noted that the Maghribi pattern of "oscillating pastoral movement" resembles that of the mountain nomads of the Near East who take advantage of "altitudinal seasonal variations" to subsist.[24] In Algeria, the nomads generally remained in the Sahara, their true home, for six to seven months, depending upon conditions. Some pastoralists possessed date-palm gardens, invariably worked by *khammas* (roughly, peasant sharecroppers) who often enjoyed patron-client relations or kinship ties (or both) with pastoral owners.[25] The rest of the year was spent in the Tell, where the pastoral nomads were an inconvenience as well as an economic asset to grain cultivators. The seasonal sojourn of the pastoralists in the north had political implications. It allowed the Turkish government and later colonial authorities to levy taxes on the tribes in state-controlled markets and meant that tribal leaders maintained ties with central authorities in the Constantine.

For example, the 'Arba'a (Larba'a) of al-Aghwat (Laghouat) and the Sa'id 'Atba of Warqala spent the summer months with their herds in the western Tell below the massifs of the Ouarsenis.[26] To the east, the pastoralists located between Biskra and Tuqqurt—the Awlad Zakri, Awlad Mulat (Moulet), Bu 'Aziz, Sharaqa, Gharaba, etc.—set out at the end of spring for the cooler high plains adjacent to Sétif or to Suq Ahras on the northeastern border with Tunisia. Those found in the immediate region of the Ziban and Wadi Righ migrated north either by going around the Awras via al-Qantara or by passing through strategic valleys in the Awras mountains, such as the pass near the village of Khanqa Sidi Naji, home to a powerful saintly lineage and Rahmaniyya zawiya by the early nineteenth century.[27]

The semiannual displacement of nomadic peoples in Algeria, a surprisingly regular, ordered process, was still partially operative in the south as late as the Second World War. Similar sorts of long-distance, desert-to-Tell migrations did not ordinarily take place in Tunisia, where pastoral displacements were much more restricted; nor did the Saharan tribes in Morocco cross the High Atlas mountains. For Algeria this pattern has historically meant that certain kinds of exchanges, particularly those involving bulk goods and food items, have tended to take place along a north-south axis; the international trade in luxury commodities and the pilgrimage traffic between Taza (in Morocco) and Ifriqiya moved along the transversal or east-west routes.[28] The semiannual movement of peoples and herds from desert to Tell was, therefore, an important structural component of the political economy of both precolonial and colonial Algeria. It had an impact upon the shape of collective action and popular protest and upon religious alliances between tribal groups and various Rahmaniyya centers controlled by privileged saintly lineages.

Until the colonial regime sought to erect a political *cordon de sécurité* around Algeria during the past century, the frontiers between the two states, which had been more or less established since the eighteenth century, were relatively porous.[29] Commercial exchanges between the Tunisian beylik and eastern Algeria flourished and were subject less to state-imposed control than to the restrictions created by tribal politics at any given moment. The very fact that recalcitrant tribes regularly fled across the fluid borders to avoid taxation constitutes in itself an implicit recognition of the territorial limits between the two regencies.

The great Sha'amba confederation, which participated in the revolt led by the Sharif of Warqala, covered an immense area in the Algerian Sahara stretching from the Mzab to the Suf in the east and as far south as Tuareg territory.[30] Depending upon the political situation in the Tunisian beylik, small groups of Sha'amba might move as far east as the Nafzawa in Tunisia to raid the local Ghrib tribe. In contrast, the pastoral nomads of the Suf did not normally cover the enormous distances of other Algerian tribes since they tended to follow an east-west axis which brought them at times into the Tunisian Jarid and Nafzawa.[31] Once over the border, their migratory regime and opportunities for peaceful or forced exchanges, were determined by the relations with the Tunisian tribes—the Awlad Ya'qub, the Banu Zid, and the redoubtable Hammama. Another factor was the beylical mahalla, whose annual tax-collecting forays into southern Tunisia, aimed principally at the prosperous, yet refractory, sedentary inhabitants of the Jarid, also discouraged, momentarily at least, tribal conflicts.[32]

The decision on the part of Saharan peoples either to take up arms or to delay collective action for a more propitious moment was often a function of the pastoralists' migratory regime. In many cases, the timing of a revolt was a function of the presence—or absence—of certain tribal groups in a particular region. Annual tribal movements were in turn dictated by the unremitting search for adequate pasturage and the agrarian cycles of the oases which demanded additional labor at specific times. Thus, an ecology of political action existed prior to 1830 and would determine the terms of the colonial encounter for decades after the French conquest.

While stock breeding and animal husbandry were the mainstays of the pastoral-nomadic economy, trade and commerce—and the closely related activity of raiding—were nearly of equal importance. Pastoralists actively participated in Saharan commerce in three basic ways: the provision of transport services, the furnishing of protection, and the distribution of their own products in markets through barter or sale. To these were added middleman functions since some of the tribes, such as the Awlad Amir of the Suf, acted as commercial intermediaries between desert and steppe economies.[33] As was the case in the oasis agrarian economy, specialization and diversification marked pastoral-nomadic production, although in rather more restricted forms.[34]

Finally, patterned economic behavior, structured by patron-client arrangements, assured the distribution of oasis surplus outside of the pre-Sahara and represented another dimension of sedentary-nomad mutualism. For example, the Sahari tribe traditionally transported dates produced in the northern wing of the Ziban to the city of Constantine for sale, while the Awlad Darraj moved oasis products to Sétif, Bu Sa'ada, Msila, and even Algiers for commercialization.[35] After 1830, and particularly with the fall of Constantine to the French army in 1837, these complex networks would be profoundly disrupted, much to the temporary advantage of oases in the Tunisian Jarid.

Commodity transfers over a wide geographical and political space were facilitated by pacts establishing patronage ties between oasis producers, traders, and pastoralists. In some cases these ties spanned the borders between the two Turkish regencies. Merchants from the Suf, who habitually traded in the Tunisian Nafzawa, maintained protection agreements with specific tribal groups in southern Tunisia.[36] As long as these pacts—a sort of "insurance" premium paid in cash or kind by the caravan traders—held, the price of commodity transport was relatively low and extralocal exchanges flourished. Yet whenever tribal warfare or excessive state fiscal pressures upon accessible nomadic groups rendered raiding more lucrative than protection, the price of transport would rise according to the dangers involved, thus wreaking havoc upon Saharan commerce.

In addition to offering security to sedentary clients, pastoral-nomadic peoples have long been pivotal in another related economic activity—smuggling and contraband. In the Maghrib as well as in parts of Iran, Anatolia, and elsewhere in the Near East, pastoralists have facilitated extralegal (from the political center's point of view) exchanges due to their involvement in transport at the margins of the state. Tribal smugglers in southern Algeria and Tunisia were inevitably associated in these enterprises with oasis merchants, port traders, and even local agents of the government. Some tribes, such as the Tunisian Ghrib and the Algerian Sha'amba, came to specialize in contraband by the middle of the nineteenth century when the booming demand for European firearms and gunpowder in Algeria encouraged the trade in these prohibited "luxury" items.[37]

As was true in sedentary-pastoralist relations, the nomads were both foe and friend of the traditional political center. If some pastoral-nomadic groups defied central governments by raiding, smuggling, and fiscal evasion of various sorts, others offered their services as irregular *makhzan* (i.e., in the service of the state) troops, especially in Tunisia, and assisted in tax collection. As Nikki Keddie has pointed out, the histories of Iran and the Maghrib are comparable in many respects, due to the predominant role played by the tribal semiperiphery in political, military, and economic relationships.[38] Tribalism, in combination with varying forms of pastoral nomadism, forged to an extent the outlines of social organization and ultimately state formation in North Africa. Thus, while the tribes were often located at the fluctuating margins of the state, they were not marginal to that state since an uneasy form of mutualism existed between political center and pastoral-nomadic society.

"Water: The Friend of the Powerful"

The inhabitants of the oases, many of whom claimed pastoral-nomadic origins, were more often than not deeply divided; these divisions frequently played into the hands of central authorities in both the Turkish and colonial periods. Moreover, tribal alliance systems, or *saffs*, discussed in subsequent chapters, were recreated within sedentary oasis societies, thus involving settled communities in much larger political contests. At the local level, however, daily conflicts erupted from the endless struggles over land and above all water—the "friend of the powerful."[39] As Valensi observed with regard to Gabis, "nothing is more complex than the system of property ownership in that oasis," an observation which applies to the vast majority of oasis societies, whether in the Maghrib or elsewhere.[40] Generally, the more slender or insecure the resources, the more intricate were the social relations managing individual or collective rights to those resources.

Islamic law and *'urf* (customary law) theoretically cede to property owners the rights to water flowing upon their land.[41] And, for the most part, French colonial jurists followed Islamic practices in matters pertaining to oasis agriculture as long as the rights of indigenous Muslims did not contradict the claims of Europeans.[42] Water, or more accurately rights to its use, however defined, enjoyed the status of *mulk* (or *milk*, roughly, private ownership) in most, but not all, cases. Water rights could be inherited and theoretically alienated—sold, lent, mortgaged, or established as *hubus* (*waqf*, or a pious endowment). Nevertheless, in some places in the pre-Sahara of Algeria, water belonged rather to the community and was collectively held.[43] Finally, no matter what status water enjoyed in law or in practice, disputes over water and its management invariably demanded the intervention of local religious notables, usually privileged saintly lineages.

Therefore, water represented more than just a scarce resource, it constituted a bundle of symbols to be fought over. As such water rights were the stuff of oral traditions and folklore which accounted either for group identities or communal antagonisms. The discourse of water, and of rights to it, constituted a language which gave expression to notions of kinship and was merged with the collective veneration of powerful saints who were the guarantors of fertility and of the social order.[44] If traditionally rank was defined, to no small degree, by access to water rights, sharp social cleavages, based solely upon that access, were partially offset by relationships of patronage, by membership in the lineage, and by shared rituals and ceremonials, especially those in veneration of the saintly notables and sufi clans.

The crucial technical as well as social problem was water distribution, and this more than anything else was the root of quotidian strife. In the Suf, underground sources were normally held and exploited directly by the owner of a particular plot, and allocation posed fewer difficulties. Yet waters flowing through extensive, complex systems, like those in the Ziban or the Jarid, had to be meticulously allotted since they irrigated gardens with numerous contiguous owners and cultivators. The most common method of repartition was by measured units of time (as opposed to volume) or a combination of time and volume units. Here the water clock, or *qadus* (*clepsydra*), played a pivotal role.[45]

The control and distribution of water were solely the domain of the local group or more precisely of notables from a particular community. Central government authorities rarely interfered in the collective administration of water resources, nor did the state, in this part of the Maghrib, levy any sort of tax upon water.[46] Responsibility for the allotment of water was frequently assigned to a committee of *kibar* (village elders), who also safeguarded the upkeep of irrigation networks by organizing village works projects. Moreover, water distribution and control were intimately associated with supernatural events and holy persons—local oasis saints, living and dead, and the organized cults honoring them.

In some parts of the Jarid and the Ziban were local elites who laid claim to vast gardens with thousands of date palms and extensive water rights. Secular oasis notables were mainly merchants, local representatives of the state, or sedentarized nomads who did not directly exploit their holdings but relied instead upon the khammas.[47] This desert bourgeoisie—the *khassa*, or "people of distinction"—was usually found in caravan cities like Tuzar, Warqala, or Ghadamis (in Tripolitania), where merchants prospered from the trans-Saharan trade and subsequently invested in land and water. Sufi notables or members of saintly lineages might also hold in various ways or have access to large tracts of land and water rights.[48] Such property rights were partially the result of saintly involvement in commerce but were more often a product of sociospiritual services and mediating functions. By the late nineteenth century, the Rahmaniyya and, in particular, the Tijaniyya shaykhs of the Tunisian Jarid and of southeastern Algeria controlled a significant share of the means of oasis production, part of which were recycled into the local economy through social welfare activities. The process of accumulation by the major sufi orders occurred over several generations and may have been related to the gradual demise of traditional secular elites under the colonial regimes in both Algeria and Tunisia. And the increased material fortunes of some sufi shaykhs, notably the Tijaniyya, explains the gradual political neutralization of these privileged lineages vis-à-vis their colonial masters.[49]

Thus, the real bases of power and wealth were land and, above all, water on the one hand and the social recognition of piety and religious learning on the other hand. Involvement in trade was important to social ranking mainly when the profits from commerce were used to acquire land and water (or more land and water).

The most equitable distribution of oasis resources was found once again in the Suf with its small family-owned and exploited gardens, a phenomenon probably related to the region's peculiar hydrology. In contrast, many of the Wadi Righ's gardens were owned by surrounding nomadic peoples, such as the Awlad Mulat who employed khammas to cultivate their holdings. Yet the sedentary populations of Tuqqurt and Warqala cannot be characterized as "serfs" (the term mistakenly used by nineteenth-century European accounts) since they were not tied to the land. Indeed, some of the Wadi Righ's cultivators periodically emigrated to more favorable parts of the Algerian southeast, particularly the Ziban, and in some cases to neighboring Tunisia. And relationships of production—or exploitation—between cultivator-sharecropper and nomadic landholders varied enormously from the somewhat subjugated peasantry of Tuqqurt to rather more equal partnerships between sedentary and pastoralist.[50] Finally, given the demographic realities of the precolonial era, characterized as relentlessly subject to "calamités démographiques en chaîne," labor was frequently a scarce commodity which militated against the abuse of cultivators.[51] In any case, if the demands upon the peasant farmer's labor became too burdensome, migration to other oases, where conditions were less unfavorable, was an option as was migration to the north.

What this imbrication of access to, and control over, resources meant was that struggles for power—local feuds, regional conflicts, or the more rare head-on confrontations with state authorities—involved both oasis sedentary populations and pastoralists. This involvement was related in part to the fact that while membership in a lineage, whether real or "fictive," was the taproot of common identities, rights, and mutual obligations, dyadic ties between groups and individuals—acquired or contractual loyalties—were also important.

The Social Morphology of the Oases

The physical morphology of pre-Saharan cities and towns was, in large measure, a reflection of ethnicity, profession, or clan-based relations forged by the permutations of centuries of tribal settlements, of saintly inmigration from Morocco, and of the traffic in humans from the sub-Sahara.

Biskra furnishes a model for social arrangements in the pre-Sahara on the eve of the French conquest. The city was divided into five factions, each having its own quarter, mosque, and gates into the gardens. One of the five main residential sections was further divided into seven smaller neighborhoods, each housing a different socioethnic group: the *dar al-'abid* was inhabited by sub-Saharan Africans; the *dar al-haddad* was occupied only by ironsmiths, universally regarded as pariahs due to their profession; another subquarter housed kin groupings of holy men of Moroccan ancestry. A second principal quarter, *bab al-khaukha*, or "gate of the peach trees," was made up of yet another saintly lineage and their khammas; a third section of the city was inhabited exclusively by those of mixed Turco-Arab descent, the consequence of the Ottoman garrison established in Biskra. The secular shaykhs of Biskra were always chosen from the Turco-Arab families. Other neighborhoods were inhabited by lineages from the Suf or Warqala, or by religious minorities, mainly the Mzabis and Jews.[52]

Nafta and Tuzar in the Tunisian Jarid displayed nearly identical patterns of ethnoresidential segregation which were not unlike those found in precolonial Tunis or Constantine. The basic unit within each quarter was the patrilineage, arranged according to households. In Tuzar, composed of seven village groupings in the past century, the main conglomeration, *madina Tuzar*, was again divided into nine distinct sections. These were separated from one another by streets and alleys that constituted veritable frontiers in times of social conflict.[53] Indeed, the old town quarters of Tuzar and Nafta still bear today the names of these lineages.

In most, if not all of the oases, city quarters and factions were organized into two opposing leagues, sometimes called saffs. These leagues were "diffused and abstract organizations, systems of political and antagonistic alliances, which may divide the village, the clan or even the family and which have . . . a potential rather than an actual existence."[54] While the operation of the saffs in the precolonial and early colonial eras is not completely understood, their contextual nature indicates that the leagues represented calculated responses to momentary situational cues rather than rigidly defined entities. Thus, their function was to manage conflict and to equalize the balance of power or, more accurately, to minimize inequities in the exercise of force rather than to prevent the outbreak of strife per se.

In terms of their dynamic, the oasis saffs often resembled those dividing the surrounding pastoral-nomadic peoples. Indeed, some of the alliance systems grouped a particular city or village quarter in the same league with a specific tribal fraction (in some cases due to earlier patterns of nomadic settlement). For example, half of Tuzar's inhabitants were allied, together with the Banu Zid tribe, in the great Bashiyya league; while the city's other inhabitants were tied to the Hammama confederation and Husayniyya saff.[55] In southeastern Algeria, these binary political alliances were invariably activated by bitter contests between the Banu Ghana (Ben Gana) and the Bu (Abu) 'Ukkaz (Bou Akkas) clans for the coveted post of shaykh al-'arab and thus for mastery of pre-Sahara. At times, these struggles spilled over into southern Tunisia as well.[56] Moreover, in the Saharan political game, changing sides or saff affiliation under certain circumstance was not unheard of, nor did shared league membership necessarily spare sedentary peoples from tribal harassment.

Saff-based quarrels might erupt due to the weakness of central government authority. At other times the leagues were manipulated by central authorities, who used them as a lever to influence local or regional politics and thereby to enhance the state's tenuous fiscal hold over semiautonomous groups. Conversely, the complex political choreography of the alliance systems could mean that government domination was only partial or short-lived, such as in the oases of Warqala or Tuqqurt. On the eve of the French invasion of Algeria, it appears that saff conflict had increased in the Ziban and elsewhere in the pre-Sahara. The political uncertainties created by the early stages of colonial occupation only intensified the league struggles as new and old contenders for power attempted to move onto the political center stage—or at least prevent rivals from so doing.

These conflicts, which incorporated ancient divisions into newer political alignments, meant that the achievement of a lasting consensus was a daunting task. Nevertheless, while the divided nature of oasis society was naturally a significant factor in the shape assumed by collective action immediately prior to and after 1830, all was not flux and disorder. Markets, temporary migration northward, and pilgrimage cycles honoring holy persons attenuated those forces for conflict, provided social order, and offered safety valves—in the case of outward "sedentary migration"—for unfavorable land-man ratios in the oases. And market centers in North Africa were universally regarded as politically neutral terrain, although it is argued here that suqs (market or bazaar), fairs, and markets were also highly charged political spaces. Thus, a distinct "market ethic" can be detected in the pre-Sahara which existed alongside the "subsistence ethic" of the cultivators and worked against what James C. Scott has wrongly called the "closed and autonomous peasant utopia."[57]

Saharan Suqs and Marketing Systems: Exchange, Communication, and Coercion

Market centers or "nodes" such as Biskra, Tuqqurt, Tuzar, and Nafta dominated attached hinterlands, composed of smaller oases, villages, and tribes, and were arranged in a solar or wheel-shaped pattern. In turn these larger Saharan trading centers constituted satellites of the two dominant commercial, cultural, and political hubs in this part of the Maghrib—Constantine and Tunis. Places like Biskra and Tuzar collected pastoral, agrarian, and artisanal products from surrounding areas and moved them up and out of the region. Conversely, "imported" items, however defined, destined for consumption in the pre-Sahara or for transshipment farther south, flowed downward through the system through chains of intermediaries.

The towns of the Jarid were particularly well placed to profit from converging trade routes since they alone were situated astride both the north-south and east-west axes of exchange. However, even prior to Ahmad Bey's (1837–1855) decrees outlawing slavery and the slave trade in Tunisia, the trans-Saharan trade was clearly languishing; thus, the Jarid prospered more from the trans-Maghribi or desert-to-Mediterranean commerce than trans-Saharan exchanges. Through the Jarid, commodities either from the Tunisian Sahil (or Sahel, meaning "olive-growing coast") or from the Tunis region were channeled into southeastern Algeria; in addition, manufactured goods from the Mashriq or from Europe were imported through the Mediterranean ports of Sfax, Gabis, and Jirba, for transshipment to the Jarid from whence they were distributed to the Algerian pre-Sahara. In addition, the Jarid was located along one of several possible overland hajj or pilgrimage routes linking the far Maghrib with Egypt and the Hijaz.[58]

The shifting importance of various trading centers and routes is difficult to assess for the precolonial and early colonial periods. The conquest of Algeria brought the demise of the trans-Saharan traffic through Algerian entrepôts since merchants and caravans avoided French-held territory, preferring to trade when possible with the other Maghribi states.[59] However, the Algerian oases of the Zab Sharqi (eastern wing of the Ziban), and the Suf traded extensively with both the northern Constantine and southern Tunisia. After 1837, and with the revolts led by Bu Ziyan and the Sharif of Warqala between 1849 and 1855, the transversal routes leading into the Jarid and the beylik increased in importance. Severed from traditional markets to the north, the inhabitants of the southeastern Algeria shifted their commercial activities to Tunisia which also allowed political protest to endure, for a time at least.

Saharan markets differed from those in the Tell or steppe regions in two related ways, both of which had political implications. First of all, they displayed the features of urban *and* tribal markets.[60] Second, they departed from the customary norms regulating the temporal-spatial occurrence of regional markets elsewhere in Tunisia and Algeria. Laurence Michalak has shown that the rotating weekly market, an ancient institution in Tunisia, did not exist in the Jarid (although today Tuzar is the site of an animated Sunday market).[61] And from the data available in Bureaux Arabes reports and travelers' accounts, it appears that some of the Ziban's markets were also daily affairs.[62] Thus, instead of the periodic suq staggered over a seven-day cycle, the large oases boasted daily markets, although naturally the Friday market was the most active. Those held during the winter date harvest attracted the largest and most diverse clienteles resulting in the highest volume of exchanges.

In addition, annual fairs were as significant to the economy and socio-cultural life of the oasis cities as they were in other regions of North Africa. In the pre-Sahara, the fairs normally coincided with the date harvest, although in Tuqqurt the salubrity of the climate played the most decisive role in timing. In all places, the annual *mawsim* (literally, season, festivity, or fair) was the occasion of a vast pilgrimage in honor of powerful saints and holy persons sometimes lasting for long periods of time. It also brought together the various fractions of a single tribe or confederacy or different tribal groups for purposes of trade and piety in a politically neutral space. Akin to the mawsim was the *zarda*, a solemn, ritualized gathering at the tomb of a powerful local saint either to call for armed insurrection or to conclude peace between two tribes after a long period of hostilities.[63] Moreover, daily or periodic markets, pilgrimage cycles, and yearly fairs offered an opportunity for central governments or local "big men" to intervene in provincial society and economy.

While central place theory accounts for the material and spatial features of exchange and distribution, it tends to neglect the coercive and communicative aspects of market systems. Since both fairs and markets brought together large groups of people in a relatively circumscribed area at regular intervals, they were the favored haunts of state fiscal authorities (in the more accessible oases) or of the agents of semiautonomous princes, such as the Banu Jallab, who exacted tribute from those trading in Tuqqurt's great winter market. And if outside interference in local affairs was sporadic prior to the 1840s, nevertheless central governments in both Tunisia and Algeria drained away considerable "surplus" from places like the Jarid and the Ziban. Thus, tribute collection was another mechanism for moving various kinds of surplus out of regional economies and into larger networks.[64]

In addition, markets and fairs were major collectors of information and news, which was then redistributed in much the same way that goods were widely dispersed. Many of the participants in today's rural suqs in Tunisia gather not only to buy or sell but also to exchange gossip and reaffirm social ties or obligations.[65] This was all the more true in the past century. Invariably present at the mawsims and markets were storytellers and bards (*maddah*) who narrated folk ballads, songs, and poetry inspired by age-old legends as well as current events. Not surprisingly, spies, either in the service of the state or of dissident groups, also frequented trading centers. And edicts and pronouncements of concern to the local community were made public. Finally, rumors ran riot in the suqs and other gathering places and as such represented the major source of information regarding events from outside.[66] Thus, the noncommercial dimensions of the market were as crucial, perhaps more so, than those strictly economic in nature. It was here that public opinion jelled; the collective sociomoral consensus regarding leaders and political circumstances formed and expressed itself in various ways. In short, the suqs represented ready-made forums for social protest under certain conditions.

The accumulation of news, rumors, and information in the oases sprang from their position as mediating centers; the presence of pilgrimage shrines and sufi zawaya also contributed to the store of information from far and wide. In addition, the dissemination of news was further tied to an older pattern of "sedentary migration" which predated the colonial era. Like the mountainous regions of the Mediterranean Basin, oases have always formed population reservoirs that exported labor either permanently or temporarily to the cities of the rain-fed coast. And rural-to-urban or interregional migrations are not only an ancient phenomenon in the Near East and North Africa but also a widespread response to adverse conditions.

The Politics of Migration

Today oasis agriculture cannot be expanded much beyond its present limits, and emigration from places like the Jarid and the Ziban is normally permanent. In past centuries, the outpouring of men from the pre-Sahara was largely, although not exclusively, a temporary survival strategy which served to integrate the desert semiperiphery into extralocal networks of exchange and communication. Yet it was not only those at the bottom of the social heap who sought to better their lot in life through journeys to the north. Ambitious members of provincial religious families inevitably gravitated to the bigger, more prestigious centers of Islamic learning—to Constantine, Tunis, or Algiers. The continual movements of people between desert and Tell served to urbanize even relatively isolated oases in much the same way that the annual hajj integrated the Maghrib into the wider Dar al-Islam.

The push-pull factors that brought Biskris, Warqalis, and Suwafa to the coastal cities in the past century resembled those attracting the Mzabis to northern Algeria and Tunisia. Although most scholarly attention has focused upon emigration from the Mzabi oases—an extreme form of labor movement—it may be that there were actually more non-Mzabis than Ibadis in Algiers. Prior to the French occupation, and for a certain period after 1830, Saharan peoples constituted a not insignificant proportion of the population of the *qasba* (casbah) in the Algerian capital. Each community inhabited a specific quarter of Algiers, formed the nucleus of a corporation under the aegis of an *amin* (head or master of the group), and specialized in certain professions or tasks whose allocation was regulated by custom.[67]

For example, emigrants from the small oasis of al-Burj (el-Borj) in the Ziban, which also boasted an important Rahmaniyya zawiya, claimed exclusive "rights" to the boatman profession in the port of Algiers. While the Mzabis traditionally monopolized the occupations of grocer, butcher, and cloth merchant, the Biskris were mainly porters or water vendors; the Suwafa inevitably were masons or dealers in whitewash. If some Saharan migrants always headed for Algiers, others (the Warqalis and Suwafa) preferred Constantine and Tunis as sites of temporary employment. In Tunis, they lived under conditions similar to those in the Algerian capital and joined other groups from the Tunisian south, like the Jaridis, in the popular Bab Swaika quarter. Some of the more enterprising Algerians in Tunis used their stays in the big city to organize contraband and smuggling operations.[68]

There were three significant features of these interregional population movements in the precolonial and early colonial eras. First, the ambiguous social status of the Saharan workers in the two capitals was reflected in the indigenous nomenclature designating their communities—*barranis*, or "foreigners." Being both a part of, yet apart from, urban life meant that they were less amenable to certain kinds of social control. Second, several of the professions they monopolized—particularly those of water vendor, porter, and boatman—allowed some of the barranis access to information not available to the ordinary citizen. Finally, under the colonial regime, which conferred roughly the same status to Saharan laborers in Algiers as under the deys, these "foreigners" acquired a distinctly political dimension because they served as a rustic press service, carrying news and rumors from the capital back to the Sahara.[69]

In the precolonial era, however, temporary labor movements did not (as far as we know) create conditions leading to enhanced politicization but rather served to reinforce the traditional order of things in the oases. Upon returning to the pre-Sahara, where the more fortunate might acquire a small garden with the proceeds from their labor, the migrants were re-inserted into a cultural world revolving around the lineage, date-palm cultivation cycle, and the local saint's shrine or sufi zawiya.[70] During the past century, the oases teemed with the awliya'—"those close to God"— who were also termed the "friends of God" or less frequently murabit, (marabout; a saint or holy man).[71] In the Jarid, for example, the saints, both living and dead, were legion and their ranks might also, but not always, include sufi shaykhs popularly regarded as holy persons, ulama, and mystics.[72] Present as well in the larger oasis cities, such as Biskra and Tuzar, were institutions of Islamic jurisprudence, administered by prominent local ulama, which served to integrate the community into the wider Dar al-Islam and provincial religious scholars into an international moral confraternity of defenders of the holy law (shari'a).

The relationship of the awliya' to water, to oasis agriculture, and to the political culture of the Sahara in general was intimate and as intricate as the irrigation systems. In most areas, the presence of springs, and thus the existence of the group and life itself, was credited to the miraculous powers of legendary holy persons, such as Sidi Bu 'Ali (Abu 'Ali) al-Nafti, the patron saint of Nafta.[73] Saints or their living descendants invariably played some part in mediating or resolving the interminable disputes over water and its distribution. And as seen from the discussion of the saff quarrels, the possibilities for conflict—involving kinship groupings, village factions, or oasis-tribal struggles—were myriad. So too were the opportunities for privileged religious lineages to acquire control over water and land by virtue of their role as highly visible social intermediaries as well as their piety, baraka (supernatural blessings), Islamic learning and literacy, and, in some cases, their knowledge of hydraulics.[74]

Therefore, the pre-Saharan communities of eastern Algeria and south-western Tunisia were marked by a peculiar human and political ecology as well as a particular spiritual ecology. And saint maps in the Maghrib were dynamic rather than static, fluid rather than fixed. Because the south maintained an abundance of ties with the north, the rise of a new saint and sufi in the Kabylia in the eighteenth century—Sidi Muhammad b. 'Abd al-Rahman—eventually transformed desert holy lineages into members of the nascent Rahmaniyya tariqa.

> Oh Sidi 'Abd al-Rahman,
> And you the saints whose tomb is decorated with ribbons!
> My heart desires to visit you
> But lacks a traveling companion.
> Protect, have mercy upon, my children
> And rescue me from the ocean into which I have fallen.[75]

2 Saint and Sufi
Religious Notables of the Pre-Sahara

And if the [Rahmaniyya] shaykh were to depart from
the zawiya to another place in the region, then the
hurma (sacredness) would [also] leave with him.[1]

The Mantle of the Saints

North Africa constitutes what might be termed the baraka belt. Its to-
pography—physical and cultural—is shaped by saintly remains which even
today inform collective popular memory and daily discourse.[2] The tombs
or commemorative shrines (*qabr, qubba, maqam*) honoring those who
were "close to God" created hierarchies of sacred space with economic and
political implications as well as spiritual, moral, and emotional content. The
saints were an expression of territorial and, by extension, historical authenticity; at the same time, many paradoxically were believed to have
come from elsewhere.[3] That elsewhere was either the cradle of Islam in the
age of the seventh-century Arab-Muslim conquests or later Morocco during the "maraboutic crisis," or saintly diaspora of the fifteenth to seventeenth centuries. In any case, the result was much the same for the
dominant style of Islam as lived in the Maghrib: descent from the Prophet,
conferring special piety and virtue, merged with the activist Islam of the
ribats; organized *tasawwuf* (sufism or mysticism); and the veneration of
holy persons.[4] And baraka was in many respects a sort of badge of holy
person status.

Baraka signified that ineffable, supernatural substance—grace, blessings, superabundance, purity, etc.—communicated from God to the faithful
through those individuals who in life and death were endowed with uncommon piety (*taqwa*) or *ihsan* (excellence).[5] Yet the act of communication
or transference was also important. Mere possession of baraka was not
sufficient to attain holy person status; the possessor had to be able to
transmit it to others. And the social recognition of baraka possession and
its unequal distribution in society were fundamental to the construction of

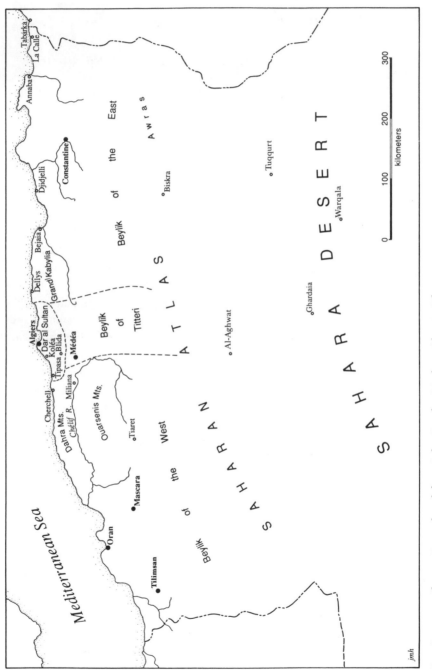

3. Ottoman Algeria. Reproduced from John Ruedy, *Modern Algeria* (Bloomington: Indiana University Press, 1992), by permission of Indiana University Press.

the saintly persona. Baraka was not only associated with persons but with specific places as well. And baraka was portable; it could be removed from spaces hitherto regarded as infused with the holy or sacred when the possessor departed. In short, baraka helped to create the holy person because it confirmed his or her privileged relation to God and thus conferred a special niche within the social order.

The most visible expression of baraka was the ability to perform miracles (*karamat*) which signaled a temporary suspension of the natural order of things through divine intervention.[6] Karamat, "gratuitous favors freely bestowed by God," assumed any number of guises—from curing and healing, to foreseeing the future, and to warding off malign spirits. Nevertheless, not all great saints and sufis were miracle workers; indeed some eschewed demonstrations of thaumaturgic powers, emphasizing instead right conduct or humility. For serious saints and sober sufis, the karamat were cited in hagiographical accounts with a didactic intent—to teach and to edify—since it was rather the heroic virtues and exalted piety of the holy persons which made them close to God.[7] Immoderate miracles could debase the currency of the miraculous and thus the holy person's piety. The miracles performed by various Rahmaniyya notables (or at least recorded by their biographers) tended to be sedate in nature. Sidi Muhammad b. Abi al-Qasim's karamat were linked to learning, purity, and moral rectitude; Shaykh Muhammad b. 'Azzuz's miracles were associated with incorruptibility in dealings with those wielding profane power. In contrast, the miraculous events ascribed to Bu Ziyan as the mahdi were more akin to *mu'jizat* (miracles performed by prophets) and regarded by his partisans as evidence of election to a divinely ordained prophetic mission.[8]

When these prodigious credentials achieved public recognition as such, they confirmed the saint or the prophet and could be instrumental in building popular followings.[9] Moreover, it is argued here that if many of the religious notables making up the Rahmaniyya were first regarded as saints by their communities and subsequently "became" sufis, the mahdi in gestation employed the implicit paradigm of the saint to construct a pious persona as well as a clientele. Conversely, there were hidden cultural norms governing the acceptable political behavior of the saint and sufi, norms which only became explicit in times of political crisis and upheaval.

Blessed with baraka, the product of their special piety and extraordinary virtue, the saints and sufis were called upon to provide a plethora of services and fulfill a number of related socioreligious roles. Protection, intercession, patronage, healing, and mediation were sought from those individuals who represented channels of grace and served as advocates as well as worthy ancestors. Some examples from the region under consideration illustrate how the ideology of baraka and collective veneration of holy persons operated in a specific environment and gave shape to its political, moral, and even ecological configuration. The oasis of Sidi Khalid near Biskra housed an ancient mosque-shrine dating from the eleventh century and dedicated to Sidi Khalid, the saint-founder. Unlike many villages in the pre-Sahara, this oasis was without fortifications. Its inhabitants, many of whom claimed descent from the saint, regarded his baraka as sufficient security against outside attack. Along the same lines of saintly patronage and protection, the miraculous intervention of a local saint in Nafta meant that the oasis escaped pillage at the hands of the Hafsid Sultan during repeated sieges between 1441–1449.[10]

Tuzar's palm groves shelter more than a hundred saints' tombs: "the saints, bearers of baraka, are the only deceased allowed burial in the gardens; to bury a non-saint there would have baneful effects."[11] In the agnatic hagiography of oasis society, kinship is expressed in relationship to a saintly ancestor, who may or may not be the group's biological progenitor. To the patron saint (or saints) of the lineage and its gardens were added saintly protectors of town quarters, factions, or entire cities; moreover, patronage and mediation, while in some respects distinct, overlapped in practice.[12] Saintly genealogy and patronage thus worked to distribute blessings and virtue in historical time and space. And cults in honor of saints assured the continual flow of baraka as well as communal access to patronage and mediation.

Organized saint veneration depends very much upon "successful shrines" where miracles, "the essential signs of the power of the saint," occur with "adequate frequency."[13] In popular theology, it was the karamat of the holy person as much as the saint himself (or herself) which attracted pilgrims and supplicants. Women in particular made daily visits to the neighborhood shrine or corner saint either to seek individual blessings or during festive occasions.[14] Saints' cults created networks of political and cultural control, and since oasis shrines attracted agriculturists and tribespeople, they reinforced rural-urban interdependence. Expressing the cultural specificity of a community, organized cults and shrines did, at times, form the locus for collective opposition to the intrusions of outside powers. Moreover, clan-dominated shrines in the pre-Sahara promoted the interests of specific religious families and challenged those of their saintly competitors.

Thus, local cult centers could be objects of rivalry in contests over various sorts of power; saints, both living and dead, represented either valuable political assets as allies or liabilities as opponents. And because holy persons were usually endowed with "potentially dangerous and anarchic" charisma, and the act of pilgrimage contained possibly "chaotic and liminal" elements, central authorities sought to regulate shrines, pilgrimages, and the collective veneration of the saints.[15] As successors to the Turks, the French colonial regime in Algeria would inherit this preoccupation with public devotional practices associated with saintly lineages and their *zawaya*.

The Political Economy of Saint and Sufi

Generally the exercise of religious as opposed to political authority tended to be distinct in eastern Algeria and can be explained in part by the historically dominant position of the city of Constantine. This contrasts with western Algeria, where sharifian aristocracies emerged in cities like Tilimsan (Tlemcen) and Mascara (al-Mu'askar). As Allan Christelow observed, "The aggressive sharifs of Mascara tried to combine political and religious roles in the Moroccan manner . . . [which] contained an implicit challenge to the authority of the Ottoman state."[16] Moreover, Amir 'Abd al-Qadir's jihad arose in Oran after 1832 precisely because profane and sacred politics were traditionally conflated in the western beylik.

In eastern Algeria, where centralization approached that of Husaynid Tunisia, the bey of the Constantine does not appear to have formally confirmed provincial or rural sufi shaykhs to leadership positions. Nevertheless, the bey selectively extended tax exemptions, fiscal privileges, and honorifics upon sufi or saintly figures. These exemptions, combined with the ritualized offerings of clients and pilgrims, often placed local religious notables in the large landholding class. For example, Sidi 'Abd al-Malik, heading one of Biskra's leading saintly lineages, was found in the 1844 census to control properties second in extent only to those held previously by the beys.[17]

In nineteenth-century Tunisia, the bey conferred letters of investiture upon the *shaykh al-shuyukh* (leader of the major sufi orders), who was frequently considered a saint and member of the ulama corps as well. These letters also served as patents of tax-free status since they publicly reconfirmed the privileged financial status of a particular zawiya and the family managing it.[18] The Husaynid state's efforts to tap into the social prestige of saints and sufi shaykhs residing on the margins of the beylik's realms are significant. First, they show that ruling elites in the Tunisian capital also subscribed to collective beliefs regarding the power of the saint and the efficacy of baraka. Second, they express the active interest that central governments took in major zawaya, even or especially those located at the limits of the state. This interest in turn suggests that the political fortunes of the beylik and its dominant classes found mainly in the capital were tied to the loyalties of provincial religious notables.[19] This fact would become all the more true after 1830.

When applied to orchards, gardens, or grain-producing fields, state-conferred fiscal exemptions could be more lucrative than the gifts or offerings that religious lineages received from their clients during the *ziyara* (the ritual visit by pilgrims, supplicants, or followers to the tomb of a local saint which was accompanied by donations; in the countryside these offerings tended to be in the form of rural produce). In the Awras, the collection of rural surplus by saintly sufi lineages through the idiom of the ziyara constituted one of the principal—if not the sole—means of capital accumulation.[20] Nevertheless, it was understood that the great zawaya of the brotherhoods performed certain crucial religious and social services for the community; thus fiscal privilege and social obligation were wedded. And religious notables, particularly in the countryside, engaged in ritualized taxation—they collected contributions in kind, and less often in currency, from clients and pilgrims. Indeed, the act of pilgrimage demanded various kinds of transactions—spiritual, symbolic, and material. From this comes the dual meaning of ziyara in the popular idiom of saint cults: ziyara signifies both the visits or pilgrimages to local shrines and the offerings made to holy persons, living or deceased, associated with a particular cult center.[21]

The death and burial of a saint, followed by the emergence of an organized cult of veneration to honor the holy person, created new "saint maps."[22] To draw up a saint map of North Africa would produce a very complex document indeed. Ritualized visits, performed individually or as part of pilgrimage cycles to a tomb-shrine, enlarged the sociospiritual capital and material assets of privileged lineages (whether biological descendants of the holy person or not) managing the shrine. Nevertheless, the ziyara was a system of reciprocity; a symmetry of exchange existed since in return the faithful received counsel, instruction, edification, blessings, and cures—in short, salvation. Moreover, generosity and charity were popularly viewed as one of the most compelling virtues of the saint and sufi. Thus much of the revenue collected was redistributed in various forms. While part was converted into the working capital of a religious center, the remainder was recycled through social welfare services and hospitality into the local economy. The single most outstanding example of this was the Rahmaniyya zawiya of al-Hamil, founded after 1850 by Shaykh Muhammad b. Abi al-Qasim and administered by his daughter, Zaynab, from 1897 on.

Moreover, the contagious quality of baraka, believed most puissant in close proximity to the saint, also gave rise to a burial business or trade. After his death in 1897, Sidi Muhammad b. Abi al-Qasim's tomb in the oasis of al-Hamil became a popular site for pious Muslims seeking a final resting place in sacred ground far removed from the contaminating influence of Algeria's European masters. Thus, colonialism both reinforced as well as altered the Maghrib's saint maps and French officials developed an intense, at times, obsessive interest in the political dimensions of spiritual cartography.

Finally, the saint's protection and patronage meant that shrines, as sacred spaces, were exempt from profane politics, at least in theory.[23] In the oases, religious establishments (mosques, zawaya, and qubbas) and the suqs were universally regarded as politically neutral terrain. The same was true in tribal regions where embryonic cult centers and "explosive markets" coexisted. There various kinds of exchanges (economic, diplomatic, and otherwise) were concluded through the sacred armistice imposed and guaranteed by the holy person's presence.[24]

Between Maghrib and Mashriq: The Rahmaniyya Tariqa, c. 1770–1830

And this saint [Mustafa b. 'Azzuz] entered Tunisian territory [from the Ziban] and disseminated the Rahmaniyya tariqa among the tribes.[25]

North African saint maps were not fixed. In times of social crisis or political upheaval, the ranks of the holy men and women tended toward inflation. The reproduction of saints was especially fecund in regions like the Jarid and Ziban, which being "axial points of the eastern Maghrib" represented crossroads for the hajj, trade, and tribal migrations as well as provincial poles of religious attraction.[26] For the Rahmaniyya tariqa, which emerged in the late eighteenth century, new and old saint maps converged to create a sufi order.

As Roy Mottahedeh observed, "Sufism was a special form of piety." From the early Islamic period, the more vaguely defined notion of taqwa, often associated with asceticism and supererogatory acts of worship, became an increasingly institutionalized ideal and mode of socioreligious behavior. While originally distinct in meaning, the three cultural personae of sufi, 'alim, and "leaders in piety" blurred over time. And by channeling piety or sanctity, organized sufism sought to control it.[27] By the eighteenth century, sufi brotherhoods had long been highly articulated organizations with clear definitions of membership, initiation rites, and elaborate ceremonials. In North Africa in particular, the *turuq* (plural of *tariqa*, literally path or way; by extension, sufi order or brotherhood) tended toward strong leadership; their shaykhs wielded considerable moral authority and social influence. And the vast majority of North African males (and to a lesser extent females) irrespective of region, social status, or occupation belonged to one or even several sufi orders.

Sufi orders often owed their origins to the travels of individuals driven by an intensely personal quest for knowledge, spiritual perfection, and the fulfillment of religious duties, particularly the hajj. The act of spiritual passage as well as physical displacement was instrumental in the creation of a number of new North African sufi orders, above all, the Rahmaniyya tariqa.[28] In the last quarter of the eighteenth century, a Berber 'alim, originally from the Ait Isma'il tribe of the Qashtula (Guechtoula) confederacy, returned to his native Kabylia after a long sojourn in the Mashriq.[29] Muhammad b. 'Abd al-Rahman had departed on the hajj in 1739–1740 and then remained in Cairo for three decades to study Khalwatiyya sufi doctrines at the feet of the order's master, Muhammad b. Salim al-Hifnawi (1689–1767–68).[30] Upon his return to Algeria in the 1760s or 1770s, the Kabyle scholar began teaching, preaching, and initiating his fellow countrypeople into the Khalwatiyya way. Backed by the enormous weight of the Azhar tradition and his own piety and knowledge acquired at the wellsprings of Islam's center, Muhammad b. 'Abd al-Rahman first became the focal point of a saint cult in his honor and subsequently the founder of a sufi order named after him.[31] While Sidi 'Abd al-Rahman and his spiritual successors viewed the Rahmaniyya as part of the eastern Khalwatiyya way, in a radically different social environment, the offshoot Maghribi tariqa assumed its own unique configuration.

The elaboration of a new sufi order represents a social movement due to the collective responses, popular and elite, to both the messenger and the message. By the eve of the saint-founder's death in 1793–1794, the Rahmaniyya had expanded considerably in terms of membership from its original matrix in the Jurjura Mountains. It counted followers in the Kabylia and Algiers region as well as in eastern Algeria, the Awras Mountains, and the pre-Sahara. Soon it would spill over the borders with Tunisia into the regions of al-Kaf and later into the Jarid. For some saintly lineages in the pre-Sahara, membership in the tariqa brought a large measure of social mobility. In part the later political behavior of these religious notables was a function of their Rahmaniyya affiliation which enmeshed previously autonomous and local saintly lineages into wider networks. Thus, the order's expansion, and the participation of provincial sufi leaders and their clients in nineteenth-century protest movements, were not distinct phenomena but were linked. Moreover, because of the nature of religious, political, and economic relationships in eastern Algeria, the development of the Rahmaniyya's Saharan branch at the eighteenth century's end was tied to the province, and particularly to the city, of Constantine.

Constantine as a Mediating Center for the Rahmaniyya

Constantine is a fortress-like city perched on a series of deep gorges over the River Rummel (Wadi al-Raml) and situated at the confluence of the ecological regions discussed in the previous chapter—the Mediterranean coast; the elevated, semi-arid plateau; and the Saharan Atlas and Awras.[32] Location made Constantine the nucleus of trade networks radiating out from the provincial capital and its hinterland and leading to seaports, to towns along the Tunisian frontiers, or to Saharan entrepôt cities.[33] Eastern Algeria's most active center for exchanges in cereals, olive oil, dates, and livestock, Constantine was frequented by desert traders and pastoralists, sedentary Berber agronomists and colporteurs, and grain cultivators of the plains, not to mention large numbers of foreign merchants, mainly from Tunisia.[34] Because Constantine's nearest port, Skikda, is fifty kilometers to the north with only mediocre maritime facilities, Tunis was its principal door to the Mediterranean and the Mashriq. Trade was brisk between regional market centers in Tunisia, like al-Kaf, Kasserine, Tuzar, and Nafta and towns in eastern Algeria.

Under Turkish rule, Algeria's eastern province was the largest, wealthiest, and most populous with the highest proportion of sedentary agriculturists and city dwellers. By the reign of Salah Bey (1771–1792), Constantine had become the most centralized of the three beyliks. Its capital historically dominated not only cultural and political life in this part of the Maghrib but also economic relations as attested to by the city's relatively flourishing commercial and artisanal industries. Trade, of whatever sort, was a monopoly of the beylik's rulers and closely supervised by them.[35] Moreover, the beys shaped the political sensibilities of religious notables, whether residing in the capital or at the margins of the province. In the city, the higher-ranking ulama—*qadis*, *muftis*, etc.—were accorded state salaries commensurate with their office. The Turks rewarded the political loyalty of Constantine's great families by parceling out prestigious religious offices; the al-Fakkun (Ben el-Faggun) clan held the important function of *shaykh al-Islam* from the late sixteenth century until the French conquest in 1837.[36] In addition, religious notables were normally not subject to taxation, and, more important, exercised theoretically exclusive control over the extensive hubus properties, a source of considerable social and financial power. Those claiming descent from the Prophet's house— and their numbers tended to swell over the centuries—were also excused from taxation as were many sufi shaykhs and saintly lineages.[37] By failing to respect ancient traditions of fiscal privilege, the French masters of Algeria created a deep sense of grievance among many religious notables after 1830.

The bourgeoisie of Constantine, whose total population is estimated at twenty-five thousand souls prior to 1830, was among the most prosperous in the region due to land holdings in the city's hinterland and involvement in local, regional, or international trade, an activity frequently combined with state office. Much to its advantage, the city enjoyed particularly close economic and cultural ties with the Tunisian beylik, resulting in a constant flow of caravans as well as students and scholars between Tunis and Constantine. In contrast to the western province, urban and rural communities were more intimately linked due to the structure of the province's ecology and economy. Some leading tribal shaykhs from the south or the mountains maintained residences in the city. And the members of aspiring religious families from the Awras or the pre-Sahara not only studied at the city's numerous madrasas but also frequently stopped off there for extended periods while performing the hajj.[38]

Unlike the Kabylia, the Rahmaniyya's original locus, Constantine was the domain par excellence of the scholar and the *faqih* (Muslim jurist); here the Islam of the countryside fused with urban, mosque-centered Islam. In 1830 the city boasted over a hundred mosques, madrasas, zawaya, and other religious establishments; the courses offered in the principal mosques drew large popular audiences as well as those versed in the religious sciences. Constantine had a substantial ulama corps, many of whom had studied in places like al-Azhar in Cairo, the Zaytuna in Tunis, or the Qarawiyyin in Fez. While the city was not as brilliant a center of Islamic learning as its competitors to the east and west, still it represented a cultural lodestar for provincial religious clans seeking to educate their sons or to enter into state service as qadis or *katibs* (scribes).[39]

Rahmaniyya Expansion from Constantine, c. 1780–1830

While the Rahmaniyya's original matrix was the Kabylia, Constantine's importance as a religious center meant that it acted as a disseminator of the doctrines of the nascent tariqa. In this the Bash Tarzi family, who as the name indicates were of Arab-Turkish origins, played a crucial role. Sometime in the 1770s or 1780s Mustafa Bash Tarzi visited Sidi Muhammad b. 'Abd al-Rahman al-Azhari at his zawiya in the Jurjura Mountains. Sidi Muhammad's reputation as an 'alim, faqih, sufi, and member of al-Azhar's inner circle had brought religious scholars from all over Algeria to his side. Swayed by Bash Tarzi's erudition and piety (and perhaps his family origins), the saint-founder initiated him into the order and designated him a *muqaddam* (sufi representative authorized to initiate others).[40] Bash Tarzi was instructed by his shaykh to spread Rahmaniyya teachings in Constantine to combat "the worldliness of its inhabitants." Subsequently he and his successors and kinsmen established several Rahmaniyya centers in their native city and its environs. Eventually the tariqa spread throughout the northern Constantine as well as along the eastern borders with Tunisia and into the pre-Sahara.

The Bash Tarzis' religious credentials were already well established prior to joining the order; they had provided Hanafi qadis and imams to the city's Islamic institutions from the early Ottoman period on. While the Bash Tarzis were eminent, they did not occupy the highest rung of the religious pecking order, long monopolized by the Banu al-Fakkun. This fact may be significant in explaining the Rahmaniyya's appeal to certain strata of religious elites. The Bash Tarzi's association with the new tariqa helped to promote the Rahmaniyya while also enhancing the family's own fortunes and social standing.[41] At the same time, social conditions in Constantine nurtured the movement represented by Sidi 'Abd al-Rahman al-Azhari. Relative to other urban areas in Algeria, Constantine was the most receptive to ideas from outside; it enjoyed close ties with Tunis and the Mashriq, and its ulama corps was firmly embedded in the city's social fabric. Moreover, Constantine enjoyed two decades of enlightened rule under Salah Bey, who, following the example of his predecessors, proved especially solicitous of the men of religion.[42]

The tariqa's rapid expansion owed much to recruitment strategies which incorporated local religious notables into its leadership. The Bash Tarzis chose privileged saintly lineages from the Ziban, such as the 'Azzuz of al-Burj, to represent the order and proselytize among the pre-Sahara's villages and tribes.[43] This was in keeping with the franchise principle which had facilitated earlier Rahmaniyya expansion in the Kabylia.[44] Rather than posing as competitors to local holy men, which in parts of the Kabylia had provoked opposition, older saintly clans in the pre-Sahara were made muqaddams; their religious clients were assimilated to Rahmaniyya networks.[45] In the southern Constantine as in the north, the Rahmaniyya was "wedded to maraboutic morphology; this led to an imbrication of the order with the Kabyle style of saint veneration."[46] And as was true of most North African turuq, Rahmaniyya *murids* (sufi novices) and shaykhs distinguished themselves by carrying a special sort of *misbaha* (prayer beads), distinctive clothing, and specific forms of address used when encountering other members. These external cultural signposts gave tangible expression to inner spiritual commitment as well as to intense socioreligious bonds.[47]

At the popular level, other forces attracted ordinary people to the Rah-maniyya. Geographically, the order gained followers in regions where the tribes' seasonal movements brought them from the desert to summer pasturage in the Tell. Moreover, the first Rahmaniyya zawaya established along the borders between Algeria and Tunisia were found precisely in market towns such as al-Kaf or Tala which handled commercial traffic between the two regencies.[48] Sa'adallah asserts that the tariqa's urban membership swelled during the late eighteenth and early nineteenth centuries due to its accessibility to those of humble rank.[49] After Salah Bey's demise, Constantine was beset by grave sociomoral dislocation and rebellions, followed by the 1805 famine which brought widespread suffering.[50] Prolonged political chaos may also have encouraged ordinary people to join the Rahmaniyya tariqa. Moreover, if poetry is an indicator of collective sentiments, Sidi 'Abd al-Rahman al-Azhari had become a heroic cult figure in Constantine's popular quarters.

One of Constantine's most remarkable poets during this period was Shaykh al-Rahmuni al-Haddad, who composed at least one *madih* (panegyrical poem) in honor of the Rahmaniyya's founder. Popular bards frequented the city's cafes, where they entertained clients with tales, songs, and ballads composed in local dialects. The poet was an important figure in the social landscape since he not only served as a barometer of public opinion but also shaped the communal moral consensus. Al-Haddad's praise poem extolling Sidi 'Abd al-Rahman's piety was recited in the city's gathering places sometime in the first decade of the nineteenth century. In it, saintly virtues were contrasted with lamentations regarding the reversal of the natural order and Islam's corruption in Constantine.[51]

Equally significant is that the poet dedicated his verses to the mahdi, the religious figure deemed capable of righting a world turned upside down. Here it should be noted that collective expectations of the redeemer's imminent appearance seem to have been heightened among most, if not all, strata of North African society from the late eighteenth century on. In part this was related to the fact that the year 1200 in the Islamic calendar came in 1785–1786; the start of a new century—in this case the symbolically charged thirteenth century—was viewed as an event of cosmic significance. And as David Robinson has shown in his study of Umar Tal's movement, many Muslims in West Africa viewed that century as holding forth the promise of "expected revival, turmoil, and possibly final judgement."[52]

While there is little hint of millenarian anticipation in Sidi 'Abd al-Rahman's original teachings, after his death, and above all, after the French invasion of Algeria, millenarian expectations reached a fever pitch.[53] Several Rahmaniyya zawaya served as cores for mahdist-led revolts which were either led or supported by sufi notables. And if the madih was a cultural medium that was widely employed in North Africa to honor saints, sufis, and the pious, later, in the context of militant resistance to the colonial order, the praise poem promoted messianic rebels. One example was Bu Ziyan, who after proclaiming himself the mahdi in 1849, launched an anti-French rebellion that was endorsed by some Saharan Rahmaniyya elites, among them, the 'Azzuz clan.

The 'Azzuz of al-Burj: The Transformation of a Saintly Lineage

Sidi Muhammad b. 'Azzuz (1756/57–1819) was among the first to introduce Rahmaniyya teachings to the inhabitants of the southern Constantine. The 'Azzuz were a privileged saintly lineage whose members had long dominated the ritual life of the oases and tribal peoples.[54] In the past century, the Ziban was composed of four clusters of oases: the Biskra area, the most important; the Zab Dahrawi, second to Biskra in population, and the site of several important Rahmaniyya centers as well as Bu Ziyan's uprising; the Zab Sharqi, the Ziban's eastern wing located along the transversal, east-west route leading to the Jarid; and the Zab Qibli, the southernmost section. As was true of most Saharan villages, stout walls protected the oases from attacks by unruly neighbors, state fiscal authorities, or the surrounding pastoral-nomadic peoples.

The Zab Dahrawi encompassed eight villages or towns, each internally organized according to kinship. In addition to engaging in date-palm cultivation, textile production, and trade, the villagers owned livestock cared for by allied pastoralists; in return, the oases functioned as storage places for the pastoral nomads during the migration season.[55] Thus, this subregion was characterized by the sedentary-nomad mutualism discussed earlier. Two towns, al-Burj and Tulqa (Tolga), were blessed with abundant water resources which accounts for their agricultural and commercial prosperity. For centuries both had served as modest outposts of Islamic learning as well as local pilgrimage sites. Due to the affiliation of religious elites with the new tariqa, al-Burj and Tulqa were the most active in disseminating Rahmaniyya doctrines.

The first detailed colonial study of the Ziban was carried out only in 1839; thus information for earlier periods is sketchy, particularly in view of the destruction wrought by the French army.[56] Al-Burj, home of the 'Azzuz, was second in size to Tulqa; both oases suffered cruelly from epidemics, particularly the plague years of the early 1820s.[57] Al-Burj counted some eight hundred people in 1839; it enclosed at least four mosques and eleven zawaya and smaller shrines, which implies a religious density—in terms of ratios between Islamic establishments and population—similar to the much larger oases of the Jarid.[58] At the town's center was the great mosque sheltering Sidi 'Abd al-Rahman b. Dalim's remains; the saint was popularly venerated as the founder and patron of al-Burj. Sidi Dalim's tomb-shrine was located near Bab al-'Ain, the main water source for the gardens, which suggests a link between his baraka and oasis fertility. The 'Azzuz claimed to be Sidi Dalim's descendants, a crucial component of their elevated socioreligious status prior to joining the Rahmaniyya tariqa.[59]

Known as the "light of the Sahara," Sidi Muhammad b. 'Azzuz was from a powerful family of awliya' who had settled in the Ziban fourteen generations earlier.[60] Most, if not all, of the region's saintly lineages traced their origins back to the Saqiya al-Hamra' in the Moroccan Sus—that breeding ground for the holy persons who unleashed the maraboutic diasporas centuries earlier.[61] These myths of origin had a double advantage. First, they bestowed an eastern Arab and, vastly more important, a sharifian genealogy upon these families—or at least made socially credible their appropriation of that ancestry. Second, that many local holy persons in Algeria and Tunisia claimed Moroccan origins conferred the beneficial status of the politically neutral "stranger" in a society perilously divided by saff affiliations. Moreover, sharifian descent and generic saintliness were closely associated in both popular lore and erudite traditions, as were two other crucial attributes of the saintly persona, science and mysticism. Until the appearance of renewed sufi orders like the Rahmaniyya and the Tijaniyya in the eighteenth century, sainthood and saintliness for most North Africans was linked to the Saqiya al-Hamra'.

Prior to becoming a Rahmaniyya notable, Sidi Muhammad already enjoyed the status of both saint and scholar due to kinship with the Prophet's family as well as his ability to work miracles, public recognition of his piety, and his advanced Islamic knowledge. As was true of other saintly lineages in the oasis environment, the 'Azzuz's moral authority and social standing had multiple sources: their monopoly of Islamic learning and literacy, baraka, their relatively large land and water holdings, and their politically ambiguous niche as "outsiders." This last factor meant that successful saints were the most effective mediators in endemic village disputes or in struggles pitting oasis inhabitants against the pastoralists.[62] Moreover, the 'Azzuz family had long administered a religious center in al-Burj—the zawiya connected with the collective devotion of Sidi Dalim—although they had not apparently belonged to any ramified sufi order prior to joining the Rahmaniyya.

Sidi Muhammad was born in al-Burj and educated by his father, Ahmad b. Yusuf, who was also venerated as a waliy. In keeping with hagiographical conventions of the period, Sidi Muhammad is credited with learning the Quran by heart as a young boy under his father's guidance; more advanced studies in the religious sciences were also completed at the al-Burj zawiya. At some point, the young man was seized by a desire to immerse himself in the study of tasawwuf; he departed for the Jurjura Mountains, then the nucleus of the newly created Rahmaniyya order still under the spiritual direction of Shaykh 'Abd al-Rahman al-Azhari. There 'Azzuz was initiated into the tariqa at the hands of the order's founder, a source of immense spiritual prestige. Sidi 'Abd al-Rahman then bade Muhammad b. 'Azzuz to seek further instruction in Constantine under Shaykh Bash Tarzi, the city's leading Rahmaniyya notable; it is uncertain, however, when this occurred or how much time 'Azzuz spent in eastern Algeria's capital.[63] There is no indication that Muhammad b. 'Azzuz ever studied in the Mashriq; thus his intellectual and religious credentials were established in Constantine, although he did journey to the Haramayn to perform the pilgrimage.

Sometime in the 1780s, Bash Tarzi appointed Sidi Muhammad as the order's muqaddam for the Ziban, an honor which he held until his death in 1819. This appointment affirmed his special place within the tariqa's hierarchy, confirmed his personal piety, and increased his stature as an 'alim. Sidi Muhammad composed a number of scholarly works related to his position within the tariqa, among them a treatise on sufism and a legal commentary.[64] Affiliation with the Rahmaniyya later increased the 'Azzuzes sociospiritual capital, making them one of the pre-Sahara's most influential families and thus a power to be reckoned with by the French. Their material fortunes may have expanded as well. An inflation in the number of clients, pilgrims, and supplicants to the zawiya brought a concomitant increase in ziyaras and pious donations. Conversely, it appears that the clan's clientele became part of the expanding sufi network; the ranks of the Rahmaniyya swelled as local saintly lineages joined the tariqa.[65] Thus, the social mobility of religious clans and the social recruitment of a embryonic sufi order were mutually reinforcing.

In the pre-Sahara, Sidi Muhammad in turn chose sufi disciples from among the leading saintly families of the Jabal Awras and Biskra region: 'Ali b. 'Umar al-Tulqi of Tulqa; Sidi 'Abd al-Hafiz b. Muhammad of Khanqa Sidi Naji in the Jabal Cherchar; al-Mukhtar b. Khalifa from the Awlad Jallal, a small oasis just south of al-Burj; Mubarak b. Khuyadim of Biskra; and Sadiq b. al-Hajj b. Masmudi of the oasis of Sidi Masmudi in the Awras. These disciple-advocates spread Rahmaniyya doctrines in ever-widening circles until the tariqa counted followers throughout the Awras, in al-Hamil near Bu Sa'ada, and as far south as Tuqqurt, Warqala, and al-Aghwat. While Sidi Muhammad b. 'Azzuz's spiritual and moral authority

preserved harmony among his sufi associates during his lifetime, competition over spiritual turf emerged immediately after his death in 1819. The
French army's arrival in the Ziban during the 1840s further complicated
relationships among notables of the Saharan Rahmaniyya.[66]

By the late 1790s, Sidi Muhammad was also initiating murids into the
Rahmaniyya in the oasis of al-Awad (El Oued) near the Tunisian border.
The shaykhs of the main sufi turuq vying for followers in this period and
later—the Rahmaniyya, the Tijaniyya, and the Qadiriyya—employed two
strategies for implanting their respective "ways" among sedentary or tribal
peoples. One was matrimonial; marriages were concluded with women
from locally prestigious lineages which served to cement sociospiritual
relations between tariqa notables and a particular family, tribal fraction, or
village. Marital alliance might also be combined with a second strategy—
designating the head of a saintly lineage to serve as a tariqa's *na'ib* (representative). In the Suf, Shaykh Muhammad's choice fell upon Sidi Salim,
a powerful but quite local saint, who headed a Rahmaniyya circle there.
Nearly a century later, the Rahmaniyya establishment in al-Awad was still
associated with Sidi Salim's progeny. By then two religious structures
dominated the Suf's capital. The older was a large zawiya built in memory
of Muhammad b. 'Azzuz in the 1820s by one of his wealthy followers. The
second building was the great mosque dedicated to Shaykh Muhammad's
son, Mustafa.[67] Situated at the base of a hill overlooking al-Awad, the
mosque's high, square minaret, constructed of several superimposed stories, can still be seen today from a considerable distance.

None of the Suf's Rahmaniyya zawaya ever attained a status similar in
reputation to those in the Ziban, Awras, or Jarid. Perhaps the competition
from traditional religious centers like al-Burj, Tulqa, Khanqa Sidi Naji, or
Nafta was too great to overcome. Then too the isolation of the Suf's oases,
with their small sedentary populations and higher percentage of pastoralists, may have worked against regional religious prominence, although
under the French regime these same conditions would confer a large measure of political autonomy. Sidi Muhammad b. 'Azzuz did not attempt to
spread Rahmaniyya teachings into the Tunisian Jarid. It was rather his son
and successor, Mustafa, who made Nafta and Tuzar into leading Rahmaniyya centers after emigrating from French-held territory in the 1840s.

Several years before his death, Shaykh Muhammad b. 'Azzuz made the
pilgrimage to the Hijaz. On this long and dangerous voyage, he was
accompanied by his closest spiritual intimates, 'Ali b. 'Umar al-Tulqi and
'Abd al-Hafiz b. Muhammad of Khanqa Sidi Naji; their selection to journey
with 'Azzuz was a sign of particular favor.[68] Sidi 'Ali b. 'Umar and Sidi 'Abd
al-Hafiz were more than mere students of Shaykh Muhammad; they were

his murids, or disciples. The master-disciple relationship was the corner-stone of the sufi way. A lifelong friendship, it forged spiritual kinship and loyalties (or rivalries) which usually endured over generations, thus re-creating the order's *silsila* (in sufism, a chain of spiritual descent) over time.[69]

Destined for Cairo and then Mecca, the Maghribi caravan which Sidi Muhammad b. 'Azzuz joined in 1816 or 1817 had initiated its journey in Morocco; among its numerous pilgrims was the future Moroccan sultan, Mawlay 'Abd al-Rahman (reigned 1822–1859). The presence of this prom-inent member of the ruling class and shurafa' furnished Sidi Muhammad with the opportunity to perform a miracle, at least according to his ha-giographer. Despite the fact that 'Abd al-Rahman was not the heir apparent, Shaykh Muhammad miraculously predicted his unanticipated accession to the throne as 'Alawi sultan.[70] How should this karama be interpreted? Whether the incident took place is irrelevant; rather it should be seen as an ideological and moral statement about various kinds of power. In the very least, the miracle underscored Shaykh Muhammad's claims to baraka. Yet the ability to foresee the political future of a scion of the Maghrib's oldest Muslim dynasty might be taken as a subtle expression of the morally superior powers of the saint and sufi. The socially leveling effect of the hajj, whose caravan juxtaposed the mighty with the humble, is another implicit theme.

Upon his return from the Haramayn, Sidi Muhammad succumbed to an outbreak of plague which reappeared several years later in a more virulent form, carrying off a good portion of the pre-Sahara's population.[71] Mu-hammad b. 'Azzuz left behind at least two daughters and six sons, some of whom continued their father's work within the Rahmaniyya tariqa. Nev-ertheless, this second generation would have to adjust to a radically dif-ferent political environment after 1830. Sidi Muhammad's tomb-shrine, located within the Rahmaniyya center in al-Burj, soon made the oasis into a favored pilgrimage site. Until well into the present century, his blessings and intercession were sought by the faithful from Algeria and Tunisia.[72] Sidi Muhammad's spiritual capital was surely enlarged by performing the hajj, since the returning pilgrim's place in local Muslim society was pro-foundly altered by fulfilling this fundamental Islamic duty. In the vicinity of his qabr, the saint's baraka was all the more potent, thus beckoning the faithful to his final resting place.

However, even before 1819, al-Burj's zawiya had attracted such a large following that it could no longer accommodate its disciples. Not all of the zawiya's visitors were necessarily Rahmaniyya members; the tariqa's lead-ership normally offered social services to the community at large, irrespective of sufi affiliation.[73] Moreover, the region's political economy—the villages served as collective tribal granaries—also played a part in the zawiya's popularity. During their winter sojourn in the oases for the date harvest, transhumant peoples visited sufi centers, shrines, and mosques. Tribal children were sent to the *kuttab* (schools) attached to the larger zawaya to learn the Quran; and the notables associated with a particular zawiya performed religious or spiritual services for the tribes.[74] Shaykh Muhammad's biographer, al-Hafnawi, mentions that he was called upon both by ordinary people, who "used to appeal to him to settle peacefully their disputes," and by the *umara'* (tribal leaders) "to quell unrest."[75] In addition, sufi zawaya served as sanctuaries for those fleeing state justice or tribal vendettas. An *aman* (amnesty) for whomever sought a zawiya's protection was often arranged for by its head shaykh; political refugees sometimes resided in sufi centers for extended periods of time. For example, the Rahmaniyya shaykh of al-Hamil, Muhammad b. Abi al-Qasim (1827–1897), sheltered dissidents in the family zawiya for decades.

To house the influx of students and scholars, the larger Rahmaniyya zawiya in Tulqa became the tariqa's Saharan center after 1819, although Sidi 'Ali b. 'Umar's selection as Shaykh Muhammad's spiritual successor played a not insignificant role as well.[76] What was at stake here was not merely spiritual authority but also charismatic leadership, which could, in the belief system of the period, be transmitted from one generation to the next. Spiritual succession often meant special access to the fund of baraka accumulated by a venerated saint and sufi.

The Saints and Sufis of Tulqa

Tulqa is situated to the northeast of al-Burj and on the route to Bu Sa'ada; some forty kilometers separated it from Biskra. Its abundant water supply supported intensive irrigated agriculture, extensive date-palm gardens, and a population—estimated at roughly four hundred households in 1839—second only to Biskra's. Despite Tulqa's relatively modest size, the oasis boasted numerous religious establishments: six mosques and at least seventeen zawaya, qubbas, and smaller shrines.[77] By the nineteenth century, the town was formed of three agglomerations, each surrounded by walls and ramparts. The oasis's numerous springs and wells moved the French painter, Eugène Fromentin, to characterize it as "the Normandy of the Sahara" during his 1848 visit.[78]

Tulqa is one of the region's oldest oases. In Roman times it sheltered a small fortress, and it figures quite early in historical accounts of the Islamic period.[79] In the first decade of the fourteenth century, a movement which was "half feud, half rebellion" against the Hafsid state erupted there. The revolt was centered in a zawiya near Tulqa and led by Sa'ada, a local holy man or murabit. Since Tulqa's importance as a pilgrimage site in subsequent centuries was partially due to this zawiya's presence and its traditions of Islamic reform as well as militant resistance to the state, it is instructive to consider Sa'ada's jacquerie.

Little is known of Sa'ada until he challenged the Hafsid governor, although as a youth he was greatly influenced by his mother, a holy woman fervently devoted to Islam. After completing religious studies in Taza, Morocco, Sa'ada returned to Tulqa, where he initiated his public ministry by admonishing the people to "command the right and forbid the wrong."[80] His message combined exhortations to return to Sunni Islam with appeals to suppress non-Quranic taxes and brigandage in the region. This program, plus the social composition of his following, which included Arab tribal leaders, humble folk, and groups normally belonging to rival leagues, alarmed the governor, who moved to expel the troublemakers from Tulqa. Naming his movement the "Sunniyya" or "murabitun," Sa'ada had the zawiya built as a locus of opposition to the state; next the rebels laid siege to Biskra on two occasions, although without success. Sa'ada's execution by the central authorities in 1305–1306 did not, however, end the rebellion, which sputtered on and off for decades. The long-term historical significance of the episode was that the Ziban's inhabitants, many of whom held Kharajite beliefs, were "reconverted" to Sunni orthodoxy. Centuries later the movement remained embedded in the popular collective memory.[81]

Bu Ziyan's 1849 revolt bears an uncanny resemblance to Sa'ada's in several crucial respects; the use of the zawiya as a matrix for concerted action aimed at overturning the political order is one striking similarity. Then too the rebellion's agenda, set by the pious, ascetic Sa'ada, who was not from the local Islamic establishment, collapsed social and economic grievances—banditry and illicit (non-Quranic) taxation—with religious renewal. Moreover, neither Sa'ada nor Bu Ziyan advocated withdrawal or avoidance protest since both rebel leaders launched offensives against Biskra, the symbol of central government authority and oppression in the Ziban. In addition, Sa'ada's revolt ended when his tribal contingents migrated to their winter pasturage in the Sahara, leaving him undermanned as state forces counterattacked; the same scenario occurred in 1849. Finally, the Hafsids skillfully co-opted the movement's religious leadership by offering the coveted post of qadi of Biskra to the local holy man heading the rebellious community after Sa'ada's death.[82] Here too there are resonances with the later reactions of some Rahmaniyya notables to the French takeover of the pre-Sahara after 1844.

Sa'ada's zawiya, however, survived its charismatic founder's death, and his clan remained in control of the religious establishment for generations. Credited with miraculous powers, Sa'ada's descendants became local saints who provided safe conduct to travelers and merchants in the region for which they normally received some kind of remuneration.[83] The provision of security to those traversing regions divided by tribal quarrels can be regarded as temporary patronage, undergirded by the principle of baraka. Thus, safe conducts guaranteed by the saints constituted portable baraka, a sort of preventative or preemptive mediation in a lend-lease form. And this was not limited to Tulqa since other zawaya and privileged lineages were still responsible many centuries later for maintaining social order along the region's trade routes.

It is uncertain whether the ancient zawiya implicated in Sa'ada's rebellion was the same religious center later administered by the Rahmaniyya shaykhs of Tulqa. According to family legend, the ancestors of Sidi 'Ali b. 'Umar al-Idrisi al-Hasani (died 1842) had emigrated from the Saqiya al-Hamra' sometime in the fifteenth century.[84] Why they were attracted to the Ziban is a matter of conjecture, although the murabitun movement centered in Tulqa may have been a factor. The town's location on the transversal hajj route from Morocco to the Haramayn may also have played a role in their establishment in the Biskra area. Until their adherence to the Rahmaniyya tariqa in the last decade of the eighteenth century, Sidi 'Ali's lineage did not belong to any of the older sufi orders. Their social status sprang from multiple roles as baraka brokers, mediators, imams, and educators; their religious establishment served as a local center of Islamic learning and culture. As was the case with the 'Azzuz, Sidi 'Ali's family had long served as intermediaries between sedentary and tribal clients as well as between government authorities and the oasis's inhabitants.[85] Indeed, Sidi 'Ali b. 'Umar's peacekeeping efforts cost him his life in 1842.

Because there is relatively more information on Tulqa for the precolonial period, the oasis can serve as a paradigm for the general arrangement of social relations and local political forces. The town was split into two saffs; the first was under the Awlad Ziyan who formed a rustic aristocracy; the second group, more heterogeneous in composition, called themselves the "ahl Tulqa," or simply the "people of Tulqa." This saff grouped together the oasis's original inhabitants and masters—before the Awlad Ziyan seized control sometime in the distant past. Since the Awlad Ziyan claimed "Fasi" origins (i.e., from Fez), they too may have migrated to the Ziban during the great maraboutic diaspora; their dominant position might have initially rested upon religious grounds.[86]

By the early nineteenth century, however, the Awlad Ziyan had evolved into secular notables with makhzan status, that is, with ties to the central government. Under the Turkish system, Tulqa's inhabitants enjoyed the exclusive privilege of serving as retainers in the great household of the dey of Algiers; whether this right was converted into local authority in the Ziban is uncertain but not unlikely. The Awlad Ziyan thus represented a group of hereditary administrators who exerted an uneasy control over the adjacent villages of al-'Amri, Fughala, and Za'atsha. In the Ottoman period, the shaykhs of Tulqa were exempt from taxation and received the burnus of investiture from the bey of the Constantine. They levied taxes upon the villagers, half of which in theory were remitted to the bey's treasury. Bloody fighting not infrequently erupted between the Awlad Ziyan and the ahl Tulqa or the other villages, inevitably provoked by fiscal exactions. In addition, quarrels and pitched battles with nearby al-Burj, which was outside of Tulqa's administrative ambit, were a semipermanent feature of oasis life. Therefore, the daunting task for religious notables, such as the 'Azzuz family or Sidi 'Ali b. 'Umar's clan, was not so much to prevent disputes as to manage social conflict when it erupted by effecting temporary reconciliations.[87] This task devolved even more so upon local Rahmaniyya shaykhs after the fall of the Turkish regime in 1830 and particularly with the French army's arrival in the pre-Sahara during the 1840s.

'Ali b. 'Umar's first encounter with the Rahmaniyya order and its founder came as he returned from a pilgrimage to the Hijaz. Stopping off in Constantine, where news of Sidi Muhammad b. 'Abd al-Rahman's preaching and miracles had created a sensation among the learned and the unlettered alike, Sidi 'Ali made his way to the Rahmaniyya zawiya in the Jurjura. (While the exact date of this is uncertain, it must have occurred prior to 1793–1794, the year of Sidi Muhammad b. 'Abd al-Rahman's death.) There Sidi 'Ali was initiated into the tariqa by Shaykh 'Abd al-Rahman himself, a sign of favor which was later converted into considerable sociospiritual prestige, for Sidi 'Ali eventually received the very important sufi honorific of *qutb* (literally, "pole").[88]

Leaving the Kabylia for his native town, Sidi 'Ali b. 'Umar began teaching Rahmaniyya doctrines in the Ziban. However, membership in the new tariqa meant that he became a disciple and subordinate of Shaykh Muhammad b. 'Azzuz of al-Burj, the muqaddam for the order's Saharan affiliates. Several decades later, Shaykh Muhammad b. 'Azzuz passed over his numerous sons and disciples to select 'Ali b. 'Umar as his spiritual heir. Sidi 'Ali held the office of Rahmaniyya *shaykh al-shuyukh* from 1819 until 1842, when death surprised him in that quintessential saintly function—mediation. In addition, Muhammad b. 'Azzuz entrusted Sidi 'Ali with the education of his son Mustafa b. 'Azzuz, who spent several years at the Tulqa zawiya as a student. The subjects offered to students were not only the Quran, hadith, and fiqh but also classical Arabic literature, *kalam* or theology, and the mystical sciences. As important, Tulqa boasted an especially fine library enclosing some three thousand manuscripts by the middle of the past century; many had been brought back from the Mashriq by Rahmaniyya notables when performing the hajj, as Sidi 'Ali had done with his spiritual preceptor, Muhammad b. 'Azzuz.[89] While the exact dates of Mustafa's stay in Tulqa are unknown, he probably studied under Sidi 'Ali in the 1820s, as first his disciple and then his future successor. Moreover, the fact that Mustafa was sent to learn at Sidi 'Ali's side indicates that Shaykh 'Azzuz had chosen this particular son to continue his work as a leading Rahmaniyya muqaddam.

Shaykh-murid ties between the 'Azzuz of al-Burj and their counterparts in Tulqa eventually spanned several generations. Following the practice of endogamy among religious clans, Muhammad b. 'Azzuz wedded one of his daughters, Dhakhira, to Sidi 'Ali b. 'Umar.[90] Thus, the two families were closely tied not only by the Rahmaniyya link but also by matrimonial bonds. Their alliance endured for nearly a century. Yet spiritual association eventually gave way to struggles between the 'Azzuz clan in the Tunisian Jarid and Sidi 'Ali's successors. Bitter quarrels over religious clients and dwindling offerings were largely the product of the 1881 French conquest establishing Tunisia as a protectorate.

The growth of the Rahmaniyya order in Tulqa, underwritten by Sidi 'Ali b. 'Umar's spiritual intimacy with both the founder-saint and Shaykh 'Azzuz, enhanced the clan's fortunes and those of the oasis. Symbolic of the older linkage between the saints and oasis economy was the location of their zawiya near 'Ain Umm Kara, the spring that furnished Tulqa with water before flowing into the gardens. The zawiya was also situated close to the town's main suqs along the road leading from Tulqa to al-Burj.[91]

Sidi 'Abd al-Hafiz of Khanqa Sidi Naji

At the oasis's center is a group of well-built houses clustered together like the buildings of a fortress; rising above them is the qubba of Sidi 'Abd al-Hafiz. The dwellings of Khanqa Sidi Naji are better kept than elsewhere in the Jabal Cherchar. The town resembles rather an Egyptian village with its small, industrious quarters; surrounding it is a wall which was recently repaired after a pitched battle with the oasis of Liana over the division of water [from the Wadi al-'Arab].[92]

As discussed in chapter 1, the southern Awras has always participated in the Ziban's social, political, and religious rhythms. Thus, the Rahmaniyya movement as well as later movements of anticolonial protest found a resonance in the region. The amicable ties uniting Rahmaniyya notables of Tulqa and al-Burj in the precolonial and early colonial eras contrast markedly with those between Sidi 'Abd al-Hafiz b. Muhammad of Khanqa Sidi Naji and his saintly nemesis, 'Ali b. 'Umar. The spiritual enmity between these two sufi centers was politically significant. It reveals the process of tariqa fragmentation that often followed the death of a charismatic shaykh, in this case Sidi Muhammad b. 'Azzuz. Moreover, rivalries among branch Rahmaniyya centers constituted an important element in "maraboutic politics" (to use Eickelman's term) and, by extension, in regional contests for power. Competition for religious hegemony shaped to no small degree the individual responses of Rahmaniyya shaykhs to the colonial regime after 1830.

The oasis of Khanqa Sidi Naji emerged during the breakdown of central government authority in the early sixteenth century. The town's founders, the Awlad Nasir b. Sidi Naji, had served as guardians of Sidi 'Uqba b. Nafi''s tomb-shrine near Biskra until endemic tribal warfare forced them to retreat into the Jabal Cherchar. In the southern Awras near the Wadi al-'Arab, they established a village and religious center that was frequented by the Namamsha tribal confederacy when migrating between the Sahara and Tebessa. Eventually, two families, the Awlad Sidi Naji and the ancestors of Sidi 'Abd al-Hafiz, shared—and disputed—control of the oasis and mosque-shrine.[93]

Shaykh 'Abd al-Hafiz's clan was yet another saintly lineage of sharifian pretensions, although they traced their origins to Fez and not the Saqiya al-Hamra'. Arriving in the Ziban sometime in the seventeenth century, the family established religious centers in Biskra and Zariba al-'Arab, an oasis immediately south of the Jabal Cherchar and located along the commercial routes linking Biskra to the Tunisian Jarid. For reasons unknown, the Awlad Sidi Naji invited the Sidi 'Abd al-Hafiz's ancestors to reside in Khanqa Sidi Naji, an offer they soon regretted; the newcomers founded a zawiya which also served as an educational establishment. Predictably, relations soured between the recent arrivals and the town's former masters; internecine struggles constantly broke out, lasting until well into the colonial era.[94] The decision by Sidi 'Abd al-Hafiz to join the Rahmaniyya order must be seen against the backdrop of these ancient disputes. Membership in the new, dynamic sufi tariqa further delineated the boundaries between the warring lineages since the Awlad Sidi Naji belonged to the older Qadiriyya order; Rahmaniyya affiliation may also have given 'Abd al-Hafiz a sociospiritual edge over his rivals, the Awlad Sidi Naji.

Sidi Muhammad b. 'Azzuz visited 'Abd al-Hafiz (1789–1850) in Khanqa Sidi Naji on a proselytizing mission sometime after being named Rahmaniyya muqaddam in the first decade of the nineteenth century. Impressed by his devout, bookish nature, Shaykh 'Azzuz initiated the local saint into the order and chose him to represent the Rahmaniyya in the Jabal Cherchar. In addition, Sidi 'Abd al-Hafiz studied at the al-Burj zawiya under Shaykh Muhammad and accompanied him on the pilgrimage to Mecca; both of these activities endowed 'Abd al-Hafiz with added moral and spiritual prestige. While the Rahmaniyya shaykh of Khanqa Sidi Naji had all the virtues expected of an 'alim, sufi, and saint—piety, erudition, and asceticism—he appears to have differed in personality from his peers. Less activist than Muhammad b. 'Azzuz or his son Mustafa, Shaykh 'Abd al-Hafiz preferred the studious calm of his zawiya to the bandwagon enthusiasm of the first generations of Rahmaniyya leaders. The shaykh's retiring, though charismatic, personality, influenced his relations with other Rahmaniyya notables and ultimately his involvement in anticolonial protest movements.

As noted above, Shaykh Muhammad b. 'Azzuz's death in 1819 produced dissension among his closest disciples. Now the leading Rahmaniyya muqaddam for the Sahara, Sidi 'Ali b. 'Umar undertook a spiritual coup against his sufi peer in Khanqa Sidi Naji. Accompanied by disciples from Tulqa, Shaykh 'Ali traveled to the Jabal Cherchar and had a mosque-zawiya constructed not far from Sidi 'Abd al-Hafiz's sufi center. The parvenus sought to woo clients away from 'Abd al-Hafiz, thereby undermining his religious authority. Spiritual competition even led to armed clashes between the two Rahmaniyya groups. The victims regarded the takeover as a provocative act, a saintly *casus belli*. Sidi 'Ali's untoward behavior suggests that he felt threatened by Sidi 'Abd al-Hafiz, or at least that he was overzealous in interpreting his mandate as Rahmaniyya muqaddam. However, the scheme failed for lack of popular support; the competing sufi lodge was abandoned several years later.[95]

Most colonial writers interpreted Shaykh 'Abd al-Hafiz's lasting antipathy toward his Rahmaniyya competitor in Tulqa as simply wounded amour propre; they dismissed intersufi contention as but another example of petty "clerical quarrels."[96] Yet the incident demonstrates both the causes of, and the forms assumed by, local maraboutic politics. It also reveals implicit contradictions in the socially constructed persona of the North African holy person. The literature, indigenous and colonial, invariably casts the saint and sufi in the role of peacemaker; yet these same religious notables might also disturb the very peace they theoretically guaranteed. Thus, pious mediators could themselves, in certain circumstances, trigger communal discord and social conflict. Moreover, the clashes that erupted between the two warring shaykhs' clienteles indicate that elite strife also directly involved the humbler members of society. Finally, this incident sheds light upon the question of acquired versus inherited loyalties within the idiom of sufism. It suggests that the older ties of religious allegiance between village or tribal clients and privileged saintly lineages took precedence over acquired loyalties to a new sufi order and its leader—Sidi 'Ali b. 'Umar—who significantly came from outside the Awras mountains.

The animosity between the Rahmaniyya clans of Tulqa and Khanqa Sidi Naji would intensify with initial colonial sweeps into the pre-Sahara after 1844. These sufi rivalries help to explain the collective and individual political behavior of Rahmaniyya leaders when confronted by the dual challenge of foreign conquest and revolutionary apocalyptic movements led by mahdis. After Bu Ziyan's defeat in 1849, Sidi 'Abd al-Hafiz's idiosyncratic form of avoidance protest expanded his fund of popular veneration to the benefit of his sons who succeeded him as Rahmaniyya shaykhs.

The social trajectory of the saints of Khanqa Sidi Naji clearly demonstrates how a strategic alliance with an energetic sufi order worked to elevate a parochial religious lineage from local to regional social prominence. Membership in the new tariqa apparently fostered friendships with "big city" ulama. Sidi 'Abd al-Hafiz resided with the Bash Tarzis at their zawiya in Constantine when en route to perform the hajj on several occasions prior to his death in 1850. His sons founded secondary Rahmaniyya centers in oases, such as Liana, Tamarza, and Khayran, located significantly on the borders between Algeria and Tunisia and later even in Tunis. At first these zawaya were under the 'Azzuz's patronage, with whom the family also concluded matrimonial ties, but they subsequently became semi-independent.[97]

Also working in Shaykh 'Abd al-Hafiz's favor was the region's political economy. Khanqa Sidi Naji lay astride tribal migratory regimes and commercial routes linking the Awras and eastern Zab with the Tunisian Jarid. Because of location, the oasis-town was a trading center that traditionally provided guides for caravans. The Rahmaniyya zawiya participated in commercial exchanges as well as extending protection to travelers, pilgrims, and merchants. Its mosque-school provided education to tribal and sedentary clients, offering subjects such as mathematics and astrology in addition to the more conventional Islamic sciences. By the middle of the past century, many of the Jabal Cherchar's inhabitants were allied, in one way or another, with the Rahmaniyya establishment under Sidi 'Abd al-Hafiz's direction.[98]

Secondary Rahmaniyya Centers: Awlad Jallal and Sidi Masmudi

Located at the base of the Ahmar Khaddu range in the southern Awras mountains, the oasis of Sidi Masmudi is sheltered in the upper reaches of the Wadi al-Abyad to the northeast of Biskra. Being of much more modest stature than Tulqa or al-Burj, the zawiya of Sidi Masmudi is difficult to document for the precolonial period; information for the post–1830 era comes mainly from its leaders' participation in rebellion. Some of the Arabic sources mention Sidi Masmudi's shaykhs only in passing, if at all.[99] The Rahmaniyya zawiya was founded by Sadiq b. al-Hajj al-Masmudi (died 1862), one of Muhammad b. 'Azzuz's disciples, and subsequently a political ally of Mustafa b. 'Azzuz. The tariqa leaders of Sidi Masmudi were intimately involved in the 1849 uprising at Za'atsha, mobilizing their intrepid tribal followers to come to Bu Ziyan's aid. Despite—or perhaps because of—Bu Ziyan's defeat, Shaykh Sadiq and his sons declared another smaller jihad in 1858; two decades later, a second chiliastic movement erupted in 1879.[100] Thus, Bu Ziyan's messianic bid for power inspired two subsequent mahdist movements led by Sidi Sadiq and his descendants. Here is evidence that a tradition of religiously based political behavior was transmitted over several generations through the medium of Rahmaniyya notables and the sufi centers they controlled.

Outside of the Awras, another secondary Rahmaniyya center grew up, one which linked the Bu Sa'ada region to the Ziban. Muhammad al-Mukhtar b. Khalifa b. Abd al-Rahman (died 1862) was yet another disciple of Shaykh Muhammad b. 'Azzuz.[101] He established a Rahmaniyya zawiya in the oasis of Awlad Jallal, located to the southwest of Biskra, sometime in the early part of the nineteenth century. The family's origins matched those of the other religious clans discussed above—sharifian descent and migration to the Ziban from Morocco centuries earlier. Prior to joining the nascent Rahmaniyya movement, Muhammad al-Mukhtar enjoyed the status of a local holy man and member of the provincial ulama. Many of the family's clients were pastoral-nomadic peoples, such as the Awlad Na'il tribe, who looked to the saints to resolve the interminable disputes over water and pasturage.[102] When the Bu Ziyan uprising broke out in 1849, Sidi al-Mukhtar joined together with the 'Azzuz of al-Burj to openly back the rebels; moreover, he had earlier dappled in rebellious activity opposing the French regime. Nevertheless, a decade after Za'atsha's defeat, Shaykh al-Mukhtar refused to lend succor to those involved in the 1858–1859 revolt led by the Rahmaniyya elite of Sidi Masmudi; he even denied sanctuary to the defeated rebels in his zawiya in Awlad Jallal.[103]

Shaykh al-Mukhtar's death in 1862 unleashed strife over the question of spiritual succession among his sons and clients. The quarrels undermined unity and ultimately worked to the advantage of the great zawiya of al-Hamil, which assumed leadership of the Saharan Rahmaniyya under Shaykh Muhammad b. Abi al-Qasim's aegis by the century's close. Shaykh

Muhammad's own brand of accommodation with and subtle opposition to the colonial regime represented both a break with and a continuation of earlier Saharan Rahmaniyya patterns of coping with unfavorable political conditions. The shaykh's death in 1897 brought his only daughter, Zaynab, to the headship of the zawiya as well as new challenges for the tariqa's religious notables.

By this time, a little more than a century had elapsed since the death of the Rahmaniyya's founder, Sidi 'Abd al-Rahman al-Azhari al-Jurjuri. In that period, the Rahmaniyya in the Kabylia and the Sahara had come to be composed of intersecting networks of zawaya, clienteles, and sacred spaces. The order's major centers were directed by saintly lineages with more or less hereditary rights to privileged positions within the tariqa's loosely defined hierarchy. Moreover, Rahmaniyya affiliation enlarged the spiritual authority and social influence of these lineages. Their local prestige, moral authority, and economic well-being were contingent upon a number of factors: the push and shove of spiritual diplomacy; ties to (or compromises with) traditional authorities; participation in the local economy; the demands of clienteles; and finally the personality of the head shaykh.

By the eve of the first colonial thrusts into the pre-Sahara, the new tariqa claimed followers in a wide region stretching from Bu Sa'ada and the Ziban to the Tunisian borders, and from the southern Awras to the Wadi Righ.[104] If the original Rahmaniyya zawiya in the Jurjura sheltering the saint-founder's remains constituted the single most important site for the entire order, the establishments in Tulqa and al-Burj were regionally prominent; while the centers at Sidi Khanqa Naji, Sidi Khalid, and Sidi Masmudi were of lesser distinction. The political upheavals of the French conquest would upset the relative importance of these sufi centers. Eventually several new Rahmaniyya complexes—in the Jarid and in al-Hamil—would partially eclipse those in the Ziban and Awras. Significantly, these two zawaya were both located outside, or at the margins of, the colonial system of domination.

Profane Politics, Sacred Politics

Older saintly quarrels, the ideology of the holy man, and the political economy of the desert shaped the later responses of religious notables to the French invasion. But what of the ties between "secular" political elites and sufi leaders of the emerging Rahmaniyya order? Information on relationships between provincial or rural Muslim notables and traditional central authorities or their local representatives is not abundant.[105] Yet these older relationships are also crucial to an understanding of the conquest era since France at first attempted to control her fractious African prize by relying upon Turkish ruling formulas. And if the deylical regime collapsed precipitously in 1830, many of the traditional political arrangements endured in one form or another for decades after the fall of Algiers.

It can be posited that the ruling caste in provincial capitals, like Constantine, bestowed honors, privileges, and other forms of both symbolic and material recognition upon desert religious notables, such as the Rahmaniyya lineages of the Ziban. Nevertheless, the Rahmaniyya's founder, a Berber from eastern Algeria, enjoyed a somewhat ambiguous relationship with the Turkish rulers in Algiers. On the one hand, according to the founder-saint's biographer, Muhammad al-Hafnawi, the pasha (dey) invited Sidi Muhammad b. 'Abd al-Rahman to the capital to instruct him and his family in sufi doctrines from the East. This the saint and sufi obligingly did, even residing in the ruler's household for a time. While al-Hafnawi cited this incident as a moral parable regarding rightful sufi *adab* (conduct) in the palaces of the mighty, he also implied that religious notables could dwell among the most powerful without necessarily incurring moral opprobrium.[106] On the other, some within ruling circles in Algiers viewed Sidi Muhammad b. 'Abd al-Rahman as a potential danger to the political order. His movement, based upon eastern Khalwatiyya reformism, was deemed menacing due to the social composition of his popular following—among the bellicose Kabyle mountain folk of the Jurjura only imperfectly within the political center's grasp. Only the saint's departure from the capital in the early 1790s, and perhaps the threat of unrest from his partisans, saved him from harm.

Moreover, the interest that governing elites took in rural or provincial holy men did not stop at the borders of the two Ottoman regencies. The Husaynid rulers of Tunis courted sufi leaders in neighboring Algeria as a matter of policy, conferring gifts and establishing hubus to their benefit. For example, both the Rahmaniyya zawiya of Khanqa Sidi Naji and the Tijaniyya centers of Gummar (Guémar) and Tammasin (Témacin) in southeastern Algeria received Tunisian subsidies. The generosity of Tunisia's princes to religious notables in Algeria would assume political importance after 1830.[107] But what of relations between religious notables and the local secular elites upon whom the rulers in distant capitals inevitably relied to govern places like the pre-Sahara?

Collective social action in the post–1830 period cannot be fully grasped without understanding the surrounding political milieu within which privileged saintly lineages had always operated. Mention has been made of the fact that saints and sufis, such as Sidi Muhammad b. 'Azzuz, were compelled by their peacekeeping functions to resolve disputes for tribal shaykhs.[108] Religious clans, like the 'Azzuz of al-Burj, were enmeshed in a political culture dominated by the play of the saffs or leagues and the struggles of tribal warlords, above all, the Bu 'Ukkaz and Banu Ghana. Moreover, the fragmentary evidence that exists for the precolonial era raises issues about the truism of the holy man's professional neutrality, which may have been in practice more nuanced than previously thought.

The Rahmaniyya of Tulqa traditionally maintained amicable ties with central authorities—or rather with their regional delegates. Sidi 'Ali b. 'Umar was the friend and adviser of the Banu Ghana's leader, who headed one of the saffs that divided the pre-Sahara's inhabitants into two political camps.[109] While the saffs were a much older mechanism for venting as well as containing political struggles, in the late eighteenth century the leagues of the southern Constantine became embroiled in a fierce contest between the Banu Ghana and the Bu 'Ukkaz for the coveted post of shaykh al-'arab, a contest discussed in detail in the next chapter. In addition to friendship and patronage with the Banu Ghana, the Rahmaniyya notables of Tulqa were also on amicable terms with the oasis's local secular shaykhs, the Awlad Ziyan. Significantly, in the Jabal Cherchar, Sidi 'Abd al-Hafiz's rivals, the Awlad Sidi Naji, were also aligned with the Banu Ghana, which suggests that the Rahmaniyya shaykh may have been on the opposing side.[110]

In contrast to the leaders of Tulqa, the 'Azzuz of al-Burj appear to have had a preference for the Bu 'Ukkaz clan. Shaykh Muhammad even sent the eldest of his eight sons, al-Hasan, to be educated from childhood on at the Bu 'Ukkaz's *zamala* (a tribal camp or settlement; in Turkish North Africa, a tribal cavalry serving the state). There Hasan was raised as a sort of warrior-marabout, reminiscent of the older Maghribi tradition of the ribat. The French commandant, Jospeh-Adrien Seroka, who eventually fought against Hasan b. 'Azzuz in the Ziban, provided this portrait of him, one of the few such descriptions of a sufi personage from the period:

> There was something extraordinary about his appearance; his
> head was as large as a bull's, his arms and legs were enormous,
> his voice was like a lion's roar. Seeing his thick mass, made
> rather for the leisure of the zawiya than the life of a soldier, one
> would never have believed that he [Hasan b. 'Azzuz] was an ac-
> complished cavalryman and fierce warrior.[111]

In marked contrast, Hasan's brother, Mustafa b. 'Azzuz was given a scholar's education and groomed as a future leader of the Saharan Rahmaniyya. Another younger sibling, Muhammad, was shaykh of the small Rahmaniyya center in the oasis of Sidi Khalid; other males in the lineage also followed religious careers. Thus, Hasan's training was unique among the eight male offspring of Shaykh Muhammad b. 'Azzuz. Confiding a son to the Bu 'Ukkaz for warrior training may have been a calculated strategy to cement relations between powerful desert warlords and a sufi order then in the process of expansion. This strategy would have protected not only the 'Azzuzes' interests but also those of the nascent tariqa. Conversely, the Bu 'Ukkaz may have sought legitimacy by associating themselves with the leader of the most dynamic sufi order in the Sahara at the time. Finally, enrolling a son in a "secular" profession ensured that sainthood, baraka, and leadership were not disputed, and thus dissipated, among family members from a single privileged lineage.

Given the close ties between the two sufi clans, the fact that the 'Azzuz of al-Burj opted for one saff while the Rahmaniyya notables of Tulqa were associated with the opposing political league appears perplexing. Nevertheless, it may have been a form of saintly realpolitik—bet hedging dictated by the rapid shifts in the political wheel of fortune as first the Banu Ghana and then their opponents momentarily gained power. This form of coping to ensure political survival was repeatedly relied upon by many Muslim notables during and after the conquest period.

From Religious Hinterland to Religious Center and Back Again

In characterizing the ulama corps associated with the Azhar mosque-university in Cairo, John Voll observed that "the various parts of the Islamic community were in constant interaction. The local religious establishment itself was not a closed corporation."[112] This observation applies equally to the Saharan sufi notables and saints just considered; many of them participated in the Islamic ecumene forged, in large part, by itinerant, cosmopolitan scholars. The continual circulation of Muslims of elevated or modest social rank to and from the Hijaz implicated religious hinterlands in larger sociospiritual currents.

The annual pilgrimage was the single most important transregional vehicle for integration into the Islamic mainstream; the hajj also frequently brought social mobility as well. Fulfilling one of the duties of Islam meant that the returning hajji or pilgrim inevitably acquired a new social status within the community. A sojourn in Mecca, regarded as a microcosm of the universe, enlarged spiritual horizons and deepened the sense of what it meant to be a Muslim.[113] In addition, the North African caravan, composed of thousands of Maghribi and West African pilgrims, disseminated new ideas, information, and rumors along the route stretching from Taza in Morocco to the Holy Cities. Several of the most activist African sufi orders of the late eighteenth and nineteenth centuries had their origins in pilgrimages to the Mashriq and Haramayn; this was particularly true of the Rahmaniyya.

Thus, the geographical displacement necessitated by pilgrimage produced other displacements as well—spiritual quests concerned with the soul's journey, the search for religious knowledge and social enhancement, were all intimately related. As seen in the biographies of Rahmaniyya notables, provincial religious figures often pursued advanced studies in Constantine, Fez, or Tunis before setting out for the Mashriq. After performing the hajj, they might linger for years in institutions like al-Azhar to complete their education. In doing so, they invariably shed their provincial status and acquired a new social rank through intimate association with the Islam's normative core. The peregrinations of these notables, their ties to the great hubs of Islamic science, integrated local patterns of religious belief and ritual into the wider Muslim community. The re-creation of Islam's universal traditions in a culturally specific setting is manifest in the Rahmaniyya libraries and manuscript collections housed in the zawaya on the Sahara's rim.

Even when travels for pious purposes took them no farther than Maghribi cities, rural religious figures frequently prolonged their stays in urban madrasas and mosque-universities for years. In the city, the more fortunate were able to form sociospiritual alliances with high-ranking ulama families. Whether temporary or prolonged, sojourns in North African capitals meant that scholars hailing from remote villages or humble towns had access to information about political events or intellectual debates from the wider Islamic world. When they returned to their respective towns or tribes, which the vast majority did, individuals like Sidi Muhammad b. 'Abd al-Rahman or Shaykh Muhammad b. 'Azzuz then served as social conduits between metropolis and countryside. In short, sufi notables of small-town origins fashioned multiple contacts with urban social milieux, whether in their own countries or more far-flung areas of the Dar al-Islam, through the mechanisms of tariqa membership, education, and pilgrimage.

Paralleling the hajj were the numerous regional pilgrimages or ziyaras in North Africa which brought together different groups from widely dispersed areas at certain times in the liturgical year. Thus, despite apparent isolation, the pre-Sahara's oasis and tribal communities shared in a number of local, regional, and transregional networks. Even the oasis peasant, seemingly tied to the relentless date cultivation cycle, participated in these networks. Along with the movement of commodities and pastoral-nomadic groups, a certain degree of labor exchange occurred between desert and coastal cities. Indeed, given the ecological restraints imposed by the environment, survival in the densely populated oases depended upon the maintenance of ties with the outside. The smooth functioning of the local economy depended upon the unhampered movement of individuals and groups, whether to trade, search for pasturage, perform the pilgrimage, or complete an education.

Like the hajj, affiliation with one or several of the great ramified sufi turuq was another element working against social closure. It was precisely this lack of closure—the cross-border relations generated by religion, commerce, and politics—that alarmed Algeria's French rulers. The vast, open expanses of the desert with its ill-defined frontiers plagued the colonial regime first in Algeria and later in Tunisia. Conversely, France's tireless efforts to close off or monitor the borders between the North African states would eventually transform the nature of the Rahmaniyya movement and the political behavior of its privileged lineages.

3 Hedging Bets in a Time of Troubles

Algeria, 1830–1849

While they were in power
The Turks were the elites among men
Each fort had its garrison.[1]

The decades immediately preceding the French expedition of 1830 are usually characterized in the literature, both colonial and recent, as the nadir of Turkish rule in Algeria.[2] However, this dismal picture must be fundamentally modified. True, the regime in Algiers suffered in comparison with Tunisia, where the Husaynid dynasty was firmly embedded in the country's political culture. And the military oligarchy of the deys and beys had always been short on religiomoral legitimacy since, unlike Morocco's 'Alawi dynasty, the Turks enjoyed little Islamic justification for their rule. Moreover, the departure of the Spanish from Oran in 1792 meant that Algiers could no longer claim to be the bulwark of Islam against the infidels. Ironically, after the deylical regime's collapse, the populace lamented the passing of the Turks; collective hopes for deliverance by the Porte remained in force until late in the century.

It can be maintained, however, that the Turkish-Algerian state was in a process of consolidation by the early nineteenth century; in the Constantine, the hereditary principle was emerging as the beys formed alliances, including matrimonial, with prominent Arab families.[3] If some historians now argue that an Algerian state—a peculiar kind of state—was in existence prior to 1830, none deny that profound reversals in the arena of Mediterranean commerce and politics had occurred.[4] As aggressive Western nations transformed the Mediterranean into a European lake, privateering, formerly so lucrative for Algiers, was eclipsed. To make up for declining revenues, the central government increased fiscal demands upon the countryside and upon groups normally excused from taxation or only lightly taxed. The shift from the earlier laissez-faire approach in governing to a more interventionist style met with radical, rural-based opposition. While the incidence of rebellion has been employed as a

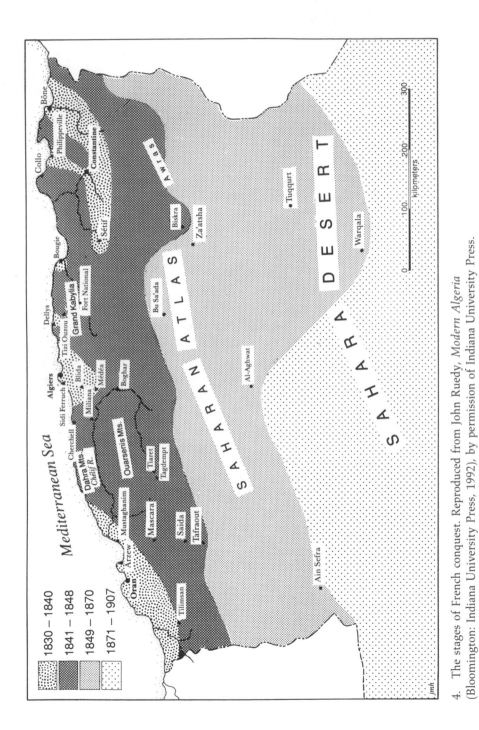

Mediterranean Sea

SAHARAN ATLAS

SAHARA DESERT

A w r ā s

1830 – 1840
1841 – 1848
1849 – 1870
1871 – 1907

Bône
Collo
Philippeville
Constantine
Bougie
Sétif
Za'atsha
Biskra
Touggourt
Warqala
Dellys
Fort National
Grand Kabylia
Tizi Ouzou
Bu Sa'ada
Algiers
Sidi Ferruch
Blida
Miliana
Médéa
Cherchell
Boghar
Al-Aghwat
Dahra Mts.
Chélif R.
Ouarsenis Mts.
Tiaret
Tagdempt
Mustaghanim
Arzew
Mascara
Oran
Saïda
Tafraout
Tilimsan
Ain Sefra

0   100   200   300
kilometers

jmh

4. The stages of French conquest. Reproduced from John Ruedy, *Modern Algeria*
(Bloomington: Indiana University Press, 1992), by permission of Indiana University Press.

compelling index of a state in crisis, the same evidence could be marshaled to argue that revolt was the response of communities striving to retain older traditional autonomy vis-à-vis a progressively more powerful center.

Rebellious activity was particularly fecund in the Oran, although the Kabylia and other parts of the Constantine also experienced local resistance. In both areas, insurgency was frequently led by militant religious figures, often of popular origins, who enjoyed tribal support. A case in point is the series of uprisings that shook western Algeria between 1783 and 1805. Initially tax revolts, these movements came under the headship of the nascent Darqawiyya sufi order (named after al-'Arabi al-Darqawi, died 1823) whose recruitment gave expression to the grievances of ordinary people in the countryside. By 1805, the stakes had been substantially transformed. The leader of the Darqawiyya in western Algeria, 'Abd al-Qadir b. al-Sharif, together with the major tribes, announced his intent of conquering the entire regency.[5] Only the energetic military intervention of Oran's newly appointed bey wrested the province from the insurgents, although the movement endured in one form or another until 1827—three years before the arrival of the French expedition.

While the Constantine was also the scene of periodic rural tax rebellions, the uprising of 1804–1807 was quite another matter for it had implicit mahdist undertones. Inspired by a Kabyle Darqawi sufi muqaddam, this full-scale revolt was greatly aided by a local Rahmaniyya shaykh, Zabbushi, from the region of Mila. Sidi 'Abd Allah Zabbushi mobilized large numbers of combatants, largely by appeal to Rahmaniyya tariqa loyalties; the rebels nearly succeeded in taking Constantine.[6] As significant were the undercurrents of millenarian fervor, particularly evident in this uprising. The tradition of collaboration between some rural sufi leaders and chiliastic figures, popularly regarded as saviors from injustice, would endure throughout the nineteenth century. Therefore traditional modes or styles of collective political action remained in force, in some cases until the early twentieth century.[7]

Before the Fall: The Pre-Sahara, c. 1800–1830

Peter von Sivers has emphasized the complexity and efficiency of the Turkish governmental apparatus, rather than its rudimentary nature, for it "was a complicated mechanism with at least five different levels of administration going from completely dominated, tribute-rendering populations to independent tribes authorized to trade in Turkish-held markets."[8] The pre-Sahara was no exception to this. In control of Biskra by the mid-sixteenth century, the central government employed the oasis as an advance post to achieve the submission, however tenuous, of more distant desert cities. Biskra served as the seat of power for the shaykh al-'arab, whose fortified residence was situated on a hill commanding the principal irrigation canals bringing water into the gardens. Thus, the oasis, and the Ziban in general, marked the fluid limits between effective Turkish rule and that of Saharan princes and tribal strong men.[9] Moreover, here contests for power tended to coalesce around the position of shaykh al-'arab.

While the Mzabi cities jealously guarded political (if not economic) independence, al-Aghwat, Tuqqurt, and Warqala were within reach of military units dispatched from Biskra. Until the late eighteenth century, Algiers left these desert entrepôts to local dynasties that rendered tribute in exchange for trading rights in Turkish-held markets. The government traditionally employed market strategies to bring the recalcitrant to heel. Particularly vulnerable were the oases and mountains, places also serving as havens for fugitives, bandits, and rebels. A blockade of strategic markets brought temporary submission and the rendering of tribute or hostages. (The French army adopted similar market strategies in its pacification of both the Kabylia and pre-Sahara.)[10] In addition, periodic expeditions to the Ziban, Wadi Righ, and Warqala reminded the fractious Saharans of Turkish authority. Nevertheless, until the eighteenth century, the returns from military intervention in the desert were scarcely worth the investment in resources.[11]

Then the traditional arrangement of force in the pre-Sahara was profoundly altered as military and fiscal activity increased. This rearrangement was partially a response to dwindling revenues from privateering, which made the oases relatively more attractive sources of revenue. The years 1785, 1788, and 1826 witnessed tax-collecting forays into the area between Biskra and Warqala. Similar sorts of fiscal pressure were exerted upon the western Sahara, culminating in sieges of the Tijaniyya stronghold in 'Ayn Madi in 1788, 1820, 1822, and 1827. These assaults upon the Tijaniyya tariqa in the Oran shaped the later political stance of that sufi order's notables toward the colonial regime.[12]

In addition to the threat of force majeure and market manipulation, the political center employed other means to coax rebellious oases into yielding tribute. Military contingents might divert the water supply from gardens or destroy precious date-palm trees until the insurgents sued for peace. This same tactic was used by the French army in the 1849 Za'atsha conflict, although without achieving the desired effect.[13] In the Constantine, the beys intervened more directly into desert politics by sowing dissension among regional strongmen. In this scheme, the post of shaykh al-'arab afforded endless possibilities for meddling in local struggles.

Theoretically, the bey governed the entire province in the name of the dey of Algiers. However, the exercise of day-to-day authority in the pre-Sahara devolved upon the shaykh al-'arab, an official normally residing in Biskra. Under him were seven great Arab tribes; the shaykh also enjoyed administrative authority over sedentary oasis populations in the region stretching from the Ziban to Tuqqurt, some two hundred kilometers below Biskra. Along with this office went the lucrative privilege of leading the winter mahalla in its annual tax-collecting duties. In return, the shaykh remitted a variable proportion of the revenues extracted, which fluctuated in accordance with the makhzan's coercive force. As was true for the Tunisian Jarid, the mahalla coincided with the autumn months when transhumant tribes descended from the Tell to the desert to search for pasturage and participate in the date harvest.[14] From the middle of the sixteenth century, the office of shaykh al-'arab was monopolized by a single clan, the Bu 'Ukkaz, an Arab tribal elite claiming descent from the Banu Hillal; since the medieval period, they had provided secular shaykhs to the southern Constantine. To counter the clan's excessive power, Salah Bey elevated an upstart lineage, the Banu Ghana to the post of shaykh al-'arab. The Bu 'Ukkaz's fall from grace upset the age-old distribution of power and meant that "the history of the [eastern] Sahara was reduced to the struggles of these two families, which the Turks supported alternately in accordance with the principle of divide and rule."[15] Employing an economy of means to rule, the beys rarely mounted military expeditions against an incumbent fallen from favor. Instead they appointed a rival clan leader to the coveted position; whoever succeeded in holding the passages between desert and Tell during the tribal migrations was subsequently invested in office.

Predictably struggles over the position found expression in the play of two saffs, or political leagues. Fallout from the saff conflict shook the Ziban, the Suf, and even oases as far south as Tuqqurt and Warqala. Biskra's inhabitants deserted the older town to disperse into a number of small hamlets scattered in the palm gardens for protection. Interminable factional strife among the ruling clans of Tuqqurt (the Jallab dynasty) and Warqala (the Allahum family) also implicated these rich oases in the Banu Ghana–Bu 'Ukkaz quarrels. Their disputes even extended into the Suf, where one coalition of oases allied itself with Tuqqurt and the Banu Ghana, another with Tammasin and the Bu 'Ukkaz. From the late Turkish period until well into the colonial era, political contests in the pre-Sahara were shaped by the intense rivalry for the office of shaykh al-'arab expressed in the war of the saffs.[16]

Nevertheless, the incessant rivalry over this office, lasting well beyond the Turkish era, constituted a significant statement about "traditional" Algerian political culture. It reveals not chaos and anarchy—as later colonial commentators would have it—but rather that indigenous elites competed fiercely for a recognized station *within* the prevailing system of power. Indeed, the ancient prestige associated with the shaykh al-'arab was too firmly embedded in Saharan political behavior for either the Amir 'Abd al-Qadir or local religious notables, like Hasan b. 'Azzuz, to overcome— even when battling the French occupiers.[17]

However, as long as the binary principle was operative, strife could be more or less managed by professional neutrals, such as Rahmaniyya sufi notables or local saintly lineages. Once a third locus of power, the colonial army, was introduced after 1830—one outside of the system at first and thus unpredictable—the role of mediators became more complex, reconciliation more difficult to achieve.[18] Indeed, in 1842 Sidi 'Ali b. 'Umar, head of Tulqa's Rahmaniyya clan and the leading sufi shaykh of the Sahara, lost his life in a mediation attempt during a three-way struggle involving the saffs and their French opponents.

Fly Whisks and Empires: The Fall of Algiers

By the eve of the 1830 conquest, order had been restored and the rebellions put down, and political calm reigned for the most part in Turkish Algeria. The real danger was not so much from within but from neighbors across the sea. Despite muted calls by some French commercial interests to rid the Mediterranean of "Algerine piracy," few prior to 1827 in Europe or the Maghrib anticipated that France would soon acquire an African "département."[19] As the Napoleonic Wars ended, France's days as a global imperial power seemed to be waning. The loss of first Canada and then India during the Seven Years' War of 1756–1763 made France a second-rate colonial power, with only small commercial enclaves in Africa, Asia, and the West Indies.

Then the French stumbled into Algeria. Eventually the North African state represented an emblem of Great Power status, a measure of national and international dignity, regardless of Algeria's economic value or cultural compatibility with the Metropole.[20] Ultimately, the impetus for new colonial holdings, particularly in the Maghrib, the Sahara, and West Africa, was to no small degree dictated by the obsessive drive to defend the oldest of France's Afro-Mediterranean colonies. In reality, the Scramble for Africa was unleashed by an imprudent dey's fly whisk in 1827 and not, as some historians of imperialism claim, a half century later.[21] Yet France was imprudent as well. Compared with other imperial ventures, Algeria's subjugation demanded the most lavish expenditure of men and materials—far greater than Britain's conquest of India. Prior to the expedition, it was calculated that no more than ten thousand troops would suffice to take Algeria; by 1847, one hundred thousand French soldiers were committed to the unfinished task of "pacifying" a population estimated at no more than three million.[22]

For obvious ideological reasons, colonial apologists maintained that the Algerian state, if indeed such existed, was tottering in 1830. Rather, the botched nature of the early French occupation, and the fierce resistance encountered, transformed Algeria into a contest state for decades.[23] Yet continuities in styles of rule and contestation persisted, principally because the French military consciously emulated their Turkish predecessors in erecting a system of domination for a country four times larger than France. The fall of Algiers was a rude shock not only to the capital's inhabitants but also to most in the regency, the Maghrib, and the Islamic world.[24] The dey's capitulation created a *sauve qui peut* mentality among traditional elites and notables, who scrambled to turn events to their own advantage. Collective opposition to the invaders was frequently combined with, or even overshadowed by, rebellions against the remnants of the Turkish ruling caste as well as ancient intraelite quarrels. The state was effectively up for grabs; yet paradoxically, those most absorbed in seizing the state were not at first the French invaders—or so it seemed to the Algerians. France's vacillations over the fate of its African prize were mirrored by military commanders in the field, whose equivocal proclamations, behavior, and policies betrayed a lack of resolve. Moreover, had not the Spanish been driven from Oran within recent memory? Could not the same destiny await the French?[25] Thus, the single most representative response on the part of many indigenous leaders was a wait-and-see position, an expression of bet hedging, which conferred considerable room for political manipulation and maneuvering. Gradually, two large-scale attempts at state building emerged: in the east, Ahmad Bey's effort to resurrect an Ottoman bureaucratic state; and in western Algeria, 'Abd al-Qadir's markedly different program of a classical tribal-based theocracy.

The Oran was the scene of the first concerted drive to right the toppled political order. Amir 'Abd al-Qadir's movement drew upon the religious legitimacy and organizational structure of the influential Qadiriyya sufi tariqa and the tribal traditions of the Eghris Plain near Mascara. Recognized in 1832 as sultan by the powerful Banu Hashim, the Banu 'Amir, and part of the Awlad Sidi Shaykh, the amir embarked upon a complex four-pronged program. First, he attacked French-held positions in Oran, while soliciting moral and material assistance from the Moroccan sultan, Mawlay 'Abd al-Rahman. At the same time, he endeavored to bring to submission Algerian tribes refusing to render tribute and thus acknowledge his authority. In addition, 'Abd al-Qadir clearly saw that control of key trading ports and towns was critical for the economic health of his fledgling state; commercial channels with Europe had to remain open to obtain needed military supplies, particularly gunpowder and firearms. Finally, the amir's dealings with the French, both in Algeria and the Metropole, displayed remarkable sophistication. Through agents, he followed debates in France over Algeria's political future and sought to bargain with local French authorities when negotiations yielded more tangible gains than did outright confrontation.[26]

The amir's approach to diplomacy and collective action served as a template for the political behavior of both secular and religious elites elsewhere in Algeria. Indeed, in the early 1850s, the Sharif of Warqala emulated the amir, after paradoxically fighting against 'Abd al-Qadir on France's side.[27] The complexity of 'Abd al-Qadir's statecraft—apparent accommodation combined with stalwart resistance and behind-the-scenes maneuvering—served to keep French commanders off guard and conferred strategic advantage.[28] As 'Abd al-Qadir's jihad gained momentum in the Oran, other experiments in reconstructing the state occurred in eastern Algeria.

The startling news that Algiers had fallen into infidel hands stirred the people of Constantine to action. By then the city's populace, under the Banu al-Fakkun's leadership, had attained an advanced, perhaps new, level of political maturity. During the tumultuous era stretching from 1792 to 1830, religious notables assumed increasingly public roles in the political fortunes of the city and province. These decades were characterized by revolts (in 1792, 1808, and 1817) or by sieges successfully repulsed (in 1804 and 1807) which politicized even ordinary people as well as making the Banu al-Fakkun more powerful than ever. Soon after the invasion, the capital's notables reinvested Ahmad Bey, who had been in office since 1823, as their ruler under the terms of a charter, specifying obligations and taxation procedures; the charter was signed by the ulama, shaykhs, and amins of the corporations.[29] All in the city, humble and mighty alike, looked hopefully, if vainly, to Istanbul for assistance.

The support of urban notables and temporizing by the Porte, combined with the political void created by French bungling, encouraged Ahmad Bey to carve out his own kingdom. To do this, rivals had to be eliminated, particularly in the pre-Sahara, where struggles over the office of shaykh al-'arab continued unabated, and with mounting ferocity. Thus, one force for political continuity between the Turkish and colonial eras was the persistence of these struggles. And the southern Constantine was one of the few regions where the two experiments in state formation, the amir's and Ahmad Bey's, collided. ˉ

The 1831 Siege of Za'atsha

The people of the Ziban are restless and turbulent in
character and much inclined toward fanaticism; the beys were
obliged on numerous occasions to resort to great severity in
repressing revolts, which at times required the use of
imposing force.[30]

Events in the north had an immediate resonance in the Ziban's oases. Yet politics in the desert were governed by the implicit principle of risk avoidance, which was dictated by the region's ecology, demographic realities, and the firepower available to indigenous leaders. There were limits to the amount of resources in men and materials any side would commit to a particular struggle; such was not, however, the case with the French army.

Ahmad Bey's nemesis, the Bu 'Ukkaz, led by Farhat b. Sa'id, employed the confusion of the 1831–1832 period to ensconce their forces in the Ziban, establishing headquarters in Tulqa. As always, the objective was to seize the post of shaykh al-'arab. The choice of Tulqa was also dictated by traditional strategic concerns. Holding this oasis conferred mastery over those tribes whose migratory regime traversed the Ziban and the gorge of al-Qantara. With Farhat b. Sa'id blocking the passages into the northern Constantine, the tribes had only one option—to fight with the Bu 'Ukkaz against the bey. Commanding superior forces with greater firepower, Ahmad Bey's forces, together with the Banu Ghana, chased most of the rebels out of the region for the moment. The victors then turned upon the unrepentant oasis of Za'atsha, which still sheltered tribal dissidents.[31]

Many small oases in the Zab Dahrawi—Tulqa, al-Burj, Za'atsha, and Lishana—were scarcely distinguishable from one another since their gardens abutted upon neighboring plantations; contiguity was frequently the source of bitter conflicts over shared water resources. Yet, during outbreaks of rebellion, as in 1831 and 1849, contiguity offered strategic advantage to villagers and tribal allies seeking to repulse outside forces. Like al-Burj, Za'atsha was surrounded by a water-filled moat and protected by sturdy walls surmounted by square towers pierced by narrow openings for firing upon assailants. Lost in a dense palm grove, the oasis was deemed impregnable by the Zab Dahrawi's inhabitants, who had always employed it as a fortified refuge. Moreover, the people of Za'atsha, who traditionally joined forces with adjoining Lishana, were regarded as intrepid warriors.[32]

While most of the Ziban's inhabitants, including the Awlad Ziyan of Tulqa, had sued Ahmad Bey for peace, Za'atsha and Lishana, feeling secure behind their walls, opted to fight. To test the rebels' resolve, the bey ordered his troops to cut down the date palms. This was not only a provocative but also a symbolically significant act. For the reaction elicited would reveal the depth and nature of grievances, signaling if mediation by religious leaders was probable. Rejecting arbitration, the two villages escalated the struggle, forcing the bey to lay a full-scale siege. Manipulating defense works effectively, the rebels inflicted such heavy losses upon the attackers that the siege was lifted. The investment in men and gunpowder was not worth the returns. As Ahmad Bey retreated north into the Tell, Farhat b. Sa'id, "the serpent of the desert," retook Biskra; the Ziban, the eastern Sahara, and the coveted post of shaykh al-'arab were his.[33]

The 1831 clash represents an important preface to the 1849 uprising because it was here that Bu Ziyan first earned a reputation for himself. Due to his energetic organization of oasis defenses, skills as a marksman, and leadership capabilities, Bu Ziyan proved instrumental in repulsing the attack. He would later draw upon the fund of prestige acquired in 1831 to advance claims as the mahdi, solicit public recognition by Rahmaniyya notables, and challenge the French colonial state. While this confrontation laid some of the groundwork for the later rebellion, it was principally a repeat performance of age-old clashes which tended to follow an established dramatic script. The Ahl b. 'Ali and Ghamara tribes, who owned the means of production in the small oasis, fought with the Bu 'Ukkaz league to repel the bey and his allies, the Banu Ghana.[34] Unlike the 1849 revolt, the 1831 resistance was a defensive type of collective political action whose main goal was to retain long cherished autonomy.

Between 1831 and 1849, however, the stakes changed drastically, although some of the traditional tactics and strategies endured. The earlier resistance lacked a religious basis, and local Rahmaniyya leaders were not involved in either the contest itself or its resolution; nor was there any hint of millenarian fervor on the part of the besieged. The 1849 movement was no longer solely defensive but was also offensive in its aims—to seize power and initiate the realm of justice as embodied by the mahdi. In the eighteen intervening years, traditions of oasis defense were gradually merged with mahdist ideology; bet hedging was no longer acceptable political behavior. If the 1831 clash created a local folk hero, Bu Ziyan, the next decade and a half undermined age-old mechanisms for managing conflict. The traditional alignments structuring the saff quarrels would eventually be upset by the entry of both the French army and the mahdi into the fray.

Unholy Alliances, 1831–1841

The history of the Biskra region is of great interest. By
knowing the principal families of the area, their hatreds, their
alliances, their vendettas, we are better able to govern them.
An intimate knowledge of the history of a conquered country
often aids the conqueror to avoid mishaps and disasters.[35]

Between 1832 and 1837, when the city of Constantine fell to General
Valée's army, the saff-based struggles in the pre-Sahara became more
complex. Disappointed by the wavering support of his protégé, Ahmad Bey
broke with the Banu Ghana's chief, thus creating a triangular struggle for
control of the Ziban.[36] In 1837 three important events transpired. One was
the conquest and sack of Constantine, which had serious economic and
political consequences for the entire province, north and south. Second, the
leaders of the two leagues sent out feelers in 1837 to French authorities
seeking military assistance against Ahmad Bey, according to the principle
"the enemy of my enemy is my friend." At first these overtures encountered evasive response because of the colonial policy of limited occupation.
Moreover, the governor-general, Valée, believed that the crucial theater of
operations lay in western Algeria, where the Treaty of Tafna had been
signed in 1837 between Amir 'Abd al-Qadir and the French government.
Finally, that same year the amir attempted to extend his authority into the
southern Constantine.[37]

The fall of Constantine was important for a number of reasons. Besieged
by two French military expeditions in 1836 and 1837, resistance was
organized and led by urban religious notables. When continued armed
opposition became futile, the terms of defeat were negotiated by Shaykh
al-Fakkun, the *shaykh al-balad* (head of the municipality). His son, Ham-
muda, was named *qa'id* (administrator) by the French and henceforth acted
as a conduit between the city's Muslim inhabitants and its new masters.[38]
Thus, for religious notables elsewhere, the city of Constantine represented
one model for proper political behavior when coping with rapidly changing
circumstances. Significant is the fact that popular protest was first mobilized and given shape by the city's leading religious families. Then, mutatis
mutandis, as the wheel of fortune turned in a different direction, they
agreed to negotiate with the occupiers; accommodation was surely viewed
as a temporary expedient.[39] After 1837 collective hopes for redemption
increasingly centered upon the great city by the Bosphorus.

Most Algerians, both ordinary and elite, looked to the Porte for deliverance. If the local Turkish oligarchy had been regarded as oppressive by

those outside of the small ruling circle, the Ottoman sultan represented the mightiest Muslim monarch and thus a potential savior. Prior to the siege of Constantine, rumors that an Ottoman fleet was headed for the Maghrib swept through Algeria. This news persuaded Ahmad Bey to suspend negotiations with the French over Constantine's political fate; Istanbul would rescue the country from the infidels. While the Ottoman navy was held off near Tripoli by a French naval squadron, the belief that military intervention by the Porte was forthcoming remained in force for much of the century. This belief also fed into the wellsprings of collective political action, encouraging resistance—or at least rumors about revolt.[40]

The misfortunes of 1837 convinced 'Abd al-Qadir that future prospects for peaceful coexistence with France were bleak. He used the reprieve created by the Treaty of Tafna to extend operations into eastern Algeria. At this juncture, the Bu 'Ukkaz's leader sought to induce the French to recognize his family's inherent rights to supremacy in the Ziban. Yet French military officials demurred, being acutely aware of their profound ignorance of the region's political geography. Failing at this, Farhat b. Sa'id then briefly threw in his lot with 'Abd al-Qadir. The amir seized this opportunity to gain a foothold in the pre-Sahara and appoint *khalifa*s (deputies) to administer the population and collect taxes in his name.[41] Hasan b. 'Azzuz, whose family origins were in some respects similar to 'Abd al-Qadir's, was instrumental in persuading the amir to follow this course of action. From al-Burj, the warrior-saint corresponded with 'Abd al-Qadir, describing the injustices wrought upon the Ziban's inhabitants by Ahmad Bey and the Banu Ghana and pleading for a new master. Significantly, the amir, whose clan had long been Qadiriyya sufi notables, also became a member of the Rahmaniyya tariqa. While piety may have been one motivating factor, 'Abd al-Qadir's main objective in joining the eastern province's most powerful sufi order was to gain support from Rahmaniyya leaders and enroll their popular followings under his banner.[42]

In 1839, Hasan b. 'Azzuz visited 'Abd al-Qadir at his headquarters in Médéa and was named khalifa of the Zab Dahrawi; the amir arranged for a military escort to accompany 'Azzuz back to the Ziban and install him in office. At the same time, 'Abd al-Qadir chose Muhammad al-Saghir b. Ahmad b. al-Hajj, a scion of a privileged saintly lineage in the oasis of Sidi 'Uqba, as his representative in the Zab Sharqi. Muhammad al-Saghir hailed from a powerful religious house claiming descent from 'Uqba b. Nafi' and venerated as the most eminent of the Zab Sharqi's *ashraf* (plural of *sharif*; designates a descendant of the Prophet Muhammad's house).[43] The amir's choice of local religious notables to represent his cause was wholly consonant with administrative policies in Oran, where a tradition of combined political and religious leadership had long existed.[44] However, such was less the case in the pre-Sahara, where the influence of the shaykh al-'arab—as either the focus of political loyalties or of contestation—was firmly embedded in local political culture. Moreover, the exercise of religious as opposed to political authority tended to be distinct in the Constantine.

As a result, neither Hasan b. 'Azzuz nor Muhammad al-Saghir was able to overcome the secular power of the Banu Ghana or the Bu 'Ukkaz in the eastern Sahara. Finally in 1840, 'Azzuz, lacking expertise as a military tactician, was roundly defeated near the strategic al-Wataya pass by forces loyal to the Banu Ghana. As always, the goal was to occupy the passages between Tell and desert which conferred mastery over migratory tribes and caravans laden with military stores and food supplies. The humiliating rout suffered by Hasan b. 'Azzuz seriously compromised 'Abd al-Qadir's jihad in the Ziban. More ominously, in 1841 General Bugeaud arrived back in Algeria as governor-general, and the earlier policy of limited occupation was discarded in favor of *occupation totale*; the era of French imperial uncertainty had ended.[45]

Despite Hasan b. 'Azzuz's short, unsuccessful tenure in office as a khalifa of the amir's fledgling state, the experiment was significant for its failure. It represented an effort, albeit a vain one, by a member of a prominent saintly lineage to fuse religious authority, political influence, and military might. However, 'Azzuz's demise was not merely the product of ineptness combined with the dominance of the saffs. Several incidents from the 1838–1840 period reveal the dilemma facing those who attempted to wield both sacred and profane power. Here some of the implicit and culturally constructed norms governing political behavior by religious notables are revealed.

In 1838 the Bu 'Aziz tribe, allied with the Banu Ghana, were trapped by Hasan b. 'Azzuz and his forces in the small oasis of al-'Amri. Al-'Amri was situated near al-Burj, seat of the Rahmaniyya zawiya administered by the 'Azzuz clan; most of the villagers were tariqa members and clients of the 'Azzuz. The Bu 'Aziz too were affiliated with the Rahmaniyya; many had been initiated into the sufi order by the great Shaykh Muhammad b. 'Azzuz or by his son Mustafa. Membership carried with it the right of protection and the duty of mutual assistance and respect. Had not the order's founder commanded the disciples in his sufi manual, *al-Rahmaniyya*, to "treat your [sufi] brothers well and serve them"?[46]

Caught between military concerns and the bonds of sufi kinship, 'Azzuz hesitated to attack the Bu 'Aziz. Into the impasse came the saint and Rahmaniyya shaykh of Tulqa, Sidi 'Ali b. 'Umar, who offered to arbitrate the conflict. In keeping with the tradition of the saint as mediator and adjudicator, Sidi 'Ali effected a compromise agreeable to all parties. The Bu 'Aziz paid blood money to 'Azzuz to compensate for the loss of warriors and defected from the Banu Ghana's league. Further turmoil was avoided, the oasis was spared a siege, and 'Azzuz's prestige was maintained.[47] In this instance, sufi ties prevailed over saff allegiances. Since a consensus still existed regarding the terms of saintly negotiation, the Rahmaniyya shaykh of Tulqa was able to hammer out a truce.

Sidi 'Ali's intercession saved Hasan b. 'Azzuz, but the warrior-saint's salvation was short-lived. The use of unstinting force to subdue the Ziban's inhabitants ultimately provoked a bitter quarrel within the 'Azzuz clan itself, one implicating other religious clans as well. Ceding to his troop's demands for war booty in 1838, Hasan b. 'Azzuz attacked a tribal fraction which had opted for neutrality. In doing so, 'Azzuz alienated the influential shaykh of Sidi 'Uqba, Muhammad al-Saghir, a fellow khalifa serving 'Abd al-Qadir's cause. Muhammad al-Saghir opposed waging war against neutrals and publicly expressed his conviction.[48] Thus in southeastern Algeria, the amir's movement was beset by internal strains similar to those in the Oran.

Hasan's actions also drew the opprobrium of some members of his own family, who may have disapproved of the efforts to conflate strongman politics with religious authority. One of Hasan's brothers, Muhammad, at the time the Rahmaniyya shaykh of Sidi Khalid and later the head of the order's zawiya in al-Qayrawan in Tunisia, was an intimate of the Shaykh of Sidi 'Uqba. Muhammad b. 'Azzuz sided with Muhammad al-Saghir and a family quarrel ensued. Mustafa and Muhammad b. 'Azzuz, the clan's two most powerful Rahmaniyya leaders, broke with their brothers, Hasan and Mabruk. A heated discussion at the family zawiya in al-Burj led to an abortive assassination attempt by Mabruk against Muhammad.[49]

The eruption of violence at the heart of a prominent religious family was shocking to the community; it left the 'Azzuz deeply divided when harmony among local notables was needed. Later Mabruk b. 'Azzuz, the youngest of Sidi Muhammad's eight sons, sought vengeance upon his brothers, particularly Mustafa. During the revolt of the Sharif of Warqala, Mabruk agreed to act as a paid French informant, providing information to military authorities in Algeria and Tunisia regarding his brother Mustafa's political activities in the Jarid.

Together these two incidents provide an unusual glimpse into sufi politics during a time of social turmoil and political uncertainty. They reveal the implicit codes of moral conduct incumbent upon religious figures, codes that conflicted with the dictates of profane contests for power. Hasan b. 'Azzuz's reluctance to wage battle against fellow Rahmaniyya members suggests that tariqa loyalties might override saff allegiances. If attacking league opponents, who were also family clients by virtue of sufi ties, was morally repugnant, then battling neutral tribes under the patronage of revered religious figures, such as Muhammad al-Saghir, was perilous. Once he had forfeited the moral backing of the Ziban's leading notables, 'Azzuz's movement—and by extension the amir's—was doomed.

Moreover, armed aggression by one member of a privileged saintly lineage upon another was popularly viewed as a scandalous act. Intrafamily disputes may have compromised the 'Azzuzes' prestige among some of their clients in the region. It might also explain in part why the Rahmaniyya shaykhs of Tulqa eventually supplanted the divided 'Azzuz clan, although Mustafa b. 'Azzuz's departure for the Tunisian beylik in 1844 shifted Rahmaniyya leadership to Sidi 'Ali b. 'Uthman. Finally, while Shaykh Mustafa's departure was primarily motivated by the Islamic duty of hijra, family quarrels in al-Burj could have made emigration a more attractive course of action.

The Perils of Saintly Mediation

In 1842 as the tribes moved north to summer pasturage, two armed contingents met before Tulqa: on one side was the shaykh of Sidi 'Uqba, Muhammad al-Saghir, still serving the amir; against his forces were ranged those of the Banu Ghana.[50] Following the lead of Tulqa's Rahmaniyya notables, one half of the oasis's population had declared support for the Banu Ghana; the rest joined the other saff now under Muhammad al-Saghir's leadership. Those in the latter league were from the "ahl Tulqa," who had long been subjected to the dominance of the Awlad Ziyan. In fact, bitter strife among Algeria's great warrior families had sparked small-scale revolts all over the country against local potentates, like the Awlad Ziyan, as well. The "ahl Tulqa" publicly signaled their rejection of the political order by murdering their shaykh, a member of the Awlad Ziyan, as he made his way to the Rahmaniyya zawiya. Tulqa's rebellious have-nots then petitioned the shaykh of Sidi 'Uqba to rule them while those villagers in the opposite league joined the Banu Ghana in giving battle; numerous casualties ensued.[51]

Seeking to avoid further bloodshed, Sidi 'Ali b. 'Umar, then head shaykh of the Saharan Rahmaniyya, offered once again to mediate as he had earlier done for 'Azzuz in 1838. Followed by a solemn retinue of sufi notables and brothers, Sidi 'Ali emerged from the entrance of the Rahmaniyya center located near the town's central marketplace. This was the *kharja*, the ritual processing of a sufi notable and his retinue from the zawiya that inaugurated festive religious occasions. His religious clients bore the banners of Sidi 'Ali's family and the Rahmaniyya tariqa; the procession's ceremonial vocabulary was a symbolically charged component of the peacemaking process. Yet the ritual of socioreligious reintegration was cut short. No sooner had the saint and sufi crossed the threshold of his zawiya then a stray bullet struck Sidi 'Ali in the breast, killing him instantly. Sidi 'Ali's murder was accidental; the bullet had been intended for the leader of the hated Awlad Ziyan. Terror stricken, the shaykh of Sidi 'Uqba ordered his forces to retreat immediately. To kill a sufi leader was to invite God's wrath; those responsible fled in panic. The battle for Tulqa was postponed, and the Banu Ghana subsequently took possession of the region by default. Sidi 'Ali b. 'Umar was buried in the family cemetery attached to the Rahmaniyya center.[52] His death brought a change in the order's leadership.

Following the pattern of alternating succession between the two leading Rahmaniyya families, the post of head shaykh reverted back to the 'Azzuz clan in 1842. That honor went to Sidi Muhammad b. 'Azzuz's favorite son, Mustafa, who had been tutored by Sidi 'Ali b. 'Umar at Tulqa, and who was the defunct saint's brother-in-law. Because of the baraka inherited both from his father and his spiritual preceptor, Mustafa b. 'Azzuz's headship of the Saharan Rahmaniyya, though short-lived, met with approval by the order's notables and rank and file. As the French officer investigating political conditions in the region after the seizure of Biskra in 1844 reported: "The Ben Azzouz [sic] exert enormous influence over the populations in and nearby to the oasis [of al-Burj]."[53]

The Two Sieges of Biskra, 1844

Even before Hasan b. 'Azzuz had been eliminated from the political stage and prior to Sidi 'Ali's death, the leader of the Bu 'Ukkaz, Farhat b. Sa'id, had withdrawn his support for 'Abd al-Qadir; defecting to France's side in 1838, he was rewarded with the post of qa'id for the pre-Sahara. While this was as yet an empty office—the pre-Sahara was completely outside of French control—still the entry of the colonial army into the tangle of desert politics eventually brought the temporary collapse of the saff mechanism. The defection of some tribal elites to the French camp also spelled the doom of the amir's movement, although these desertions should be read as another expression of bet hedging. For tribal big men, like Farhat b. Sa'id, the aim was not so much to advance France's cause as to manipulate support from the French military to overcome local indigenous rivals.

By the end of 1843, 'Abd al-Qadir's jihad was faltering; he was forced to retreat into Moroccan territory, where he requested asylum. General Bugeaud's crusade for total occupation and his scorched-earth policy had shattered the amir's movement. From this period on, his partisans could only muster local solutions to the problem of local order. Moreover, the continual turmoil ravaging the pre-Sahara convinced French authorities in

Constantine that a military expedition to the Ziban was imperative. In 1844 for the first time a colonial army crossed through the Awras via the al-Qantara pass, arriving at the gateway to the Sahara in March; this represented the earliest direct French contact with desert peoples. Led by the Duc d'Aumale, several thousand soldiers took the oasis of Biskra after a brief siege; organized resistance was minimal since many had fled at the army's approach. Remaining in Biskra only two weeks, the duke hastily improvised a rudimentary administrative apparatus which drew consciously upon Turkish modes of control. The real exercise of power was conferred upon the Banu Ghana, who had solicited the office of shaykh al-'arab from the French. Believing the Ziban sufficiently pacified, the expeditionary force withdrew late in March 1844, leaving behind a handful of French officers commanding units of indigenous (*tirailleurs*) troops.[54]

The political and administrative system devised by the Duc d'Aumale to govern the unruly pre-Sahara was modeled upon colonial practices in the north, where a resident Arab khalifa supervised a largely sedentary population of peasants and townspeople. Conditions in the desert, however, were quite different. The Duc d'Aumale's failure to appreciate those differences ultimately led to disaster.[55]

The Ziban was far from pacified. Two months later the entire French garrison—some 116 European soldiers—was massacred by the native troops, who mutinied. The soldiers then joined together with a contingent of rebels from the oasis of Sidi 'Uqba under Muhammad al-Saghir, whose large popular following in the pre-Sahara owed more to his family's ancient religious notoriety than to association with the amir. The mutiny and revolt brought a second siege of Biskra by a French army dispatched from the northern Constantine in May of 1844. Outnumbered and lacking artillery, the shaykh of Sidi 'Uqba and his forces prudently retreated into the Awras, which represented a no-man's-land that sheltered dissidents for decades to come. Fearing reprisals, a large number of Biskra's inhabitants followed Muhammad al-Saghir into exile. The next year, they left the Awras for Tunisia, seeking asylum with Shaykh Mustafa b. 'Azzuz at his Rahmaniyya zawiya in Nafta. Between 1845 and 1849, the shaykh of Sidi 'Uqba remained in the Jarid; once rumors of revolt reached him, he and his followers returned to the Ziban to take part in Bu Ziyan's movement.[56]

Learning a lesson from the 1844 debacle, the French army built a fort in Biskra on the site of the old Turkish garrison, created a permanent military presence for the pre-Sahara, and set up a customs office.[57] Three years later the oasis boasted a Bureau Arabe supervising some 125,000 people in the vast expanse between the southern Awras and Tuqqurt. Biskra became the *chef-lieu* of a *cercle* encompassing the eastern Sahara and attached to the subdivision of Batna; a commanding officer governed largely through local indigenous chiefs and religious notables.[58] The heavy reliance upon Algerians—instead of Europeans—was due to the fact that prospects for settler colonization, based upon capitalist control of resources, were slim at best. What amounted to indirect colonial rule over an immense swatch of territory could be accomplished only by co-opting native cadres, a solution that offered advantages but carried perils as well. Between 1840 and the late 1850s, military authorities strove to fashion a loyal indigenous aristocracy in areas where Europeans declined to dwell. This failed to yield the expected fruits—easy pacification of traditionally unruly areas such as the mountains and desert. Instead the political instability and uncertainty created by this *aristocracie manquée* were decisive elements in repeated outbreaks of unrest, drawing France into local struggles for power deep in the Sahara and toward the borders with the two adjoining states.[59]

Emigration, Avoidance Protest, and Accommodation, 1843–1849

The responses of local religious elites to Biskra's occupation were far from monolithic, in part because repeated clashes among indigenous political actors had sowed dissension even before the French drive into the pre-Sahara. The diversity of reactions was molded by changing perceptions of the invaders and their intentions, by traditional relations between religious clans or between tribal leaders, by news and rumors from elsewhere, and by geographical location vis-à-vis Biskra, which at first represented but a tenuous colonial outpost.

In Tulqa, the Rahmaniyya shaykh Sidi 'Ali b. 'Umar had been characterized as "hostile" to France and to the colonial regime.[60] However, the shaykh's death in 1842 was traumatic for his clan and had unequivocally demonstrated the dangers inherent in acting as a power broker. In addition, the massacre of Biskra's garrison in March 1844 placed the saints of Tulqa in somewhat of a quandary. The only Frenchman to survive the disaster was Major Pelisse. Pelisse had been visiting prostitutes from the Awlad Na'il tribe in Biskra's red-light district when the surprise attack came and was spared; sensuality had its rewards. Major Pelisse, together with the French-appointed qa'id of Biskra, a member of the Banu Ghana, sought asylum in Tulqa's Rahmaniyya zawiya. Because of the duty of protection, which sufi centers extended to all seeking refuge from harm, Shaykh 'Ali b. 'Uthman (the dead saint's nephew and successor) was obliged by custom to receive the two men.[61]

Sheltering the French officer may have represented a first, tentative gesture of accommodation by Tulqa's religious notables; the colonial regime chose to read it as such. Once order had been restored in Biskra by May 1844, the Banu Ghana, longtime friends of Sidi 'Ali b. 'Uthman's family, received the coveted post of shaykh al-'arab. Thus, the politically circumspect stance of Tulqa's Rahmaniyya shaykhs toward their French masters, who in any case governed through local elites, emerged in this crucial period. The Bu Ziyan uprising and its destructive aftermath would only prove the wisdom of cultural survival through neutrality for the Rahmaniyya clan of Tulqa. Moreover, the contours of an implicit pact can also be detected—one establishing a quid pro quo relationship between local sufi notables and French military officers residing in nearby Biskra. As long as order was maintained, there was to be little colonial interference in the socioreligious activities of the sufi zawiya or its members.

Other religious lineages in Ziban followed suit; Sidi 'Abd al-Malik, head of Biskra's most powerful saintly clan, submitted to the French army in 1844 under circumstances similar to those obtaining in Constantine seven years earlier.[62] Sidi 'Abd al-Malik's extensive oasis properties may also have encouraged him to support (or not openly oppose) whoever appeared capable of restoring calm. As important was the Duc d'Aumale's appointment of his nephew to an administrative office.[63] Older religious quarrels were partially at work, too. Sidi 'Abd al-Malik's clan had long been spiritual rivals of Sidi 'Uqba's shurafa' headed by Muhammad al-Saghir; apparently rule by the Banu Ghana was preferable to that of saintly competitors. Finally, location played a not insignificant part in determining the political behavior of Muslim notables. If Biskra hosted a formidable French military presence, the rest of the Ziban was not yet fully subdued. Those outside of Biskra had a marked advantage in maneuverability over those residing within the oasis.

Biskra's fall provoked further splits within the 'Azzuz family of al-Burj; some elected to remain in the region; others chose avoidance protest as a course of action. After Sidi 'Ali b. 'Umar's death in 1842, Mustafa b. 'Azzuz acceded to the post of head Rahmaniyya shaykh. For political and religious reasons, Sidi Mustafa soon chose to abandon his homeland and his ancestor's zawiya. After the French army retook Biskra, he and a group of tariqa disciples emigrated to the Tunisian Jarid to seek the protection of the Husaynid Bey, Ahmad, and fulfill the Islamic duty of hijra from infidel-held lands. Based upon later participation in the 1849 revolt, other Rahmaniyya leaders, such as Shaykh al-Mukhtar of the Awlad Jallal, who stayed behind, were scarcely reconciled to the new political order of things.[64]

In Khanqa Sidi Naji, Shaykh 'Abd al-Hafiz chose neither flight to a neighboring Muslim country nor apparent accommodation. His form of avoidance protest was a mode of political behavior adopted by many in

Algeria and later in Tunisia after 1881—withdrawal. To escape contamination by the infidels, the shaykh retreated into the isolation of his zawiya in the Jabal Cherchar, where according to popular rumors, he had himself enclosed in a coffin. Here physical retreat gave expression to ritual norms concerning pollution and religious purity. Whether the rumor concerning the coffin was taken as fact by the shaykh's following, or rather interpreted metaphorically, his actions had immense symbolic meaning and may have done much to shape collective behavior. In effect he became a "social banner," signifying rejection of foreign rule. However, once Bu Ziyan unfurled another banner—that of the mahdi—Sidi 'Abd al-Hafiz would be compelled by his disciples to relinquish retreat as a stratagem for coping.[65]

What was the reaction of ordinary people to the arrival of the French on the desert's rim? If information for provincial religious authorities in this period is sparse, sources for nonelite responses, aside from rebellions, is even less abundant. It appears that ordinary people—cultivators and tribespeople—sought the counsel of their religious leaders in deciding upon a particular course of action. This was seen among Tijaniyya clients in the eastern Sahara. The shaykh of the Tijani zawiya in Tamalhat (near Tuqqurt) was Sidi 'Ali b. 'Isa (died 1844), then spiritual leader of the entire tariqa. As the Duc d'Aumale's army approached Biskra for the second assault, delegations from the Suf, Tuqqurt, and Biskra were sent to Sidi 'Ali b. 'Isa seeking his guidance. The Tijaniyya shaykh preached calm and submission, informing the delegations that "God gave Algeria to the French; it is He who protects their domination. Remain in a state of peace and do not make war. God has delivered you from your oppressors [the Turks] who observed no law but that of violence."[66]

Sidi 'Ali b. 'Isa died a few months later. His son and later head of the Tijaniyya order, Muhammad b. al-'Id (1814–1876), while outwardly reconciled to French rule, engaged in behind-the-scenes political activity against France during the Sharif of Warqala's revolt in the early 1850s.

Secular political leaders in the desert chose strategies similar to those of local religious notables. In the Wadi Righ, the sultan of the Banu Jallab also recognized French suzerainty in 1844. In exchange for the right to purchase grains in French-held markets, Tuqqurt's princes rendered a modest annual tribute. The terms of the agreement were almost identical to those customarily concluded with the Turks. Seen in retrospect, Tuqqurt's obeisance was an expedient device, imposed largely by economic necessity; in any case, the colonial regime's presence was scarcely perceptible south of Biskra.[67] The same was true for many tribal leaders in the Awras and other inaccessible parts of Algeria; infidel rule was temporarily accepted until the strength and intentions of the conquerors could be tested.[68] Here, too, 'Abd al-Qadir's example of momentary acquiescence to superior forces may have had a determining influence. Another critical factor was risk avoidance, dictated not only by ecological and demographic realities but also by the availability of military supplies, particularly contraband gunpowder and European firearms. Finally, political behavior and decision making on the part of religious notables and secular leaders were influenced to no small degree by the kinds of information available to them. And Algeria reverberated with rumors.

Saharan Trade and Commerce in an Era of Uncertainty, 1830–1849

Nearly two decades of unrelieved strife in the pre-Sahara placed intolerable strains upon the already precarious agrarian and pastoral economies. The 1837 conquest of the eastern province's center, Constantine, brought further economic dislocation as well as outbreaks of cholera; in 1838 severe drought occurred. In 1846 an invasion of locusts devastated crops, and the "drought which visited the pre-Sahara during [the previous] winter . . . almost completely destroyed the harvest."[69] From the 1831 siege of Za'atsha until 1845, pitiless raids were inflicted upon oasis dwellers and pastoralists by the warring saffs. Thousands of date palms and fruit trees were destroyed; flocks and herds were lost as well. Even the villages of the distant Suf were not spared. Between 1835 and 1841, the princes of Tuqqurt mounted several military expeditions to the Suf, resulting in the partial destruction of gardens. When the French official, Prax, visited Al-Awad in 1847, he was struck by the devastation.[70] Finally, as first the Banu Ghana and then the Bu 'Ukkaz momentarily claimed the post of shaykh al-'arab, tribute was extracted from the hapless populace.

Taxation is a disputed element in debates over the causes for the Za'atsha uprising. Some colonial writers maintained that injudicious tampering with the ancient fiscal regime after 1844 was to blame for political discontents. Others categorically deny that taxation was a causal factor. What can be ascertained is that the new French-appointed qa'ids and their subalterns went about tax-collecting duties with unaccustomed energy; in some locales, the impositions were extraordinarily heavy.[71] Surplus extraction, which had earlier been a matter of bargaining and negotiation as well as contention, was now regularized. In addition, social groups traditionally exempt, particularly religious notables, were included on fiscal rolls, while others were arbitrarily granted exemptions. Moreover, French military officials in Biskra unwisely increased the tax assessed per date-palm tree by at least 50 percent and, worse still, applied this assessment uniformly without consideration of productive capacity.[72] These measures forced some families to sell their plots—or the rights to the produce of the gardens—to meet the new more onerous fiscal obligations.[73]

Among the groups most adversely affected were the Ghamara, the chief property holders in Za'atsha. It was this lineage, part of a larger tribal fraction, which later formed the backbone of Bu Ziyan's rebellion; they provided combatants and provisions and pressured nearby pastoral nomads to join the revolt. By the eve of the insurrection, French-decreed changes in taxation had been integrated into the popular rumor mill; some rumors had it that the burdensome taxes would be repealed. The very fact that ordinary people were exchanging information on fiscal matters is significant and suggests that economic grievances were part and parcel of public opinion.[74]

Colonial policies also adversely affected local, regional, and transregional trade currents; while total occupation was the declared objective after 1840, the French military lacked the means to achieve that occupation. As discussed in chapter 1, the seasonal movements of the pastoralists between Tell and desert was, under the Turkish regime, a more or less orderly and strictly supervised operation. Turkish authorities would only permit the tribes to move down to their winter pasturage in the Sahara grouped together in units under the guidance of the shaykh al-'arab, whose task was to guarantee order. From 1830 on, that vast movement of peoples and herds was increasingly chaotic; struggles erupted among the tribes, migrating willy-nilly, which adversely affected all along the migratory route.[75]

Merchants are rarely risk takers but rather strive to minimize risks whenever feasible; one method for doing this is to devise alternative trade channels. In this period, trade, which had traditionally linked the oases of the Algerian pre-Sahara to the northern Constantine via Biskra, shifted to the Tunisian Jarid; that is, commodities previously procured from cities such as Algiers and Constantine were increasingly sought in Tunisian markets, to the benefit of traders and producers there. Continual unrest in the region between the northern Constantine and the Ziban discouraged commercial exchanges, encouraging the tribes of the southern Constantine to rely upon the Jarid to supply firearms, gunpowder, and other manufactured products.[76] The reliance upon southwestern Tunisia for products no longer readily available in parts of Algeria, as well as the emigration of Algerian tribal and religious leaders to the beylik, ultimately drew Tunisia into across-the-border politics and social movements.

Moreover, the older symbiotic relationship between oasis producers and pastoralists appears to have suffered a number of rude shocks between 1830 and 1849. Nomadic peoples had always served as intermediaries between oasis producers and distant markets in northern Algeria, particularly for the triangular exchange of dates, textiles and raw wool, and wheat. The large numbers of soldiers in Algeria stimulated an insatiable demand for wool which was reflected in exceedingly high prices for woolen products. Attracted by the higher prices, some traders and pastoral groups preferred to sell wool in French-held markets rather than supply traditional customers—oasis or village weavers who used the proceeds from textile production to provide for household needs, for exchange, or to pay taxes and ensure subsistence.[77]

Equally ominous for all Muslims, but particularly for members of the ulama and the sufi turuq, were the decrees of 1843 and 1844, a product of increased European settlement and demands for land. These placed hubus lands, or pious endowments for the collective good of the Muslim community, under the administration of the Domaine, which then, by denying the inalienable legal status of these properties, made them available for purchase by settlers. The appropriation of the hubus was regarded as an attack upon Islam and upon the religious notables who had traditionally administered these properties.[78] In places like the Ziban, where hubus properties were numerous and characteristically held by the major sufi zawaya, when those properties were not seized they were subjected to taxation for the first time.[79]

In addition, changes in demography and the institution of slavery may have contributed to social disorder and created a sense of collective grievance. By the middle of the century, the slave trade through Algeria was languishing for a number of reasons; slaves from Bornu and Hausaland were mainly sent to Morocco and Tripolitania. Tunisia outlawed slavery and the slave trade by 1846 through a series of measures enacted by the bey.[80] In Algeria, slaves were predominantly female and employed mainly in domestic service by the great families. The number of slaves in the colony was relatively low—somewhere between eight thousand and eighteen thousand in the 1840s, compared with an indigenous population of about three million. Nevertheless, "the possession of slaves had more of a psychological than economic importance. The owning of slaves was an index of the master's wealth and increased his social standing."[81] Some of the Bureaux Arabes reports from the pre-Sahara observed that the abolition of slavery in April 1848 was an unpopular measure among local elites. Indeed, Bu Ziyan himself had been involved in a violent confrontation with French authorities over a female slave whom the authorities forcibly removed from his household.[82] Moreover, labor was in short supply in many parts of Algeria due to exceedingly high mortality rates, mainly provoked by military pacification, deteriorating health conditions, and disease and famine.

The pre-Sahara had suffered cruelly from the 1835 cholera epidemic that decimated much of the Constantine. The pandemic, which began as early as 1827 in Asia, may have been introduced to the Maghrib by merchants and pilgrims returning from the East. The French army was also beset by cholera; large-scale troop movements throughout Algeria spread the disease far and wide.[83] Its effects upon the densely populated oases was devastating. In some villages, like al-Burj, Za'atsha, and Lishana, many of the sedentary cultivators were carried off; in some places, pastoralists from the surrounding area took over abandoned gardens and houses. Demographic catastrophes had depleted the Ziban, which despite its ancient traditions of rebellion, made the region appear incapable of sustained resistance. According to Carette, writing in 1839, the population was "diminished to the point that they totally lack political potential and would be unable to fend off a French attack."[84]

So it seemed in the decade prior to the Za'atsha uprising. In the winter of 1849–1850, cholera reappeared in the southern Constantine in the wake of the French army's advance. For a while at least, the epidemic was a boon to the insurgents during the long bitter siege.

By the eve of Bu Ziyan's millenarian movement, many indigenous political actors had either been defeated, exiled from the country, co-opted by the colonial regime, or had withdrawn momentarily from politics. The bid by one member of the region's leading sufi clan, Hasan b. 'Azzuz, to conflate religious authority with secular power had failed singularly. Other religious notables had taken flight or retreated into temporizing and bet hedging. The ancient saff mechanism for managing conflict had been destabilized and political energies dissipated in endless struggles. For the most part, the French army had not been directly involved in these struggles, being preoccupied with the amir's jihad in western Algeria. Colonial authorities generally watched from the sidelines as native opponents slugged it out. French support was, however, offered to one side and then another, which was read by many Algerians as an index of colonial indecision at best, at worst as pusillanimity.[85] As one Bureau Arabe officer reported from Biskra in 1846:

> It is better to provide ample support to the shaykh al-'arab since it is practically impossible for a French officer, no matter what support he has been given, to replace the influence of the shaykh which has been in place for centuries; it is dangerous to attempt to place our flag in the midst of conflicts and disorders that, for so long, have divided the tribes of the south.[86]

Then in December 1847, 'Abd al-Qadir surrendered to the Duc d'Aumale and was sent into exile with his partisans; the next year Ahmad Bey was captured along the borders between Algeria and Tunisia by the French army and imprisoned.[87] Collective hopes for the re-creation of various kinds of Islamic states in eastern and western Algeria were extinguished. That same year, 1848, the Second Republic was proclaimed in Paris; the new constitution stated that Algeria had the special status of French territory unlike the rest of France's colonies. Nevertheless, the disorders accompanying the Second Republic's troubled birth in the Metropole had an immediate resonance in Algeria's cities, bringing uncertainty about France's intentions in North Africa; some Algerians interpreted the burst of pro-republican sentiments in Algiers as a sign that an immense shift was under way. The mahdi's path was clear.

Toward Za'atsha: The Master of the Age

By 1848 unbearable pressures had been brought to bear upon those regions of Algeria where colonial rule was not yet firmly implanted but indigenous governing institutions had been partially uprooted.[88] Moreover, popular traditions of protest gradually fused with elite disaffection; the removal of the tax-free status, traditionally enjoyed by religious notables, meant loss of privilege and income. As important, however, was the rapidity of the various changes imposed by the colonial regime without prior knowledge of local conditions. As Herbillon observed during the siege of Za'atsha: "We entered much too precipitously into the internal affairs of the peoples of the south."[89] Sudden, precipitous shocks to a social order and economic system are one of the preconditions of rebellion, particularly when "adaptive or survival strategies" no longer secure a morally grounded subsistence level.[90] And prophets (and rumors) tend to arise in periods of intense social disorder and chaos marked by a "pervasive sense of the unpredictable."[91]

Most of the Constantine's traditional secular leaders—the Muqrani of the Majana, Turkish officials, and leaders of the great saffs—had been compromised in nearly two decades of unrelieved fighting; their rivalries had inflicted material and moral duress upon the pre-Sahara. While contests for power in these decades were expressed in the vocabulary of the saff principle, as more contestants crowded the political stage, the conventional framework for politics was eroded, only to collapse just prior to Bu Ziyan's rebellion. Moreover, local conflicts had prompted some groups—such as the ahl Tulqa—to attempt to overthrow the traditional hierarchy.

The French military's erratic meddling in as yet unfamiliar political terrain intensified social turmoil, particularly the *politique des notables*. Hastily elaborated by French officers without consideration for customary practices, this policy only heightened administrative disorder. In some places obscure holy men, seduced by offers of minor posts, were elevated to positions of authority over autonomous tribal groups. Singularly unprepared to assume these duties, and lacking support, local saintly figures met with resistance. As one French military officer remarked in 1844 "the shaykhs of the tribal *noblesse militaire* in the Awras and Hodna feel humiliated by their political subjugation to the authority of a marabout appointed by the Duc d'Aumale."[92] The politique des notables was not only resoundingly unsuccessful in restoring a semblance of normality, it fueled further discontent, not only in the Ziban but also in the adjacent Awras and Hodna.[93] The very social order itself was at stake.

After fifteen years of French colonial rule, Algeria—or many of its regions—was more of a contest state than ever. This created a political environment conducive to radical kinds of solutions to the problem of social order and justice. And since the mahdi was from outside that contested state, collective hopes for salvation became riveted upon the Muslim redeemer. Popular millenarian traditions had long associated widespread chaos—the world turned upside down—with the mahdi's appearance. And in the eighteenth century, a powerful desert saint, Sidi al-Aghwati, had, through his prophecies devoted to the savior's appearance in time, fused the mahdi's advent with the degradation of infidel rule in the collective consciousness.

In many parts of Africa and Dar al-Islam, beliefs regarding the redeemer's imminent arrival heightened at the eighteenth century's close.[94] Moreover, these expectations were found both among the simple and the erudite; while they existed mainly in the rich oral traditions, they were also found in texts. As discussed in the previous chapter, this phenomenon can in part be linked to the onset of the thirteenth Muslim century. Nevertheless, the mahdi as a social actor has always been a vital, if at times subterranean, component of political life in North Africa. From roughly the time of al-Kurtubi (died 1272 A.D.), the Maghribi traditions held that the mahdi would first appear in the Sus region of southern Morocco, perhaps in the ribat of Massa, prior to his journey to Mecca to receive "a second oath of allegiance."[95] The privileged place accorded to the western Maghrib in eschatological lore concerning the mahdi is significant; until the present century, certain groups in North Africa still looked to Morocco or the Sahara as the site from whence the long awaited one would arise.[96]

Particularly influential in the Sahara were the prophecies of Sidi al-Aghwati, the venerated holy man from the oasis of al-Aghwat. In his writings and visions, the saint miraculously foresaw that the infidels would invade the Maghrib. After several decades of humiliation at the hands of the unbelievers, the mahdi would deliver the faithful from oppression and establish the realm of justice. According to Sidi al-Aghwati's widely believed predictions, the date of that event of cosmic significance was the year

1271 A.H./1854 A.D. The timing of the redeemer's arrival was inextricably linked with the degradation of infidel rule.[97] And Sidi al-Aghwati's prophecies were both read and disseminated by word of mouth well into the nineteenth century.[98]

Human and natural disasters, along with social and political upheaval, forged an overwhelming sense of the unpredictable among many North Africans. And collective expectations of the mahdi's imminent arrival—as well as rumors of such—appear to have intensified that sense of the unpredictable.

4   Mahdi and Saint
The 1849 Bu Ziyan Uprising

> It has been well known (and generally accepted) by all
> Muslims in every epoch, that at the end of time a man
> from the family (of the Prophet) will without fail make
> his appearance, one who will strengthen the religion and
> make justice triumph. The Muslims will follow him, and
> he will gain domination over the Muslim realm. He will
> be called the Mahdi.[1]

Of the many rebellions that rocked Algeria throughout the nineteenth
century, Bu Ziyan's was the most dramatic. Based in the small village of
Za'atsha, near the Rahmaniyya strongholds of Tulqa and al-Burj, the
mahdist uprising was quelled only after the French army engaged in a long,
bitter siege. By December 1849, the village was totally demolished, its
inhabitants put to the sword, and the region devastated; thousands fled the
ensuing repression; many more succumbed to the cholera epidemic unleashed by the confrontation. Lest others be thus tempted, the French
commander had Bu Ziyan's severed head exhibited on a pole at the entrance
to Za'atsha's ruins as a warning to future troublemakers.

As a vehicle for entering into the religiopolitical culture of nineteenth-
century North Africa, Bu Ziyan's movement raises a number of issues.
Why did a movement of violent social protest arise in the pre-Sahara nearly
two decades after the French invasion and five years after Biskra's pacification? What part did Rahmaniyya or other sufi leaders play in either
promoting or blocking the revolutionary potential of the self-proclaimed
mahdi? What can this spectacular, if short-lived, rebellion tell us about the
cultural norms governing the political behavior of religious notables? How
did the experience of Za'atsha mold the subsequent positions of religious
notables vis-à-vis the colonial regime and how did this eventually shape the
course of Algerian and North African history?

Bu Ziyan's challenge to the colonial regime also represented a challenge
to the Ziban's leading sufi notables—a dare or summons to political action
of a particular and peculiar sort. While the sufi zawaya and their shaykhs
nurtured traditions, both written and oral, regarding the "rightly guided
one," the mahdi's appearance was fraught with perils. Chiliastic move-

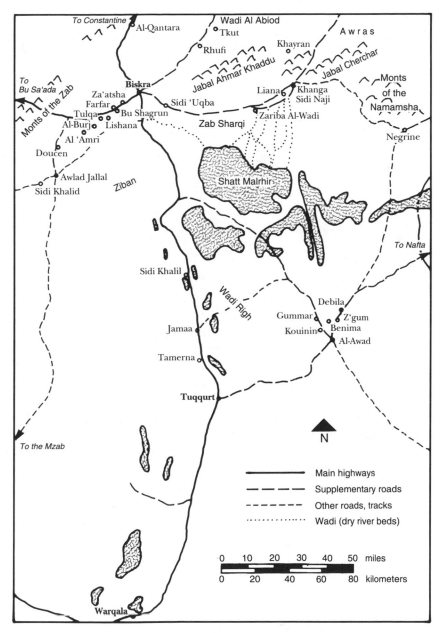

To Constantine

Al-Qantara

Wadi Al Abiod

Tkut

Rhufi

Khayran

Awras

Jabal Ahmar Khaddu

Jabal Cherchar

To
Bu Sa'ada

Monts of the Zab

Za'atsha

Farfar

Tulqa

Al-Burj

Al 'Amri

Doucen

Biskra

Bu Shagrun

Lishana

Sidi 'Uqba

Liana

Khanga
Sidi Naji

Monts
of the
Namamsha

Zariba Al-Wadi

Zab Sharqi

Negrine

Awlad Jallal

Sidi Khalid

Ziban

Shatt Malrhir

To Nafta

Sidi Khalil

Wadi Righ

Debila

Z'gum

Gummar

Benima

Kouinin

Al-Awad

Jamaa

Tamerna

Tuqqurt

N

To the Mzab

	Main highways
	Supplementary roads
	Other roads, tracks
	Wadi (dry river beds)

0   10   20   30   40   50   miles

0   20   40   60   80   kilometers

Warqala

5. The Ziban, Suf, Tuqqurt, and Warqala

ments under the mahdi's leadership threatened to vent popular social forces which could only be controlled with difficulty. More ominous was that false prophets might arise in guise of the Muslim redeemer. The task facing the sufi establishment, as guardians of the sacred law, of correct belief and right conduct, was to discern the base pretender from the one who would "fill the earth with justice."[2]

The task facing the historian is rather different in nature, although no less daunting. "Historians prefer the curtain up and the lights on," observed Eugen Weber in his reappraisal of peasant politicization in nineteenth-century France.[3] Yet quite the opposite prevailed during the Za'atsha revolt. In addition to the fragmentary or recondite nature of available written sources, many of the significant events preceding the 1849 rebellion were played out on an ill-lit stage with partially drawn curtains; others occurred backstage or outside the theater of action. Much of the information about what really transpired was buried, along with the rebels, under the debris.

The Antecedents

Between 1844, when Biskra fell, and 1849, as revolt took the French by surprise, an uneasy calm fell upon the pre-Sahara's oases. However, two millenarian movements erupted in 1845 as 'Abd al-Qadir's jihad approached its final denouement. Political circumstances in the north had an immediate impact upon the southern Constantine and may have paved the way for Bu Ziyan.

In 1845 a self-proclaimed prophet named Jamina organized and led a small anticolonial insurrection in the region of el-Arrouch. Jamina was well known to the Ziban's inhabitants since he had resided in the oases for at least a year before publicly advancing claims to mahdihood. There he had initially acquired a reputation as a local holy man through demonstrations of miraculous powers to the villagers who constituted his first popular following. Leaving the Ziban in 1844, Jamina and his partisans launched a rural protest movement the next year among the tribes just north of the city of Constantine, where progressive settler land expropriations were making inroads into the local agrarian economy. Jamina exchanged letters with Bu Ziyan, some of which were intercepted by French officials, until the eve of the 1849 Za'atsha insurrection.[4] However, this particular rebel was not alone; there were other chiliastic figures creating unrest in the countryside during the same period.

The Dahra insurrection, inspired by Bu Ma'za, emerged from the intersection of two forces which also directly affected the Za'atsha uprising: the waning of the amir's movement and with it collective hopes for an Islamic state; and the indiscriminate application of harsh colonial "native policies" upon even those Algerians opting for nonresistance to France. Since the humiliation of submission to the infidels carried no tangible rewards, this rendered "l'authorité française insupportable."[5] In 1845 another rebellion broke out under the guidance of a young man of no more than twenty years. Popularly known as Bu Ma'za (Abu Ma'za, or the "man with the goat"), he assumed the provocative *nom de guerre* of Muhammad b. 'Abd Allah, the name inevitably associated with the mahdi. Revered among the sedentary tribal populations of the Chélif Valley and Ouarsenis Mountains as an ascetic and holy man, Bu Ma'za promised to drive the Europeans into the sea. Rebellions soon broke out in the Hodna and the Titteri and Kabyle Mountains, regions thus far little touched by the conquest but whose people were fiercely attached to their native land. During the repression that followed, the French army resorted to the cruelest of measures in "pacifying" the Algerians. In one instance, Pélissier, a future governor-general and marshall of France, caused eight hundred unarmed villagers to be methodically burnt to death in the caves where they had taken refuge.[6]

During its latter stages, the Dahra movement found a resonance in the Ziban. In 1847, Bu Ma'za and a band of supporters drawn from the Awlad Na'il confederacy were chased into the oasis of the Awlad Jallal where Shaykh al-Mukhtar al-Jallali headed the Rahmaniyya zawiya. So great was Bu Ma'za's reputation as the redeemer and an intrepid warrior that the indigenous troops under General Herbillon's command fled in terror at the sight of the rebels' flags and messianic banners. Apparently even those Algerians who had enrolled in the French army preferred the dangers of desertion to fighting the mahdi. The news of Bu Ma'za's approach encouraged the oases of Sidi Khalid and Awlad Jallal to engage in their own rebellious behavior; the populace besieged the French-appointed qa'id in his residence.[7] Significantly, the mahdi sought the assistance of the Rahmaniyya shaykh of Awlad Jallal, neither the first nor last example of political collaboration between a powerful sufi leader and a messianic figure. With the full backing of Shaykh al-Mukhtar, the insurgents used the fortified oasis as a base of resistance. Employing habitual tactics of retreat, the rebels withstood a first, devastating assault by the French army, offering a "vigorous defense."[8]

Customary oasis warfare was effective as long as both sides marshaled roughly similar sorts of military technology; it was also predicated upon the principle, dictated by prevailing demographic structures in North Africa, that no side could afford to lose more than a restricted number of fighting men.[9] In this confrontation, the besiegers enjoyed access to machines of war unavailable to the rebels—artillery. Moreover, by the mid-

1840s, France had committed tens of thousands of troops to the conquest of Algeria. The match was grievously unequal. Suffering heavy casualties from the extraordinary force of artillery attacks, the oasis of Awlad Jallal eventually sued for peace. After rendering war indemnities and hostages, the villagers were accorded an official pardon. Bu Ma'za, however, escaped the dishonor of defeat by fleeing the region but was finally captured elsewhere by General Saint-Arnaud in April of 1847. As for the hapless Rahmaniyya shaykh, Sidi al-Mukhtar was forced to abandon his sufi residence in Awlad Jallal to seek refuge among his tribal supporters, the Awlad Na'il. There he remained until 1849. Then the news of Bu Ziyan's prophecy prompted Shaykh al-Mukhtar to return to the Ziban, where he resumed militant politics, once again in concert with a mahdi.[10]

Here several implicit patterns in the social construction of the mahdi can be detected. First, would-be rebels chose sites traditionally employed as retreats from central government oppression—the oases or mountains—as places to patiently fashion a clientele. Second, a mahdi-in-the-making invariably manipulated the cultural paradigm of the saint, blessed with baraka and the ability to perform miracles, to establish credentials as a holy person. And finally, self-appointed mahdis carefully solicited the moral sponsorship of recognized religious notables often associated with the great sufi orders, particularly the Rahmaniyya.

What the preceding indicates is that the Za'atsha revolt was not a purely local phenomenon, isolated from transformations elsewhere in Algeria or—as will be seen—from changes occurring in neighboring Tunisia and even France. In addition to the economic and social devastation that the pre-Sahara's peoples had endured for so long, the example of rebellious prophets may have inspired the Ziban's inhabitants, and particularly Bu Ziyan, to undertake uncommon forms of collective action.

These forms were unusual in that subordinate peoples elected, whenever feasible, to work "the system [of domination] to their minimum disadvantage," rather than engage in suicidal frontal assaults upon the oppressors.[11] This had often been the case under the Turkish regime; this approach was also employed by 'Abd al-Qadir. In addition, mahdist solutions to political and social crises, while increasingly prevalent after 1845 in Algeria, were not the only type of collective action in North Africa's political repertoire. That mahdist-led revolt became the preferred mode of collective behavior for several decades indicates that other styles of protest had been discarded as ineffective or ignoble; traditional stratagems for foiling outside interference were exhausted.[12]

For many Algerians avoidance of protest as a strategy for coping was relinquished at precisely the moment when the mahdi offered an alternative program for righting a topsy-turvy world. And the single most appealing element in that program was the promise of justice in an era when the administration of the law, whether indigenous or colonial, had ceased to function. If the time was indeed out of joint, that temporal disjointedness was most apparent in the realm of justice.[13]

Nevertheless, popular protest depends to no small degree upon "opportunity," combined with a shared, profound sense of grievance. This means a fortuitous conjuncture or favorable set of circumstances for mobilization and militant action to eliminate the source of oppression. Ordinary people, believing that "the time is right," embark upon a selected course of action while jettisoning others. Even extraordinary people—those sent from God—were sensitive to the calculus of timing.[14] In this respect, the field of power in Algeria was increasingly informed by a new rhetorical field of information about the detested Europeans, one composed of rumors, improvised news, gossip, and hearsay.

Migration, Information, and Social Movements

Timing and opportunity were closely linked to the fact that information networks crisscrossed the Mediterranean between Europe, particularly France, and North Africa even in the pre-wireless age. The heady, intense political ferment provoked by the 1848 revolution was not confined to the Metropole. Turbulence in Paris attending the birth of the Second Republic was recreated among the European colons in Algeria, many of whom immediately embraced republicanism and the revolution. Indigenous Algerians witnessed feverish political activity in places like Algiers, the scene of mass demonstrations, meetings, and public gatherings by civilians. The army, still ostensibly in control of the colony, but whose administration was increasingly resented by the settlers, appeared no longer fully in command. All of this was interpreted in a specific way by some Algerians, who, seeing the obvious discord among the conquerors, believed that the appointed hour for deliverance was at hand.[15] Integrated into translocal networks of work, trade, and religion, the Ziban's inhabitants were soon aware of the European revolutions of 1848. News of civil strife in Paris and Algiers was rapidly carried from the coastal cities to the southern Constantine by the "Biskris," or migrant workers from the oases. In 1843, officials noted that the number of Biskris working in urban areas had increased relative to previous years. Another official report from 1855 showed that out of a total Muslim population of eighteen thousand in Algiers, some seven thousand were barranis living there temporarily.[16] This may have been a direct response to unfavorable social and economic conditions in the pre-Sahara, a product of over a decade of political upheaval.

The activities of the Biskri community were, moreover, directly linked to rebellion in the oases. To explore the relation between labor migration, the dissemination of information, and the timing of popular protest, the barrani phenomenon needs additional amplification.

Thiriet, a colonial administrator investigating patterns of temporary labor exchange involving Saharan peoples, observed: "This form of sedentary nomadism propels migrants not toward the steppes to engage in pastoralism but toward the cities in the springtime and summer; there they trade or work at various jobs to provide their families with resources beyond those available from the date harvest."[17] The continuous comings and goings of the Biskris, who returned after extended sojourns in the north, meant that some members of oasis society had at least a limited knowledge of European ways, the French language, and the contours of the colonial system.[18] Indeed, it was the Saharan barrani community in Algiers that furnished military officers, such as Antoine Carette, with information regarding conditions in the great desert even before the French ventured into the region.[19] To others in the colonial system, the labor migrants were a source of disorder. In 1852 a Bureau Arabe officer in the Ziban characterized the Biskris as a sort of rustic news service. Upon returning to the oases, they "spread about the most dangerous news and information. Their activities should be restricted in order to dampen insurrectionary ardor."[20]

Many Biskris had witnessed the proclamation of the Second Republic in the capital and its attendant mayhem. And because some Biskris held the customary job of port worker, they were able to observe troop movements in and out of Algeria. Seeing contingents embarking for France during the 1848–1849 era, the Biskris spread the news that the soldiers were abandoning Algeria to defend their mother country against the English. Another rumor current at the time was that Great Britain—then regarded by the North Africans as a counterpoise to French imperial designs upon the Maghrib—had declared war against France.[21] All of this information was distributed willy-nilly around Algeria (and surely enriched as it was passed along by word of mouth) and worked to undermine French authority at the local level.

In the words of one officer reporting from the period: "Between Algiers and the Ziban there exists a very active exchange of information through which the most absurd lies circulate. The natives are saying that the governor-general has promised a tax exemption for the Ziban and that Biskra's commandant has been removed from office."[22] Also integrated into this network of spontaneous news was Jamina's jihad, then spreading into the Collo region in opposition to expanding colonization schemes which threatened the Algerian peasant with further loss of land.[23] The

Biskris moving south from the Constantine or Algiers brought back information about Jamina's revolt. More provocative was that French troops were redeployed from Biskra's garrison to the north to quell Jamina's rebellion. This too was viewed by the Ziban's inhabitants as a signal of military impotence; tongues began to wag furiously and hopes for deliverance were raised.

Nevertheless, not all rumors were necessarily detrimental to French rule; indeed, colonial authorities promoted the dissemination of certain kinds of information favorable to France's interests. For example, in 1846 news of the Tunisian bey's official voyage to France was carefully spread around the Constantine. Ahmad Bey's state visit, characterized as the "great symbol," was full of ironies for Algerian political aspirations and hopes of salvation by Muslim rulers. The first such visit by a Muslim head of state (in this case de facto) to Europe, Ahmad's resolve to journey to France was prompted largely by unconfirmed rumors that the Ottoman sultan aimed to reimpose direct authority over its autonomous beylik. According to the North African rumor mill, the Ottoman fleet was en route to Tunisia in 1845 to chastise the Husaynid prince.[24] While the rumor proved unfounded, Ahmad traveled to Europe to seek French guarantees of Tunisia's autonomy vis-à-vis the Porte—something Paris was happy to provide in view of France's long-standing diplomatic position regarding the Ottoman Empire's integrity. Thus, if the Algerians regarded the Tunisian bey as a potential savior from French colonialism, the Husaynid dynasty looked to King Louis Philippe to defend the beylik from Istanbul's centralizing embrace. According to the Bureau Arabe officer reporting from Biskra in 1846, the news of Ahmad's state visit

> produced an excellent impression upon the [Algerian] population. By showing them the amicable relations that bind together our government and that of the Tunisian prince, the news of Ahmad Bey's trip to France must have silenced those who attempt to represent the Tunisian government as hostile to us and Tunisian territory as a safe asylum for our enemies.[25]

Events, of course, were to prove otherwise. What emerges from this is that information, as much as access to contraband military supplies or popular support for political agendas, was a precious commodity, one fought over and bargained for.

Thus set in motion, the rumor mill continued to run along well-greased wheels and through intricate channels all over North Africa. Colonial officials in Algeria, and French diplomats and spies in Tunisia, complained throughout the century that the indigenous population frequently knew of events in the Maghrib—or even in Europe—before they did. Small wonder that military officers repeatedly advocated that the movements of the Biskris between Tell and desert, or of other peripatetic groups, particularly popular religious preachers, be strictly curtailed. Only then would the insidious flow of rumors and information deemed harmful to France's imperium be halted.[26]

Rumors of Revolt

While the written religious word reigned sovereign in nineteenth-century North Africa, oral communication was the principal information duct for the unlettered, who were in the majority. As seen in chapter 3, Algeria was awash in rumors; the political word-of-mouth pamphlet, as a genre of communication, flourished with peculiar intensity. In their spontaneity, rumors might be conceived of as verbal graffiti—as statements about power by the preliterate in a society in which full-blown literacy was difficult to achieve and thus traditionally restricted to urban or rural elites.[27] Rumors can be political gossip writ large and democratically. Endless numbers of people, whether ordinary or otherwise, can actively participate as purveyors of improvised news, without the burden of written verification, although rumors often have a symbiotic relationship with writing.[28] Rumors are rhetorical dialects or communicative vernaculars that employ persuasive language to interpret events as well as create facts. If their original inspiration may have been the written word, the persuasive power of orally conceived rumors might also cause them to be committed to writing. Thus, rumors about politics were akin to verbal revolutionary tracts.

The information transferal process itself produced endless virus-like mutations as news made the rounds from mouth to mouth and ear to ear. Nevertheless, rumors are grounded in fact, the realm of the possible or the arena of the desired; they must have an aura of half-truth about them at least. And rumors are a statement about power—the power of words, information, and communication to affect individual and, particularly, collective behavior. Finally, political rumors decenter the controlling discourse of ruling elites to the social periphery or margins since they represent ideological statements about what ordinary people think the normative should be.

Rumors and prophets thrive in situations of uncertainty, social dislocation, and political incoherence. In May 1849 Biskra's Bureau Arabe officer reported that "news [had] begun circulating in the region regarding the arrival of a mahdist leader who [was] endowed with superhuman powers and [would] chase the French out of Algeria."[29] This statement was recorded at the very moment when Bu Ziyan's movement had already assumed a particular configuration, that of a millenarian movement. To understand how that configuration came to be, two fundamental issues must be addressed: the nature of collective visions of the Muslim redeemer in nineteenth-century North African society; and how expectations regarding the mahdi were channeled to, and received by, ordinary people and elites alike.

Speculations about the mahdi's imminent arrival appear to have been integrated into the general fabric of village talk during the past century in much the same way that an upcoming wedding would dominate coffeehouse palaver. And it was the maddahs who were largely responsible for disseminating the popular eschatological traditions regarding the "master of the hour."[30] As discussed in chapter 2, poems and ballads extolling religious paragons—venerated sufis, saints, and even the mahdi himself—or tribal heroes were recited in rural and urban gathering places. Ruling authorities, deemed unworthy, were also mocked or satirized, a subtle yet potent symbolic expression of contestation.[31] In the countryside, annual mawsims honoring tribal saints or village festivals were enlivened by storytellers, bards, and the maddahs. Even today in the Sahara, "there is always present everywhere a floating population of wandering entertainers, itinerant musicians, magicians, and storytellers who are constantly traveling about, singly or in small groups, from oasis to oasis all over the area."[32] In the past century, this was all the more true. And since the maddah invariably came from the ranks of ordinary people, he spoke for and about them.

The *jasus* (spy) was another key figure in the exchange of information, although the art of espionage predated the colonial era.[33] Due to its vulnerability, the Saharan trade had always attracted spies and counterspies. Merchants and caravan leaders often employed paid informants to alert them of the presence of bandits. Desert highwaymen—Saharan pirates—also used espionage to discover caravan departures, itineraries, and the nature of the goods transported. In addition, as the anthropologist van Gennep reported at the turn of the century, "all along the lines of springs and wells are caravan meeting points; here people quickly exchange news and information."[34]

Through the spy's mediation, certain kinds of information were transmitted from one cultural zone, the European, to the other, the indigenous Muslim Algerian. Both communities covertly monitored each other's activities since, to a large degree, their strengths were inversely related, thus interdependent. Commerce, colportage, and spying naturally went hand in hand. Jean Mattei was a long-time resident of Tunisia whose profession as a merchant caused him to trade frequently with the beylik's southern tribes. In 1856 Mattei reported that "in the tribal tents the written and popular [i.e., oral] prophecies about the 'Master of the Hour' [sahib al-zaman] are constantly discussed."[35] Mattei's command of Tunisian Arabic and appearance were such that he easily passed as a North African; he was also a spy for the French consulate in Tunis and frequented the beylik's coffeehouses, gathering politically useful information. Indigenous spies, paid by colonial authorities in Algeria, also reported similar conversations regarding the mahdi in town gathering places until late in the century. Moreover, Mustafa b. 'Azzuz's estranged brother, Mabruk, was employed by the French to monitor the seditious activities of the Rahmaniyya zawiya in Nafta during the Sharif of Warqala's mahdist rebellion.[36] Thus, spying and rumor mongering were interrelated activities which mediated communications between two otherwise antagonistic communities; indeed spies probably provided much of the grist for news grapevines.

Collective expectations regarding the redeemer's appearance thus fed into the pulsating North African rumor mill which resonated in the countryside and the cities' densely populated Muslim quarters. Rumors accompanied spies, migrant workers, pilgrims, sufi couriers, and colporteurs on their journeys and then were disseminated in markets, mosques, zawaya, and cafes, where more rumors were collected. The return of the hajj caravan from the Hijaz set off a new salvo of hearsay as did the seasonal migrations of the tribes. Contained within the informal news pipeline from roughly 1830 on were endless reports of a mahdi-savior who was making his way from the Sus in Morocco or from the deep Sahara to save Algeria. Frequently rumors about the redeemer were intertwined with news that the Tunisian army was crossing the border to assist the mahdi in delivering the country from the rule of the impious. Another variation on the theme of external salvation was that the Ottoman sultan was poised for a military expedition. On the eve of Bu Ziyan's uprising, hopes for deliverance by Muslim rulers were not extinguished after two decades of colonial rule.[37] And evidence suggests that the bey of Tunis may have actively sought to nurture those hopes among the Algerian populace.[38]

Letters exchanged between sufi shaykhs in southeastern Algeria and southern Tunisia in the 1850s report similar sorts of news—the rise of a new mahdi from the Maghrib al-Aqsa (Morocco) and forthcoming military assistance from Tunis, Istanbul, and even the British government.[39] Because they were visited by travelers, pilgrims, students, and merchants, often from distant places, rural or urban sufi centers functioned as major collectors and distributors of information. Moreover, sufi shaykhs maintained a fairly sophisticated system of couriers who carried letters between affiliated zawaya. In the Sahara, Rahmaniyya and Tijaniyya lodges were scattered along major trade routes. Therefore, due to numerous social welfare functions, the major sufi centers fed into sinuous information circuits.

Concerted colonial efforts to block the circulation of politically "inflammatory information" proved futile. Dismissed by French officials as nothing but vicious *bruits*, the rumors (*akhbar*, or "news" in Arabic) flourished with peculiar intensity in the chaos and uncertainty of mid-nineteenth-century Algeria. Rumors are not, however, idle gossip or meaningless chatter. As Anand A. Yang demonstrated for India under the Raj, they "emerge purposively rather than accidentally as they represent the preoccupations of a 'public' seeking to comprehend the exigencies of their precarious situations."[40] In a society under siege, the rumors reveal not only what large numbers of people talked about but also how they interpreted events and what the public believed to be within the realm of possibility. As such, they offer an unusual glimpse into popular *mentalités*. The fact that sufi notables committed some of these rumors to writing indicates that the learned class shared the public's perceptions of the mahdi as heroic savior. Shaping and reflecting collective opinion, the hearsay also worked to maintain millennial aspirations and fervor at a heightened pitch.[41]

Nevertheless, can a causal link be established between inflammatory information and apocalyptic sentiments, on the one hand, and mass political behavior, on the other? Key here is the implicit linkage made in the public mind between what appeared to be weakening French resolve to retain Algeria and the redeemer's advent. Rumors about the revolutions in Europe, settler unrest in Algiers, and French troop movements coalesced with the news of the mahdi's arrival—the time was "right." In the months preceding Bu Ziyan's rebellion, the Biskris transmitted unsettling information from the capital to the oases which had a perceptible influence upon indigenous attitudes toward those ostensibly in authority. Emboldened by the promise of the approaching "final days," several of Biskra's inhabitants threatened their French-appointed native administrator with the news of the mahdi's appearance. An unambiguous warning to collaborators, this threat represented the first small-scale rebellion against the prevailing system of domination, a prelude of things to come. Despite disturbing reports from other regions and untoward conduct by the subordinate, the markets of Sidi 'Uqba and Biskra remained open and seemed reasonably tranquil. Local French officials read calm in the suqs as a sign that nothing was amiss because political unrest usually erupted first in the markets, the single most important public forum for resistance. Nor were there any apparent preparations for combat. All was well—or so it seemed in the early months of 1849.[42]

Thus, the confluence of a number of forces determined the timing of the 1849 revolt. Lacking was a catalyst or prime mover to transform economic grievances, perceptions of moral disarray, and deeply felt social malaise into a politically focused movement. It was Bu Ziyan who suc-

ceeded, where others had failed, in reinterpreting events, embodying discontents, and constructing an acceptable yet alternative program of social
action. He collapsed the Sahara's tribal warrior ethos with traditions surrounding the mahdi and the activism of the medieval North African ribat;
in so doing he achieved popular mobilization that momentarily tran-
scended local divisions and antagonisms, something even powerful religious notables had failed to accomplish.

Who Was Bu Ziyan?

Nothing in Bu Ziyan's past made him a particularly likely candidate for the
role of "Master of the Hour." One element working against his mahdist
pretensions was that he was already well known to the region's inhabitants
due to his part in the 1831 attack upon Za'atsha. Notoriety meant that Bu
Ziyan could not claim to have been sent by heaven, as the Sharif of Warqala
later did.[43] Nor was the hero of Za'atsha, as far as we know, in any way
connected with local religious elites. Had Bu Ziyan enjoyed sufi connections, his prophecy would have confirmed a pattern seen among other
charismatic leaders, who frequently came from the margins of the Islamic
establishment.[44] As discussed in chapter 3, Bu Ziyan's fame rested upon
military prowess rather than piety, miracle working, or religious scholarship. Predictably, later French colonial writers dismissed him as simply
a "semi-fanatic, semi-brigand agitator."[45] Nevertheless, military officers
directly involved in suppressing the revolt extolled Bu Ziyan's valor and
leadership qualities, while also employing that great explanatory device—
Muslim fanaticism—to characterize the movement.

The sources are in apparent conflict regarding his exact social origins.
One alleged that he had been a water carrier in Algiers in the 1830s, one
of the occupations traditionally monopolized by the Biskris.[46] Others maintained that Bu Ziyan had been a middling sort of landowner in the Ziban
prior to his appointment as a local administrator by 'Abd al-Qadir.[47] Lieutenant Seroka, perhaps the best informed, stated that he hailed from the
Awras—from the Burj Awlad 'Aruz of the Wadi 'Abdi—and was of "humble rank."[48]

Given the nature of the region's economy, it is possible to reconcile the
contradictions in Bu Ziyan's biography; these diverse elements are not
necessarily mutually exclusive. He could well have been of modest substance and sought work in Algiers, prior to returning to the pre-Sahara with
some capital to invest in the date-palm gardens—as the Biskris had traditionally done. Moreover, if Bu Ziyan had indeed labored as a water carrier
in the capital, it would confirm a second pattern in the recruitment of
millenarian figures seen elsewhere, most notably in sub-Saharan Africa.

Not infrequently, those who declared jihad against the European occupiers had previously been in sustained contact with the "White Man's ways"; thus, cultural familiarity with, rather than distance from, colonial masters bred discontents.[49]

Since Bu Ziyan did not leave behind any written accounts, speculations regarding how he gradually assumed the persona of the mahdi are perilous. It is known that he had been a partisan of 'Abd al-Qadir and held the minor post of shaykh of Za'atsha for several years until the French army took the Ziban in 1844. Then the position was taken away—perhaps in retaliation for Bu Ziyan's support of the amir—and given to an inept and despised figure, 'Ali b. 'Azug, who enjoyed no popular support in the oasis.[50] Another source claimed that Bu Ziyan was a disappointed office seeker in the new political order established after 1844. His preference for the Bu 'Ukkaz saff, however, had disqualified him from any stake in that order since the opposing Banu Ghana clan were given direct control over Biskra by French commanders.[51] These elements alone, however, hardly suffice as explanations for his later course of action, although between 1844 and 1849 he probably realized there was no room for him in the Banu Ghana brokered armistice. More significant is that Bu Ziyan assumed the mantle of the "expected one" in a period when millenarian expectations approached their zenith and had already been translated into rural mahdist-led movements in several places, notably the Dahra.

Declaring oneself the redeemer, on the one hand, and persuading a potential audience of this so as to construct a following, on the other, may appear to be sequential activities, structured in a cause-and-effect relationship. However, the ability to build a clientele could, in the cultural system of nineteenth-century North Africa, also validate the authenticity of the religious mission; the lines between cause and effect were blurred and could be reversed. In convincing ordinary people of his messianic claims, Bu Ziyan closely adhered to an implicit mahdist "script" and appears to have been fully conversant with the popular traditions concerning the signs, personality traits, and attributes identifying "the one sent from heaven." Simply stated, the creation of a community of devotees and the construction of the mahdist persona were simultaneous and mutually reinforcing activities.

"The Christians Will No More Enter Za'atsha Than They Will Enter Mecca"

In the early months of 1849, Bu Ziyan was beset by divinely inspired visions and disturbing dreams, universally regarded in that society as constituting a means of "access to the invisible world."[52] He dispatched emissaries to the Awras and Biskra to inform the populace of these portents from on high. Before long Bu Ziyan's otherworldly experiences entered into the rumor mill: "People were constantly speaking about [him] and much preoccupied with this man from Za'atsha who had seen the Prophet and grouped around him numerous partisans."[53] In addition to publicizing these supernatural visitations, which brought the pious and the curious to his side, Bu Ziyan also proceeded quite methodically to fashion a base of support by sacrificing sheep every day and distributing food to the poor; he held lavish banquets and entertained visitors. Since these rituals of sacrifice and the cultural behavior normally associated with them were outside of the normal liturgical cycle, they may have signaled a break in the ordinary flow of time, thus hinting at the mahdi's arrival.[54] However, up to this point, there was not much to distinguish Bu Ziyan's gradually emerging call to prophecy from the initial stages of the saint in gestation. Then came more visions and supernatural signs; the Prophet Muhammad announced in a dream that Bu Ziyan was the mahdi. The suspension of historical time was near; conquering piety was at hand.[55]

Nevertheless, some refused to believe that the Prophet had so honored the man from Za'atsha. To win over skeptics, Bu Ziyan predicted that other signs would soon follow. Once again the Prophet appeared in a nightly vision and seized Bu Ziyan by the hand, which turned green in color, a manifestation of *mu'jizat*, or those miracles attributed to prophets. The crowds gathered to behold the mystery, and his residence became a pilgrimage site as villagers arrived from far and wide. Divine election was finally confirmed—and any remaining skeptics won over—when the Prophet reappeared a third time, informing Bu Ziyan that "the reign of the impious had come to an end and the rule of the true believers is about to commence."[56] Having convinced an audience of his prophecy, Bu Ziyan then expanded the public nature of his preaching; his message combined exhortations to piety and right conduct with moral censure of local religious notables, who were upbraided for the "disorders of their private lives." At the same time, the new mahdi capitalized upon widespread dissatisfaction with the recently imposed colonial fiscal regime.[57]

Only in May 1849 did French officials have an inkling of the unfolding movement. By now the authorities sensed that the calm was deceptive but were frustrated in attempts to gather information through paid spies; apparently even indigenous informants had defected to Bu Ziyan's cause. Lieutenant Seroka, then a Bureau Arabe officer in Biskra and later wounded during the siege, was sent to investigate the rumors. Among them were disquieting reports going around the oases that "Algeria would soon be ruled by the Muslims again." The Ziban's French-appointed representative, Muhammad al-Saghir b. Ghana chose to ignore or minimize the explosive situation. Engaged in behind-the-scenes bet hedging, he surmised that rebellion would not be detrimental to his own interests, neither the first nor last time that supposed French allies turned a conveniently blind eye to unrest from below.[58]

At this critical juncture, blunders by those ostensibly in power served to transform an incipient movement of militant opposition into a full-scale uprising. Discovering the source of popular agitation, Seroka, and a small band of soldiers sent from Biskra, attempted to arrest Bu Ziyan in Za'atsha's marketplace in full view of the crowd. The mahdi miraculously escaped for a time. A second effort failed once again in the suqs when the people, by now carrying arms, rushed to Bu Ziyan's defense, delivering him from the French. Outnumbered, Seroka and his troops fled ignominiously for their lives. The populace interpreted this initial victory as evidence that their colonial masters were no longer equal to the task of ruling. Soon after, jihad was solemnly proclaimed from the minaret of the mosque attached to the Rahmaniyya zawiya; other oases in the Zab Dahrawi also declared open support for the insurrection.[59]

More than a month elapsed, and still the French did nothing to punish the villagers; this too was read as an indication of weakness. Finally, a small contingent of French soldiers led by Colonel Carbuccia arrived in July to end the sedition. The rebels retreated to Za'atsha, where they were protected by dense palm groves and shielded by walls and moats. Undermanned and unfamiliar with the peculiar exigencies of oasis warfare, the French contingent was forced into humiliating retreat the next day after costly losses. News of this second victory spread like wildfire and provoked further unrest in the Ziban, the Awras, and Bu Sa'ada.[60] The hour of deliverance was at hand.

Between July and September, however, no further clashes occurred in the pre-Sahara, mainly because the French army was distracted by insurrection in the northern Constantine. Moreover, a full-scale military expedition was virtually impossible due to the intense heat of summer. Another key element in the delay of hostilities was the annual migration of the Saharan tribes. Until the first autumn rains brought adequate pasturage, the tribes were absent from the Ziban, having moved tents and flocks over the mountains into the cooler, grain-growing plains. Without the additional manpower of tribal allies, the sedentary population of the oases was insufficient to withstand a long siege. Both sides—French and Algerian—bided their time.

The rebels used this reprieve to organize and prepare for the forthcoming Armageddon. Bu Ziyan continued to preach jihad from the Rahmaniyya zawiya in Za'atsha; significantly, he called for the taking of Biskra, the symbol of France's presence as well as the gateway to the eastern Sahara and the Tell. By capturing Biskra, Bu Ziyan's forces could then advance into the northern Constantine to expel the infidels. While assuring his followers that victory would come from God, Bu Ziyan also undertook practical measures to achieve large-scale mobilization. He turned to adjacent regions which traditionally maintained religious, commercial, and political ties with the Ziban. Letters and emissaries were dispatched far and wide to solicit material and moral support. Many villages and tribes beyond the southern Constantine also declared their support; a local uprising was assuming the proportions of a transregional movement.[61]

The response of Bu Sa'ada's populace underscores many of the forces for political action just discussed. Under the leadership of a local saintly figure, Muhammad b. Shabira, who maintained a constant correspondence with Bu Ziyan, Bu Sa'ada also recognized the mahdi.[62] But first specific anxieties had to be identified with the savior's call to arms. Muhammad b. Shabira, a member of Bu Sa'ada's shurafa', had not engaged in political activities until Bu Ziyan launched his jihad in 1849. A peaceful man of religion, Shabira was propelled to militant action by rumors, spies, and popular fears about European interference in the oasis's internal affairs. In addition to unsettling letters from Bu Ziyan calling for holy war and rumors about "the man with the green hand," news of Colonel Carbuccia's setback reached Bu Sa'ada. At this juncture, colonial officials sent an indigenous spy to investigate the extent of the hubus properties held by sufi and other religious notables; these properties were targeted for possible incorporation into the French-controlled public domain. A tactless move, it only inflamed indigenous elites and ordinary people alike. Other rumors circulated that the infidels sought to create a European settler presence in Bu Sa'ada. Thus threatened, Shabira and his followers declared holy war. Here we can see how quite local concerns were collapsed into the mahdi's program for universal deliverance.[63]

As Bu Sa'ada and other oases prepared for combat, the inhabitants of the Ziban, and particularly Za'atsha, stockpiled their villages with provisions ample enough to endure a long assault. The rebels concocted bullets made of date pits and covered with a thin layer of lead since this precious war metal was in short supply; they mined the houses with gunpowder, some of which may have been supplied by Shaykh Mustafa b. 'Azzuz, then residing in the Rahmaniyya zawiya in the Tunisian Jarid.[64] Finally, as autumn approached, noncombatants—children, women, and the elderly— were sent away for safety, although Bu Ziyan's extended family remained in the oasis as a sign that victory was assured. Nevertheless, a number of women elected to stay and fight along with their menfolk. If Bu Ziyan was a visionary, he was also a pragmatic mahdi who drew upon his prior experience as the spearhead of the 1831 uprising. His worldly brand of millenarianism contrasts sharply with other messianic leaders in North Africa or elsewhere, who often were singularly indifferent to the material dimensions of militant social protest since divine intervention would preserve them from harm.[65]

On the eve of the great conflict, Bu Ziyan had acquired many of the essential attributes expected of a mahdist leader in North African society: charisma, religious legitimacy conferred by the Prophet Muhammad and evidenced by mu'jizat, a large popular following, and a prophetic program to inaugurate the realm of justice and remove the source of evil and oppression. To these were added his own personal qualities of military prowess, which was prized in desert society, and political astuteness, perhaps acquired through earlier contacts with the colonial regime. Colonial authorities themselves contributed to Bu Ziyan's movement by failing to arrest him, which was read as yet another miraculous event, confirming his prophecy. Moreover, military officials did not immediately respond to the developing challenge to their authority. This too was interpreted as a symptom of feebleness; European might was crumbling in the face of the mahdi's power. By the summer of 1849, Bu Ziyan "was the real master of Za'atsha and his numerous partisans in the oases of the Sahara and in the Awras Mountains made him a dangerous personage."[66] Despite his revelations and proficiency in achieving popular mobilization, the mahdi felt compelled to seek the patronage of the region's sufi leaders and saintly lineages.

The "Rightly Guided One" or Base Impostor?

In many respects, desert sufi elites resembled their urban counterparts, the big-city ulama, in their predilection for social order over disorder as long as the holy law was upheld. As men of the pen, most preferred the zawiya's studious calm to the boisterous game of tribal politics—Sidi 'Abd al-Hafiz of Khanqa Sidi Naji is a perfect example of this position. If the saints championed communal opposition to wicked rulers, since they enjoyed a theoretical immunity from state repression, at the same time the ideal of saintliness was that of flight or retreat from violent confrontations.[67] Nevertheless, saintly leaders had to be responsive to the demands and needs of their clienteles since one of the social indicators of sainthood was collective recognition of piety expressed in the form of popular followings. Thus, the political behavior of religious notables was governed by clusters of implicit cultural codes that were highly contextual in nature.

The myriad responses of local religious notables to the French advance into their respective spiritual bailiwicks were examined in the previous chapter. During this critical period, the different, if ambiguous, positions of Rahmaniyya and other sufi leaders toward the colonial regime and its native allies began to congeal. Moreover, avoidance protest, bet hedging, and apparent accommodation were not mutually exclusive strategies for beleaguered religious notables. Procrastination and temporizing represented attempts to cope until the true intentions of the infidels could be ascertained. At the same time, confusion over France's aims in the Sahara—bolstered by colonial pacts with desert princes like the Banu Jallab of Tuqqurt—added to the collective sentiment of uncertainty but also conferred some measure of political maneuverability. Bu Ziyan's public prophecy abruptly ended the era of ambiguity and feigned compliance. An event long anticipated yet feared, it raised even more catastrophic uncertainties about the true identity of the would-be redeemer.

If the rise of a new saint was a cause for rejoicing within the community, the coming of the mahdi provoked both jubilation and trepidation among religious authorities. The traditions regarding his appearance in time were contradictory; they also warned that impostors would arise to lead the unwary into error. The dilemma faced by members of the provincial Islamic establishment—local saints and sufi notables—was to distinguish the divinely guided from the vile pretender.[68]

What then was the reaction of Rahmaniyya shaykhs to Bu Ziyan's self-proclaimed mission? Tulqa's sufi elite had already opted for political neutrality and nonresistance as early as 1844. After Mustafa b. 'Azzuz's departure for southwestern Tunisia that same year, Sidi 'Ali b. 'Umar's nephew, 'Ali b. 'Uthman (died 1898), assumed direction of the Tulqa Rahmaniyya center and its secondary zawaya in the Ziban.[69] Based upon his behavior even before the long siege, Sidi 'Ali b. 'Uthman and his family demurred to publicly recognize the authenticity of Bu Ziyan's mahdist claims; the outbreak of warfare failed to shake their resolve to eschew militant politics. Throughout the cruel siege months, Shaykh 'Ali of Tulqa continually offered his good offices, vainly seeking to effect reconciliation between French authorities in Biskra and the rebels, many of whom were Rahmaniyya brothers. Resolving traditional oasis conflicts was one of the functions expected of saintly mediators; mediating an apocalyptic struggle pitting the infidels against members of the community was new. Nevertheless, Shaykh 'Ali's refusal to sanction Bu Ziyan's movement did not discourage Tulqa's inhabitants from joining in the rebellion. They not only sent fresh recruits to Za'atsha but also dispatched a small band to attack the residence of the shaykh al-'arab in Biskra.[70]

The stance of Tulqa's sufi leaders toward the mahdi may have been determined by more than theological doubts regarding the legitimacy of Bu Ziyan's divine calling. Older saintly quarrels may also have been at work. After Mustafa b. 'Azzuz's hijra to Tunisia in 1844, any semblance of unity among the Saharan Rahmaniyya was effectively ended. Shaykh 'Ali b. 'Uthman was opposed by some Rahmaniyya figures, most notably Sidi 'Abd al-Hafiz of Khanqa Sidi Naji. The lack of cohesion among Rahmaniyya notables at this pivotal juncture was one element working against concerted political action. Clearly evident here is the interplay between older "maraboutic politics" and anticolonial resistance, including mahdist-led movements.

In contrast to those in Tulqa, the region's other Rahmaniyya leaders decided to confer their sociospiritual support to the rebellious prophet by the summer of 1849. On the eve of Colonel Carbuccia's abortive attack, Rahmaniyya shaykhs and their followers gathered in the oasis of Sidi Khalid, not far from Za'atsha. There Mustafa b. 'Azzuz's brother, Muhammad, headed the order's small zawiya. After much discussion, a general call for jihad was publicly announced. The 'Azzuz clan of al-Burj threw in their lot with the rebels; one of Mustafa b. 'Azzuz's brothers joined the battle as a combatant and lost his life in the final showdown. Another sibling, Mabruk b. 'Azzuz, earlier estranged from his family, fought for a time with Bu Ziyan but managed to escape the carnage of late November. In the oasis of Sidi Masmudi, the Rahmaniyya shaykh also lent moral support to Bu Ziyan's movement by preaching jihad to clients in the Awras. A large number of peasants and tribesmen from Sidi Masmudi participated in the hostilities.

When the news of Carbuccia's defeat reached Sidi al-Mukhtar, head of the Rahmaniyya zawiya in Awlad Jallal, he returned to the Ziban from his refuge with the Awlad Na'il. Shaykh al-Mukhtar recruited insurgents from the oases around Awlad Jallal and drew the great Saharan tribe of the Awlad Sassi into the insurrection. As he had done two years earlier during Bu Ma'za's revolt, Shaykh al-Mukhtar was instrumental in achieving popular mobilization based upon tariqa loyalties and patronage ties with tribal groups. In addition, he offered his services to Bu Ziyan in the event of an attack upon Biskra.[71]

In the Jabal Cherchar, however, Bu Ziyan's prophetic claims initially encountered skepticism. Sidi 'Abd al-Hafiz, whose influence stretched from the Zab Sharqi to the southeastern end of the Awras, hesitated to sanction the mahdi. The shaykh entertained grave doubts about the authenticity of his messianic pretensions, particularly Bu Ziyan's dreams in which the Prophet announced his selection as the "rightfully guided one." Perhaps too the fact that Bu Ziyan was not a member of the region's religious establishment prior to 1849 made his calling suspect. Despite his own personal misgivings, Sidi 'Abd al-Hafiz eventually, albeit reluctantly, joined with the rebels. Intense pressures from below—from the shaykh's tribal clientele in the Awras—forced him to alter his stance.[72] Here is a striking example of how ordinary people, the rank and file composing the popular followings of revered religious figures, also molded the political behavior of these notables. The unlettered mountain folk exerted their own form of moral suasion from below to force reluctant sufis out into the political arena. Thus, despite—or perhaps because of—his supernatural visions, Bu Ziyan sought the backing of sufi notables and their public acknowledgment of his prophecy. However, the important matter of sequence remains largely unknown: did Bu Ziyan wait until the movement had acquired a critical mass among the villagers to solicit Rahmaniyya confirmation of his mission? Or was his following in the oases dependent upon the blessings of certain activist sufi notables from the start? What is significant is that the endorsement of some prominent Rahmaniyya leaders transformed a local rebellion into a regional and transregional insurrection and that the would-be mahdi felt obliged to court those leaders. This hints at a symbiotic relationship between popular messianic figures and the rural Islamic establishment.

"Bu Ziyan and His Followers Are Like the Prophet's Companions"

A pragmatic millenarian, Bu Ziyan also sought to enlist outside help; letters were sent to the Tunisian ruler, Ahmad Bey, soliciting assistance.[73] This effort at international diplomacy raises several issues about how the rebels viewed their undertaking. If indeed God was on their side, why was additional support deemed necessary? And if the realm of justice was imminent, what role would established dynasties, such as the Tunisian Husaynids, play in the new socioreligious order? Importuning Ahmad Bey for help does, however, suggest that those preparing for the coming battle believed in the rumors then raging about forthcoming military assistance—indeed they probably contributed to the fund of improvised news.

By the autumn of 1849, Bu Ziyan had come to incarnate divinely ordained opposition to the French for many in Algeria and elsewhere in the Maghrib. The battle cry of the insurgents—"the Christians will no more enter Za'atsha then they will Mecca"—is symbolically suggestive of how the movements' participants interpreted their cause. The universal, normative core of Islam—the sacrosanct city—had been conflated with the rebellion's locus, a small oasis on the Sahara's brow; thus, the great religious "center out there" and the local center of revolt were one and the same. And in their struggles against the impious, Bu Ziyan and his partisans had been transformed by the collective religious imagination into the Prophet's companions.

Moreover, the mahdi had convinced his partisans by miracles, words, and deeds that they would defeat the French as they had the Turks. God had ordained total annihilation for the Europeans, who, in the popular discourse, were "worse than the Turks." Rumors ran riot. According to one, the infidels were trapped by the Kabyles, who had retaken Skikda, and by the Tunisians, who held Annaba; thus, the French army's access to the sea was blocked. This kind of news attracted fighters from outside of the pre-Sahara, who swelled the ranks of the insurgents. Bu Ziyan sent letters to areas as far removed as the Jurjura Mountains calling for jihad. Among those responding from the northern Constantine was al-Hajj Musa, the Darqawi leader who had earlier opposed 'Abd al-Qadir in the 1830s due to the amir's negotiations with the French. Sidi Musa brought with him to Za'atsha some sixty followers. Another religious charismatic, Muhammad ibn 'Abd Allah, the instigator of a small uprising near Collo, also arrived in the oasis. In addition, many religious leaders who had fled the Ziban in 1844 returned to the region. The former shaykh of Sidi 'Uqba, Muhammad al-Saghir, left the safety of Nafta's Rahmaniyya zawiya, crossing the border with his forces in an attempt to link up with Bu Ziyan. French spies in the Tunisian Jarid reported that Shaykh Mustafa b. 'Azzuz was also involved in the Za'atsha affair, mainly by supplying gunpowder and preaching revolt.[74]

As the French army began moving contingents down from the northern Constantine in September, victory over the unbelievers seemed assured. Then came a serious setback, a sign of what lay ahead. In the middle of September, Shaykh 'Abd al-Hafiz, pushed by his restive tribal clients to assume a front-line part in the uprising, reluctantly left his zawiya in the Jabal Cherchar. While popular pressures were probably the decisive factor in moving the aging shaykh to action, saintly disputes may also have been a factor. 'Abd al-Hafiz's adversaries—the Rahmaniyya of Tulqa and the Awlad Sidi Naji of Khanqa Sidi Naji—were in the opposing Banu Ghana camp, which probably made Bu Ziyan's cause all the more attractive. Sidi 'Abd al-Hafiz's entire life had been devoted to study, teaching, and spiritual exercises, thus he was especially unsuited for the rigors of militant action. At the head of several thousand warriors from the Awras and Zab Sharqi, the sufi shaykh established a bivouac near the small oasis of Sariana commanding the route to Biskra. The objective was to join up with Bu Ziyan's forces; together they could take the Ziban's capital, which many predicted would "fall without firing a shot." Believing that the French army was enfeebled and that Sidi 'Abd al-Hafiz's baraka was potent, many of the tribesmen arrived poorly armed or without weapons at all; the saint's blessings were deemed sufficient protection. Some villagers, anticipating the material rewards of apocalyptic victory, rode mules loaded with empty sacks in order to partake of war booty or to raid Biskra's lush gardens. They were cut to ribbons in a rapid surprise attack. Commandant Saint-Germain and his vastly superior forces led a nocturnal assault upon Sidi 'Abd al-Hafiz's band outside of Sariana as September drew to a close. Those who were spared retreated in confusion back to the mountains.[75]

The Rahmaniyya banners, tent, and baggage belonging to Shaykh 'Abd al-Hafiz were captured during the rout. The saint, who desired nothing but the serenity of his zawiya far from the rigors of war, fled into the Awras "almost naked." Despite this crushing contretemps, the shaykh appears to have been convinced by then of the authenticity—or at least the urgency—of Bu Ziyan's mission. A month later as Za'atsha was besieged by the French army, Sidi 'Abd al-Hafiz joined forces with the Rahmaniyya leader of Sidi Masmudi and the shaykh of Sidi 'Uqba, Muhammad al-Saghir, in a second assault upon Biskra, which was also repelled by superior French forces and armaments.[76]

The quandary that Bu Ziyan's jihad posed for sufi leaders, like Shaykh 'Abd al-Hafiz, is poignantly illustrated by the saint's behavior on the eve of his ill-fated military campaign. Striving to meet the demands of religious clients—to fulfill his obligations to disciples and preserve his prestige—the shaykh also made covert diplomatic overtures to the enemy. He wrote a conciliatory letter to colonial officials in Biskra in a last ditch effort to remain in good standing should the unthinkable occur. In his letter the shaykh declared that he had no reason to oppose French rule. Pressed by his clients to lead the jihad, he as their religious patron was obliged to follow suit.[77] Ultimately the decision to engage in popular protest would make Shaykh 'Abd al-Hafiz a political exile. The sufi notable's actions might be interpreted as merely self-interested equivocation. Yet this incident lays bare all the competing, contradictory social forces confronting religious notables during the conquest era. It also reveals that ordinary people wielded influence over the political behavior of privileged saintly lineages in certain circumstances.

The Final Showdown: The Siege of October to November

On 7 October, General Herbillon, commander of the province of Constantine, and four thousand French and indigenous soldiers arrived before Za'atsha with munitions and supplies sufficient for a prolonged siege.[78] Soon other contingents poured in until eight thousand men were assembled. To determine the rebels' resolve, Herbillon ordered the date-palm trees demolished; this was met by rifle shot indicating that negotiations were futile.

While the technological odds were on their side—the French army was equipped with heavy siege craft—lack of experience in oasis warfare hampered the colonial war machine. As the siege dragged on, morale deteriorated among the French soldiers since living conditions were miserable. An outbreak of cholera, introduced into the pre-Sahara by battalions from Sétif, decimated the army, further undermining esprit de corps. Moreover, the rebels were by then well organized and displayed the utmost indifference to death as they made sorties from the fortified oasis to attack the infidel encampment. While Bu Ziyan's forces killed a number of soldiers, the epidemic carried off many more.[79] The deadly confrontation became a test of France's will to retain the entire Sahara; eventually the fallout from Za'atsha would extend the turbulent colonial frontiers ever further in the desert.

With the cooler weather, the tribes began moving their flocks down from the Tell to the desert winter pasturage. This alarmed the French military; a rapid, decisive defeat was imperative since the pastoral-nomadic groups would most likely join the insurrection. Learning of the demoralized state of the European soldiers, the Sharaqa and Bu 'Azid tribes decided to lend aid to the besieged; they assembled in a small oasis near the Wadi Jadi for an attack from the rear. Alerted in time, General Herbillon mounted another nighttime sortie, which overwhelmed the tribes since it caught them by surprise; their chiefs surrendered on 15 November, and those who could escape fled south toward Tuqqurt. The rout was interpreted as a portent of doom by some of the Ziban's people; many sought to flee Za'atsha, now nearly encircled by soldiers and continually pounded by deadly artillery. Even al-Hajj Musa, an intrepid warrior, counseled Bu Ziyan to consider departing. Then the Rahmaniyya leader of Awlad Jallal, Shaykh al-Mukhtar, one of the mahdi's most fervent supporters, had disturbing visions. The Angel Gabriel (Jibril) had appeared to him in a dream warning that the Muslims would suffer ruin at Za'atsha and their leaders would perish. Despite the inauspicious news, Bu Ziyan persisted, believing that divine assistance was forthcoming as promised by the Prophet. His courage and steadfastness convinced many to take heart and remain, although much more than personal valor was at stake. Za'atsha's fate was seen as "a supreme struggle that would determine the authenticity of Bu Ziyan's prophecy and whether the last hour had arrived for the Christians."[80] To depart would have belied his own claims to be the awaited one. And should the mahdi prove to be a base pretender, his supporters would suffer heaven's displeasure.

As long as Za'atsha's gardens were not severed from the adjoining villages, resistance was possible since fresh combatants from contiguous oases replaced the dead or wounded. Women too were among the fighters.

During the fifty-two day ordeal, village women helped in repulsing the attack. Not only did they exhort their menfolk to acts of bravery, as was the custom in the Sahara, but they also took up arms, fighting alongside the men. Then the cholera epidemic began to take its toll among the rebels as it had already done among the Europeans. Exacerbating the losses from disease was the punishment that modern firepower bestowed on the oasis's ancient defenses, so invincible when faced by traditional foes. Here, as in innumerable other encounters between colonial armies and indigenous forces in Africa or Asia during the nineteenth century, the advanced military technology available to Europeans proved decisive.[81] In addition to intimidating cannonry, other tools of empire were at work. By 1849, the French army in Algeria was equipped with a new type of rifle, the *carabine à tige*, or bolt-action rifle, which replaced the older, and much less accurate, *carabine à munition*. Bu Ziyan's followers, in contrast, were armed with muskets of diverse origins and uncertain quality. Finally, after great losses, the French had completely encircled Za'atsha; a military *cordon sanitaire* isolated the village from other oases in the Zab Dahrawi.[82]

By 26 November the end was in sight; both sides knew what the future held. The relentless artillery had carved gaping breaches in Za'atsha's walls, and soon soldiers poured into the narrow, debris-strewn alleys and garden pathways. Bu Ziyan convened his followers in the town mosque. After leading them in prayer, he enjoined the few survivors to fight to the death. Later that day, French troops trapped the mahdi, together with his family— two young sons, a daughter, his wife, and mother—in the abandoned residence of the French-appointed qa'id. The mahdi emerged from the house brandishing a rifle; "I am Bu Ziyan," he calmly stated to the officers as he knelt down to pray. After being forced to witness his family's massacre, the rebellious prophet was placed against a wall, the order given to prepare arms. "You were the strongest; God alone is great, may His will be done" were his last words. Shots rang out, and the hero of Za'atsha fell to the ground. Bu Ziyan's head was offered as a prize of war to General Herbillon, who had it displayed on the gatepost for all to see. Throughout the remainder of the day, the silence was broken only by the sound of explosions as soldiers detonated gunpowder caches underneath the few houses still standing.[83]

The Aftermath

The revolt was immensely costly for both sides. Its suppression involved the French army in the longest, bloodiest siege experienced thus far in Algeria. Over fifteen hundred soldiers and officers perished in combat, and perhaps as many again died from cholera. Predictably, Za'atsha produced a number of ex post facto studies of oasis warfare in French military circles in anticipation of future such insurrections.[84] Analysts of the period regarded the battle as the most grueling test to date, far more so than the two sieges of Constantine over a decade earlier. Moreover, this epic confrontation in a small oasis on the Sahara's upper rim proved significant to the history of Algeria writ large. The commitment of so many soldiers and resources to the battle diverted attention away from other rebellious regions, delaying the Kabyle campaign, which began in earnest only in the 1850s. As the news of the terrible suppression spread, it instilled fears of similar reprisals among the Ziban's populace, who demurred, for the most part, to support openly the Sharif of Warqala's jihad several years later.[85]

Beyond the purely military or political realms, the Za'atsha affair directly affected colonial attitudes and policies toward sufis, saints, and holy men in North Africa. It raised the level of French consciousness regarding the potentially revolutionary role of popular and elite religious figures in collective protest. From 1850 on, a distinct genre in colonial historiography and in quasi-scientific studies of indigenous society emerges—the corpus of literature devoted to the turuq, the saints, and the so-called marabouts.[86] Obsessions with a "sufi menace" dominated French colonial thinking until at least the turn of the century.

The Ziban's inhabitants interpreted the fall of Za'atsha as a judgment from God and the outbreak of cholera as divine retribution visited upon those who had not perished as martyrs during the siege. In the epidemic that ravaged the region for several years after 1849, some oases lost nearly three-quarters of their population. The nearby pastoral-nomadic peoples suffered cruelly as well. Many fled Algeria for Tunisia to escape vengeance, disease, and the devastation inflicted upon the Zab Dahrawi, where some ten thousand date palms—the very basis of the economy—were systematically cut down by the French army in retaliation. From the ruins of Za'atsha—the town was thoroughly demolished and its gardens destroyed—eight hundred bodies were uncovered. As a warning to future insurgents, the French army chose to leave the razed village as it was; no one was permitted to reside there again. In the words of one contemporary witness, Za'atsha constituted a monument to "des horreurs qui n'avaient pas de nom" ["indescribable horrors"].[87]

The events of 1849 provoked different sorts of responses, ranging from passive resistance to mass emigration not only to neighboring Tunisia but also to more distant lands.[88] That same year a Kabyle Rahmaniyya shaykh, Sidi al-Mahdi, publicly called upon his clients to emigrate from the colony to Syria; some three thousand people eventually departed for the Ottoman-ruled Mashriq.[89] In December 1849, the governor-general of Algeria,

Cavaignac, wrote a letter to the minister of foreign affairs in Paris deploring the movements of Algerians, both ordinary people and elites, out of the colony.[90] Since the porous frontiers between Tunisia and Algeria were a favored escape route, the Tunisian beylik became increasingly critical to French imperial strategy.

For those religious notables who had participated openly in the Za'atsha movement, emigration or withdrawal to inaccessible regions was imperative for survival. Commanding tribal warriors from the Tunisian border regions, the shaykh of Sidi 'Uqba had sought to coordinate operations with Sidi 'Abd al-Hafiz and the Rahmaniyya shaykh, Sadiq b. al-Hajj, from the oasis of Sidi Masmudi in the Awras. Together they aimed to relieve Bu Ziyan by supplying fresh combatants, although their coalition collapsed after several defeats at the hands of the French army. The shaykh of Sidi 'Uqba withdrew once more from the Ziban, seeking refuge in the no-man's-land between the Suf and the Tunisian Jarid until the Sharif of Warqala declared revolt in 1851. Likewise, the Rahmaniyya leader of Sidi Masmudi escaped to his sufi sanctuary in the mountains, still outside of French control; a decade later a small mahdist uprising erupted from the zawiya under Sidi al-Sadiq's auspices.[91]

Twice defeated in 1849, Sidi 'Abd al-Hafiz also retreated back to his Rahmaniyya zawiya in Khanqa Sidi Naji. Because of his advanced years and spiritual authority, colonial authorities officially pardoned him in January 1850. Nevertheless, remaining in Algeria was intolerable for the Rahmaniyya shaykh; soon thereafter, he went to Nafta to reside with his sufi associate, Sidi Mustafa b. 'Azzuz, in accordance with the duty of hijra. While in the Tunisian Jarid, Shaykh 'Abd al-Hafiz succumbed to the cholera epidemic still raging in the region. He died in July 1850; his body was transported from the Jarid back to the family Rahmaniyya center in the Jabal Cherchar.[92] According to popular lore, however, the shaykh had not perished. Rather he was once again enclosed alive in the tomb, from which he continued to bestow his baraka upon clients and family members. His sons were regarded by ordinary people not as his spiritual heirs but as mere representatives of the still-living saint.[93]

Elsewhere in Algeria, Za'atsha's repression brought to heel other rebellious groups who had emulated Bu Ziyan by raising the flag of revolt. As discussed above, Bu Sa'ada's inhabitants had rallied around a local saintly leader, Shabira, who kept in touch with Bu Ziyan and convinced the townspeople to participate in jihad. There "the market became the rendezvous of the insurgents; the rebels bought arms and ammunition in the city's markets for holy war and everywhere in the streets, in the houses, gunpowder was being made."[94] By 9 November, however, Bu Sa'ada's populace realized that they were outnumbered by French forces and laid down their arms. When the nearby tribal peoples of the Awlad Na'il learned of Za'atsha's fate and the execution of the mahdi and his family, they also sued for peace. Soon thereafter, a military headquarters, including a fort and a local Bureau Arabe, was established in Bu Sa'ada, to supervise the townspeople and the pastoral nomads, above all the Awlad Nail, who traded in the markets there. The cruel lessons of Za'atsha were not lost on a religious notable residing in a small oasis not far from Bu Sa'ada—Sidi Muhammad b. Abi al-Qasim of al-Hamil. The saint had only recently in the village created a madrasa, which would later serve as the nucleus for one of the largest Rahmaniyya complexes in Algeria. Shaykh Muhammad's strategy for containing foreign domination through nonviolent means was surely a consequence of the events of 1849. Finally, the mahdi's demise may have also vindicated the neutralist position of political fence-sitters like the Rahmaniyya notables of Tulqa who had preached calm and compromise.

Nevertheless, the deeper social significance of Za'atsha did not end at mid-century; many refused to believe that Bu Ziyan and his family had died. Rumor had it that the mahdi had foiled death by flight; others held that one of his sons had survived the carnage. Several years later, another Saharan rebel, the Sharif of Warqala, claimed to be associated with Bu Ziyan's son, al-Qasim, whose body was never recovered from the ruins. By tapping into the reputation of the hero of Za'atsha, the sharif attempted to incite another uprising. Paradoxically, defeat only served to increase Bu Ziyan's stature as a paladin and legend whose deeds were incorporated into the fund of local epic lore. Through the cultural medium of oral ballads and poetry, the events of 1849 were woven into the collective historical memory; Za'atsha remained vivid in the popular imagination long after the final showdown.[95]

Collective Memory, Poetry, and Social Protest

Thus far the narrative of the 1849 uprising has largely been based upon written accounts left by European participants in the struggle. Most of the rebels were illiterate, although as mentioned above the French army uncovered letters in Bu Ziyan's house; some of the mahdi's correspondence was intercepted en route by colonial authorities.[96] Viewing the events from the perspective of the mahdi's followers is, however, rendered less daunting because several fragments of praise poetry composed in Bu Ziyan's honor were recorded at the time in their original vernacular Arabic.[97] These ballads are significant not only for what they say but also for how they came to be. Their existence points to a much larger fund of verse inspired by rebellious prophets and disseminated in popular milieus. And the two ballads offer clues about the channels through which millenarian traditions were transmitted to ordinary people.

Poetry dedicated to local folk heroes—whether saints, rebels, or mahdis—was recited during social or religious gatherings by rural and urban
maddahs, often to the accompaniment of music.[98] In North Africa, the word
maddah traditionally had a wider connotation than the more restricted
classical meaning of "panegyrist." Beaussier's dictionary of Algerian Arabic, first published in 1897, defines the maddah as "a kind of religious
minstrel who attends festivals to sing the praises of the saints, of God, and
of holy war, and who is accompanied on the tambourine and flute."[99] In
the largely oral society of the countryside, poets represented the collective
historical memory of the community as their verses were passed on by word
of mouth across generations. But they were more than mere chroniclers,
satirizers, or entertainers. The maddahs were "arbiters of words" in the
same way that the saints were the arbiters among men or between hu-
mankind and God.[100] And through the mediation of the local bard, eschatological lore, conserved in the countryside by sufi zawaya, was woven
into publicly narrated epics.[101]

As discussed in chapter 2, popular poets wielded considerable political
clout since they both shaped and reflected public opinion—much as rumors
did—a fact recognized by indigenous North African leaders and colonial
authorities. Even 'Abd al-Qadir cringed at the satirical verses composed by
one recalcitrant maddah from the Oran when the amir's jihad was in its
most exalted phase.[102] Bu Ziyan, however, had nothing to fear from the
Ziban's bards, who were florid in their praise. But these verses were more
than popular eulogies for they were intended to make sense of disturbing
events in much the same way that rumors did. Indeed, given the cultural
fact that storytelling talents were so widely diffused throughout the society, rumors and ballads were mutually reinforcing; both mirrored public
opinion, which viewed the coming struggle as the decisive moment in the
long-awaited final showdown between good and evil.

The first ballad was attributed to Muhammad b. 'Umar of the small oasis
of Lishana which adjoined Za'atsha; his verses were composed before the
movement's demise in November 1849. Two years later, in 1851, Muhammad b. 'Umar was incarcerated by French officials in Biskra for singing
this same ballad during village festivals. The maddah was deemed a threat
to public order solely by virtue of his poetry, which indicates the potential
political influence of both the poet and of the Za'atsha epic.[103]

Muhammad b. 'Umar refers to Bu Ziyan as both the mahdi and the "bey
of the Sahara," which indicates that the hero of Za'atsha had collapsed both
the warrior traditions of the desert with those of the redeemer. The rebels
were, according to the poet, armed in a manner that would excite the
admiration of any tribesman. They carried "richly ornamented pistols,

long-barrelled rifles, and curved daggers," and were amply supplied with British gunpowder, the most coveted ammunition in North Africa at the time since it was believed the most deadly. Backing the combatants were their womenfolk, whose shrill cries exhorted them to brave deeds, a reference to culturally acceptable female participation in desert warfare. Moreover, the struggle was situated not only within the sociocultural milieu of the Sahara but also within its recent historical context. The poet portrayed the French siege as the culmination of a long series of confrontations with outsiders. Just as the 1831 attack by the last bey of the Constantine failed before Za'atsha, so would the present assault by the Christians. In concluding his ballad, Muhammad b. 'Umar once again waxed eloquent over the virtues of British gunpowder, then compared his verses to the beads of a Muslim rosary.[104]

The second ballad, by another local maddah, 'Ali b. Sharqi, also glorified Bu Ziyan and his uprising, although its tone was somewhat more doleful than the first. Here we also see how the besieged viewed their situation during the fifty-two–day ordeal. Hordes of infidel soldiers from all over Algeria had converged upon the oasis like "a plague of locusts."[105] Cannon shot and the smoke of firearms filled the air as did the thunder of the enemy's drums. Yet with the help of God and Bu Ziyan, the hero of holy war, the impious will be buried at Za'atsha, sang 'Ali b. Sharqi. So great was Bu Ziyan's reputation that he was known in the Tunisian cities and tribes; even the Ottoman sultan had heard of him.[106]

Each of the poems depicted Bu Ziyan as both the long-awaited one and a local folk hero; valor on the battlefield earned him as much popular veneration as did his divinely ordained mission conferred by the Prophet Muhammad. Thus, powerful symbols and historical events were refashioned and interpreted in such a way as to give the movement's supporters some measure of certainty of what lay ahead—triumph—after decades of uncertainty. Here it should be pointed out that the maddahs did more than narrate stories; they were regarded as blessed with the power of divination. And in the early autumn months of 1849 the future appeared to be guaranteed by Bu Ziyan. Through the mahdi's leadership, the community's collective redemption would be attained: "Bu Ziyan will assure our salvation in this world and in the next, . . . the man with the sword. . . . Bu Ziyan and his followers are like the Prophet's companions. . . . I sing the praises of my hero, . . . the first among the faithful. . . . Even the angels say that Bu Ziyan will be victorious, . . . the valiant, the one who does not yield."[107] The appeals to reigning Muslim rulers and princes for legitimacy suggest that the besieged situated their struggle within the much wider politicoreligious context of the Islamic *umma* (community of believers),

which implicated all Muslims in the confrontation.[108] While the beleaguered Tunisian prince, Ahmad Bey, certainly entertained no thoughts of
coming to the aid of rebels holed up in Za'atsha, documents in the Tunisian
state archives indicate that officials in the beylik were anxiously awaiting
the siege's outcome. A letter written by the Jarid's governor to Tunis in
November 1849 noted the *harb shadid* (violent war) then raging in the
Ziban and recorded the death of Bu Ziyan in a terse manner.[109] The fact
that Ahmad Zarruq, the Tunisian governor, did not feel obliged to provide
officials in Tunis with any further details regarding Bu Ziyan's identity or
the nature of his movement implies that beylical authorities were already
conversant with events in the Ziban. Moreover, letters discovered by
French officers in Bu Ziyan's headquarters in the demolished oasis showed
that he had corresponded with the Tunisian central government. Compromising letters from a number of indigenous Algerian leaders, who
ostensibly had submitted to France and were regarded as colonial allies,
were also uncovered. Whether Ottoman officials in Tripolitania had a hand
in the uprising as the French maintained at the time is, however, a matter
of conjecture.[110] However, Bu Ziyan's movement was deemed important
enough by British officials to earn space in the London *Times*.[111]

In the eyes of the North Africans, the battle for Za'atsha was an epic
struggle—comparable to those waged by the Prophet Muhammad and his
Companions against the polytheists of Mecca in the early seventh century—to right a world turned upside down by foreign conquest. The
movement's constituency is a powerful indicator of the revolt's nature and
ideology. Among those battling the forces of evil, "who swarmed like
locusts" upon the village, were individuals from places far removed from
the Ziban: Algerians from the Oran, subjects of the Tunisian bey and the
Moroccan sultan, and even some Arabs from the Hijaz. In addition, twenty
different tribal groups from the eastern Sahara sent contingents.[112] Bu
Ziyan had indeed succeeded—for a brief time at least—where others had
failed; the older saff divisions had been overcome for a while, and a
translocal coalition of forces put together, consolidated by their collective
belief that the realm of justice was within reach.

The ballads praising Bu Ziyan were recited long after the mahdi's death.
His story was integrated into the Sahara's folkloric and cultural traditions
and became part of collective historical memory. Thus Bu Ziyan could claim
a certain victory in defeat. According to a Bureau Arabe officer in Biskra:

> We have often said that the memory of Za'atsha has remained in
> the heart of the Ziban like a ferment of hatred which will not be
> dissipated for a long time. The defense of the oasis, the battles
> waged there, have become the theme of popular songs. Bu Ziyan
> and the heroes of jihad are therein glorified. It is known that

these songs have been recited publicly in the oases, particularly during religious festivals which draw large crowds.[113]

The rumors that nurtured Bu Ziyan's movement did not cease with the oasis's destruction; rather more improvised news, now confused with the horrors of cholera, both fueled and reflected the collective sense of anguish. In response to the devastating epidemic of 1849–1851, a program to introduce basic European medicine was initiated in the Ziban.[114] Efforts by local officials to inoculate indigenous children encountered determined opposition; the events of 1849 were again evoked by the distrustful parents. Biskra's inhabitants were ordered to bring their children to the French doctor for inoculation; fifty youngsters were vaccinated. Wary of foreign medicine and of colonial intentions, the populace soon spread the rumor that the French were forcing families to give up their offspring and that the vaccination program was but a pretext to abduct Muslim children. Convinced by the rumors, the parents refused to obey, saying that they "would rather be buried under Za'atsha's ruins" than render their children.[115] Za'atsha had became a poignant symbol of passive resistance in nonviolent confrontations with French authorities.

Thus, this bitter conflict in a rather remote corner of the pre-Sahara was regarded by many in North Africa as a decisive encounter—as decisive as the 1885 clash between General Gordon and the Sudanese Mahdists in Khartoum or 'Abd al-Qadir's last stand on the Mulwiyya in 1847.

The Algerian Pre-Sahara in the Aftermath of 1849

The Za'atsha insurrection provoked a sea change in colonial thinking about and strategies for policing the Sahara and its diverse populations. After 1849, new military and administrative policies were elaborated in which the oases and pastoral nomads figured prominently for the first time.[116] By 1850, the French military had come to realize that a stranglehold over key markets was as important to pacification as battalions of soldiers. Thus, colonial strategists more or less consciously emulated their Turkish predecessors, who had always employed economic or market pressures to bring their more restless subjects to heel; Turkish blockades of vital foodstuffs and supplies had on more than one occasion coaxed insurgents to lay down their arms. And possession of Biskra, the heart of the Ziban, meant that the colonial regime held one of the main passageways between Tell and Sahara after 1849.

Nevertheless, when the passes into the north were closed, rebellious groups situated near the frontiers with Algeria's neighbors unfailingly turned to Tunisia or Morocco for grains, guns, gunpowder, and other necessities. In addition, the Ottomans lodged a garrison in Ghadamis, a strategic oasis-emporium for the trans-Saharan trade, in 1842. The Ottoman drive to reassert direct sovereignty over Tripolitania after 1835 made French penetration of the eastern Sahara all the more imperative. Yet without the 1849 revolt and, above all, the Sharif of Warqala's jihad further military expansion into the desert would have been less urgent.[117] In addition, Shaykh Mustafa b. 'Azzuz's across-the-border activities, and the migration of Algerian dissidents to his zawiya in the Tunisian Jarid, focused colonial attention upon the beylik as well.

For colonial officials in Algeria, victory at Za'atsha assured the continued occupation of Biskra, portal to the Sahara, while at the same time necessitating future campaigns southward which thrust the edges of the colonial state outward. In terms of geopolitics, the 1849 victory gave the French military a desert beachhead from whence the pacification of more distant oases could be undertaken, although not without encountering more mahdist-led resistance: al-Aghwat fell in 1852, followed by Tuqqurt, Warqala, and the Suf by the end of 1854. Propelled by the activities of rebellious prophets and dynamic sufi leaders, the turbulent frontier was being relentlessly expanded until it reached the Tunisian borders in the mid-1850s. While nearly three more decades elapsed before Tunisia was added to France's African possessions, the first calls for the beylik's occupation were made in this period. And in these calls for French overlordship of Tunisia, Mustafa b. 'Azzuz of Nafta figured prominently.

In contending with rapidly changing political conditions after 1830, Sidi Mustafa b. 'Azzuz embraced a course of action different from some of his Rahmaniyya sufi peers in the southern Constantine—hijra to a neighboring Muslim country. From his sufi zawiya, constructed in the Tunisian Jarid after 1844, Shaykh 'Azzuz was involved in both the Za'atsha and Warqala jihads. And while Sidi 'Azzuz did not lead bands of armed rebels, he was instrumental to the elaboration of movements of social protest. Like other Rahmaniyya notables, Shaykh 'Azzuz combined strategies of apparent accommodation, when circumstances demanded, with rejection of colonial hegemony. If he chose not to confront European technological and military might head on, nevertheless, Sidi Mustafa's response to French domination paralleled in a sense the reaction of Bu Ziyan and his supporters. By the rebellion's later phase, the Za'atsha insurgents sought to create a "city of God" in the desert which, after the final triumphant encounter with the forces of darkness, would usher in a new social order. In the same period, Shaykh 'Azzuz was also engaged in laying the basis for a new social and political order—on the other side of the Algerian border. And his style of moral combat drew Tunisia and the Tunisians into the political wilderness of *Algérie Française*.

5   Baraka and Barud
Sidi Mustafa's Emigration to Tunisia

> We have everything to lose from the ruin of the Algerian
> people; the damage will be even greater if the Algerians
> begin to emigrate. This is quite easy for the population
> of the Ziban so close to Tunisia.[1]

The establishment of colonial regimes in nineteenth-century Africa raised
anew the issue of the Islamic duty of hijra and demanded a redefinition of
the concept of Dar al-Islam.[2] Hijra, like travel, can be politically subversive
in certain contexts. Political or social movements in Africa frequently had
their genesis in the removal of pious Muslims from territory ruled by the
impious. Thus, hijra could be the prelude to jihad, to the rise of a new sufi
order, or to mass withdrawal to a space untainted by Europeans.[3]

Compared with Bu Ziyan or the Sharif of Warqala, Mustafa b. 'Azzuz
embarked upon a different course of action in his 1844 hijra to Tunisia—an
apparent retreat from violent confrontations with Algeria's French masters.
However, emigration did not constitute the final chapter of his political
involvement. Rather emigration allowed Shaykh Mustafa to provide the
institutional, material, and ideological components for sustained collective
action. From his newly created sufi center in the Jarid, Sidi 'Azzuz channeled provisions, arms, counsel, and information to those opposing French
rule across the border. Even without frontline participation in jihad, provincial notables heading large, prosperous, and strategically located zawaya
could offer support to dissidents.

Hijra also provoked changes in collective notions of religious center and
periphery. As the turbulent colonial frontiers were pushed relentlessly
outward in Algeria, regional or local centers of Islam also shifted—south
into the desert or across the frontiers into the Tunisian beylik. If the city
of Constantine had long served as the Islamic core for eastern Algeria, after
1837 places like Tunis and the Jarid increasingly replaced Constantine as
vital poles of attraction for Algerian Muslims.[4]

By their political behavior, sufi notables, such as Mustafa b. 'Azzuz,
reconstructed the relationship between center and periphery; indeed the

125

ALGERIA

Tamarza

Shatt al-Gharsa

Tuzar

Nafta

To Suf

Shatt al-Jarid

From Tunis

Gafsa

To Sfax

Shatt al-Fajaj

Mediterranean Sea

Gabis

JIRBA

Zarzis

Kabili

Duz

Matmata

Madanine

Tatawin

TUNISIA

ALGERIA

LIBYA

N

| 0 | 25 | 50 | miles |

| 0 | 50 | 100 | kilometers |

Ghadamis

6. Southern Tunisia and the Jarid

drastically transformed conditions in Algeria demanded such. Nevertheless, 'Azzuz's decision to depart was not in keeping with the responses of his Rahmaniyya associates in the Ziban. Most religious figures, and even many members of the 'Azzuz clan, elected to remain, despite social turmoil and the growing colonial presence, although, as discussed in the previous chapter, the Za'atsha revolt constituted a sea change in the political stance of sufi leaders residing in the Awras and pre-Sahara.

The Hijra of 1844

In the months between the first French incursions into the Ziban and the second taking of Biskra in May 1844, Mustafa b. 'Azzuz emigrated to the Tunisian Jarid. He was accompanied by Rahmaniyya disciples as well as family members—his wife, several daughters, and at least two young sons.[5] While there is no information about the hijra itself, 'Azzuz and his followers probably traveled with a merchant caravan from the Ziban to Nafta via the oases of the Suf. The émigrés could have settled in the Suf since it was still completely outside of colonial control, remaining so until the defeat of the Sharif of Warqala's jihad in 1854. In 1844 there was no indication that the French would move against the quasi-independent Suwafa, whose salvation lay in isolation and the region's treacherous terrain. Moreover, in the Suf were several Rahmaniyya centers established earlier in the century by Muhammad b. 'Azzuz. Yet Sidi Mustafa chose instead to traverse the fluid frontiers into the beylik, although the 'Azzuz clan neither owned property nor had any sufi establishment there.[6] Perhaps Sidi Mustafa's departure was initially intended as a temporary expedient since many Algerians at the time viewed the infidel occupation as a passing affliction.

Symbolically, the hijra was of immense importance. It signaled a refusal to reside in territory whose status had precipitously changed from Dar al-Islam to *Dar al-Harb* (enemy territory).[7] As such it was an expression of avoidance protest, in this case elite protest based upon religious duty, directly linked to Biskra's capitulation to the French army. Nevertheless, events in the Ziban prior to 1844 may also have shaped the decision to emigrate. Sidi 'Ali b. 'Umar of Tulqa, Shaykh Mustafa's spiritual preceptor, was killed in 1842 during the interminable saff struggles. And splits within the 'Azzuz clan itself had erupted over the warrior-saint Husayn's political activities, to which were added older divisions among Rahmaniyya notables in the Awras and Ziban. In addition, some of the great families of eastern Algeria—the Banu Ghana and the Muqrani, for examples—had concluded unsavory alliances with the colonial regime to advance their interests against those of rivals. Indeed, Sidi Mustafa's older brother, Hasan, had been captured by French officials in 1841 largely due to al-Muqrani's betrayal.[8] By this time too, the French army had proven a formidable opponent against which new strategies had to be deployed.

Southern Tunisia represented a haven for organizing political action against the neighboring colonial state. Historically the Jarid had provided refuge to political agitators fleeing central government oppression. Due to location on the hajj route, its oases were in constant contact with Tripolitania, then an Ottoman regency, the Mashriq, and Hijaz.[9] In addition to being a holy city, popularly regarded in the beylik as second only to al-Qayrawan, Nafta was strategically situated on the route to southeastern Algeria. Establishing a zawiya there placed Mustafa b. 'Azzuz in an optimal position for waging across-the-border holy war through the vehicle of the tariqa. At the same time, Shaykh 'Azzuz and his family were soon under the protection of the Tunisian ruler, Ahmad Bey, and within the confines of Dar al-Islam. Thus hijra embodied both physical movement and a spiritual odyssey offering purification for the polluting influence of the unbelievers.[10] Flight from Biskra represented the fulfillment of religious obligation as well as a pragmatic response to unfavorable sociopolitical circumstances.

Moreover, the Jarid offered opportunities for expanding Rahmaniyya membership and networks in socioecological conditions identical to the Ziban. Emigration eventually conferred upon Mustafa b. 'Azzuz an altered spiritual identity as he became the focal point of a semi-independent sufi order whose members referred to themselves as *'Azzuziyya* [followers of Sidi 'Azzuz]. (Indeed even today in Tala and the Jarid, people refer to the Rahmaniyya tariqa as the 'Azzuziyya in deference to the saint and sufi's memory.) Thus, physical withdrawal from one political zone to another conferred upon the emigrants an altered sense of religious place. Viewed from the long term, relocation brought the 'Azzuz family a degree of social mobility in subsequent generations which might not have occurred otherwise. Just as affiliation with the nascent Rahmaniyya tariqa transformed parochial saintly lineages into sufi notables by the early nineteenth century, emigration to the beylik eventually conferred *baldi* status upon some of Sidi Mustafa's sons and grandsons in the Tunisian capital at the century's end. Integration into the Jarid's political economy and saintly ecology through the idiom of sufism helped the 'Azzuz clan overcome their *gharbi* (i.e., from the West or Algeria) origins. Overcoming their *afaqi* (provincial) status resulted from the collective recognition of Shaykh Mustafa's piety, learning, and baraka, from his resistance to the French regime, and from his part in shoring up the Husaynid dynasty during the great revolt of 1864.[11]

But first, what kind of social environment awaited the newly arrived émigrés from the Ziban? How did they employ the Jarid's geopolitical possibilities to engage in transborder political movements? In which ways did Tunisia's relatively greater integration into Mediterranean commercial and other networks shape political action? And to what extent was the spiritual ecology of sainthood and sufism in the North African context subject to ecological constraints upon collective social action? Simply stated, how did hijra influence the range of political options open to Sidi Mustafa b. 'Azzuz and his partisans?

Bilad al-Jarid: The Tunisian Pre-Sahara

Along the route leading from the Algerian Suf into the Tunisian Jarid, the sand dunes change subtly in color from white to amber; the distance from al-Awad, capital of the Suf, to Nafta is roughly 140 kilometers.[12] In the past century, a loaded caravan reached Nafta, the first oasis on Tunisian territory, in three days; four days were needed to arrive in Tuzar, the region's provincial capital. Compared with the Suf's oases, which resembled large villages, Nafta and Tuzar were towns or even cities, as *madina* was understood in the cultural vocabulary of the period.[13]

The bilad al-Jarid is located in southwestern Tunisia between the Shatt al-Gharsa to the north and the Shatt al-Jarid to the southeast. In a sort of isthmus separating the two shatts are the oases of Nafta and Tuzar, historically the most important Saharan towns in Tunisia; to the north are smaller oases such as al-Hamma and al-Widyan. The climate is typically pre-Saharan with insignificant rainfall and summer temperatures sometimes exceeding forty degrees centigrade. Intense heat, combined with abundant underground springs, make the Jarid one of the world's leading producers of high-quality dates. As Muhammad b. Salama, *qadi al-mahalla*, wrote in the late 1830s, "the best date is the daqla al-nur [whose] equal is not found outside of the Tunisian Jarid."[14]

As was true for the Ziban, palm cultivation formed the linchpin of the Jarid's economy; textile production was also an important economic activity which undergirded commercial exchanges with other parts of Tunisia and Algeria as well.[15] In the middle of the past century, the Jarid proper enclosed some 770,000 date palms.[16] The wealth, power, and prestige of the clan were calculated by the number of gardens and trees to which it laid claim. Profits derived from trade and commerce, a crucial adjunct to agriculture, allowed merchant families to purchase more land, trees, and water rights.[17] If the date-palm plantations permitted human life to exist in an unforgiving natural environment, trade and commerce, based upon agrarian surplus, allowed the oases to flourish by sending out economic and social runners far and wide.

The Jarid's geographical situation was indeed fortuitous. Among the largest, wealthiest, and most active North African oases, Nafta and Tuzar owed their prominence to location. Both lay astride the intersection of two complex trade routes: the transversal or east-west line offered easy access to the ports of Gabis and Jirba only several days march from the Jarid; the north-south route reached Tunis through interior cities like Gafsa or al-Qayrawan.[18] Moreover, as Antoine Carette shrewdly observed in 1844, Tunisia was "both the Paris and the London of the eastern Maghrib." Not only did the beylik supply Algeria with a wide array of manufactured goods and foodstuffs but also the Tunisian piaster was the preferred coinage for the Constantine. Areas as far removed as the Mzab, Ghadamis, and the Touat employed Tunisian currency. Even after 1830, the piaster retained its dominant position in the Algerian Sahara over the *duro*, a coin introduced by the colonial regime to exert tighter control over the fiscal, economic, and political life of desert communities.[19]

Because of the beylik's geography, both the long-distance, luxury trade and the traffic in regional bulk commodities, often less valuable in worth, flowed through the Jarid's oases. The stock of the long-distance trans-Maghribi caravan trade was more likely composed of luxury goods that commanded high prices but were light in weight: fine Jaridi finished textiles, European cottons, silks from the Mashriq or Leghorn, perfumes, gold, or beautifully wrought firearms from Tunisian producers.[20] Tuzar and, in particular, Nafta were Tunisia's Saharan ports opening onto a line of oases stretching nearly one thousand kilometers to the west, while at the same time funneling trade from Metlilli, Warqala, Tuqqurt, and the Suf either through southern Tunisia to the coast or up to Tunis.[21]

The Jarid's two main oases served as vast entrepôts for products of diverse provenance—from the Maghrib, the Mashriq, Europe, or sub-Saharan Africa; these commodities were then distributed throughout the Constantine, the Algerian Sahara, and southern Tripolitania. More significant from a political viewpoint was the fact that the Jarid-Gabis region represented southeastern Algeria's outlet to the Mediterranean; the journey from Tuqqurt or the Suf to the sea via southern Tunisia was several days shorter than the routes through northern Algeria. And for decades after 1830, the Suf-Jarid-Gabis routes were beyond the colonial regime's grasp. This was a decisive factor in the contraband trade in armaments and other forbidden commodities and in the shape of political action along the Tunisian-Algerian borders.[22]

Finally, the Jarid was also connected by caravan routes to southern Tripolitania, a source of grave concern to colonial authorities since the Ottomans in Istanbul had reasserted direct control over the Regency of Tripoli in 1835.[23] A set of routes led across the Shatt al-Jarid's salt flats from Nafta directly to Ghadamis. Before Ahmad Bey outlawed the slave trade in Tunisia (by 1846), the Jarid had attracted caravans from Fazzan and Ghadamis bearing gold powder, ostrich feathers, and human cargo; slaves formed one basis for trans-Saharan exchanges in the period before abolition.[24] Nafta's desert cosmopolitanism was reflected by its ethnic composition, in part the by-product of trade, migration, and the wages of tribal politics. The Banu Zid hailed from Biskra; while the Masa'ba and Zibda tribes were originally from the Suf, having settled in the Jarid in recent times. The inhabitants of Zawiya Sidi al-Ahmadi, a small oasis in Nafta's suburbs, claimed descent from the Awlad Sidi 'Abid in the Awras. Still other groups had come from Ifriqiya, the Nafzawa, the Wadi Righ, or sub-Saharan Africa.[25] But there was another force that brought outsiders to the Jarid.

Linking Maghrib to Mashriq was the North African hajj, whose southern route followed the string of oases on the Sahara's upper lip from Morocco to the Jarid. Thousands of pilgrims arrived in southern Tunisia with the hajj caravan—as many as six thousand annually—bringing with them goods from the sharifian empire or Algeria. Enjoying close relations with the Hijaz and Egypt, the Jarid was also a cultural relay for parochial religious notables from places like Mali or Mauritania, who lingered there while en route to Tunis or points further east.[26] With the establishment of effective French rule over northern Algeria at mid-century, the desert hajj route was preferred by many North Africans seeking to avoid restrictions imposed on the pilgrimage by colonial authorities, who were ever mindful of the political aspects of hajj. After Tunisia's incorporation into France's African empire in 1881, both Tunisians and Algerians used the southern pilgrimage itinerary to combine hajj with permanent migration to the Ottoman Empire. As late as 1885, the French ministry of war characterized Nafta as "a most active religious center; between Nafta's numerous zawaya and the holy cities of Islam, there exists a constant exchange of emissaries and propaganda."[27]

From Tunis to the Jarid: Center-Periphery Relations

The winter mahalla dispatched from the capital to collect taxes and dispense justice reached the south only after a laborious journey of several weeks.

The central government's presence there was symbolized by several small garrisons and the dar al-bey in Tuzar, a somewhat dilapidated structure occupied solely during the annual winter expedition. The welcome accorded to the mahalla in any given year constituted an index of collective popular sentiment toward the state. It was not uncommon for some of the Jarid's more unruly inhabitants to attack the departing mahalla in a quixotic gesture of defiance, killing or wounding those hapless soldiers who had straggled behind.[28] The French vice-consul to Tunis, A. Marcescheau, accompanied the 1826 expedition to the pre-Sahara. In addition to fiscal objectives, the mahalla served "to show to the inhabitants of the interior and along the frontiers as well as to neighboring peoples the sight of a prince at the head of a strong army and to consolidate the ruling family's authority by rendering justice and distributing [government] posts."[29]

Thus, the beylical camp's yearly sojourn in the Jarid can be compared to the "royal progress" in Morocco; as such it was a visible expression of central government authority, however tenuous. Distance from Tunis did not mean that the elites in the capital were indifferent to their fractious province. The oases of the Jarid were far too prosperous, strategically located, and densely populated to ignore. The tribute rendered by the Jarid, however grudgingly, to the treasury was twice that extracted from the Sahil; Nafta alone paid more taxes than Baja, the regency's grain basket.[30] Thus for the Husaynid state, the Jarid represented a crucial source of revenue, which contrasts with the historic relationship between the adjacent Algerian Suf and central governments based in Algiers. Until the French army suppressed the Sharif of Warqala's revolt in 1854, the Suf's oases were left undisturbed since the resources demanded to collect tribute or impose order were scarcely worth the effort.

The Jarid's unfortified towns could not dispense with the central government, even one that attempted so little. The oasis communities were encircled by a number of redoubtable tribal groups—the Hammama, the Banu Zid, etc. In addition, Algerian tribes periodically crossed over the fluid borders for trade or plunder or both. Through the institution of the beylical camp, the central government resolved disputes involving the pastoralists and oasis dwellers—in periods when the state disposed of the means of violence to enforce its will.[31] The political center prudently avoided entanglement in conflicts beyond its military or administrative capacity to resolve. More localized social struggles were left to the mediation of saintly lineages, local notables, or tribal big men. Thus, the political center was mainly concerned with large-scale political contests threatening the regency's tranquillity and the process of surplus extraction. In return for rudimentary justice and security under the state's thinly protective mantle, the Jarid reluctantly rendered tribute to the Husaynid dynasty.[32]

Housing the mahalla's forces, the dar al-bey was located on Tuzar's central square, which dominated the marketplace and suqs. The beylical camp's visit coincided with the winter date harvest, the period of the most intense economic activity for the oases and their surrounding pastoral-nomadic populations. Fairs held in Nafta and Tuzar attracted traders, merchants, and pilgrims from other parts of Tunisia, Algeria, and the deep Sahara. Caravans heading for the Suf left Jaridi towns almost daily in this period as did those moving east to Gabis, Jirba, and above all, Sfax, the south's principal seaport. Other merchant caravans, loaded with the region's prized textiles, dates, and other products destined for distribution in northern Tunisia, were organized during the winter harvest season; often they traveled back to Tunis with the beylical column, which provided protection in return for specified fees. Mahalla and market were, therefore, interlocking mechanisms for appropriating surplus and distributing goods across a wide region. And the mahalla-market symbiosis—a fiscal, commercial, and political complex—integrated cities on the Saharan semiperiphery into the wider economy and social fabric of the Husaynid state.

Despite long-standing ties to northern Tunisia, history and ecology fashioned a special cultural identity for the Jarid. Even in modern-day Tunisia, the Jaridis are regarded as somehow "different," a distinction they take pride in and cultivate. This finely tuned sense of otherness resulted in part from an ancient system of local self-rule intact until the reforms of Ahmad Bey. Fiscal semiautonomy in the pre-1837 era meant that local notables monopolized the privilege of assessing and collecting taxes, also acting as intermediaries between the political center and oasis lineages.[33] Finally, the Jarid had an abiding tradition of defiant resistance to outside interference. The qa'ids' reports, dating from the first years of Ahmad Bey's reign, described the *ahl al-Jarid* as intractable, especially when it came time to render taxes to the central government. "And all of the Jarid is insolent and impudent; we who are here in Tuzar among the populace fear for our lives," wrote the qa'id to the *khaznadar* (state treasurer) in 1844.[34]

After 1837, several forces for change intersected with peculiar intensity in southern Tunisia. Although many of these were present elsewhere, their confluence was heightened in the Tunisian pre-Sahara due to geography and age-old transborder ties. France's pacification of neighboring Algeria had an immediate impact upon the region. The colonial onslaught next door sent waves of political and religious émigrés into the Jarid. Intensified European interference in the Tunisian beylik, another expression of larger imperial thrusts throughout Africa and Asia, spurred the Husaynid prince, Ahmad, to embark upon his own version of Tanzimat (the Ottoman Empire's official reform program). Moreover, pressures exerted upon Ahmad Bey by European suitors were prompted by political events along the Tunisian-Algerian borders. In short, the Jarid constituted the terrain par excellence for observing the local impact of global transformations and how provincial elites strove to manipulate those changes to their own purposes.

The Religious Ecology of the Jarid

Upon reaching Nafta in 1844, Shaykh Mustafa b. 'Azzuz immediately began constructing a sufi center, one of the largest in the oasis.[35] Even today, the zawiya remains standing in the town's southwestern corner, located a certain distance from older saintly shrines such as the tomb of Sidi Bu 'Ali or the qubba of Sidi Brahim (Ibrahim) which also served as the Qadiriyya zawiya (see map 7). The latter is found in the oasis's ancient northern quarters along the rim of the "corbeille," a bowl-shaped depression some thirty meters deep where waters from underground springs well up to form a single wide stream before emptying into the gardens. Significantly, Sidi Mustafa chose to situate his new zawiya on the edge of Nafta's vast date-palm plantations, close to the only route leading to the Algerian Suf. Spatial location—distance from preexisting zawaya—translated and defined spiritual relationships with the older, more established oasis saints and their cults.

The Jarid was densely populated by saintly cohorts; historically it constituted a religious pole of particularly irresistible attraction. Not only did the region draw students and scholars from the central Tunisian steppes, the southeastern beylik, and eastern Algeria but its zawaya and centers of Islamic instruction also furnished pious, learned men to neighboring areas, including the pastoral-nomadic communities. The Jaridi tradition of religious education, including tasawwuf, in a crossroads context offered a fecund milieu for the production and reproduction of saints—for saintly inflation and for transregional veneration of especially virtuous hometown saints, such as Sidi Bu 'Ali. For both men and women, the networks of zawaya and shrines informed the rhythms of daily existence, defining spirituality and piety in culturally specific terms.[36]

In addition to the ramified sufi orders, socioreligious life and spiritual allegiances revolved around local or regional saint cults and shrines, controlled by holy lineages such as the Shabbi clan of Tuzar.[37] Among the plethora of oasis holy men, Sidi Bu 'Ali al-Nafti was the most revered; even today his tomb-shrine stands in the middle of a lush palm grove and is still the object of daily prayer sessions and an exuberant annual mawsim.

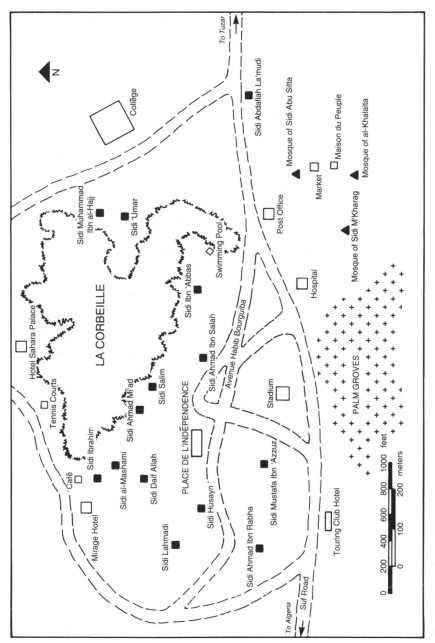

7. Nafta in the Jarid

Known by the sobriquet "sultan-saint of the Jarid," he was believed to have come to southern Tunisia from the Moroccan Sus around 1200 A.D. after a sojourn in Biskra. Strong Kharajite tendencies still existed in southern Tunisia and Algeria at the time, and the saint was credited with coaxing the region's inhabitants back into the Sunni orthodox fold.[38] While the saint was honored for over half a millennium because of his triumph over heterodoxy, by the early twentieth century the popular beliefs and practices associated with his cult were viewed with distaste by some reform-minded ulama in the cities.[39]

Even before the French invasion, sufi notables from the Tijaniyya, Rahmaniyya, and reformed Qadiriyya turuq began arriving in the Jarid. In 1826 Algerian Tijanis from the Suf and Tamalhat created an establishment in the Jarid; the zawiya's extensive hubus properties were alienated to the benefit of the Tijani shaykhs of Tamalhat near Tuqqurt. Within Tuzar itself, an older saintly shrine was converted into a Tijaniyya zawiya in 1834. Other centers sprang up, invariably receiving tax exemptions from the Tunisian beys, many of whom, particularly al-Sadiq Bey (1859–1882), looked with special favor upon the Tijaniyya order.[40] And as mentioned above, Tunisian state patronage of the Tijaniyya did not stop at the borders. Husayn Bey (1824–1835) conferred large sums of money upon the Tijani leader of Tamalhat, Sidi 'Ali al-Tammasini, who used the funds to build a mosque and *hammam* (bath house). Subsequent Tunisian beys offered lavish gifts to embellish Tijaniyya centers in southeastern Algeria.[41]

With Biskra's capitulation to the French army in 1844, Rahmaniyya and Qadiriyya sufi notables arrived from the Ziban and began initiating followers into their respective "ways" as well as founding zawaya. While both Nafta and Tuzar boasted numerous religious establishments prior to this period, the activities of the major turuq in the region resulted in an even greater luxuriance of qubbas, mosques, and sufi centers. By the century's end, when the first statistics were gathered, Nafta boasted some 108 mosques, zawaya, qubbas, and shrines. In 1885, Tuzar counted fifty religious establishments.[42]

The deeply rooted popular veneration for Sidi Bu 'Ali was not to be challenged by the bearers of reformed sufism in the nineteenth century. Traditionally, the annual pilgrimage in Sidi Bu 'Ali's honor attracted the faithful not only from southern Tunisia but also from the Awras, the Ziban, and even western Algeria. The saint's cult was at the center of a ramified network of zawaya and clients which made it into a sort of local brotherhood. In Tunisia, followers were found in Tuzar, Tunis, Gabis, and Sfax; in Algeria, Bône, Guelma, Khenchela, Biskra, and al-Awad had sizable followings.[43] As was true in the Kabylia during the time of Sidi 'Abd al-Rahman, sufi notables arriving in the Jarid from elsewhere sought accommodation with existing saintly lineages, sometimes incorporating older religious clans into the spiritual lexicon of the new. Indeed, the leading Qadiriyya muqaddam in Tuzar attempted to associate his tariqa's teachings and "proselytizing" with Sidi Brahim's cult. Somewhat later the Sanusiyya apparently did much the same with another saint and his cult, wedding the small Sanusi presence in the Jarid with that shrine.[44]

However, there are hints of competition either between the old saints and the new or between the shaykhs of recently imported tariqas in the Jarid. For example, gentle rivalry for spiritual prestige and popular followings between the Rahmaniyya and reformed Qadiriyya is still remembered in popular lore as a sacred tournament. In a saintly contest pitting Sidi Mustafa b. 'Azzuz against Sidi Brahim b. Ahmad, the "winner" was selected by the miraculous intercession of Sidi Bu 'Ali at the shrine of Nafta's patron saint. Contention between oasis holy men cloaked several layers of social conflict—that of sufi orders and zawaya as well as that of town quarters and lineages—in a sacred idiom.[45]

If one saint interceded on behalf of another, sufi-saintly figures could be made to intervene historically in the invented genealogies of the lineage. Through the manipulations of collective memory, saintly origins were conflated with those of the local clan, creating a double myth of origin. By the end of the nineteenth century, the Banu 'Ali of Nafta advanced sharifian claims by portraying themselves as the biological descendants of Mustafa b. 'Azzuz. Even though 'Azzuz had only settled in the quarter of Nafta belonging to the Banu 'Ali in the 1840s, the clan attributed Andalusian origins to Sidi Mustafa, who was later said to have resided there since the ninth century. And by linking Sidi Mustafa to themselves and to Andalusia, the Banu 'Ali thus tied the Algerian Rahmaniyya shaykh and their own lineage to one of the exalted hubs of Islamic mysticism in the medieval Muslim west.[46]

The central government and its representatives were solicitous of the Jarid's older saintly clans or turuq and the newly arrived sufi notables from across the borders. Gifts, honors, religious endowments, and exemptions from most forms of taxation were granted to the oasis holy men. Side by side with the zawaya and local shrines were madrasas constructed by Tunisian rulers to win favor in the region.[47] Moreover, religious edifices were considered *haram* (sacred), and those seeking asylum normally found protection within their walls; the sacred and therefore politically neutral space of these establishments was usually, although not always, respected by government authorities.[48]

Thus, in the Jarid as elsewhere in North Africa during the period, distinctions between the 'alim, saint, and sufi blurred. The compromise between the orthodoxy of the urban mosque or the state-endowed madrasa and the vibrant populist spirituality of the saint's shrine and cult still held; reform-minded, activist sufism coexisted in harmony, for the most part, with older expressions of collective piety.

The Growth of the Rahmaniyya-'Azzuziyya, 1844–1866

In a remarkably short period of time, Shaykh 'Azzuz and his disciples constructed one of the wealthiest and most powerful of North Africa's Rahmaniyya centers, giving concrete expression to the shaykh's moral and spiritual authority as well as his social empowerment. In creating a sub-stantial popular following, Sidi 'Azzuz retraced the earlier steps of his sufi master, Sidi Muhammad b. 'Abd al-Rahman al-Jurjuri, although in radi-cally changed, politically charged circumstances. In part the expansion of the 'Azzuz-directed Rahmaniyya after 1844 was effected through the growth of Shaykh Mustafa's own family. Two more sons were born shortly after the hijra to Nafta. Of his many daughters, two were eventually married to provincial religious notables in northwestern Tunisia. Ruqaya was given to Sidi al-Hajj Mubarak in Tala and al-Hajja to Shaykh 'Abd al-Malik of Tebursuq; both of these small towns, close to the borders with Algeria, boasted Rahmaniyya centers established in the early decades of the century. Two other daughters were wedded to religious families in al-Aghwat and Syria; the rest apparently remained in Tunisia. The choice of spouses for Sidi 'Azzuz's daughters was in concert with endogamous sufi marriage practices and served to cement ties between the 'Azzuz of Nafta and religious notables elsewhere.[49] In addition, one of Mustafa's seven brothers, Muhammad, assumed the headship of Rahmaniyya members in al-Qayrawan and among tribal groups in that city's hinterland. The re-mainder of Sidi Mustafa's brothers appear to have resided in Algeria, where they continued to direct Rahmaniyya establishments. Nevertheless, family visits between the two countries, clandestine or otherwise, were frequent. After 1881 French colonial authorities on both sides of the borders at-tempted to monitor such visits; requests for travel permits by sufi figures were denied as often as they were conferred.[50]

Sufi notables performing the hajj frequently initiated members into their tariqas during journeys to the Haramayn. Shaykh Mustafa b. 'Azzuz made the pilgrimage to Mecca on at least one occasion around 1850–1851. This explains the existence of Rahmaniyya-'Azzuziyya members in the oases along the Tunisian-Tripolitanian borders and even in Ghadamis; these disciples were most likely introduced to the Rahmaniyya "way" by Shaykh 'Azzuz while en route to the Hijaz. Until recently in Lebanon, Syria, and Medina there still existed Rahmaniyya-'Azzuziyya circles whose silsilas revealed their creation a century earlier by Shaykh Mustafa b. 'Azzuz of Nafta.[51] Thus, the hajj produced a curious twist to Rahmaniyya religious geography for the order returned to its original eastern matrix.

Due to Sidi Mustafa's energetic proselytizing, the Rahmaniyya spread from the Jarid into southeastern Tunisia and then the Regency of Tripoli. Tariqa circles and secondary zawaya paralleled the east-west caravan routes linking the Ziban and Suf with the Jarid and Mediterranean ports along the beylik's southern reaches. Many communities located along the commercial trunk line connecting southwestern Algeria with Tunisian seaports were Rahmaniyya disciples attached by patron-client ties to the 'Azzuz clan of Nafta.[52] Secondary zawaya were created in the Nafzawa, Gabis, Jabal Matmata, and Zarziz. Important tribes, like the Farashish and Majar of the central Tunisian plains between Gafsa and al-Kaf were religious clients as were the Marazig and Awlad Ya'qub. Also regarded as 'Azzuz followers were the Awlad Ahmad and the Farjan, who camped on the Tunisian-Algerian borders.

In 1860 one European traveler witnessed how ordinary people honored sufi notables and how popular veneration was translated into collective rituals. In the course of his journey from the Suf to the Jarid, Henri Duveyrier, the French explorer and spy, traveled with a caravan of merchants and pilgrims from Tunisia, Tripolitania, and Algeria. Many were brothers affiliated with the Nafta Rahmaniyya. While the caravan labored across the dunes separating the Suf's oases from the beylik, 'Azzuz's followers chanted prayers to the accompaniment of music. Then, "a Jaridi man, seated on a camel, seized a drum and recited a long, improvised ballad dedicated to the marabout of Nafta, Sidi Mustafa b. 'Azzuz; the refrains of the song were repeated by other young men in the caravan singing in unison as a choir."[53] Rituals of veneration were a visible expression of implicit transactions between religious patron and client; protection was perhaps the most important return expected from the ziyara.

Duveyrier's account reveals how the saint's patronage facilitated both commercial and spiritual exchanges or pilgrimage between regions and groups in the Sahara. Desert holy men often furnished travelers, merchants, and pious wayfarers with the *'inaya*, a sort of passport guaranteeing safe passage through the *balad al-barud* (the land of gunpowder) and underwritten by the saint's baraka. Duveyrier witnessed the 'inaya at work during his 1860 trip, one fraught with dangers from bandits and turbulent tribesmen. While en route from al-Awad to Nafta, advance scouts for the caravan warned that an encampment of unruly Hammama warriors was nearby, blocking the main passageway into the Jarid. Fearful, the members of the caravan refused to proceed any farther toward their destination. An emissary was dispatched to Nafta to seek Sidi Mustafa b. 'Azzuz's counsel. Apparently, the shaykh furnished a safe conduct to the caravan for it reached Tunisian territory shortly thereafter without incident.[54]

Finally, a nexus between pilgrimage, trade, and information networks can be posited based upon eyewitness accounts by Duveyrier and other travelers. Upon arriving in Nafta, the members of caravans proceeded immediately to the residence of Shaykh 'Azzuz. There they rendered homage to their patron, offered thanks for his role in ensuring a safe journey, and made pious offerings. It can be assumed that the travelers also brought news of events across the border in Algeria. Like desert markets, Saharan sufi centers functioned as collectors not only of religious tribute but also of information, which made them "bureaus of public opinion."[55] Roughly two decades after his hijra to the beylik, Sidi 'Azzuz counted numerous followers in many places in Tunisia and Algeria; roughly three-quarters of the Suf's inhabitants considered themselves associated in one way or another with the saint and sufi of Nafta.[56] Religious affiliation was articulated by specific forms of public behavior which gave outward expression to inner commitment: "The followers of Shaykh Mustafa b. 'Azzuz, leader of the Saharan Rahmaniyya, can be readily distinguished by a long white chaplet which they wear upon their necks and under their burnus; the brothers associated with the Rahmaniyya greet each other in a manner different from other orders by crossing their hands twice, one after the other."[57]

Along with the growth of a following, the 'Azzuz family soon acquired substantial property in the Jarid and elsewhere. A little over a decade after their arrival in the beylik, the zawiya in Nafta controlled nearly seven thousand daqala al-nur date palms and over one thousand ordinary trees. Date-palm gardens, water rights, and other forms of productive wealth alienated to sufi notables were generally held as hubus. Prior to the institution of the 1841 *qanun* (tax) on date palms, part of Ahmad Bey's overhaul of the fiscal system, date palms held as hubus by saintly lineages were subject to a tax in kind, the *tamr al-hubus*. Yet this was a much lighter imposition than those taxes levied on other social groups and reflected the state's deference for religious rank. After 1841, religious properties were totally exempt from taxation.[58]

Due to the 'Azzuz clan's sufi prominence and sharifian descent, their tax-free status was periodically renewed by the central government in written decrees; however, this privilege was in exchange for the socioreligious services provided by the Nafta zawiya to those in need.[59] One such decree dated 1859–1860 stated: "We renew our decree to the pious, blessed, pure shaykh and saint, Sidi Mustafa ibn 'Azzuz, regarding the privileges [attached to] his zawiya found in the region of Tuzar."[60] Reconfirming the privileged financial and socioreligious status of the zawiya and its leadership, the decree also reveals the active interest central governments took in sufi shaykhs located at the state's limits, even—or particularly—those who had recently emigrated from Algeria. After 1854, when the French army established a permanent presence just across the beylik's frontiers in the Suf, courting religious notables in strategic places like the Jarid became all the more compelling.

Control of the means of production, tax privileges, and the offerings of the pious furnished Shaykh Mustafa with the wherewithal to fulfill the social mandate expected of him—charity, education, and mediation. The social welfare dimension of the Saharan zawaya was observed by the British explorer James Richardson. During his 1845 journey in the Jarid, Richardson visited the Rahmaniyya center of Sidi Mustafa b. 'Azzuz then only recently established: "There were at the time of our visit to him [Shaykh 'Azzuz] about two hundred people in his courtyard who all subsisted on his charity. We were offered dates, couscous and a seed which had the appearance of a dried apple seed. The saint also distributed beads and rosaries, giving some to one of our party."[61]

Tax exemptions aside, whether the bey or his local representatives bestowed any other favors or material prerogatives upon Sidi Mustafa prior to his role in quelling rebellious behavior during the 1864 insurrection is unclear. However, Shaykh Mustafa was held in high esteem by both Ahmad Bey and the governor appointed to the Jarid in 1850, Ahmad Zarruq. The bey met personally with Sidi 'Azzuz "more than once," although when and where were not specified.[62] Toward the end of his life Ahmad Bey frequently enjoyed "social intercourse with people of distinction such as Shaykh Mustafa b. 'Azzuz."[63] Apparently the shaykh made periodic trips to Tunis, and while in the capital Sidi Mustafa resided in a small zawiya not far from the qasba which served as a place of retreat.[64] No wonder that Jean Mattei, the French consular agent in Sfax, informed the French representative in Tunis that "Mustafa Ben Azouz [sic] feels that he is strongly protected by the Bardo."[65]

Ahmad Bey's solicitous treatment of Sidi Mustafa reflected his general posture toward other Algerian notables residing in the beylik. From the 1830s until 1881, many members of Algeria's religious or political elites, including the last bey of the Constantine, were welcomed by Tunisia's rulers, who also provided the immigrants with financial resources to lead lives consonant with their social rank. After the Sharif of Warqala's defeat in 1855, Sliman b. Jallab, the former sultan of Tuqqurt and the sharif's comrade in arms, found comfort and a modest pension—for a time—at the bey's court. Two years later, Sidi al-Hajj 'Umar, head Rahmaniyya shaykh in the Jurjura, fled to Tunis after the Kabylia's tribes were crushed by the French army. There Muhammad Bey (1855–1859) granted Sidi al-Hajj 'Umar a subsidy; from the beylik's capital, the sufi notable attempted to direct the religious affairs of the distant Kabyle zawiya. Finally, as mentioned above, beylical largesse toward powerful sufi figures did not stop at the borders with Algeria. The beys of Tunis periodically accorded rich offerings to the Rahmaniyya of Khanqa Sidi Naji and the Tijaniyya of Tammasin and Gummar.[66]

In providing for Algerian refugees, the beys were moved by a number of motives both pious and pragmatic. The Rahmaniyya tariqa, and especially the Tijaniyya order, were highly esteemed by ruling circles in Tunis; Muslim solidarity with the besieged Algerians was also a factor. Courting sufi leaders established along the confines with the colonial state was a way of controlling, perhaps even encouraging, their politicoreligious activities. And the bestowing of gifts upon those notables still residing in colonial Algeria might also be read as a subtle reaffirmation of the transborder strength of Islamic ties. This was not lost on Léon Roches, appointed as French consul to Tunis in 1855. Roches reported to the governor-general of Algeria, not without some trepidation, the lavish reception that Ahmad Bey accorded the Tijani shaykh of Tammasin in 1856 during the sufi shaykh's visit to Tunis while en route to the Haramayn.[67] What really incensed Léon Roches was the Tijani leader's hostile public stance toward France while in the Tunisian capital. For were not the Tijaniyya of Algeria loyal to French interests?

The Zawiya as Political Refuge

Like the Suf, the Jarid had a natural vocation as a refuge for political malcontents. Each uprising in Algeria during the colonial offensive sent rebels across the borders into the Jarid or other parts of Tunisia. In addition, Muslims seeking asylum from infidel rule often made their way into the beylik via Nafta. Some remained there for generations; others relocated in Tunis or the Mashriq, particularly after the 1881 French invasion. This movement of peoples from Algeria into Tunisia is an extremely significant phenomenon for both countries, yet its importance is often overlooked in histories of the past century. While accurate figures are difficult to come by, the migratory pump to Tunisia apparently created enough of a critical mass to change local politics and the local economy in certain border regions. Moreover, since migration is a specific kind of transformational displacement affecting individual and communal political consciousness, it was not accidental that the twentieth-century Tunisian nationalist movement involved a number of Algerian exiles, the best example being 'Abd al-'Aziz al-Tha'albi, leader of the Old Dustur party.[68] Thus forced emigration frequently led to a heightened degree of politicization.

The colonial regime's response to Algerian emigration to Tunisia (or Morocco) was somewhat belated. In 1850 a series of draconian ordinances were passed to circumscribe the displacements of Muslim Algerians, whether for purposes of trade, religion, or family affairs. In the Constantine, where these laws were first applied, the measures were prompted by the Za'atsha uprising and the colonial regime's gradual discovery of the sufi turuq and their significance to society.[69] Moreover, from mid-century on, the intricate social networks, historically joining the Algerian Sahara to Tell, encountered growing obstacles as civilian settler communities expanded into the fertile northern plains.[70] This rerouted socioreligious and other types of interchanges to the southeastern routes linking Algeria to Tunisia and to Ottoman-ruled Tripolitania. Saharan provinces under the fitful jurisdiction of indigenous elites, nominally allied to France, became all the more attractive as avenues of escape.

Sidi Mustafa received a steady stream of Algerian visitors to his sufi center, among them pilgrims, students, and political refugees. Some were only sojourners impelled by the Islamic duty for religious instruction. One important notable seeking learning at the Nafta zawiya was 'Ali b. 'Uthman, the nephew of 'Ali b. 'Umar of Tulqa and a kinsman of Sidi Mustafa's through marriage. After Mustafa b. 'Azzuz's departure from the Ziban in 1844, 'Ali b. 'Uthman had become head shaykh of the Rahmaniyya in the Algerian pre-Sahara. At some point, Shaykh 'Ali studied at Sidi Mustafa's side in the Jarid; the fact that he returned subsequently to French-ruled Algeria indicates that the borders were still sufficiently porous to permit such displacements.[71] Sidi 'Abd al-Hafiz, leader of the Rahmaniyya zawiya in Khanqa Sidi Naji, also maintained close ties with Shaykh Mustafa after 1844. Indeed with the defeat of Bu Ziyan's movement late in 1849, Sidi 'Abd al-Hafiz fled to Nafta, where he succumbed to the cholera epidemic then raging; his sons remained allied with the Tunisian branch of the 'Azzuz clan until late in the century.[72] This too indicates that decrees passed in Algiers were difficult to enforce until 1881, when Tunisia passed under direct French rule.

The learned and the pious were not the only visitors welcomed at the 'Azzuz zawiya in the Jarid. During the turbulent period between 1844 and 1866, the year of Sidi Mustafa's death, a number of political activists sought refuge there. After the second siege of Biskra, the shaykh of Sidi 'Uqba, Muhammad b. Ahmad b. al-Hajj, and his supporters joined Shaykh 'Azzuz temporarily in the Jarid. In 1846, Muhammad b. Ahmad was even received with great pomp and circumstance in Tuzar by the bey al-mahalla (the heir apparent to the Husaynid throne) then leading the annual tax-collecting column. Also present at the time was a French official, E. Pellissier de Reynaud. Outraged at the welcome accorded the shaykh, who had, among other things, led the attack against the Biskra garrison two years earlier, Pellissier made official protests to the bey. Describing the shaykh of Sidi 'Uqba as "a rebellious French subject" and "dangerous" to France's interests, Pellissier demanded that Tunisian officials intern him in a province well away from the borders with Algeria. Ahmad Bey countered that the honors bestowed upon 'Abd al-Qadir's former khalifa were consonant with his family's prestigious origins as shurafa'. The bey cunningly attempted to draw distinctions between the religious realm and the strictly political, an argument that France rejected. Despite constant pressures, Tunisian officials refused to forcibly remove the shaykh of Sidi 'Uqba from the Jarid, and unending French demands that the same be done with Shaykh Mustafa b. 'Azzuz also went unheeded.[73]

Not by coincidence, Lieutenant Prax was dispatched to the Jarid the following year. Prax was a French naval officer and amateur ethnographer of Saint-Simonian persuasion. In 1847 he was entrusted with an exploratory mission to collect information about the oases and peoples of the pre-Sahara. Significantly, he had been sent to the Sahara by the ministries of war, foreign affairs, commerce, and education in Paris. His official instructions were to travel to al-Awad and Tuqqurt via the Tunisian beylik and to cross into the colony from Nafta—instead of following the more conventional itinerary from northern Algeria. In the Jarid, Prax gathered information regarding the political and commercial influence exerted by Tunis upon the Suf and Tuqqurt and the degree of beylical support for Algerian refugees, including the shaykh of Sidi 'Uqba. This appears to have been the first unequivocal demonstration—at the level of Parisian ministries—of Tunisia's importance to colonial strategy in the Maghrib; in this strategy, primacy of place was accorded to the oases of the Jarid.[74] In large measure, that primacy was the consequence of Mustafa b. 'Azzuz's hijra to Nafta and the presence of Algerian émigrés along the beylik's borders.

During the revolt inspired by the Sharif of Warqala, the zawiya's role as a haven for dissidents would become glaringly apparent. As that uprising ground to an inglorious halt, the shaykh of Sidi 'Uqba again looked to the 'Azzuz of Nafta for protection and asylum. To shield his own family from the rigors of combat, the shaykh of Sidi 'Uqba placed them in Mustafa b. 'Azzuz's care; in 1857 Muhammad b. Ahmad al-Hajj died at the Nafta Rahmaniyya zawiya, where the 'Azzuz clan ministered to him. Another participant in the Warqala movement, Nasir b. Shuhra, a former French ally, also employed the Nafta zawiya as a base of operation. With the rebellion's final rout late in 1855, the sharif himself sought and found solace at Sidi Mustafa's side.[75] The tradition of political protection was carried on even after 'Azzuz's death in 1866. During the aborted revolt centered in al-'Amri, a small oasis in the Ziban, one of the movement's leaders, Sidi Mustafa b. Mabruk, fled to the Jarid in 1876. And after the great 1871 Muqrani insurrection in the northern Constantine, which provoked unrest in southeastern Algeria, some of the rebels again sought asylum at the Rahmaniyya-'Azzuziyya center in southern Tunisia.[76]

The Jarid's zawaya were able to provide material support to activists largely because of integration into the local political economy. In Nafta, the Rahmaniyya zawiya controlled by the 'Azzuz owned camels, placed in the care of client pastoralists, which were used for transport. The zawiya also served as a storage place for goods. Also housed there were arms and supplies acquired through razzias by dissident Algerian tribal leaders, participating in the Sharif of Warqala's movement.[77] Its location, therefore, made the Rahmaniyya zawiya in Nafta particularly well suited to facilitate the traffic in contraband gunpowder between southern Tunisia and eastern Algeria.

Nevertheless, migrants and refugees invariably provoke unwelcome changes. As growing numbers of Algerians settled in the Tunisian oases to escape French rule or unfavorable economic conditions, Sidi Mustafa was called upon to mediate disputes between the Jarid's inhabitants and the newcomers. With Tunisia's economy deteriorating mainly due to unfavorable world market forces after 1850, relations were increasingly strained as letters from the Jaridis to local authorities reveal. One complaint filed with Tuzar's *majlis* (council) by the oasis's inhabitants in 1861–1862 contained the following economic grievance: "[We] have suffered injury and heavy loss in livelihood from the mass of immigrants from Algeria. . . . the newcomers, tempted by the life of ease, have bought up cooking oil [and other commodities] so that the price of these items has been raised and there are shortages."[78] Among the Algerians seeking refuge in the Jarid were also French-paid spies, one of whom was Muhammad b. Rabih. At some point, Rabih agreed to act as France's consul in Tuzar and to discretely monitor Shaykh Mustafa's political activities for the French representative in Tunis. Despite his somewhat ambiguous—even compromised—position vis-à-vis his own countrypeople, Rabih later stipulated that he was to be buried in the cemetery attached to the 'Azzuz's zawiya in close proximity to the very special dead.[79] Apparently espionage for the infidels did not preclude veneration for saintly patrons.

Cross-Border Manipulations: The Affair of the Shurafa'

The period between Ahmad Bey's reforms and the great revolt of 1864 represented a long season of discontent in Tunisia. In the Jarid the bey continued to rely upon traditional notables to implement new fiscal measures until 1849. The next year Ahmad Zarruq was named governor. Zarruq was an authoritarian, energetic figure regarded as doubly foreign by the Jarid's inhabitants; he was a member of the ruling elite in Tunis and worse a *mamluk* (literally, "owned" or "possessed") by birth from the house of Larbi Zarruq Khaznadar. His mandate was two-fold: to end the Jarid's ancient autonomy by instituting a new fiscal system and to construct an administrative apparatus placing local notables more firmly under the political center's thumb.

Zarruq's assumption of office encountered immediate resistance in the Jarid; letters of objection poured into the capital complaining of his conduct. Things came to a head in the spring of 1851 when missives from the Jarid's shaykhs decried the outbreak of "disturbances owing to violence and extortions in tax collection."[80] Soon thereafter a large contingent of Nafta's population left Tunisia for the French-ruled Suf in a collective expression of protest rejecting Zarruq and the bey's reform program. Since ancient times, kinship, religious, and commercial ties had existed between the Suf and the Jarid. Estimates of the numbers of people involved vary from five hundred to seven hundred.[81] This migration placed Ahmad Bey in a quandary.

Fleeing over the border to evade taxes or beylical justice was by no means a novelty for some subjects in nineteenth-century Tunisia. Pastoral-nomadic groups had always done this; recalcitrant tribes habitually crossed into the Constantine as the mahalla approached only to return home when the coast was clear.[82] Yet the presence of the French army along the frontiers complicated cross-border movements not only for ordinary people but also for Tunisian rulers. Profoundly troublesome for Ahmad Bey was that the emigration of 1851 involved a somewhat unusual community— prestigious religious notables, the shurafa' of Nafta, who by seeking asylum in the Suf came indirectly under French rule. Naturally, colonial authorities in Algeria eagerly seized upon the incident as proof that the Husaynid prince was unequal to the task of governing effectively.[83]

By resorting to migration as a political tool, the Tunisians sought to force the bey to dismiss a state agent deemed odious; at the same time, their pardon by the Tunisian ruler would remove the stigma attached to asylum with the infidels. A series of letters setting forth the emigrants' grievances were sent to Tunis; the charges leveled against Zarruq entailed not only fiscal improprieties but also transgressions of customary religious norms: "We have fled from Nafta to the Suf and abandoned our homes because he who governs, Ahmad Zarruq, violated the sanctity of the zawaya of the Jarid and established tradition; we have nothing left; we fled barefoot and naked; we fled out of fear of total ruin in torment."[84] From the letters, it appears that Nafta's zawaya had been used as fiscal-political havens, according to custom, and that the governor had refused to honor the sanctity of those establishments. In addition, a deputation of forty notables from the shurafa' traveled to Tunis to plead their case directly before Ahmad Bey in June 1851.[85]

Unmoved, the bey ordered the shurafa' to pay their taxes to Governor Zarruq; to do otherwise would set dangerous precedents. The group returned to French territory. Predictably, the incident sparked rumors, one of which held that the émigrés had organized a delegation to go to Istanbul and petition the Ottoman sultan, Abdulmejid.[86] While this cannot be confirmed, the rumors reveal once again what people believed to be within the realm of possibility and indicate that even the bey's subjects looked to the Porte for redress of grievance. The imbroglio ended with the eventual return of the shurafa' to the Jarid after mediation by colonial authorities—an ominous event. However, Ahmad Bey's worst-case scenarios— that the Ottomans in Tripolitania would intervene or that the colonial regime would manipulate the incident to annex the Jarid—went unrealized.

The 1851 emigration, which paralleled the inverse movement of Algerians to the beylik, is significant for a number of reasons. We can see one of the strategies available to provincial communities for deflecting unjust central government interference into local matters, which constituted a violation of the older moral economy. Moreover, the incident embodied growing popular dissatisfaction which also may explain the initial appeal of the Sharif of Warqala's rebellion to Tunisian subjects. Viewed in the *longue durée*, these discontents represented harbingers of things to come in the next decade—the great Tunisian uprising of 1864. State intrusion into the fiscal, and thereby social, relations of the Jarid, so long accustomed to semiautonomy, may have expanded the ranks of Sidi Mustafa's clients due to the increased demand for intermediaries. Finally, the incident provides evidence that Sidi Mustafa's rapidly expanding religious following was the product not only of participation in Algerian resistance but also of his ability to focus and interpret disturbing changes in Tunisia for ordinary people.

It is unknown if Mustafa b. 'Azzuz was present in Nafta during the initial stages of the 1851 clash. Sometime in 1850 he performed the hajj to the Haramayn, returning to southern Tunisia via the port of Gabis only in March 1851. The French commercial agent in Gabis, Augustin Espina, observed Shaykh 'Azzuz's entry into the town from the Hijaz, also noting that local opposition to Ahmad Bey's fiscal reforms had increased palpably:

A few days ago Mustafa ibn 'Azzuz arrived in Gabis; it would appear that the visit of the shaykh had as its objective anti-French propaganda. 'Azzuz is a famous marabout who is very much ven-

erated and who is extremely influential in speaking. Ordinarily
he resides in Nafta but he has just returned from Mecca and
was greeted by the leading notables of Gabis. Upon his departure
for the Jarid, the local authorities accompanied him on his journey to a place some twenty-five miles outside of Gabis [on the
route toward Nafta]. This dangerous man is hostile to the French,
whom he accuses of advising the bey to impose extraordinary
taxes this year. Wherever he goes, 'Azzuz preaches jihad; however, if in terms of influence he is another 'Abd al-Qadir, 'Azzuz
does not have, judging from his past, either the courage or the
military prowess of the Amir.[87]

Here the rhetorical power exerted by the saint and sufi as moral preceptor and guide emerges. Shaykh 'Azzuz interpreted distressing changes
for the populace so as to make sense of disorder; he also exonerated the
Tunisian ruler, his patron. Opprobrium for unpopular tax measures was
placed upon the Europeans, whose meddling in the beylik's internal affairs
was increasingly apparent by the 1850s. While there is no information on
the shaykh's activities while in the Haramayn, his stay there may have
enhanced 'Azzuz's awareness of European inroads elsewhere into Dar al-
Islam since the Hijaz functioned as a collector and distributor of news from
all over the Muslim world. By virtue of his travels, hijra, and position as
head shaykh of a crossroads zawiya, Mustafa b. 'Azzuz too sat at the center
of a network of communications. This conferred upon him access to information unavailable to others. Finally, Sidi Mustafa's energetic denial of
Ahmad Bey's responsibility for the beylik's financial malaise anticipated
the shaykh's later support for the regime during the 1864 uprising.

Thus, Mustafa b. 'Azzuz's emigration in no way hampered continued
involvement in collective bids to reshape politics in southeastern Algeria
but rather made involvement possible. At the same time, residence in
Tunisia spared him from concessions to the infidels, an advantage not
enjoyed by his sufi peers remaining on French-held soil. In Algeria, other
Rahmaniyya notables, such as the shaykh of al-Hamil, Sidi Muhammad b.
Abi al-Qasim, were forced by political circumstances to rely upon internal
hijra or withdrawal to engage in cultural survival.

The Shaykh, the Beylik, and the World beyond Tunisia

Shaykh 'Azzuz is a dangerous individual who should be
interned as far from the borders with Algeria as possible.[88]

In November 1851, the French consul in Tunis officially protested to
Ahmad Bey, as many subsequent consuls would, about the political ac-

tivities of religious notables enjoying beylical protection. On this particular occasion, the object of Gallic wrath was the 'Azzuz family of Nafta. Accusing Shaykh Mustafa of inciting rebellion from his zawiya in southwestern Tunisia, the consul demanded that Ahmad Bey curb the shaykh's "subversive behavior." Among the charges levied against the Rahmaniyya leader were spreading rumors inimical to France's interests, disseminating hostile propaganda, and harboring Algerian rebels at his sufi residence. To bolster his case, the consul presented the bey with a letter written by Shaykh Mustafa to another sufi leader still residing in Algeria; the missive, carried by a sufi courier, had been intercepted by colonial authorities several weeks earlier. In the letter, 'Azzuz sought to dissuade a Tijaniyya shaykh from fleeing to the Jarid, assuring him that the appointed hour to chase the infidels from Algeria had arrived. The Tunisian ruler's response to French allegations was predictably equivocal. Soothingly, Ahmad Bey replied that the religious authority of Nafta's Rahmaniyya shaykh was a sufficient guarantee of order and security along the borders; the representative of France to the Bardo was needlessly concerned.[89]

Much of the information about Mustafa b. 'Azzuz in the post–1844 era was generated by his unfailing involvement in across-the-border politics as well as in Tunisian affairs. French officials (and to a lesser extent British agents) in North Africa kept abreast of his various activities through native spies and European informants. This has prejudiced the data toward the "political" as understood in the vocabulary of nineteenth-century Europe. Lamentably, the few Arabic sources available from the period carefully skirt the issue of the more mundane features of activist sufis and saints, in keeping with the traditional hagiographic paradigm for holy persons. Ahmad ibn Abi al-Diyaf noted tersely that Sidi 'Azzuz was revered by the people because he "renewed the faith of the tribes, urged people to accomplish their religious duties, and worked miracles."[90] This could fit any number of provincial religious notables in North Africa; what is not stated is more significant than what is. Also absent from al-Diyaf's account are the larger, more ominous forces gathering around Tunisia by the time of Ahmad Bey's reign.

By the 1840s, the fate of Husaynid Tunisia had become entangled in the Eastern Question; both France and Great Britain feverishly courted the bey and Tunisian ruling elites.[91] Jealous competition for Tunisia's hand in a political marriage also included the Ottomans and later the Italians; these passionate diplomatic courtships had a resonance in the pre-Sahara as well. The number of European visitors to the Jarid in the nineteenth century is remarkable in view of the uncertainty of the journey, its length, and the imminent danger of attack from tribes or bandits. Normally the visitors traveled south with the annual beylical mahalla or appointed escorts; the rulers did not generally authorize foreigners to travel in the hinterland unaccompanied by Tunisian dignitaries. This was more out of fear of retribution from more powerful European governments—should some mishap occur—than a desire, as seen in Morocco at the time, to limit foreign penetration of regions beyond the government's effective grasp. The presence of foreigners in southern Tunisia was not fortuitous but rather part of the process whereby the outside world increasingly encroached upon the beylik.[92]

French and British travelers in the Jarid arrived with several objectives in mind. Frenchmen had basically two goals: to assess the Tunisian state's clout in the countryside and to monitor the activities of Algerian émigrés as well as the beys' involvement in things Algerian. The British had similar objectives but additionally desired to probe and check French influence upon the Tunisian realm where possible. At least four Europeans met personally with Sidi Mustafa between 1845 and 1860, recording their impressions in detailed reports that also contained specific information on trade, tribal politics, and other provincial notables. These sources naturally reveal the prejudices of foreign observers but can be employed as eyewitness accounts as long as their Eurocentric bias is flushed out.

James Richardson, a well-known English explorer, traveled to the Jarid in the winter of 1845 with the mahalla, then under the command of Ahmad Bey's cousin and later successor, Muhammad al-Sadiq. Significantly, Richardson was accompanied by the son of the British consul in Tunis, Richard Reade. Richardson's 1845 report, later submitted to the British consul, judges Shaykh 'Azzuz quite favorably, although the Englishman generally viewed Tunisian society with a jaundiced eye. The oasis of Tuzar was dismissed as nothing but a "miserable assemblage," yet Nafta's Rahmaniyya shaykh was praised:

> As soon as the native escort of troops entered Nafta, they went directly to the shrine of Sidi Bu 'Ali according to the custom. There are two famous saints here, one of them [is Sidi Bu 'Ali]; the other is Sidi Mustafa ibn 'Azzuz [who] has the character of being a very clever and good man which also his intelligent and benevolent appearance betokens and [is] not a fanatic like Sidi 'Umar 'Ubayda of al-Qayrawan.[93]

Five years later the Frenchman Ducouret, journeying in the guise of a convert to Islam under the name of Hajji 'Abd al-Hamid Bey, also wrote of his passage through the Jarid in 1850. Ducouret was undoubtedly a spy gathering information for several French ministries in Paris; while his intelligence mission does not necessarily flaw the data, his report, like that of any European, must be used with caution.

> One sees at Nafta two or three beautiful mosques and a number of maraboutic centers, the main one being that of Sidi Mustafa ibn 'Azzuz [who is] the former khalifa of 'Abd al-Qadir and the declared enemy of France, whom he still opposes daily by unleashing upon her territory numbers of brigands who are his followers. Sidi Mustafa is very rich and an intimate friend of General Zarruq as well as a friend of Sidi Ahmad [Bey]. It is imperative, therefore, that this individual be brought to the government's attention for sooner or later he will create for us grave difficulties.[94]

Ducouret's observations reveal Parisian ministerial interest in provincial religious leaders, an interest which evolved into the French maraboutic myth and obsession with sufi orders by the century's end. While it is uncertain whether his lengthy report reflected official beliefs in the Metropole or helped to shape them, still Ducouret's account shows what colonial officials in Algeria and France believed. And while Ducouret was most probably a mountebank, nevertheless his assertion that Sidi Mustafa was an intimate of both General Zarruq and Ahmad Bey can be verified by reference to Ahmad ibn Abi al-Diyaf's work.

The 1850 mission was soon followed by another, that of the French diplomatic officer (*elévè-consul*) Charles Tissot in 1853. Tissot's trip with the mahalla to the Jarid that year may have been prompted by Ducouret's findings submitted to the ministry of war in Paris. As the military column laboriously made its way south to the oases, Tissot noted a Rahmaniyya zawiya located near Tala and recently built at the expense of the 'Azzuz clan of Nafta.[95] Tissot's preoccupation with Shaykh 'Azzuz was clearly motivated by the Sharif of Warqala's rebellion, which by 1853 was assuming alarming proportions in neighboring Algeria. In that year the sharif and his followers had abandoned al-Aghwat after a bloody French siege and taken refuge in the region between the Mzab and Tuqqurt. The Frenchman was clearly attempting to measure the degree of popular or elite support for the insurrection among the inhabitants of the Suf and Jarid. Tissot's report was based upon a meeting held in the Nafta zawiya between Shaykh 'Azzuz and a native North African, Ahmad b. Abi Ilah, who acted as a guide and interpreter.

> I [Tissot] have spoken of a famous marabout in Nafta, Mustafa ibn 'Azzuz, who has in this oasis one of the Regency's largest zawaya. His influence in the country is immense and stretches all

over Algeria, and particularly in the south in Tuqqurt, Warqala, Tammasin, and the Suf, where he has followers who are as numerous as they are devoted to him. The saint complained politely [to the interpreter] that he had not been visited by the representatives of France during their stay in Nafta and expressed fears that this was the result of false rumors spread about by his enemies implicating him in the latest uprising in Algeria. Far from being an opponent of France, he [Sidi Mustafa] more than anyone understood and accepted the Divine will that had placed Algeria in French hands; no one deplored more than him the shedding of blood, spilled by the false prophets who provoked warfare in God's name.[96]

Not content with verbal pledges of loyalty to France, Sidi Mustafa wrote two letters restating his lack of enmity toward the French masters of Algeria; one was for the governor-general of Algeria, Randon, the other for the director of the Bureau Politique of the Bureaux Arabes. Both missives were entrusted to the Algerian interpreter, who was to transmit them to colonial officials across the border. Tissot concluded his report by observing that the sufi leader's energetic denials of involvement in Algerian insurrections had convinced him of quite the opposite. Moreover, Tissot, as Ducouret had claimed three years earlier, contended that he had obtained irrefutable evidence regarding the Rahmaniyya shaykh's participation in the arms and gunpowder trade through southern Tunisia. "Mustafa ibn 'Azzuz is the most active agent in the contraband gunpowder traffic which is ceaselessly carried on between Gabis and Algeria."[97]

Tissot's meeting with the saint and sufi is replete with significance. Shaykh 'Azzuz's actions demonstrate that he was entirely conversant with the command structure of French Algeria as indicated by his letters addressed to the most powerful officials in the colonial hierarchy. The saint's protests about his political innocence, advanced to counter allegations concerning rebellious activities, reveal that the Rahmaniyya leader was well apprised of what French officers in Algeria were saying about him. This information had surely been acquired through the rumor mill and purveyed to Nafta by spies, pilgrims, or traders. Moreover, since most of his kinspeople still resided in Algeria, Sidi 'Azzuz prudently sought to stay within the good graces of French authorities, even from the safety of the beylik. Finally, 'Azzuz's reference to "false prophets" indicates that he was aware of the Sharif of Warqala's movement and of the colonial nomenclature employed both to describe—and dismiss—mahdist-led uprisings.

This same appreciation of the nature of the European challenge is revealed in Shaykh Azzuz's 1860 meeting with the explorer Henri Duveyrier. While Duveyrier's account is subject to some caution, particularly in view of his later alarmist work on the Sanusiyya order, the veracity of his observations from this period can be ascertained by reference to other sources.

> The saint ['Azzuz] received me in a very polite manner and he took pains to make me understand that all beings, Muslims, Jews, and Christians, were his children, all those whom God had created. He gave his approval to my studies and blessed us. His zawiya was full of people, notably the Suf's inhabitants who had come with me in the caravan. Shaykh 'Azzuz asked me to give him a great deal of detailed information regarding electricity, steam engines, and many other similar things. In sum, I think that he is an enlightened man, quite above the ordinary.[98]

The fact that Shaykh 'Azzuz questioned his French visitor at length about steam engines and electricity suggests that the sufi and saint grasped, if only dimly, the material bases of European power, which, after three decades of French military pacification, were painfully apparent to many North Africans. By 1860 the steamship crossing from Marseille to Algiers had been reduced from five days to forty hours; many North African hajjis were beginning to make the voyage to the Holy Cities on European steam vessels. Moreover, the land telegraph, a form of electronic imperialism, had already made its appearance in parts of Algeria; in 1861 it was supplemented by a submarine cable linking the Metropole with Algiers. The shaykh's awareness of the "tools of empire" indicates that he had access to information, provided by other North Africans, about the curious, if repellent, infidels.[99] Finally, if the reports of Ducouret, Tissot, and other colonial writers are accurate, it seems that the Rahmaniyya leader realized that some kinds of power came out of the barrel of a rifle.[100]

Barud and Baraka

The Rahmaniyya leader appears to have been associated with the commerce in munitions flowing between southern Tunisia's coast and Algeria by the late 1840s or early 1850s—that is, during the period of the movements led by Bu Ziyan and the Sharif of Warqala. Nevertheless, the sufi shaykh did not fashion the intricate sequence of exchanges making the arms trade possible. Rather Sidi Mustafa's participation in that trade sprang from the fact that he headed a zawiya situated near the fluid borders in a region where Mediterranean and Saharan commerce converged. By aiding Algerian political figures in obtaining desperately needed gunpowder, Shaykh 'Azzuz merely drew upon existing tariqa and commercial networks. Moreover, Sidi Mustafa had a compelling example in the Amir 'Abd al-Qadir, who had been in the arms business throughout his jihad as were numerous West African religious leaders in the century.[101] Indeed, Ahmad Bey himself was accused by the French of sending arms to 'Abd al-Qadir by way of Biskra in 1841.[102]

The Jarid's location on the margins of the state made these activities feasible—despite efforts by Tunisian central authorities and French officials to end the trans-Mediterranean trade in firepower. The illicit traffic in munitions was part and parcel of a larger series of exchanges termed "contraband" or "smuggling" by both the Husaynid dynasty and the colonial regime. While the ability of both states to intervene in the affairs of the previously autonomous periphery escalated in the century, some age-old strategies for survival endured and new ones were created.[103]

The active participation of a saint and sufi in the international commerce in the instruments of warfare may seem paradoxical. Yet Shaykh 'Azzuz's actions reflected a long North African tradition whereby the divinely conferred protective powers of the holy man encompassed the salvation afforded by firearms. Barud, like baraka, had in the popular imagination something of the miraculous and magic about it.[104] The amazing grace of rifles and gunpowder was intimately linked in popular discourse to legends about saints and their karamat. One leitmotiv was the immunity of some holy persons—whether mahdi, waliy, or sufi—from the destruction wrought by guns. The nearly universal claim of aspiring mahdist leaders was that "powder counted not against him" or that his adversaries' bullets would be miraculously deflected in flight or transformed during their trajectory into watermelons, raindrops, etc. Numerous examples from nineteenth-century ethnography confirm that the magical, the sacred, and North African hopes for deliverance from French oppression were symbolized by gunpowder.

In the Kabylia, the inhabitants of the village of Koukou conserved earthen jars containing gunpowder bequeathed by a powerful saint who had died several centuries earlier. According to legend, the miraculous transformation of the substance into high-grade gunpowder would signal that the appointed hour for the infidels' expulsion had arrived.[105] When a Turkish army threatened the Tijaniyya center at 'Ain Madi in the first decades of the past century, the inhabitants implored Ahmad al-Tijani, then in Fez, to save them—either by his saintly presence in the oasis or by furnishing them with arms to resist the invaders.[106]

Not only did the mantle of the saints include protection against firepower but also rural zawaya in some parts of the Maghrib supplied clients with munitions. The Mzabis habitually stored armaments in their mosques, and the Darqawi zawaya in Algeria housed both arms depots and workshops for repairing firearms. By the end of the past century, some Sanusiyya centers deep in the Sahara enclosed veritable arsenals of largely European weaponry in response to the growing threat of foreign occupation. Finally, among the articles brought back by Algerian hajjis from the Haramayn were both firearms and gunpowder, prohibited by colonial laws; these were often concealed in trunks or in vials ostensibly filled with water from the sacred springs.[107]

Borders and Guns: The International Arms Trade

Whatever happens we have got the Maxim gun and
they have not.[108]

The international arms traffic between Europe and the Maghrib sprang from the fact that the Mediterranean's southern shore had become a new frontier in Western struggles for global hegemony. While the French conquest of Algeria in 1830 did not initiate the transfer of military technology from one side of the Mediterranean to the other, that conquest—and the resistance it encountered—accelerated the transferal. From 1830 until the imposition of the 1881 protectorate upon Tunisia, French diplomatic and military correspondence revolved obsessively around three related issues—the borders between Algeria and Tunisia, guns, and sufi orders. There were endless calls for sealing the frontiers, limiting the movements of Algerians, particularly religious figures, and suppressing the "contraband" arms trade between the two countries. While French and Tunisian authorities had more or less delimited the northern borders by the 1840s, the vast desert expanses between southwestern Tunisia and the southern Constantine remained a "hotbed of quasi-permanent political disorder," at least in colonial eyes.[109]

In large measure, the turbulent frontiers were the product of collective protest in Algeria, which found a resonance in the beylik due to refugees like Mustafa b. 'Azzuz, who provided comfort and support to rebels. Sedition along the borders convinced colonial lobbyists in Algeria and the Metropole that Tunisia must be appended to France's African *département* to bolster Algerian security. Indeed, some writers at mid-century began referring to the Jarid as the "natural annex" to the southern Constantine.[110] As the century wore on, French pressures upon the beys to police regions adjoining the frontiers mounted until the Tunisian Khrumir tribe provoked yet another border incident in 1881, thus providing the long-awaited pretext to invade. One of the clauses of the Bardo Treaty, imposed upon Muhammad al-Sadiq Bey in May 1881, enjoined the ruler to terminate the clandestine arms trade and restrict the legal sale of armaments as well.[111]

Thus, the arms trade between Europe, Algeria, and Tunisia in the post–1830 period was the product of a number of conjunctures: shifts in the balance of power between Europe and adjacent Muslim empires, relations among the Great Powers vying for spheres of influence, and quantum leaps in Western arms technology after 1850. The rapidly outmoded military stocks of European arms factories eventually found their way via the world market into non-Western regions.[112] Moreover, the colonial advance into Africa was as much the cause as the consequence of new forms of warfare and violence, which developed with pitiless efficiency after the introduction of the quick-firing breechloaders in the 1870s. At the same time, technology, and especially military prowess, became the European gauge par excellence to calibrate the cultural development of non-Western societies.[113] While the military component of Western technological virtuosity has received by far the most scholarly attention, the actual processes and mechanisms by which some of that technical superiority filtered down to non-Western peoples is still only imperfectly understood.

For indigenous political actors in the Maghrib or elsewhere, access to European military might was the sine qua non of political action. Continued unrest in Algeria until, and even after, the great revolt of 1871, fueled a relentless demand for ever greater quantities of gunpowder and firearms. Before the introduction of rapid-firing rifles, North Africans possessed arms more or less equal in quality to those issued to the French army, although never in sufficient quantities.[114] European muskets fell to the tribesmen from desertions by native troops or captures of munitions depots. 'Abd al-Qadir obtained firearms both through regular channels— agreements with the French and the Moroccan sultan—and smuggling operations with British suppliers via Gibraltar.[115] However, the arms race posed two great difficulties for the North Africans: guaranteeing steady supplies of imported munitions and, once obtained, maintaining firearms in working condition. Few tribes or villages boasted artisans skilled enough to effect repairs on the newer European rifle models. While there were indigenous specialists who had traditionally manufactured firearms and gunpowder (for examples, the Kabyles, the Mzabis, and skilled artisans in Tunis), they were not organized to produce in mass quantities; moreover, locally made gunpowder was often of uncertain quality.[116]

One of the components needed for making gunpowder—sulfur—had to be imported for the most part. The price of sulfur in North African markets fluctuated in direct proportion to the fortunes of war, or peace, at any given moment. Another essential ingredient, potassium nitrate (or saltpeter), was found in pure form throughout the Maghrib, usually near the desert shatts. Beginning in the 1840s, French officials imposed severe import restrictions upon sulfur coming in from Tunisia as part of a larger effort to erect a commercial and political quarantine around Algeria.

These measures were designed to impede extralegal exchanges of any kind, particularly those involving gunpowder, firearms, or the components for making gunpowder. However, these labors were doomed to failure in the period since the land borders with Tunisia, particularly in the south, were impossible to supervise; and Tunisian ports, from whence much of the contraband armaments originated, were only imperfectly policed by beylical authorities. Thus, France's control over the arms business in Algeria—indeed mastery over her rebellious African *département*—depended to no small degree upon the good will of Tunisian rulers and upon the Husaynid state's ability to govern its own provinces.

Tunisia in the Age of Change from Above

Paradoxically, a sequence of changes initiated by Ahmad Bey after 1837—together with the spillover effect of collective protest in Algeria—inadvertently accelerated the international arms trade, and other extralegal exchanges, between Western Europe and the Maghrib. And if Ahmad's reform agenda was intended to fortify his realm against outside interference, quite the opposite eventually transpired. Moreover, local resistance to the Tunisian version of Tanzimat may have enhanced the sociospiritual authority of religious notables, such as Mustafa b. 'Azzuz.

Ahmad Bey's reign represents a sea change in modern Tunisia's history, mainly, but not exclusively, because of the reforms imposed upon his largely unwilling subjects. His modernization program bore a resemblance to that of Muhammad 'Ali Pasha of Egypt; indeed Ahmad may have consciously emulated the Egyptian ruler. Upon taking the throne, the bey inaugurated new fiscal policies, organized a conscript army, and established modern commercial, industrial, and educational facilities, patterned upon Western institutions with assistance from European advisers. It was a delicate, and ultimately, ruinous balancing act. Only internal consolidation of Tunisia's population and resources could thwart the political ambitions of European and Ottoman suitors; yet his subjects had to remain reasonably content as well. In some cases, Ahmad Bey's reforms expanded state power at the expense of provincial autonomy. Yet in regions distant enough from the political center—four hundred kilometers separate the Jarid from Tunis—some of these reforms had at first little immediate impact. Others, mainly fiscal changes, or the abolition of slavery and the slave trade, directly touched local communities and economies, although unevenly.[117]

Compared to Muhammad 'Ali Pasha, Ahmad Bey's reform program was less radical; nor did Tunisia have an internal communications system similar to the Nile or a crop eagerly sought on world markets like cotton. And Ahmad, again unlike Egypt's wily Pasha, was not particularly enamored of the mundane details of day-to-day administration. In contrast to policies in Egypt, Ahmad Bey's modernization decrees did not include expanded bureaucratic structures for the Tunisian hinterland. Aside from the regular correspondence maintained between regional administrators and the capital, few innovative institutional linkages between ruling elites in Tunis and the countryside were devised. Instead the traditional pattern of "concessionary administration" was reinforced and augmented in the beylik.[118] The political center's laissez-faire approach conferred a degree of maneuverability upon some social groups since Tunis lacked loyal cadres in sufficient numbers to enforce its policies. Even the French protectorate, armed with an eminently more formidable bureaucracy, proved unequal to the task of policing Tunisia's tribes and frontiers until early in the present century.[119] Nevertheless, the sedentary grain-growing populations of the north and the Jarid's oases were within relatively easy reach of Ahmad's fiscal reform measures.

In the early 1840s, the Jarid's age-old fiscal autonomy faced its first assault. Beylical decrees extended government monopolies to include salt, hides, and tobacco, important items in the Jarid's economy. In addition, the *mahsulat* (indirect tax upon commodities sold or bartered in oasis or tribal markets) was imposed upon the Jarid for the first time. These greatly augmented the total amount of revenue owed to the central government. Moreover, customs duties on caravans entering southern Tunisia were raised, which together with the ban on slavery after 1841, discouraged trade with Ghadamis and other Saharan emporia, or at least rerouted it. In the Mediterranean ports, customs duties on exports—Jaridi dates and textiles, grains, raw wool—and imports were either raised significantly or subject to taxation for the first time.[120] Finally, the bey's agents attempted to co-opt Jaridi notables, such as the shaykh of the Awlad al-Hadif clan in Tuzar, with offers of the *lizma* (or tax farm) for the new mahsulat.[121]

In states poised between tradition and modernity, provincial or rural peoples frequently had at their disposal a ready cache of stratagems for thwarting the smothering embraces of ruling elites—the "weapons of the weak." The very existence of strategies to preserve local autonomy was precisely what compelled reform-minded rulers, like Ahmad Bey, to embark upon ambitious overhauls of the system.[122] Many of the responses of both ordinary people and local notables in Tunisia to increased fiscal pressures after 1837 resembled those found elsewhere in the Ottoman

Empire, particularly Egypt. Short of militant protest, these included evasion, bribery of local officials, emigration or flight, banditry, black markets,
and smuggling—neither new nor mutually exclusive defense mechanisms.
What was novel for Tunisia after Ahmad ascended the throne was the larger
political matrix within which his centralizing program, and the responses
it generated, became ensnared. Ironically, some reforms, originally intended to enhance the center's control over its periphery, actually reduced
its coercive force. Local opposition to the state, combined with world market
forces and colonial policies in next-door Algeria, ultimately undermined
the Tunisian experiment in Perestroika. In short, heightened fiscal demands
presented enough of a threat to older currents of exchange to induce a
number of people to engage in risk-taking enterprises such as smuggling.

Smuggling and Smugglers: An Overview

Tunisia's ancient, very intense involvement in the Mediterranean world is
dictated by her geography. The coastline stretching from the Cap Bon in
the north to her southernmost tip invites "unregulated commerce," or,
from the state's perspective, contraband. No mountain chains rise up to
sever the interior from the sea as in the Tabarka region or along most of
Algeria's Mediterranean littoral. As one drives along the coastal road from
Sousse to Gabis at midday, land and water seem to merge. Sandy inlets,
and flat, protected beaches offer endless nooks and crannies for landing
small craft undetected; once ashore, easy access to the hinterland is assured.

The very notions of smuggling and contraband are state centered. After
1840, moreover, the definition of what constituted illegal or extralegal
exchanges was expanded. For both the colonial and beylical governments,
contraband was the sale, importation, or exportation by nonstate agents of
commodities legally subject to state monopolies—firearms, ammunition,
tobacco, and agrarian products such as grains and olive oil.[123] For local
communities, smuggling was in part the continuation of older patterns of
exchange which, because of state regulation, now had to become clandestine. In some cases, alternative black markets were organized to frustrate
meddling by the political center. In the inaccessible reaches of Tunisia's
interior, covert rural suqs were set up, often with access to Algerian
markets, to evade local tax farmers.[124]

From the reign of Ahmad Bey on, smuggling evolved into an increasingly institutionalized mode of exchange so that a dual or shadow economy
eventually resulted. Cunning entrepreneurs engaged in contraband and
black market operations to circumvent monopolies, market taxes, onerous
customs duties levied in ports or on the overland caravan trade, and the
periodic prohibitions on the import or export of certain commodities. Most

in demand were the very instruments granting a measure of local empowerment in the face of the state's intrusive power—European gunpowder and firearms—items theoretically the exclusive purview of central governments.

The sub rosa trade was exceedingly complex; it was not confined to North Africa but was a Mediterranean-wide system or systems of interlocking exchange that grew steadily in scale and intricacy as the century wore on.[125] At times the transfer of military technology from Western manufacturers to African or Asian markets was carried on with the blessings of European governments; at others it was regarded as inimical to the interests of European nations struggling for global superiority.[126] For Tunisia, the contraband traffic held perilous international as well as domestic repercussions since many coastal smugglers were members of the beylik's resident foreign community. Above all, the Maltese, who numbered in the thousands and were British protégés, acted as mediating agents in illegal networks of exchange.[127]

The contraband trade, whether in firearms or other commodities, involved diverse congeries of people: oasis dwellers, pastoral nomads, foreign traders, native merchants, and sometimes provincial religious notables. Impecunious functionaries—beylical port officials or qa'ids along the borders—charged with stifling unregulated commerce could be persuaded to turn an obliging blind eye when need be. Smuggling functioned as a relay operation composed of interlocking chains of petty importers, retailers, middlemen, and transporters. Particularly well situated to deal in forbidden goods were traders in oases or southern ports and those communities located near the pervious frontiers. Nevertheless, the contraband traffic was not confined to these areas since the sources mention endemic clandestine exchanges in Tunis, the Cap Bon, and Sousse.[128] Aside from the Maltese, and perhaps the Algerian Suwafa, a professional "class" of smugglers does not appear to have evolved during Ahmad Bey's reign as was the case in Anatolia under the European Tobacco Regie.[129] By the 1870s, however, Tunisians and Algerians living near the borders had formed business associations specifically designed to procure firearms and gunpowder for sale in black markets.[130] Not surprisingly, these transactions were most frequently concluded by barter. One consular report from 1864 stated that "the Tunisian tribes come to the beaches near Gabis to trade their olive oil [with the Maltese] for British gunpowder with which they are increasingly supplying themselves." Yet when circumstances demanded, even tribal customers found currency to purchase contraband munitions.[131]

Accurate assessments for the volume or value of economic exchanges effected through irregular channels are naturally difficult to come by.

Informed observers from Ahmad Bey's reign maintained that the customs receipts from Sfax reflected only a fraction of the total amount of imports; if smuggling were taken into account, the volume of trade would have to be doubled or tripled. Estimates of exports from Sfax must also be increased substantially to account for the total value of commercial movements, including contraband, from southern Tunisia's most active port.[132] The American representative in Tunis reported that in April 1864, admittedly an unusual year, he was "assured by trustworthy merchants who possess ample means for obtaining practical knowledge that the exports and imports of the regency are probably five or six times greater than represented [in official records]."[133] Even the bey himself encountered the problem of smuggling as the following incident demonstrates. A Sardinian merchant in Tunis who routinely furnished the court with European goods sold imported luxury textiles valued at 150,000 piasters to Ahmad Bey. The ruler, desiring to know the textiles' declared value, requested the customs receipts from the port of La Goulette. There were none; the goods had been brought into the beylik illicitly.[134]

The increasing state regulation of both domestic and international trade in Tunisia came at precisely the moment when the demand for Tunisian products soared in Algeria due to the French conquest. Evaluating the volume or value of overland caravan exchanges between the beylik and Algeria at mid-century is hazardous. Impressionistic sources reveal, however, that commercial exchanges between the Jarid and eastern Algeria were at least as important as those between southwestern Tunisia and the rest of the beylik. Moreover, the trade balance was probably in the Jarid's favor, particularly after the 1837 fall of Constantine severed the oases of the Ziban, Wadi Righ, and Suf from northern Algeria, making Tunisian markets more attractive.[135]

This was not lost upon colonial officials, although French authority in the southern Constantine was largely nonexistent before 1844 and only partially, if brutally, restored after the suppression of Bu Ziyan's rebellion in 1849. After 1844, a *douane* was established in Biskra, and the customs bureau succeeded at times in discouraging (or more likely rerouting) smuggling between the Ziban and Tunisia. In addition, the colonial regime passed a number of laws to inhibit the arms trade and restrict overland commerce involving the two countries; decrees were enacted in 1843, 1851, 1860, and 1867. While the French military occupations of al-Aghwat, Tuqqurt, Warqala, and al-Awad from 1852 to 1854 enhanced political and economic control over Saharan merchants and markets, parts of the Suf and Mzab continued to operate as freewheeling desert "free ports" until late in the century.[136] A similar situation obtained along Algeria's western frontiers with Morocco, where smugglers conducted a flourishing contraband trade in staples and guns until the present century.[137]

French military authorities in Algeria simply lacked the means to survey closely desert trade or to curtail the movements of peoples. Each new customs office, law, and mounted patrol inspired enterprising smugglers to work out counterstrategies for circumventing state regulation. From the 1840s on, growing quantities of Tunisian products and European goods, above all, British gunpowder, originally imported into the beylik, were introduced fraudulently into Algeria. These were distributed all over the Sahara and as far north as Constantine and Sétif, usually, though not always, in markets unfettered by colonial supervision. Some contraband merchandise from Tunisia found its way into French-held markets, where it was passed off as "indigenous" products from the Suf.[138] Not insignificant quantities of Tunisian dates and olive oil, imported into Algeria illegally, were then sent to France under the guise of colonial products, which enjoyed duty-free status in the Metropole. (In contrast, products from the Jarid exported directly to Europe had to pay hefty export duties and also import duties in Marseille.) Also smuggled between the two countries were salt and the components for making gunpowder, sulfur and saltpeter. Tobacco grown in the Suf was clandestinely transported to the Jarid for sale despite—or because of—the beylical monopoly.[139]

As crucial as armaments to popular protest were grains—wheat and barley—the demand for which constituted the flywheel of the desert to Tell exchanges. Depending upon the annual harvest, wheat in Tunisia was frequently subject to export restrictions. During outbreaks of rebellion in Algeria, the price of wheat rose precipitously due to scarcity, particularly in Saharan markets. To contain the Sharif of Warqala's long insurrection, French authorities severed defiant oases from customary grain sources in Biskra's markets. Rather than lay down their arms, the rebels turned to the Tunisian Jarid for foodstuffs and supplies, furnished by traders in the Suf. Smuggled wheat from northern Tunisia nourished insurgent Algerian tribes and oases during the early 1850s, permitting the sharif's movement to endure as along as it did.[140]

But there is another crucial piece to our trans-Mediterranean contraband puzzle. While many native Tunisians and Algerians participated, the fractious Maltese made smuggling their commercial fiefdom. The Maltese formed the single largest resident European community in Tunisia. This was the result of Malta's propinquity—a mere 320 kilometers separate it from Tunisia—and of a demographic boom which by the 1820s had rendered the island one of the most densely populated in the Mediterranean world with 350 inhabitants per square kilometer. Thus, unfavorable economic conditions in Malta sent waves of migrants to the Tunisian littoral and eastern Algeria in search of a better life. Moreover, the Maltese were culturally akin to the Tunisians; they spoke a form of Tunisian Arabic and some had converted to Islam, although the vast majority were Catholic. While the Maltese occupied the lowest social niche among the Europeans in North Africa, official if grudging British protection, combined with integration into Tunisian society, allowed them to act as primary conduits for trans-Mediterranean exchanges. One of the mainstays of the Maltese island economy, so poor in natural yet so abundant in human resources, was either the production of local gunpowder or the transshipment of British armaments to North Africa. During the turbulent 1850s in the Italian peninsula, Maltese smugglers supplied rebels there with gunpowder as well.[141]

The Maltese in the beylik tended to live either in the capital or in seaports scattered along the inviting Tunisian coastline, where they organized the nocturnal unloading of goods at unsurveyed points: Italian and British textiles as well as products from Great Britain's colonies, English hardware, rifles, and gunpowder. Conversely, the Maltese smuggled Tunisian commodities out, avoiding the expense and bother of obtaining an export license—the *tadhkira*—from officials. Many exported goods were destined for Malta since the island was chronically short of foodstuffs and raw materials: dates, olive oil, wax, hides, and wool. Consular documents in French and British archives for the 1840–1870 period report that Jaridi dates, an important dietary source of sugar, were exported fraudulently from Sfax and Gabis to Malta and elsewhere in the Mediterranean. The contraband trade in dates spiraled after 1868 when Tunisian state export duties were raised from one piaster per fifty kilograms to twenty-five piasters, an increase of 2,500 percent.[142]

Thus, contraband, smuggling, and black market operations represented local responses to increasing central government regulation in Tunisia and Algeria as well as to global transformations in the balance of power. As defense mechanisms of the weak, these responses, taken in the aggregate, partially attenuated the Tunisian state's (and Moroccan kingdom's) extractive power, its control over trade and commerce, and its monopoly over the means of violence.

Shaykh Mustafa b. 'Azzuz and the Contraband Trade

As the Sharif of Warqala's rebellion peaked in the early 1850s, the contraband gunpowder traffic between Malta, southern Tunisia, and Algeria flourished as never before, although Bu Ziyan's movement and others like it had earlier nurtured the trade. In addition to supplying Algerian rebels with firepower, this commerce gave some Tunisian tribes access to European military technology. While a few traders and caravans specialized in armaments, more frequently firearms were transported along with Tunisian foodstuffs and other commodities, which found a ready market in Algeria due to the disruptions of war. Gunpowder imported from Malta was unloaded either at unguarded inlets along the Tunisian coast or right in the ports with the complicity of underpaid customs officials. Then the smugglers could chose between several possible routes leading to Algeria.

From Gabis, caravans generally crossed the oases of the Nafzawa directly to the Jarid; from Sfax, however, smugglers went to Gafsa. In Gafsa several alternative routes existed; choice of routes was dictated by the presence of beylical authorities, French military operations along the borders, or the geographical placement of Algerian demand. Just beyond Gafsa, one road led to Kasserine, Tala, and Qal'a al-Sanam, eventually reaching Suq Ahras, Guelma, and finally one of Constantine's suburbs which functioned as a distribution point for contraband firearms and gunpowder. A second route connected Gafsa with Tuzar and Nafta and the Jarid with the Suf; once in al-Awad, a bifurcation led some caravans south to Warqala, Tuqqurt, the Mzab, and even al-Aghwat. The inhabitants of the Suf and the Mzab specialized in the arms trade and in general were regarded as inveterate smugglers.[143] Other caravans took gunpowder from the Suf to the Ziban, where the oasis of Sidi 'Uqba was an active shipping center for munitions, supplying the Jabal Awras, Bu Sa'ada, and the Awlad Na'il. Some European firearms and gunpowder thus introduced into Algeria eventually reached as far west as Morocco.[144] Finally, to facilitate redistribution, concealed munitions depots were created at relay points near crossroads; for example, contraband gunpowder was stored in al-Manzil on the outskirts of Gabis, and at Khaba, to the south of al-Kaf. Despite precautions taken by smugglers, mounted French patrols and customs officials periodically surprised the unlucky, thereby providing documentation for clandestine traffic.[145]

Let us track a shipment of gunpowder being transported from the southern Tunisian coast to markets in Algeria during the early 1850s. In this particular instance, Maltese purveyors unloaded small boatloads of gunpowder and other products coming from Malta onto the beaches adjacent to Gabis after greasing the palms of customs agents. Then part of the shipment was sold to another Maltese trader, Francesco Bartalo, a middleman and longtime resident of Gabis. As most of his fellow smugglers did, Bartalo stored the contraband munitions in his home in the European quarter. (On more than one occasion, this produced tragic accidents when casks of gunpowder exploded.) Since smuggling operations were small in scale, and organized along family lines, and because the Maltese had been placed under Great Britain's flag, Tunisian or French authorities had difficulty suppressing the traffic. From Gabis gunpowder caravans, organized by native Tunisians often from the commercially important Jewish community, set out west across the Nafzawa. Tribal groups specializing in transport furnished animals, usually camels, to carry the contraband to Nafta. Involved in this were the Marazig, the Ghrib, and the Banu Zid, among other tribal groups, most of whom were religious clients of Mustafa b. 'Azzuz in Nafta.[146]

Once in Nafta, the gunpowder was turned over to the shaykh of the Rahmaniyya center. In Tissot's words, the contraband was "placed under the protection of Sidi Mustafa" and most likely stored at his zawiya in the oasis, which being a sacred and inviolable space, was off limits to authorities. The gunpowder was then resold at a profit to a group of merchants from the Suf who had traveled to Nafta expressly for this purpose. The Suwafa were led by Sahili b. al-Hajj 'Umar, who, acting as yet another middleman, had the smuggled items transported over the frontiers by the Sha'amba tribe. From the Suf the gunpowder was subsequently sold again to various clients and customers by Algerian merchants. In Tissot's 1853 report, the only named purchasers were religious figures—the Tijaniyya shaykh of Tammasin and Muhammad b. 'Abd Allah, the Sharif of Warqala; in addition to gunpowder, these leaders had also had foodstuffs imported from the Jarid's markets into southwestern Algeria. While the sharif had declared an anti-French jihad in 1851 and desperately needed firepower to pursue his rebellion, the involvement of the Tijaniyya is more problematic. By the middle of the nineteenth century, the Tijani elites of both western Algeria ('Ain Madi) and the eastern Algeria (Gummar and Tammasin/Tamalhat) were ostensibly among France's staunchest indigenous religious allies.[147] Nevertheless, in the turbulent conquest years, access to firearms represented an insurance policy against the future wages of war both for sufi leaders and their followers.

While calculations regarding the quantities involved in the gunpowder traffic are no more than "guesstimates," Tissot reckoned that between 2,500 and 3,000 camel-loads of gunpowder—roughly 60,000 kilograms—passed through southern Tunisia to Algerian markets in 1852. Seizures made by Tunisian or French officials in the period suggest that Tissot's estimate may not be too exaggerated; smaller quantities of firearms were also confiscated.[148] After the final defeat of the Algerian phase of the sharif's rebellion late in 1854, the head of the Bureau Arabe, Warnier, took inventory of the forbidden goods available in the Suf's markets:

> The contraband trade has no agents more active or intrepid than the Suf's inhabitants. It is the Suwafa who, despite all the measures enacted, have caused this great stream of British and Tunisian products to flow into our markets. When we arrived here, we found in the villages of the Suf a great quantity of rifles, almost all of British manufacture; their price varied from thirty to thirty-five francs. Gunpowder is also found in abundance; the Suwafa told us that they acquire these munitions from Sfax and Gabis, where entrepôts are found belonging to Maltese traders. In these last years, the Suwafa imported a huge quantity of British gunpowder and a good portion of it was sent to the Kabylia.[149]

Moreover, other Rahmaniyya-'Azzuziyya zawaya may have participated in the trade between Algeria and Tunisia. One secondary zawiya affiliated with Nafta was located in Tala and under the spiritual administration of Sidi al-Hajj Mabruk, who was Mustafa b. 'Azzuz's son-in-law. In the middle of the past century, the village of Tala consisted mainly of a large armaments depot and the sufi center, associated with the 'Azzuz clan and situated on a principal caravan route linking the beylik with Tebessa. While the involvement of Tala's Rahmaniyya zawiya in the arms trade is a matter of speculation, it is not unlikely given that the village functioned as an important relay station in the transborder traffic.[150]

Conclusion

The hijra of Shaykh Mustafa, and others like him, entangled Tunisia in the political and economic forces that were transforming her hapless neighbor into an eternal piece of French soil. While eastern Algeria had historically maintained multiple ties with Tunisia, these changes differed substantially in nature, scale, direction, and international implications. Ironically, the efforts of Algerian exiles, perhaps with behind-the-scenes encouragement from Tunisian authorities, to check the French advance in their homeland ultimately jeopardized the beylik's precarious independence vis-à-vis the Great Powers. Moreover, the elaboration of the arms traffic across southern Tunisia provided tribal groups with firepower which eventually reduced effective Husaynid control over its periphery, thus providing justification for increased French intervention. By manipulating trans-Mediterranean and trans-Maghribi commercial, religious, and communications networks to local advantage, Shaykh 'Azzuz and other activists unwittingly brought the turbulent frontier onto Tunisian soil; in 1881 the long-term consequences of this became painfully apparent. Energetic religious notables like Sidi Mustafa 'Azzuz thus undermined the very social order they strove so mightily to defend and preserve.

In its latter stages, the Sharif of Warqala's rebellion drew anticolonial protest squarely into Tunisian territory for the first time, mainly due to Shaykh Mustafa b. 'Azzuz's presence in the Jarid. And if the fiscal and other reforms initiated by Ahmad Bey drove some to construct alternative marketing strategies—branded as contraband by the state—local opposition to the same changes imposed from above explains why the sharif's jihad, originally centered in Algeria, elicited popular support for a time from among the bey's subjects as well.

6 The Sharif of Warqala's Jihad, 1850–1866

> We are approaching the era foretold in the prophecies
> when the mahdi will make his appearance and while the
> natives have a semblance of nearly total tranquillity,
> they are in the throes of feverish expectation which is
> exploited by agitators of all sorts. The conviction that
> [the Algerians] hold of inevitably chasing us from
> Algeria is for them an article of faith.[1]

The uprising inspired by the Sharif of Warqala had several matrices: saff
quarrels, popular millenarian expectations which peaked at mid-century,
the colonial policy of indirect rule with its clumsy, half-hearted co-optation
of local elites, and the example of Za'atsha, which paradoxically spurred
communities farther south to violent protest. Another related cause was the
eruption of bitter struggles within Tuqqurt's ruling elite, the Banu Jallab.
Support for Muhammad b. 'Abd Allah's jihad by a powerful faction of the
Jallab family transformed a localized rebellion into a regional insurrection
that eventually ground to an inglorious halt in Tunisia. Thus, events in the
antechamber of the Sahara, Tuqqurt, must first be examined.

Tuqqurt: The "Stomach of the Sahara," c. 1750–1830

Tuqqurt, located two hundred kilometers due south of Biskra, is the Wadi
Righ's capital. A long, narrow valley situated near sea level, the Wadi Righ
is composed of sabkhas, broken by scattered date-palm oases whose groves
enclosed over one million trees in 1851. In the past century, the region
counted twenty-five small towns and villages with a total population of
roughly thirty thousand souls.[2] Viewed from the northern caravan route,
the oasis of Tuqqurt, which the tribes called "the stomach of the Sahara,"
resembled a broad green curtain; its countless date palms nestled in a
bowl-shaped depression surrounded by sand dunes.

Centered in the gardens was the walled city, constructed in a circular
pattern reminiscent of medieval Baghdad. In the nineteenth century, Tuqqurt was shielded by a moat; narrow maze-like streets and covered bazaars
protected its inhabitants against a merciless sun.[3] Indeed, the city's

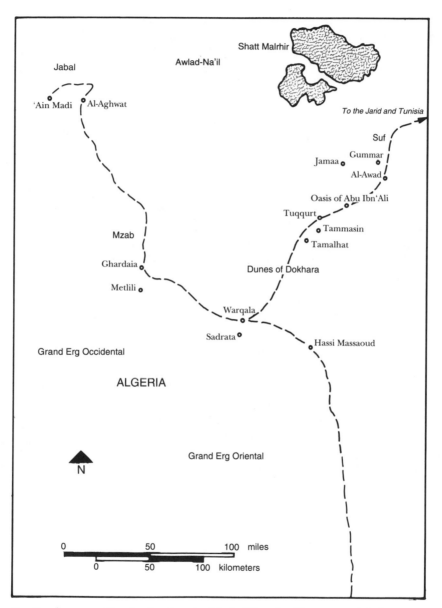

8. Southeastern Algeria showing the Mzab, Warqala, Tuqqurt, and Suf

architecture betrayed the nature of rule by its Saharan princes. A large market area occupied the inner labyrinth of the desert fortress; above was perched the qasba, the seat of the Banu Jallab and a symbol of their ancient supremacy. The city's dominant religious structure was the great mosque, built by Tunisian architects and regarded as the most remarkable edifice of its kind in the eastern Algerian Sahara. When L. Charles Feraud visited the mosque, its minaret still bore the marks of the 1788 artillery attack by Salah Bey, neither the first nor the last attempt by central powers in the north to take the city.[4]

Tuqqurt sat on one of the principal southern hajj routes leading from Morocco to the Mashriq. Its written and popular traditions were peopled by numerous saintly figures from the Maghribi "Far West," whose settlement in the Wadi Righ was accompanied by miraculous deeds, political realignments, and new religious establishments. Moreover, the Banu Jallab claimed to be the last descendants of the Marinids, a tribal dynasty that seized the Moroccan state in the mid-thirteenth century. To bolster these claims, the clan patterned their court and ruling system on that of the Moroccan sultans. One borrowed institution was a praetorian guard of black slaves, immune in theory to the temptations of local politics and intrigues.[5]

While the exact origins of the Banu Jallab remain obscure, they had secured command of Tuqqurt by the early fifteenth century. Their rise to power was accomplished largely with the backing of two pastoral-nomadic tribes, the Awlad Mulat and the Dawadida.[6] Despite incessant family feuds over succession, the dynasty displayed an astounding longevity, almost without counterpart in this part of North Africa. Its long tenure in office was due to the quid pro quo relationship with nomadic supporters and to a geographical location which allowed the regime to tap into the Saharan trade in gold and slaves with only sporadic interference from central governments until the eighteenth century. Nevertheless, unlike other Saharan or maraboutic dynasties, the Banu Jallab's authority had no religious basis; they ruled exclusively by force majeure. By the beginning of the past century, however, Tuqqurt's prince represented the last piece of a political mosaic engendered by the disintegration of the great Berber empires and states of the late medieval era.[7]

The Banu Jallab had always represented a kind of litmus test for measuring the Turkish regime's effective hold over the Sahara; the very existence of the desert kingdom made Algeria into a contest state.[8] From 1552 until the arrival of the French army on the desert's rim, Tuqqurt's rulers (as was true of Warqala and Tammasin) paid tribute only irregularly, if at all, to Algiers. In the early Ottoman period, the Banu Jallab rendered "gifts," as opposed to taxes, an important political distinction, to the dey. As their economic fortunes plummeted and the Ottoman's political clout swelled in the eighteenth century, Tuqqurt's oligarchy grudgingly agreed to recognize the bey of the Constantine in exchange for the right to trade in markets controlled by the central government. When the tribute promised was not forthcoming, the bey strove to install his protégés, the Banu Ghana, in power over the Wadi Righ; this largely unsuccessful move further complicated the political tug-of-war in the southern Constantine.[9]

Until they became embroiled in the abortive revolt led by the Sharif of Warqala, the Banu Jallab ran their internal affairs quite in the manner of a Machiavellian city-state. They commanded their own tribal makhzan troops, the Awlad Mulat, who extracted taxes from the sedentary oasis inhabitants and formed a cavalry corps, armed and mounted at the sultans's expense. The Awlad Mulat enjoyed tax exemptions, owned many of the oasis's palm groves and extensive flocks, and constituted a cast of warrior-nobles. Other pastoral-nomadic groups in the Wadi Righ also laid claim to a large proportion of the means of production, employing khammas to cultivate oasis tracts.[10]

Since most of the pastoral nomads and local religious notables paid no tribute to the Banu Jallab, fiscal exactions fell heavily upon the cultivators, whether khammas or small family landholders. By the eve of the French conquest, regular impositions, in kind and specie, as well as extraordinary taxes upon the gardens and domestic looms, appear to have increased. While the dearth of scholarship on the Banu Jallab makes speculation hazardous, dwindling revenues from the trans-Saharan trade may have induced the ruling elite to compensate by skimming off more agricultural surplus. To escape growing fiscal oppression, some of the Wadi Righ's cultivators emigrated to the Ziban, the Jarid, and even Tunis, where conditions were more favorable. Another response by villagers residing on the Wadi Righ's northern lip was to recognize the shaykh al-'arab of Biskra, and thus indirectly the bey of the Constantine, as their fiscal master instead of Tuqqurt's princes.[11]

Despite political semiautonomy, Tuqqurt and its hinterland participated in commercial and social exchanges extending far beyond the valley. Dates grown in the region, while inferior in quality to those of the Jarid, were exported to Biskra's markets. From the Ziban, the Wadi Righ's inhabitants obtained grains bartered for textiles and pastoral products. Female weavers produced a special type of *huwli* (woolen cloak) for sale in northern markets. Tuqqurt also traded extensively with southern Tunisia via the oases of the Suf. In 1845, General Daumas noted that commercial transactions between the Wadi Righ and the beylik consisted of rifles, pistols, sabers, and *shashiyyas* (felt caps)—the Tunisian product par excellence—as well as other items either of Tunisian or Mediterranean provenance. Although small quantities of firearms and gunpowder were produced in Tuqqurt as in the Mzab, most munitions were obtained from Tunisia because of their higher quality.[12]

Thus, the Wadi Righ historically maintained varying economic and other ties with coastal Algeria, the cities of the Mzab, al-Aghwat, and Tunisia. As was true of much of the trade in this region and period, commercial operations were organized into series of relay traders; while the great caravans might transport merchandise from Morocco or the deep Sahara, exchanges with the Tunisian beylik were generally effected by more modest caravans originating in towns and villages stretching along the route from Tuqqurt to the Suf and the Jarid. Merchants from Tuqqurt, who traded in the beylik, first journeyed to Nafta and then to Tunis under the protection of the beylical mahalla; they returned to the Wadi Righ after July when the tribes were occupied with the harvests or had moved to the Tell for pasturage. Therefore, Tuqqurt, the largest entrepôt of the Wadi Righ, acted as a collection and redistribution center for diverse commodities.[13]

Underwriting the Banu Jallab's wealth and power was the great winter market held in a vast terrain between the suburb of Nazla and the city walls. In terms of its volume and value, this huge Saharan fair constituted the real fortune for the entire region; its prosperity functioned as a gauge for the dynasty's economic and political well-being. The fair operated only in the winter months, when the climate was sufficiently salubrious to permit large numbers of people to gather. Throughout the rest of the year, especially during the summer heat, fevers caused by stagnant drainage water assailed the populace, carrying off or debilitating those not acclimated. The endemic fevers, called *al-wakham* (literally, "unhealthy air"), sent many of Tuqqurt's inhabitants to the Suf, where they resided for the summer months; this also explains the close sociopolitical ties between the two regions.[14]

The winter market attracted merchants, traders, and pastoral nomads as well as rebels and rogues from all over Algeria, Morocco, Tunisia, and the deep Sahara. In 1851, Tuqqurt's fair was described in the following manner:

> It is a mobile city [which is] ten times larger than the city of stones. Here are found the Arba'a, Harzaliyya, Awlad Na'il, Suwafa, etc. All of the nomads from the Ziban arrive in caravans of 20 to 100 or 500 camels. The shaykhs [sultans] of Tuqqurt levy a tax of ten sous per camel and duties upon a certain portion of all goods brought to market.[15]

It was here that Muhammad b. 'Abd Allah was able to provision his forces during several years of opposition to the French army established in the Ziban—a critical element in the longevity of his jihad. The Banu Jallab's downfall resulted from a particularly vicious round of intraclan strife, in part related to the colonial policy of indirect rule, which drew Tuqqurt and the Wadi Righ into the millenarian solutions offered by the Sharif of Warqala. Until 1849, however, Tuqqurt's sultans adopted a wait-and-see policy not unlike the bet-hedging and fence-sitting positions of the pre-Sahara's leading Rahmaniyya and Tijaniyya notables and secular tribal elites discussed previously.

Saharan Princes and Desert Politics, c. 1830–1850

Like other desert elites, the sultans of Tuqqurt sought to exploit the opportunities offered by the precipitous collapse of the deylical regime. As early as 1833 several of the great Arab warrior chiefs, exasperated by Ahmad Bey's sanguinary conduct, approached French authorities for an alliance against the last bey of the Constantine; among them was 'Ali b. Jallab, who concluded a gentleman's agreement with military officers.[16] As long as the colonial regime did not tamper with the customary political and economic relations from which the sultans derived their power, the Banu Jallab pledged neutrality if not outright loyalty to France. The infidels were not regarded as terribly bothersome at first, mainly because they were distant from Tuqqurt and their attention was diverted elsewhere. Indeed, French rule appeared as more of a boon than a burden since the army had eliminated the Banu Jallab's bête noire, the Bu 'Ukkaz, from the political stage and elevated Tuqqurt's old ally, the Banu Ghana, to the post of shaykh al-'arab.[17]

Thus, until the third decade of French rule, the relationship between the sultans of Tuqqurt and the colonial administration remained much as it had been under the Turks. The rulers paid a largely symbolic tribute to France of some fifteen thousand francs which secured the right to trade in colonial-held markets. At the same time, the Banu Jallab flirted surreptitiously with 'Abd al-Qadir after his 1838 victory over the Tijanis of 'Ain Madi made the amir appear, momentarily, as a rising power to be reckoned with.[18]

In 1844, Sultan 'Ali b. Jallab formally recognized French supremacy, which was interpreted by Tuqqurt's rulers as an implicit pact giving them carte blanche in the Wadi Righ. The sultans used the alliance to try to subjugate their ancient rivals in the nearby oasis of Tammasin, which had always remained outside of Tuqqurt's political orbit. Until the eve of Bu Ziyan's uprising, the Banu Jallab and their tribal allies waged constant warfare against not only Tammasin but also against the oases of the Suf. This brought the usual turmoil and often implicated groups that were theoretically French allies, complicating the situation for the colonial military establishment. After a crushing defeat of Tammasin in 1848, 'Abd al-Rahman, on Tuqqurt's throne since 1844, agreed for the first time to receive French officials within the walls of his oasis city-state; among the visitors was the head of Biskra's Bureau Arabe. Misreading French intentions, the sultan next sought military assistance in taking the independent oases of the Suf and even traveled to Biskra to personally petition Saint-Germain for support. Received there with all due honors, the sultan left empty-handed and visibly discontented. He was coming to realize that his French benefactors had other schemes for governing the Sahara.[19]

Tuqqurt's relentless assaults upon Tammasin and the Suf deflected colonial attention away from incipient unrest in Za'atsha in 1848 and early in 1849. Then came Bu Ziyan's self-declared prophecy and the long siege which engrossed the military and colonial bureaucracy. By 1850 the marriage of convenience between the desert princes and French officials showed strains; the "politique des notables" was increasingly bankrupt. The sultan was dismayed by the new administrative order imposed after the Za'atsha revolt, particularly since Tammasin had been removed from Tuqqurt's grasp and handed over to a French indigenous ally who was loathsome to the Banu Jallab. For their part, French officials in Biskra now viewed their erstwhile ally as more of an irritating liability than an asset to the emerging colonial order.

'Abd al-Rahman b. Jallab's political behavior in the aftermath of the 1849 uprising had been unblushingly disloyal. Not only had he welcomed dissident tribes, such as the Salmiyya and the Rahman, to his oasis but he had also allowed them to trade in Tuqqurt's winter market, delaying their submission to France. In Seroka's words, "the market [at Tuqqurt,] as we were to see on so many occasions, dominated the entire politique of the Banu Jallab."[20] This would remain true throughout the sharif's rebellion.

The sultans of Tuqqurt were never very secure on their thrones since their numerous offspring created a huge pool of potential contenders, and a clear-cut principle of succession did not exist.[21] In 1851 family quarrels, forever bubbling just below the surface, came to a head. A cadet member of the clan, Sliman (Sulayman) staged a palace coup against his cousin, perhaps because of 'Abd al-Rahman's pro-French stance. Seeing the imminent danger, the incumbent frantically sought to counter Sliman's growing political influence. Sliman and his party then took refuge with Tuqqurt's nemesis, Tammasin, in March 1851, shrewdly making overtures to the French military for assistance. Yet the heat of summer with its murderous fevers discouraged authorities in Biskra from taking action; moreover, it was not yet clear where France's interests lay—with the upstart Sliman or with their beleaguered ally still perched precariously on his throne in the round city.[22]

Had the situation farther south in Warqala at the time been otherwise, the unfolding conflict would have degenerated into a two-way struggle between competing family factions with the French army ultimately throwing its weight behind the likely victor. A political contest of this sort would have been mainly limited to the region between the Wadi Righ and oases of the Suf. This scenario, however, did not materialize because another movement, mahdist in inspiration, was already gathering force in the oasis of Warqala. Upon hearing about the charismatic figure in Warqala, the parvenu Sliman b. Jallab immediately sent out political feelers to Muhammad b. 'Abd Allah. By then the pious stranger from the east had formed a cohort of partisans in Warqala, based largely upon peacemaking activities in the divided oasis and his claims to be the mahdi.

Warqala: Queen of the Desert

The valley of the Wadi Mya lies 160 kilometers to the southwest of Tuqqurt, and stretches some 60 kilometers in length. Enclosing a number of villages and towns, the Wadi Mya's most important city was Warqala, the largest of all Algerian oases. Allied with Warqala was the nearby village of Ruissat; another more distant oasis was N'gusa (N'goussa), a longtime rival and arch foe. In the past century, Warqala probably counted a sedentary population of between three and five thousand people; the surrounding pastoral-nomadic communities numbered about the same.[23]

Today's Warqala sits at the epicenter of one of the Sahara's richest oil deposits and has been subjected to the social stresses inevitably introduced by high-technology enclave industries. Before the discovery of black gold, the oasis was celebrated by medieval writers, most notably by Ibn Khaldun, for its dominant role in the gold trade linking the Niger Basin with the Mediterranean. Between roughly the eighth and sixteenth centuries, Warqala (the Warjilan of classical Arabic geographers) was among the most prosperous of the mighty desert entrepôt cities, a busy caravan and commercial hub linking the Maghrib with sub-Saharan Africa. It was probably the lure of gold, slaves, and tribute that drew the Turkish army as far south as Warqala in 1552 to effect Tuqqurt's temporary submission to Algiers.

Warqala's relationship with the Turks resembled the arrangement concluded between the Banu Jallab and the deys. By rendering a modest tribute in slaves, a large measure of autonomy was secured. However, the political situation was complicated by the forced entry of the Moroccan Sa'adians into the Wadi Mya in the early seventeenth century. The Moroccans installed a client sultan, chosen from the Allahum (or Alahun) lineage, upon Warqala's throne. Eventually breaking with their Moroccan patrons, the Allahum dynasty retained nominal suzerainty over the oasis until the mid-nineteenth century. Whenever Ottoman control over the Sahara loosened, the Banu Jallab of Tuqqurt strove to extend their authority over Warqala.[24]

Long before the French invasion, Warqala had lost much of its former commercial glory to the Mzabi cities, which captured large shares of the diminishing trans-Saharan trade along with some of the Tell-Sahara commerce. And ownership of the Wadi Mya's date-palm gardens, containing an estimated half a million trees in the past century, had passed into the hands of Mzabi merchants as well as the Sha'amba tribal confederacy for whom some sedentary cultivators became khammas.[25] While Warqala's declining fortunes can mainly be traced to the drying up of—or shifts in—the gold and slave trade, local and regional political quarrels also were at work.[26] All that need be said regarding the tangled, treacherous flow of politics in Wadi Mya is that, as elsewhere in the Sahara, two warring saffs emerged. And until Muhammad b. 'Abd Allah's advent, political alliances tended to coalesce around this binary system.[27]

Thus, on the eve of French military expansion into the region, the "queen of the desert" had for the most part been dethroned. Her urban population was enmeshed in endless bickering that pitted city factions against one another. Continual strife also broke out between Warqala and her nemesis, the *qsar* (fortified oasis) of N'gusa, situated twenty-four kilometers to the north. If the Mzabis had become the commercial overlords of the Wadi Mya, its political masters were the pastoral nomads—the Sha'amba, Sa'id 'Atba, and Banu Thur. By the middle of the past century, outsider hegemony over principal trade routes into the valley and over the means of agrarian production within the oases, combined with the saff conflicts, limited the Allahum dynasty's effective power to the walls of their desert stronghold.[28]

Muhammad b. 'Abd Allah: The Sharif of Warqala

Before it was partially razed by the French army in 1861, the oasis-city of Warqala perched on a limestone terrace that dominated the dense palm groves stretching as far as the eye could see. Surrounded by ramparts, the elliptical qsar was constructed of roughcast stone, its narrow streets covered by vaulted roofing. Viewed from its suburbs, the city had a curious appearance due to the square minaret of the principal mosque "leaning like the tower of Pisa."[29] By then Warqala lacked the architectural dignity as well as the wealth of her counterpart, Tuqqurt. Nevertheless, it had some attractive features, mainly its remoteness. In its heyday during the medieval period, it had sheltered religious dissidents; its isolation, caused by its fall from grace in the trans-Saharan trade, made Warqala a place of refuge. Throughout the Ottoman centuries, political figures from the Ziban or Tuqqurt, who had suffered defeat at the hands of local rivals or the central government, habitually found a haven there.[30]

In the early months of 1851, a pilgrim arrived before the city's walls seeking asylum. Warmly received by Warqala's people, the individual, who was accompanied only by his wife and a servant, soon fashioned a local following through his rigorous asceticism and acts of piety.[31] In effect, the stranger seized upon the paradigm of the holy person, who represents an exemplar of right conduct and focuses social grievances for which he proposes solutions. Set in motion, the rumor mill portrayed the unknown holy man as blessed with a rare saintliness and destined for extraordinary feats.[32]

For many North Africans, the timing of the stranger's appearance was replete with meaning. The eighteenth-century desert saint and mystic Sidi al-Aghwati had predicted the redeemer's advent, after several decades of infidel rule, sometime in the 1850s.[33] And despite defeat, Bu Ziyan's revolt had raised popular millenarian expectations upon which the sharif capitalized. Thus, the third decade of French rule was a period rife with mahdist pretenders in Algeria and, to a lesser extent, in Tunisia. Like Bu Ziyan's movement, Muhammad b. 'Abd Allah's revolt demonstrates the symbiotic relationship between Saharan sufi elites, such as the Rahmaniyya and the Tijaniyya, and rebellious prophets. However, unlike the hero of Za'atsha, the sharif had originally come from the margins of the rural religious establishment in western Algeria. Because he had served the colonial regime for several years, Muhammad b. 'Abd Allah provides another example of protest leaders who were familiar with European ways; his variegated career puts him in the category of "charismatic adventurers."[34]

Naturally French military officials characterized Muhammad b. 'Abd Allah as belonging to a long line of "maraboutic impostors who, under the pretext of religion, have so often succeeded in attracting a following of unfortunate, superstitious people or bandits desiring nothing but booty."[35] While there is an element of truth to this, Muhammad b. 'Abd Allah's real significance lay elsewhere. The grievances of ordinary people as well as the interests, ambitions, and political platforms of desert big men coalesced around him into a series of related movements for which his mahdist claims provided the connective tissue. Nevertheless, in the eyes of Warqala's inhabitants, who formed his primary following, the mystery of the sharif's origins, and his status as a devout hajji and sufi arriving in the oasis from the Mashriq, held forth the possibility that he was the long-awaited one.

Unfortunately for the historian, scarcely more is known of Muhammad b. 'Abd Allah than of his apocalyptic predecessor, Bu Ziyan; the sharif's birth date, family background, and real name remain a matter of dispute.[36] What is certain is that he had been a *faqir* (wandering ascetic) from the maraboutic tribe of the Awlad Sidi b. Yusuf, who occupied the territory north of Tilimsan. Prior to 1830, he had been a student at the zawiya of Sidi Ya'qub of the powerful maraboutic tribal confederacy, the Awlad Sidi al-Shaykh. During the early years of 'Abd al-Qadir's jihad in the Oran, Muhammad b. 'Abd Allah earned local notoriety through his self-inflicted deprivations and extreme mystical practices at the tomb-shrine of Tilimsan's patron saint, Sidi Abu Madiyan. For several years, the future mahdi engaged in unremitting devotions at the shrine, spending entire nights in prayer and meditation, much like any Maghribi saint in gestation.[37] And acts of self-denial were very much part of the spiritual armature of the waliy and sufi.

Muhammad b. 'Abd Allah might have ended his days in relative obscurity in the service of Sidi Abu Madiyan had he not been enmeshed in the political turmoil that rent western Algeria in the 1840s. As his reputation for holiness grew, Muhammad b. 'Abd Allah caught the attention of both French authorities, then battling the amir, and one of the amir's *agha*s (local representative), Mulay Shaykh. By 1841 Mulay Shaykh desired to distance himself from 'Abd al-Qadir's faltering movement. Seeking to manipulate the faqir to his own ends, Mulay Shaykh associated himself with the local holy man to appropriate his popular religious following and baraka and thus pose as a contender to the amir. Failing at this, the traitorous agha subsequently concluded an alliance with the French but was later outmaneuvered by Muhammad b. 'Abd Allah, whose religious clientele brought him into the political limelight. Named khalifa of Tilimsan in 1842 by General Bugeaud, who sought to counter the amir's authority by promoting another religious leader, Muhammad b. 'Abd Allah soon proved an inept military leader and, worse, a decidedly uncooperative French ally.[38]

After several military debacles which pitted the holy man ineffectively against the amir, Bugeaud decided to rid himself of a political embarrassment. Exiled from the colony, Muhammad b.'Abd Allah was dispatched on a state ship to Alexandria, from whence he set out for the Hijaz sometime in 1845 or 1846 to perform the pilgrimage. While in the Haramayn, he spent three or four years studying at the zawiya of Muhammad b. 'Ali al-Sanusi (1787–1859) in Mecca. The founder of the Sanusiyya brotherhood was also from western Algeria and had left the Mashriq to take up residence in al-Bayda (in Cyrenaica), which served as the Sanusi center from 1842 until 1857. By this period, Muhammad b. 'Ali al-Sanusi was already lending moral and material support to Algerian opponents of the French colonial regime via the sufi network.[39]

Once again there is little information on the future mahdi's activities while in the Holy Cities, apart from vague references to his Meccan sojourn in letters addressed to tribal followers in the Sahara sometime after 1851. In these missives, Muhammad b. 'Abd Allah stated that for four years he had studied in Egypt and the Hijaz, where he encountered Muhammad b. 'Ali al-Sanusi (date unknown) who commanded him to preach jihad in Algeria.[40] Another source claims that while in the Mashriq he had established relations with Mecca's "Arab elite"; since the leader of the Sanusiyya had returned to the Hijaz in this period, it is not unlikely that the two men met there.[41] Whether or not he encountered Mustafa b. 'Azzuz, who was also performing the hajj at the same time, is a question worth raising in the light of their later collaboration.

Sometime around 1850, the sharif resurfaced in the Regency of Tripolitania, where he was received with honors by the Ottoman governor, Izzat Pasha. The reasons prompting Muhammad b. 'Abd Allah's return to the Maghrib are unknown; his arrival in Tripoli provoked consternation among French officials, who had native spies tracking him there as well as in Tunisia and Algeria. From Tripoli, he journeyed south to Ghadamis, where he befriended the Ottoman *mudir* (governor) with whom the mahdi later corresponded.[42] Departing southern Tripolitania, he went to the Tunisian Jarid, where he may have resided at Mustafa b. 'Azzuz's zawiya in Nafta; he then crossed into Algeria to the Suf and Tuqqurt. Feraud maintained that while in the Suf, Muhammad b. 'Abd Allah attempted unsuccessfully to mobilize the people against the depredations of the Banu Jallab.[43] Eventually he reached a zawiya in Warqala's suburbs sometime in the early spring of 1851.

Bearing letters from the Sanusiyya shaykh, Muhammad b. 'Abd Allah met an enthusiastic reception from Warqala's leading female saint, Lalla Zuhra, venerated for her piety and gift of divination. Lalla Zuhra later pronounced him to be "the one sent from God," and prophesied a brilliant future for the mysterious guest as "sultan and terror of the Christians."[44] One of the letters from the Sanusiyya shaykh, which bore his personal seal, read as follows:

> Here is a pious man who fears God and who has influence in the Tell, where the most important tribes of the West have recognized him as their leader; he has come, scorning the ephemeral things of this world, avoiding the French, whom he detests, in search of tranquillity and happiness in the midst of palm trees to await better days.[45]

In addition, Muhammad b. 'Abd Allah enjoyed the immediate support of a leading tribal notable from one of the city's warring factions, Shaykh 'Abd

Allah b. Khalid, who provided the stranger with accommodations in his own home. In contrast to Bu Ziyan, the sharif initially encountered little difficulty in convincing a potential constituency of the authenticity of his divinely ordained calling. (It was only later, when the promised victory in battle proved elusive, that his mahdist claims met with growing skepticism.) Thus, from the start of his prophetic mission, Muhammad b. 'Abd Allah solicited and received the backing of local religious and secular elites.[46]

Warqala in this period was a rather modest desert religious center; the oasis boasted two large congregational mosques and a number of zawaya representing turuq from both western and eastern Algeria—the Shaykhiyya, Qadiriyya, Rahmaniyya, and Tijaniyya, to name only the most important. Among the sufi orders there, the Rahmaniyya claimed the second-largest popular following; perhaps as many as one-third of Warqala's population was affiliated in one way or another with the tariqa. The Rahmaniyya presence resulted from missionary activity by both Muhammad b. 'Azzuz and his son Mustafa. As was the case in the Jarid and the Suf by this time, many Rahmaniyya followers called themselves "'Azzuziyya" to signify their special spiritual attachment to the 'Azzuz clan of al-Burj and Nafta. Warqala's sufi orders do not appear to have been divided in this period by the kinds of "maraboutic rivalries" found elsewhere. And the sharif did not court any particular sufi elite or order in his jihad but rather appealed to all for assistance.[47]

The choice of Warqala as the site for an anticolonial rebellion—if indeed that was Muhammad b. 'Abd Allah's original intent—was probably dictated by moral as well as strategic concerns. The desert was considered one of the few places left unsoiled by the infidels, who by 1850 were the undisputed masters of most of northern Algeria, the Berber Kabylia aside. And many North Africans expected the Muslim redeemer to arise from the Sahara. "For them, our presence in Algeria is only a passing affliction, an atonement. They always have their eyes fixed upon the south from whence the mahdi, whose mission is to expel us from Dar al-Islam, will make his appearance."[48] Moreover, the oasis was situated on several transversal desert routes leading either to the Tunisian Jarid or to Biskra; it could with some difficulty be reached from Ghadamis in southern Tripolitania. At the same time, Warqala had always been just outside the grasp of central governments. The last time a Turkish army had occupied the city was in 1821 and then only briefly. After 1830 the French military left the region to its own devices, being completely absorbed with pacification in the north. With the crumbling of the local Allahum dynasty after 1842, Warqala fell into a state of anarchy, subjected to years of interminable saff quarrels which could be resolved only by someone neutral to these bitter conflicts.[49] Thus, a resident "outside saint" was needed to restore order.

When French colonial officials finally turned their attention belatedly to the Sahara in 1850, they found that the political vacuum in Warqala had aroused the territorial ambitions of both of its neighbors, the Banu Jallab and the Babiyya clan of the nearby rival oasis of N'gusa. In 1851 the shaykh of N'gusa, al-Hajj b. Babiyya, opted, purely from self-interest, for collusion with the French and was duly appointed to a largely fictitious *khalifalik* (an administrative post headed by a khalifa or subaltern), encompassing the entire Wadi Mya. This naturally alarmed Warqala's inhabitants as well as other oases and tribal leaders. In fact, the timing of the sharif's public declaration of both his prophecy and jihad was tied to Warqala's refusal to acknowledge the authority of the new French-appointed khalifa, al-Hajj b. Babiyya. Seeking to take command of his as yet unsecured office, the khalifa and his forces mounted several unsuccessful expeditions against the oasis-city and in August 1851 were preparing another military offensive.[50]

Khalwa and Jihad

Between February and August 1851, Muhammad b. 'Abd Allah engaged in a rigorous *khalwa* (mystical retirement from the world); he spoke but rarely, and he avoided contact with Warqala's populace. As he had earlier done in Tilimsan, he spent day and night in prayer, self-denial, and meditation in an outward expression of interior, mystical hijra. This behavior naturally aroused popular curiosity; people began talking about the stranger, and the rumor mill ran wild. Then in August as another military assault from N'gusa loomed on the horizon, the sharif accepted the vacant post of sultan of Warqala, yielding to the entreaties of the city's notables and masses with seeming reluctance.[51] His populist election was due to his role as a pious outsider, untainted by association with any single faction, to the backing of local political leaders, and to the blessings of the city's patron saint, Lalla Zuhra.

Nevertheless, indigenous political actors from outside may also have played a part in the sharif's elevation to power. The Mzabis and the chief of the powerful Awlad Sidi al-Shaykh confederation, Sulayman b. Hamza, had both viewed the promotion of N'gusa's shaykh to khalifa status with extreme trepidation. Since one of the sharif's first declared objectives was to rid the Sahara of French native allies, Sidi Hamza initially pushed Muhammad b. 'Abd Allah's mahdist claims, viewing with favor his selection as Warqala's sultan.[52]

The first civic act of the newly elected sultan-saint was to abandon his modest quarters in the house of his host and take up residence in the qasba, a significant move since the citadel was historically a highly charged and visible political space. Eventually the sharif's partisans constructed a palace for him in Ruissat; it resembled a medieval ribat combining religious, political, military, and administrative functions in a single architectural complex.[53] His initial program aimed to impose peace upon the Sahara by uniting Warqala's factions, defeating the French-backed khalifa of N'gusa, and driving the Christians from the desert. This plan emerges from the sharif's letter to the governor of Ghadamis written in 1851: "When I arrived in the region of Warqala, it had come to pass that the Muslims were under the rule of the Christians, and their khalifa (al-Hajj b. Babiyya) was there."[54]

As Bu Ziyan had done two years earlier after his following had reached a certain critical mass, the sharif upped the ante. His letters, designed to mobilize supporters for the jihad, were signed with the name invariably ascribed to the mahdi, Muhammad b. 'Abd Allah. Whether he actually claimed to be *the* redeemer, instead of the mahdi's precursor or messenger, is uncertain. In his letters written early in 1852, the sharif refers to his teacher, Muhammad b. 'Ali al-Sanusi, as the "master of the hour," an epithet commonly ascribed to the Muslim savior.[55] However, the nuances of eschatological doctrine were probably inconsequential to his tribal followers, who appear to have firmly believed that he was the one sent from God to deliver them from oppression and institute the realm of justice. Yet, the precise form that the kingdom of God on earth would ultimately assume was viewed differently by the myriad groups, each with its own expectations, converging under his banner.

The mahdi's message was simple and universal in its appeal for socio-spiritual regeneration. Algeria had fallen into Christian hands because the Islamic community had strayed from the right path; reform and renewal of the faith were incumbent upon all. It was the sharif who would replace discord with social harmony; the weakness of Warqala's inhabitants vis-à-vis the French was the product of their own divisions. Unified they would "march together like brothers." With God's protection and that of the Prophet, victory was assured, rich booty would be theirs. The true religion would triumph; the humiliation of subservience to unbelievers would end.[56] At the same time, specific events and deeply felt local grievances undergirded the call to arms. The vaccination campaign, then under way in Algeria due to the devastating cholera epidemic of 1849–1850, was greatly feared; rumor had it that the French were inoculating Muslim children in order to mark them with evil intent. And heaven's wrath with the Muslim Algerians had brought down upon them pestilence, drought, and a plague of locusts as punishment for submission to France.[57]

Several issues regarding the movement's origins and its organizer's initial intent must be addressed at this juncture. French military writers from the period, some of whom fought against the sharif, were naturally attracted to conspiracy theories. Many assumed that Muhammad b. 'Abd Allah had arrived in the remote oasis with the clearly formulated scheme of launching an anticolonial rebellion throughout the Sahara. Moreover, since the Sanusiyya scare soon overtook the colonial bureaucracy, later writers maintained that the sharif had been entrusted with this mission by the Sanusiyya leader.[58] Yet, Muhammad b. 'Abd Allah may have aimed first at the moral-religious uplifting of the Algerians by exhortations to virtuous conduct, perhaps through the medium of a new sufi tariqa or association with the Sanusiyya. In marked contrast to what Europeans at the time said and wrote about him, Muhammad b. 'Ali al-Sanusi had always privileged interior or spiritual jihad. In his numerous writings, the founder of the Sanusiyya advocated nonviolent means for achieving *islah* (reform, renewal) within Muslim society, urging removal from areas directly under European influence rather than confrontation. And initially the sharif sought to emulate his Sanusiyya master in words and deeds.

Whatever the sharif's motives prior to his election as sultan of Warqala, by late in the summer of 1851 he had moved (or been maneuvered by others) dead center into the vortex of Saharan politics, struggles, and alignments. As his coalition enlarged in size and complexity, rumors about the pious stranger grew accordingly, eventually reaching colonial officials in Biskra.

More Rumors of Revolt

For several months the North African rumor mill had been preoccupied with the stranger from the east. News about the sharif increased in the autumn of 1851 as he and his armed forces went on the offensive, perhaps to certify his mahdihood to any remaining skeptics. The sultan's first militant deed was to demand that the oasis of N'gusa recognize him as ruler, a command met by scornful refusal. The sharif then undertook a spectacular raid against tribal allies of Tuqqurt's Banu Jallab, who were defeated; the proceeds served to enhance his own prestige and that of his cause. Feeling vulnerable in his khalifalik, the leader of the Babiyya clan fled to his French benefactors in Biskra in September. The next month N'gusa's inhabitants rendered homage to the sharif, formally recognizing him as their shaykh. To forestall future unrest, they were forced to relocate to Warqala, where they could be easily controlled.[59] Emancipated at last from the oppression long suffered at the hands of its nearby foe, the oasis of Warqala became the rebellious capital of a movement enduring for three more years.

These events naturally were eagerly discussed, repeated, and probably embellished as they were told and retold all over Algeria. According to the grapevine version, not only did the sharif govern the Wadi Mya through popular consensus but also the surrounding tribes, and even the people of the Mzab, had submitted to him. (The submission of the Mzab to Warqala would have represented a decided reversal of prevailing economic and political realities.) At first, the French military dismissed the news as "nothing but an Arab rumor," and thus inherently spurious. Officials in Biskra's Bureau Arabe were distracted in 1851 by events along the Tunisian-Algerian border—the emigration of Nafta's shurafa' to the Suf—and by Bu Baghla's revolt in the northern Constantine. Like Bu Ziyan, the sharif was the subject of endless rumormongering and speculation, the stuff of improvised news. Significantly, Muhammad b. 'Abd Allah was associated in oral information circuits and popular thinking with the 1849 uprising. Bu Ziyan's second son, whose body had not been recovered from Za'atsha's detritus, was believed still alive. It was said that he had joined with the sharif, accompanying him on expeditions through the Sahara. Not believing or not wanting to trust this unsettling news, French military authorities were finally convinced of the situation's seriousness by their indigenous allies, who arrived from the desert with reports about the mahdi.[60]

As the year 1851 drew to a close, the rebels, still based in Warqala but emboldened by initial victories, widened their military objectives to include northern Algeria. Now the declared goal was to march an army to the north, where they would expel the foreigners. In the battle plan, Biskra once again figured prominently as the gateway to the Tell and the seat of French military administration; due to Biskra's strategic location, it would have to be taken next. The sharif sent spies to the oasis of Sidi 'Uqba to assess the Ziban's political climate and its caravan activity and to gather intelligence about French activities. Information was gleaned from as far away as Algiers, probably through barranis living in the capital. By then the rebels believed that Biskra would prove an easy prize since outside military assistance was at hand, according to the rumor mill.[61]

As in 1849, many people still looked to the bey of Tunis for deliverance. It was said that Ahmad Bey, angered by a French-imposed territorial concession, had collected a large army and was coming forthwith to embrace the sharif's cause. (This particular piece of political gossip writ large has two basic elements which can be traced to verifiable fact. The French had forced the Tunisian government to renounce claims on contested territory, and Ahmad Bey had indeed organized a new European-style army since 1838, although certainly not with any Algerian adventures in mind.)[62] Moreover, rumor had it that the Ottoman sultan was sending military assistance from Istanbul. Algeria would return to the Ottoman-ruled fold since her coastal cities were without French troops; the Turkish contingent would meet little resistance. This last bit of improvised news concerning the Sublime Porte would reappear constantly in Algeria throughout the century and in Tunisia during the French occupation of 1881–1882. Finally, in this period, the Sanusiyya's head shaykh entered into the serpentine North African information ducts; Sidi Muhammad b. 'Ali al-Sanusi was presumed to be in the Tunisian Nafzawa, massing his followers to aid the sharif's jihad.[63]

For the historian seeking to reconstruct the rhetorical universe of collective social action and to make sense out of what was dismissed as "nonsense" by colonial observers, these rumors are significant. Indeed the rumors provide virtually the only window into the aspirations of the unlettered supporters of the rebellion. The news linking the sharif to Bu Ziyan's son indicates that Muhammad b. 'Abd Allah had convinced many of the authenticity of his calling and had also been assimilated into the pantheon of local folk heroes. In addition, this suggests that the sharif's jihad was regarded as the successor movement to Za'atsha. Conversely the sharif may have consciously tapped into the fund of popular veneration for Za'atsha martyrs to garner added legitimacy for his prophecy and jihad. Moreover, as was true in 1849, rumors played several functions. First, they persuaded the rebellion's constituency that their cause was just, its victory assured, since they were not alone in the struggle; the might of the Tunisian bey and the Ottoman sultan were on their side. Second, the rumors reveal once more what the movement's shock troops believed to be within the realm of possibility. Finally, because both leaders and followers acted upon information fed to them by the rumor mill, improvised news was a powerful force in shaping collective behavior. But rebels need more than rumors to survive, particularly in the parched desert regions.

Markets, Grains, and Political Action in the Sahara

Before Biskra could be taken, however, Tuqqurt, which had pitilessly tyrannized the region, would have to be subdued for use as a base of action. Warqala was too isolated, impoverished, and thinly populated to support a sustained uprising; its location made it vulnerable to economic pressures exerted by cities to the north. The battle for the "stomach of the Sahara" involved as much desert market strategies as the settling of old political accounts by Tuqqurt's ancient enemies. While the Wadi Righ traditionally acquired most of its grains from the Algerian Tell, after the occupation of Biskra in 1844, cereals from the Tunisian beylik, imported from the Jarid via the Suf, became increasingly vital for both Tuqqurt and Warqala. Therefore, control of Tuqqurt would assure grain supplies imported from Tunisia.

By September 1851, the sharif had a multitude of desert forces enrolled under his banner. Contingents from Tammasin, Warqala, and al-Awad as well as tribal groups from the Sha'amba and Larba' confederacies gathered to topple the Banu Jallab and reap the rich prizes promised by their leader. The French sent native troops and supplies of grain from Biskra to Tuqqurt to relieve their terrified ally. 'Abd al-Rahman b. Jallab also begged for European artillery so that the increasingly menacing insurrection would not, in his words, "turn into another Za'atsha." By this time, the family rebel, Sliman b. Jallab, had enlisted the sharif's aid in dislodging his cousin from power. Finally, the nomads were once again moving down from the Tell to the Sahara in September, further complicating the political game. In contrast to Za'atsha, where the French military strove to prevent the transhumant tribes from regaining the desert, colonial officers now pressed the Salmiyya and Rahman to hasten back to the Wadi Righ; there they owned palm gardens and could be counted on to defend Tuqqurt against attack.[64]

In October the insurgents arrived in Tammasin, whose markets, while not as well stocked as Tuqqurt's, could supply basic provisions demanded by militant action. Ordered by French officers to erect an economic blockade, the hapless sultan, 'Abd al-Rahman, made a genuine effort, for the first time, to close markets in the Wadi Righ to the rebel force. In the Ziban, colonial authorities did the same for French-held markets, measures which made supplies a critical element in the insurrection. Indeed, throughout the sharif's long and wide-ranging movement, access to desperately needed provisions, more than any other material factor, shaped the rebellion's geopolitical trajectory.[65]

The next month battle was joined before the walls of Tuqqurt. The city, however, was not taken, mainly because the attackers lacked siege craft and were less numerous than the Banu Jallab's forces swelled by French army contingents. Moreover, the commercial blockade of Tammasin, the rebels' base, meant that provisions from elsewhere could reach the oasis only with some difficulty. The clash ended in a stalemate but was interpreted quite differently by the sharif, who declared victory since his troops, though outnumbered, had killed a goodly number of the enemy and the sultan was holed up pitifully in his walled city. Muhammad b. 'Abd Allah's supporters chose thus to read the confrontation as divine confirmation of their leader's mahdist pretensions. From this period on, many in the Sahara referred to Warqala's sultan as the mahdi. The Sha'amba constructed a maqam (or shrine) of stones to honor the one sent from God and designate the place sanctified by his presence.[66]

During this period, Muhammad b. 'Abd Allah also turned his attention to the Mzab. If the cities of the Pentapolis could be brought into his campaign, a vast midsection of the central Sahara would be in revolt. However, the characteristically independent Mzabis declined to open their doors to the rebels in December 1851, although they did allow that if the sharif proved mighty enough to oust the infidels then they would consider joining his cause. Wisely, the sharif did not press the Mzabis further; a siege of their fortified oases would have been futile anyway. Nevertheless, the Mzab's professed neutrality meant that the movement's western flank was free for the moment from danger.[67]

Soon after came the news that Tuqqurt's ruler was near death; 'Abd al-Rahman finally succumbed in January 1852, and Sliman took over the oasis, welcoming Muhammad b. 'Abd Allah and his forces. If the Banu Jallab's leader depended upon the mahdi for legitimacy, Muhammad b. 'Abd Allah needed the desert prince for material support. The sharif even ritually installed Sliman on the throne in a ceremony held two months later, although the new sultan may have espoused the mahdi's cause less from ideological or religious commitment than from economic and political self-interest. Whatever the motivations, their respective fates became intertwined, to Sliman's eventual detriment since he ended his days in exile in Tunis.

Mindful of the threat from the French army poised in Biskra, Sliman attempted to soothe colonial officials in 1852 by disingenuous letters assuring them of undying fealty. This effort encountered skepticism, tinged with resignation. As Seroka observed in the period, French sovereignty in the Sahara was such that France was condemned to "simply endure the *faits accomplis* of desert politics."[68] Nevertheless, the French tried, unsuccessfully, to woo Sliman away from his religious patron, the sharif, during the next three years. Moreover, events in Tuqqurt had come to the attention of authorities in Tripolitania, for Sliman received a delegation, seeking to determine the state of affairs in the Algerian Sahara, from either the Ottomans or the Sanusiyya.[69]

No sooner had he come to power than Sliman b. Jallab immediately made the winter fair available to rebellious tribal groups, a reckless gesture of insubordination to France. Without access to Tuqqurt's vast markets, the sharif's movement might well have collapsed in 1852 since insufficient supplies had brought hardship and dissent to his camp. Now the mahdi's army could use the products of their razzias, mainly flocks, to purchase grains, dates, gunpowder, and firearms from the Suf and Tunisia. But there were some items that even the Suf's intrepid traders could not easily obtain. Thus, Sliman and the sharif both sought across-the-border assistance from the Tunisian bey, requesting that he furnish cannon and soldiers to the rebellion. By then painfully aware of his own vulnerable position vis-à-vis France, Ahmad Bey prudently rejected the audacious request.[70] The Tunisian head of state's refusal to get involved deprived the movement of added legitimacy, although it did not extinguish hopes for future succor.

The End of the Rebellion's Algerian Phase, 1852–1854

Prior to moving against Biskra, the sharif sent letters soliciting moral assistance from Rahmaniyya notables residing in the villages of Awlad Jallal and Sidi Khalid in the Zab Qibli. Under the moral ascendancy of local saintly lineages affiliated with the Rahmaniyya, these small oases had tenaciously supported Bu Ziyan's uprising three years earlier. Moreover, the word-of-mouth epic or rumor regarding the coalition between Bu Ziyan's miraculously risen son and the sharif had been disseminated from the Ziban. Due to its military garrison, Biskra was the most firmly under colonial rule; yet expressions of popular unrest surfaced as the rebel forces neared in May 1852. Several of Biskra's inhabitants hired musicians and storytellers to sing the praises of Za'atsha's martyrs in public places, resulting in arrests. And Bureau Arabe officers observed that popular support for Muhammad b. 'Abd Allah was high among the region's tribes and oasis dwellers.[71]

At last the long-awaited battle between the forces of good and evil occurred in May 1852 in the Zab Qibli, south of Biskra. Never a great strategist in warfare, the sharif and his contingents were beaten back by the better armed, organized, and equipped French army. Moreover, the sharif's forces were fighting in unknown territory; the advantage was clearly on the enemy's side. This was the first encounter between a modern, European contingent and the sharif's coalition, since previous clashes had involved French native allies who fought on terms roughly similar to those of the rebels. As was true in 1849, the match was grievously unequal, mainly because colonial soldiers wielded superior firepower. The sharif and his armed followers were impelled ignominiously into retreat, and Biskra remained in infidel hands; thus the way to the north was blocked. Had Muhammad b. 'Abd Allah been able to carry the day, most likely the rest of the Ziban would have revolted.[72] Nevertheless, without an initial victory to prove the would-be redeemer's claims to divine guidance, and with the memory of Za'atsha still fresh in the minds of many, the Ziban remained largely quiet during the confrontation. In retrospect, the failed Biskra campaign was the beginning of the end; the real turning point in the insurrection's fortunes transpired late in 1852.

Failing in the southern Constantine, the sharif was compelled to look elsewhere in the Sahara for conquest and booty to keep his tribal followers content. Nasir b. Shuhra, head of the powerful Arba'a confederacy, encouraged the sharif to shift operations to southcentral Algeria. His attention was drawn to the large, relatively prosperous oasis of al-Aghwat, located some four hundred kilometers south of Algiers.[73] Since 1844, the oasis had been under a French-appointed ruler, Ahmad b. Salim, whom the Arba'a chieftain sought to overthrow with the mahdi's assistance. Due to popular discontent with the French-allied khalifa, Ahmad b. Salim was forced from office and al-Aghwat's populace opened their doors to the sharif and his followers. However, the rebels remained in control of the strategic oasis, dominating the routes leading to Biskra, the Mzab, and the Oran, for several months only. By then al-Aghwat was deemed critical to Governor-General Randon's future plans for a French Saharan empire stretching deep into the desert. Under Generals Yusuf and Pélissier, the oasis was taken by storm on 2 December 1852, resulting in thousands of casualties on both sides during an "atrocious carnage." It proved to be one of the bloodiest episodes in the conquest period; 2,300 men, women, and children were killed and al-Aghwat's streets ran with blood.[74] The horrors of the siege, which surpassed even Za'atsha, passed into the collective historical folk memory of the region and were remembered by al-Aghwat's remaining inhabitants in the guise of popular religious dramatic rituals reenacted regularly until the eve of Algeria's independence.[75]

Prior to the final assault by the French army, both Nasir b. Shuhra and Muhammad b. 'Abd Allah managed through a ruse to escape from al-Aghwat—miraculously so in the minds of their partisans. In January 1853, the sharif retreated to his palace complex in Ruissat, where he was joined by the leader of the Arba'a tribe. As was true of other tribally based mahdist movements, such as those led by Bu Himara and Bu 'Amama in Morocco, the sharif's clientele expanded with victory only to dwindle after defeat.[76] Had he limited his movement to the Tuqqurt-Suf area, Muhammad b. 'Abd Allah could have posed a serious threat to colonial interests in a strategic crossroads region opening onto the eastern Maghrib, Sahara, and the Mashriq. Yet in his relentless quest for support and supplies, he was drawn into other Saharan battles and political programs; this deflected the jihad from its original aim—initiating the realm of justice on earth—and channeled it to more mundane objectives.

From 1853 on, the movement's millenarian core was gradually replaced by a much less stable nucleus of shifting desert coalitions. Campaigns were waged more in the manner of tribal razzias than anything else. By now popular fervor for the mahdi was wearing thin; some began to question the authenticity of his prophetic calling. Significantly in this critical period, the mahdi began increasingly to rely upon sorcery and magic to convince his reluctant partisans of his divinely conferred mission.[77]

By mid-1853, both the sharif and his comrade in arms, Sliman b. Jallab, faced growing disenchantment from their constituencies in Tuqqurt and

Warqala. As economic conditions deteriorated, many within the Banu Jallab clan began to cast about for other family members to supplant the sultan, whose defiance of the French had brought little else but misery. As long as the caravans could travel safely from the Tunisian Jarid to the Suf and Tuqqurt, militant opposition to France was feasible. However, raids by French military patrols began to impede the caravan trade between the two countries, which in any case could supply the rebels only with food-stuffs if harvests were plentiful in the beylik. In the spring and summer of 1853 grain harvests in the southern Constantine and in parts of Tunisia failed due to drought; a devastating series of epizootic diseases decimated herds and flocks. The oases of Warqala and Tuqqurt begged colonial authorities for permission to trade in well-stocked French-held markets, which nevertheless remained closed to them. Some, however, clung to their faith in the mahdi's cause, perhaps for lack of alternatives. In Tuqqurt, religious notables led processions to the city's sufi zawaya, seeking divine guidance; local holy men consoled the populace with their supernatural visions and dreams, which promised that the French would not take the oasis that year. Their visions proved correct for a time.[78]

Before internal revolt against the sharif and Sliman reached the boiling point, betrayal from outside dealt the fatal blow to the jihad's Algerian phase. As mentioned above, Muhammad b. 'Abd Allah had enjoyed the backing of Sidi Hamza, leader of the powerful Awlad Sidi al-Shaykh confederacy, when the movement was in its early stages during 1851.[79] A fearless tribal warrior as well as a saint, Shaykh Sulayman b. Hamza had been captured by the French military and incarcerated for two years between 1851 and 1853. During his prison years, he appears to have undergone a change of political heart and defected to France, at least momentarily. In return for collaboration, Sidi Hamza was freed and named *bash-agha* for the western Sahara. His first task was to quell the sharif's uprising, which Sidi Hamza went about with his customary vigor. In November 1853, he arrived in the Wadi Righ with a large army to take on Muhammad b. 'Abd Allah, who counted only a handful of stalwart partisans. Soundly defeated at the seat of his power, the sharif managed once again to evade his would-be captors—mirabile dictu—by fleeing to the desolate area between al-Awad and the Jarid. The sharif's palatial headquarters in Ruissat were reduced to rubble, and by the end of 1853 Warqala was added to the growing list of colonial outposts in the Sahara.[80] Only Tuqqurt and the Suf remained unrepentant and unchastised.

The next year, 1854, witnessed a desperate rearguard action by Sliman b. Jallab and the sharif, by then confined to Tuqqurt, which was still under economic blockade. While some of the Suwafa were still loyal to the rebellion, many no longer dared to openly lend material support since native troops under Sidi Hamza moved throughout the region. As the cool months of autumn approached, the pastoralists prepared to migrate south from the Tell. This forced the hand of colonial officials in Biskra, who rightly feared that the Salmiyya, the Rahman, and the Awlad Mulat would aid the faltering movement out of economic self-interest.[81] Soldiers from the Ziban were rushed down, and by December the oasis was encircled by advancing colonial troops. The two rebel leaders decided to depart rather than attempt a last stand, which would have resulted either in a dreadful siege similar to Za'atsha and al-Aghwat or might have brought their murder at the hands of Tuqqurt's thoroughly exasperated and demoralized population. By now Sliman b. Jallab was completely compromised in the eyes of French authorities and destined to follow the sharif's rapidly fading star. Together the two men retreated to the Tijaniyya center in Tammasin, where Muhammad b. 'Abd Allah placed his family under Tijani protection. In the Suf, they were joined by Nasir b. Shuhra with some 450 tents from the Arba'a and other recalcitrant tribal groups. At the end of December the political refugees crossed into the safety of the Tunisian Jarid, where they were welcomed by Shaykh Mustafa b. 'Azzuz of Nafta.[82]

That month General Desvaux occupied both Tuqqurt and the Suf with relatively little sustained opposition; Tuqqurt's inhabitants were spared the sword and disarmed by the army, rendering up thousands of rifles.[83] In a ritual ceremony meant to symbolize France's new political order for the Suf, General Desvaux conferred the white burnus of investiture upon the Suf's first qa'id, Sidi 'Ali Bey b. Farhat, whose father had headed the Bu 'Ukkaz saff. At this juncture, the Tijaniyya shaykh of Tammasin, Sidi Muhammad b. al-'Id (1814–1876), arrived in al-Awad. Accompanied by his large retinue and bearing the religious banners of his tariqa, the Tijani leader officially placed himself under France's rule. Shaykh Muhammad also pledged to act as the new French-appointed qa'id's preceptor in fulfilling the duties of office, an offer eagerly accepted by colonial officials, despite some lingering doubts about the behind-the-scenes role of the Tijani shaykh in the sharif's rebellion.[84] At the same time, 'Ali Bey b. Farhat was instructed by his colonial masters not only to cultivate amiable relations with al-Awad's elders through gifts and offerings but also to treat Tijaniyya notables with due respect for therein lay the key to political quiet along the borders.[85]

The Mahdi and Saharan Sufi Elites

Thus far we have followed the sharif and his movement in its peregrinations throughout the Algerian Sahara. The part that religious elites played—or declined to play—in the jihad needs to be examined to underscore similarities as well as differences between the 1849 revolt and its successor movement. This examination will render explicit some of the implicit cultural norms governing sufi political behavior. It also explains subsequent postures assumed by religious notables toward colonial regimes both in Algeria and later in Tunisia.

Bu Ziyan and the sharif solicited the religiomoral backing of sufi leaders and local saints to confirm their mahdist pretensions and legitimize their jihads. Because the Za'atsha uprising developed in the Ziban, where the Rahmaniyya tariqa counted numerous followers and prominent sufi centers, the blessings of families like the 'Azzuz were crucial to large-scale mobilization. Nevertheless, several other significant dimensions of religiously based popular protest emerged in 1849. The political responses of Rahmaniyya notables to both the self-declared redeemer's cause and to the growing colonial presence were neither uniform nor monolithic. Tulqa's Rahmaniyya elite eschewed, at least publicly, taking sides, and Shaykh 'Abd al-Hafiz attempted to remain uncommitted as long as possible. As important, neither Sidi 'Abd al-Hafiz nor Shaykh Ali b. 'Uthman al-Tulqi could dissuade their clients from joining the rebels. Despite what the colonial sufi vulgate held regarding the blind obedience of tariqa members toward their religious patrons, ordinary people did on occasion follow political paths ostensibly divergent from those of powerful religious leaders. Moreover, intense popular pressure from Sidi 'Abd al-Hafiz's tribal clientele in the Awras actually forced the diffident shaykh out of retreat to throw in his lot with Bu Ziyan.

Even prior to making public his mahdist claims, Muhammad b. 'Abd Allah sought the spiritual imprimatur of Warqala's local saints, although he also drew upon the tradition of the pious reformer who achieves popular recognition of his message through uncommon forms of devotion. The sharif came to the Wadi Mya in 1851 bearing letters from the head of the Sanusiyya order, then centered in Cyrenaica, which appears to have convinced many of his religious legitimacy. However, the Sanusiyya did not then or later command large numbers of devotees in Warqala. And during the rebellion's prehistory, the oasis's local sufi establishment does not appear to have been instrumental either in promoting collective action or in opposing it. Due to its poverty and isolation—the oasis was not on the hajj route—Warqala boasted no large or regionally powerful zawaya such as those found in Tammasin, Tulqa, or Nafta. Thus, instead of translocal sufi ties, Muhammad b. 'Abd Allah's following derived more from his personal piety, the backing accorded him by Lalla Zuhra, and the social crises rocking Warqala for which the stranger proposed solutions. Once the conflict widened beyond Warqala's confines, the encouragement of Sidi

Hamza, who wielded both religious and secular authority as head of the Awlad Sidi al-Shaykh confederacy, and that of Nasir b. Shuhra, a leading tribal chieftain, was critical for mobilization.

By employing Tammasin as a base of operation in the fall of 1851, the rebellion moved squarely into territory under the Tijaniyya's moral and socioreligious influence. The tariqa's eastern branch dominated the Wadi Righ's oases from its wealthy sufi complex in Tammasin's suburb, Tamalhat. In addition, another important zawiya existed at Gummar in the Suf, serving as the Tijaniyya headquarters during the summer months when Tuqqurt's climate was unhealthy. In theory, the Tijaniyya leadership of 'Ain Madi in the Oran had embraced the French cause in 1844. Yet in eastern Algeria, Tammasin's Tijaniyya notables had thus far been spared difficult choices regarding public stances toward France since the army had not yet penetrated this part of the Sahara. Muhammad b. 'Abd Allah's move to launch his desert jihad from Tammasin brought anticolonial protest to the Tijani's back door, confronting the sufi shaykhs with dilemmas similar to those faced by the Ziban's Rahmaniyya elite in 1849.[86]

Since Tammasin had long been a rival to Tuqqurt, the sharif actively cultivated popular animosity against the Banu Jallab to enroll the oasis's inhabitants in his movement. Publicly at least, the Tijani shaykh, Sidi Muhammad b. al-'Id attempted to dampen revolutionary ardor by adopting a neutral stance. This was in keeping with his father's earlier position during the 1844 siege of Biskra when Shaykh 'Ali b. 'Isa had cautioned his sufi followers against violent confrontations with the French army. In 1851, however, Tammasin's populace welcomed the sharif to the oasis, provided decisive military assistance in men and arms, and continued to aid Muhammad b. 'Abd Allah throughout the Algerian phase of the rebellion.[87]

Whether or not Shaykh Muhammad b. al-'Id was playing a double game is open to question. The benefits of loyalty to France were not yet evident— nor were the dangers of sedition—and the self-proclaimed mahdi was, after all, bent upon destroying Tammasin's mortal enemy. Based upon reports from contemporary observers, Shaykh Muhammad b. al-'Id may not have been the pillar of the regime as colonial officers wanted to believe. As the rebel army approached Tammasin in 1851, some sources maintained that the Tijani leader privately viewed their cause with a favorable eye. And the Tijaniyya of Gummar may have even entertained the notion of fleeing the colony for the safety of Tunisia, as Mustafa b. 'Azzuz had earlier done. Two years later, Tissot reported that Tammasin's Tijaniyya center was receiving shipments of gunpowder from merchants connected to Mustafa b. 'Azzuz of Nafta. And during his 1856 visit to Tunis while en route to the Haramayn, Sidi Muhammad b. al-'Id's behavior toward French diplomats in the

Tunisian capital raised troubling doubts about the sufi leader's true feelings toward his colonial mentors.[88]

When confronted with the risks of collective protest under the mahdi's banner, the Tijaniyya elite of the eastern Sahara opted for the quite pragmatic strategy of bet hedging and fence straddling. In 1851, Muhammad b. 'Abd Allah's rebellion was but nascent, its outcome uncertain. The intentions of the French were unfathomable since some colonial authorities betrayed a lack of resolve when confronted with desert politics. Therefore, the Tijaniyya's risk-avoidance strategy resembled the stance adopted by some Rahmaniyya notables in 1849. Until Bu Ziyan scored several tangible victories over the French army—signs of Heaven's pleasure—some sufi leaders declined to openly sanction his cause. Some writers explain the Tijaniyya shaykh's political diffidence toward the sharif by positing that he viewed the redeemer as a spiritual competitor rather than a savior from infidel rule, which is to miss the point.[89] To publicly sanction the mission of an impostor in guise of the mahdi was a morally perilous course of action. Highly visible social intermediaries, such as Sidi Muhammad b. al-'Id, more often than not chose to temporize until both popular pressures and auspicious portents from on high combined to compel them to action.

By 1854 much had changed for the Tijaniyya of Tammasin. The sharif's movement was clearly bankrupt, at least in Algeria. More important, in 1853 Muhammad b. al-'Id had obtained the coveted post of head shaykh of the order's two branches, east and west, something he could not have done without implicit colonial approval. Moreover, the French recognized the Tijaniyya's growing authority in the Sahara by bestowing honorifics and privileges upon their shaykhs. Finally, the old Bu 'Ukkaz saff, for whom the Tijaniyya had always shown a marked preference, were reinstated in power in the Suf under the French-backed qa'id Sidi 'Ali Bey b. Farhat. From 1854 rather than the previous decade, the eastern Algerian Tijaniyya reluctantly realized that their best interests lay—for the moment—with the colonial order. And that order was still distant enough from their desert zawaya to be a tolerable, if unpleasant, reality.[90] From this period on, the Tijani shaykhs of Tamalhat peddled their influence by acting as brokers for French authorities in both Algeria and Tunisia as seen during the 1864 revolt led by the Tunisian rebel 'Ali b. Ghadhahim.[91]

As the geographical trajectory of the sharif's rebellion shifted so did its political content and local constituency. Moving north from Tuqqurt and Tammasin to the Ziban in 1852, Muhammad b. 'Abd Allah's movement reached an area where local religious notables were mainly, although not exclusively, drawn from the Rahmaniyya. As significant, the revolt was now in close proximity to France's mighty desert outpost in Biskra. By then any lingering political unity among Rahmaniyya notables had ceased, a product of the brutal Za'atsha defeat.

In the mountain fasts of the southern Awras, the shaykh of Sidi Masmudi, Sadiq b. al-Hajj, represented the Rahmaniyya order. During the 1849 uprising, he had mobilized tribal forces to come to Bu Ziyan's defense. By 1850, Shaykh Sadiq b. al-Hajj appeared momentarily resigned to French rule and was officially pardoned for his participation in the Za'atsha affair. Together with his family and clientele, Sidi Sadiq withdrew to the isolation of his zawiya. However, in 1851 he provoked considerable unrest in the Awras by exhorting his followers to perform the hajj en masse to seek pardon for their tepid faith. This may be interpreted as both the result of Za'atsha, which many pious Algerians viewed as a manifestation of divine wrath, and as an omen of things to come. Large numbers of Sidi Sadiq's religious clients left permanently for the Haramayn, a departure that colonial officials were powerless to prevent. Whether the migrations from the Awras were linked to widespread millenarian expectations and the news of the sharif's jihad is uncertain. Seven years later the Rahmaniyya shaykh of Sidi Masmudi instigated his own ill-fated mahdist rebellion, which was quickly quelled. This brought the French army into the heart of the Awras, although the region remained as late as 1954 one of the least touched by colonialism.[92]

Even after the debacle of 1849, the Rahmaniyya leader of the oasis of Awlad Jallal, Sidi al-Mukhtar, hesitated at first to officially recognize French authority. Because of his popular following and prestige, Shaykh al-Mukhtar was treated deferentially by colonial officers; the next year he came to Biskra to offer his outward submission as other Rahmaniyya notables had done. The shaykh, however, was clearly not reconciled to the new political order in the Ziban. In 1852 he maintained a written correspondence with Muhammad b. 'Abd Allah through the sufi network during the aborted attack upon the Zab Qibli. But once again without a decisive victory by the rebels to buttress the sharif's claims to be the mahdi, Sidi al-Mukhtar could scarcely convince his clients to lend open support to a movement that might have repeated the disastrous lessons of Za'atsha. With the demise of Muhammad b. 'Abd Allah's movement in 1854, the Rahmaniyya notables of Awlad Jallal retreated into avoidance protest as a means of coping. They eschewed relations with the Europeans as much as possible, assuming a mien of subdued hostility when contact could not be avoided. Shaykh al-Mukhtar's death less than a decade later triggered a bitter dispute over spiritual succession between the defunct saint's progeny and other Rahmaniyya elites. This deflected attention away from external political matters and eventually resulted in the creation of a new, rival

Rahmaniyya center in al-Hamil that steered a rather novel course in the struggle for cultural survival after midcentury.[93]

Predictably, during the sharif's assault upon the Ziban, Sidi 'Ali b. 'Uthman of Tulqa remained neutral and continued to maintain cordial, if distant, relationships with nearby French officials and their native allies. For the rest of the century, the saints and sufis of Tulqa neither actively sought nor sullenly dodged contact with the foreigners. After 1850 the fortunes of the Tulqa Rahmaniyya complex expanded as numerous students and pilgrims flocked to the oasis to pursue studies in Islamic Law and other religious sciences, the consequence of the closure of rebellious religious establishments elsewhere. The social service and educational activities of the Tulqa zawiya received the sub rosa blessings of the colonial regime due to its leadership's accommodating stance. While Sidi 'Ali agreed to mediate between rebels in the southern Constantine and French officials, he rebuffed offers of official posts or functions out of a desire to remain strictly within the increasingly restricted boundaries of his sociospiritual station. Nevertheless, he was characterized by local officers as "playing a double game." This meant that the Rahmaniyya shaykh was privately less than an enthusiastic supporter of a political system intent upon destroying the cultural foundations of Algerian Muslim society. Sidi 'Ali b. 'Uthman thus chose the path of educational and charitable activities as a means of contending with the unfavorable circumstances in the Ziban. His example was followed by the founder of the al-Hamil Rahmaniyya zawiya, Sidi Muhammad b. Abi al-Qasim. As part of his bet-hedging policy, Sidi 'Ali b. 'Uthman created secondary sufi centers in the Jarid and acquired substantial property in southern Tunisia, a form of insurance, since the future in *Algérie Francaise* appeared less than bright for Muslim notables.[94]

After their father's political mishaps of 1849, the two sons of Sidi 'Abd al-Hafiz also renounced overtly militant anticolonial resistance. Avoiding the company of native French allies in the Jabal Cherchar, the Rahmaniyya notables of Khanqa Sidi Naji devoted their energies instead to creating small sufi centers in the oases of Negrine and Tamarza, located strategically near the Tunisian borders; the two sons also remained closely linked to the 'Azzuz clan of Nafta. Thus, Shaykh al-Hafnawi, the eldest son, also chose as a mode of survival physical withdrawal to an area spared from colonial interference. Then in 1853, during the sharif's rebellion, another mahdist pretender arose along the frontiers near Tamarza. Professing to be the long-awaited redeemer, 'Umar b. al-Jadid led an ephemeral revolt which failed resoundingly, largely because Sidi al-Hafnawi refused to publicly declare this particular figure as the mahdi. Shaykh al-Hafnawi's objection to sanctioning 'Umar b. al-Jadid, a blacksmith by profession, may have been the consequence of his behind-the-scenes support for Muhammad b. 'Abd Allah.

Once the sharif moved his base of operations over to the Jarid, Shaykh Mustafa b. 'Azzuz openly embraced the rebellion. Influenced perhaps by his sufi mentor in Nafta, Sidi al-Hafnawi appears to have provided clandestine backing to Muhammad b. 'Abd Allah. In April 1855 it was reported: "Sidi al-Hafnawi has traveled to the Nafzawa from time to time and is in correspondence with the sharif of Warqala." Orders were issued for Sidi al-Hafnawi's arrest should he be rash enough to promote the sharif's cause too fervently, which he did not. Between the sharif's demise and the 1881 occupation of Tunisia, Sidi al-Hafnawi avoided political entanglements by dwelling in the seclusion of the small oasis located in the arid foothills of the mountains separating the two countries. There he directed a small Rahmaniyya center and ministered to the villagers' spiritual wants and social needs. France's invasion of Tunisia unsettled the Rahmaniyya shaykh of Tamarza, by then an old man. As the French army moved south in Tunisia to pacify rebellious communities, al-Hafnawi, beset by terrifying visions and dreams, sought to raise up the oasis's inhabitants by appealing to millenarian sentiments and wielding mahdist symbols and rituals.[95] The aging saint and sufi's revolt was quickly put down.

Relative to their sufi associates in the Rahmaniyya Saharan leadership, the 'Azzuz lineage of al-Burj and Nafta displayed much more diversity in terms of political behavior and response; this was true both during Za'atsha's aftermath and the sharif's rebellion. The greater complexity may be explained by the family tradition of activist sufism, inherited from the previous generation, by intraclan squabbles, and above all by the fact that a key 'Azzuz family member—Mustafa—had earlier chosen hijra as a means of coping with unfavorable political circumstances. The last element rendered engaging in anticolonial resistance less hazardous since there existed an avenue of escape—to the Jarid and Sidi Mustafa's prosperous zawiya—should the political wheel of fortune turn in the wrong direction.

Muhammad b. 'Azzuz, the Rahmaniyya shaykh of Sidi Khalid, fought beside Bu Ziyan and his forces; yet when the movement appeared doomed late in 1849, he escaped from the besieged village and left Algeria for Tunisia, where his brother had already been residing for five years. In the beylik, Muhammad b. 'Azzuz assumed spiritual headship of the Rahmaniyya members in the region of al-Qayrawan. From the scanty evidence available, it seems that he joined his brother in endorsing Muhammad b. 'Abd Allah's movement by exhorting the family's clients back in the southern Constantine to jihad through the medium of letters and emissaries, a powerful form of moral persuasion.[96]

The case of Mustafa b. 'Azzuz's estranged brother, al-Mabruk, who had earlier made an assassination attempt upon Muhammad during a family quarrel, is indeed a bizarre story. Al-Mabruk (died 1890) further alienated the leading Rahmaniyya clans in Tulqa and al-Burj by eloping with the daughter of a locally prestigious lineage related through marriage to Sidi 'Ali b.'Uthman. Completely out of favor with his family and sufi peers, al-Mabruk took refuge with the Awlad Na'il tribe in the Bu Sa'ada region. There he passed himself off as a muqaddam of the Rahmaniyya until the news of Bu Ziyan's uprising reached him. After fighting with the insurgents in Za'atsha, al-Mabruk also managed to flee prior to the final showdown. From the Ziban, he traveled to al-Aghwat, then under the French-allied khalifa, Ahmad b. Salim, and created a small Rahmaniyya zawiya in the oasis. Early in 1852, as the sharif's campaign was raging in the area between Tuqqurt and the Ziban, al-Mabruk b. 'Azzuz submitted a written proposal to French authorities in the Constantine, soliciting an official pardon and the post of khalifa of Warqala. In exchange, he offered to defeat Muhammad b. 'Abd Allah, restore peace to the Sahara, and establish French hegemony in the Wadi Mya. Because of his shady reputation and past behavior, French military officials judiciously rejected his offer, also citing as reasons the anticolonial stance of other members of his clan. Undaunted, al-Mabruk on his own initiative enlisted with General Yusuf's native troops to take part in the 1852 siege of al-Aghwat. This apparently convinced French authorities that he could be of some use in imperial schemes. It was al-Mabruk b. 'Azzuz who later as a paid spy furnished the French in Biskra with intelligence about his older brother Mustafa. Among the information furnished by al-Mabruk was a report on Sidi Mustafa b. 'Azzuz's untiring efforts to promote the sharif's movement in the Jarid.[97]

Thus the earlier saintly quarrels—maraboutic politics—that rent the 'Azzuz of al-Burj during the turbulent 1840s era were paramount in subsequently shaping the political behavior of religious notables. Yet other forces dictated the political behavior of religious notables and desert communities.

Guns, Wheat, and Rebellion: The Suf

The orders incumbent upon 'Ali Bey b. Farhat, as newly appointed qa'id to the Suf, revealed not only colonial apprehensions about politics along the borders but also a growing appreciation of Tunisia's significance to Algerian insurrections. He was instructed to "ceaselessly keep abreast of the activities of Sliman b. Jallab and the sharif" by then safely in the beylik. By gathering news and rumors provided by the Suf's inhabitants, who traveled constantly between southern Tunisia and Algeria, 'Ali Bey was to assess the collective state of mind of the people. In addition, he was instructed to place spies in the oasis of Nafta, which had already proven instrumental to Algerian resistance.[98]

Even before he sought refuge in the beylik in December 1854, the sharif had dispatched agents to ports in southern Tunisia; there they acted as brokers between suppliers of arms and gunpowder from Mediterranean sources and the rebellion's supporters. One informant revealed that the sharif was negotiating the clandestine purchase of small cannon and siege craft from a French manufacturer through purveyors residing in Tunisia's coastal cities.[99] Islamic states on the Mediterranean's African shores had for centuries obtained armaments from various European powers. Yet in this period a significant difference emerged. The booming smuggling economy with its contraband networks permitted nonstate agents access to the instruments of warfare on a scale much larger than ever before. In this the Suf's inhabitants played a vital role as intermediaries due to the region's position astride the east-west trunk line linking the Mediterranean and the Jarid to the southern Constantine and Sahara.

Despite its small population, isolation, and meager resources, the Suf was pivotal to the larger checkerboard of desert politics and commerce for both Algeria and Tunisia.[100] Eight in number, the Suf's oases resembled Berber republics in terms of sociopolitical organization; its villages were divided into two warring camps of four each, according to saff loyalties. Yet when collective commercial interests were at stake, the Suwafa readily put aside, at least temporarily, age-old vendettas to engage in their preferred métier—trade.[101] The Suf's oases, whose inhabitants also provided indispensable services to caravans as guides and underwriters, acted as a desert pipeline for trade between southeastern Algeria and the sea.[102]

In addition, the region represented a haven for smugglers, rebels, and outlaws. This remained true even after the French army established nominal authority over the Suf in 1854 by driving the sharif of Warqala's movement over the border into the Jarid. Prior to this, however, the fortunes of the sharif's jihad were largely dictated by fluctuating economic conditions in these oases so close to the permeable borders with Tunisia.

The Suf's stance vis-à-vis France was ordained not by politics or religion but rather by commercial concerns, above all, by the availability of grain. For the region produced no cereals of its own and was forced to rely upon grains grown elsewhere. The incessant search for wheat and trading outlets involved the Suwafa in far-flung networks stretching into the Jarid, Nafzawa, and the Tunisian littoral, and as far south as Ghadamis and Ghat.[103] After 1844, the Suf's trading enterprises shifted perceptibly to take advantage of rapidly changing market conditions. The traffic in Tunisian grains, European arms and ammunition, and other items assumed increasing significance in the region's political economy. As one Bureaux Arabes officer remarked during the sharif's rebellion, "the economic interests of the Suwafa are in Tunis and in the markets of the Regency; this is the cause of their continual insubordination [to France]."[104] Thus, the Suf's peoples were consummate bet hedgers, largely due to the precarious ecological niche they occupied.

By 1852 military authorities in Biskra realized that the Suwafa's commercial activities posed serious political obstacles to colonial hegemony in this part of the Sahara. Such had been the case ever since Biskra's capture eight years earlier. While they had welcomed 'Abd al-Qadir's rebellious khalifa, Muhammad b. Ahmad al-Hajj, in al-Awad from 1844 on, the Suwafa had also made friendly overtures to colonial officials to forestall the closure of French-held markets to their merchants. Even as delegations of notables were dispatched periodically to Biskra to assure the Bureau Arabe of everlasting devotion, the Suf's oases were busy selling provisions to France's opponents. The small-time rebel and mahdi, Sharif Ahmad, who attempted to foment an insurrection among the Namamsha of the Awras, looked to the Suwafa for supplies as did Bu Ma'za in the mid-1840s. The colonial riposte—excluding the Suwafa from French-held markets, merely harmed commerce since it further diverted trade away from Algeria and toward Tunisia.[105]

In retaliation for support of the sharif's uprising, colonial officials closed Biskra's markets to the inhabitants of Warqala and Tuqqurt and declared the passages into the Tell off limits as well. Only the Suf remained to funnel grains, arms, and other commodities necessary for survival. Impelled as much by economic opportunity as ideological commitment, the Suf's merchants sent caravans to the sharif's camp loaded with grains and foodstuffs obtained from the Jarid. In this period the contraband arms traffic between southern Tunisia and eastern Algeria reached one of its peaks. Amply resupplied with the material components of populist protest, provided at a price by the Suf, the rebels again assumed the offensive in the spring of 1852 to take the coveted goal, Biskra. While the oasis remained firmly in French hands, the perfidy of the Suf's inhabitants was not lost on Biskra's military command.[106]

In 1852 the Suwafa had been caught red-handed once more—abetting the enemy. However, the most compelling element shaping their subsequent political behavior was the repeated failure of Tunisian grain harvests after 1852; with the beylik's supplies dwindling, and deprived of access to the Ziban's markets, the Suwafa were in straitened material circumstances. Forced by 1854 to chose between anticolonial resistance and assured food supplies, the Suf's people opted for submission to France. A huge war contribution was levied upon al-Awad, the most culpable oasis in the rebellion. Its wealthy inhabitants, prosperous from their myriad commercial dealing, including the arms trade, paid the indemnity in only two days. The solution that Captain Warnier and other Bureau Arabe officers proposed to ensure the Suf's political fealty was to reorient commercial relations away from Tunisia and solely toward the colony's domestic trade networks.[107]

Yet, until the French occupation of the Jarid in 1881–1882, the Suf eluded effective colonial control, remaining a desert stronghold for religious resistors, bandits, and smugglers. Moreover, its was the Suf's intimate connection with the beylik that drew both the sharif and French colonial authorities into southern Tunisia.

The Tunisian Phase, 1854–1856

Even prior to the terrible disaster at al-Aghwat late in 1852, Muhammad b. 'Abd Allah had made overtures to religious and secular notables in Tunisia. Responding favorably was Muhammad b. Abi 'Allag, chieftain of the redoubtable Tunisian tribe, the Awlad Ya'qub, who supplied the rebels with horsemen. Local Tunisian officials also helped the movement to endure as long as it did; their motivations were probably based upon Muslim solidarity as well as economic self-interest. When the self-proclaimed mahdi appeared briefly in the Jarid before his 1854 defeat in Algeria, Nafta's qa'id allowed him to purchase grains and sell some of his flocks in the oasis's markets. It was reported that the rebels disposed of considerable sums of money and hundreds of sheep and camels, probably obtained through razzias.

Elites in Tunis viewed the situation quite differently. Fearing French military reprisals, and perhaps unrest among his increasingly disaffected subjects in the south, Ahmad Bey directed General Zarruq to forbid officials in the Jarid from trafficking with Muhammad b. 'Abd Allah and Sliman b. Jallab. Nevertheless, the qa'id of Tuzar, 'Abd Allah b. Sudani, was on friendly terms with the rebels and extended some material assistance. Also sympathetic to their cause was the powerful Wirghimma (Ouerghemma) tribal confederacy of southeastern Tunisia.[108] Here it can be posited that local shows of support for Algerian agitators—against the wishes of ruling elites in Tunis—may have also been an implicit critique of Ahmad bey's centralizing program, which by the 1850s had created grave discontent.

During his 1853 trip, Tissot carefully noted the political orientation of the region's sedentary peoples and leading tribes toward the sharif's rebellion. The Tunisian tribes of the southwest were then undecided about which course of action to pursue—momentary neutrality or active, militant support for the insurrection. It was the latter option that French colonial authorities naturally feared most. The mahdi's presence along the frontiers and the emissaries and letters he dispatched to Tunisian political and religious notables inevitably churned up rumors and improvised news. Moreover, the outbreak of the Crimean War, in which Ahmad Bey participated by furnishing the Ottoman sultan with a military contingent, also provided additional grist for the rumor mill. In the beylik it was said that "the day has arrived when the flag of Islam must replace the images [suwar] of the Christians and Algeria will be delivered forever from the yoke of the infidels."[109]

A rare insight into how native Tunisians viewed the revolt is provided by al-Hajj al-Lus, a merchant from Sfax who traded frequently with the Suf's inhabitants. Returning to Gabis in April 1854 after a stay in al-Awad, al-Lus spread the news that the sharif had scored a spectacular victory over Algerian tribes allied to France. The rumor spread like wildfire and increased Muhammad b. 'Abd Allah's credibility in Tunisia, further fueling millenarian speculations about the arrival of the "Master of the Hour."[110] Many believed that the insurgents were undertaking another attack upon Biskra as the prelude to driving the French from North Africa. Since it was also rumored that Algeria's coastal cities were wanting in colonial troops, many Tunisians, including al-Hajj al-Lus, were convinced that the Ziban's capital would fall shortly to Muhammad b. 'Abd Allah. As our merchant from Sfax put it: "The moment has arrived to return Algeria to her rightful ruler, the Ottoman sultan."[111] Once again this interpretation of political events, based upon orally transmitted news, was a reflection not only of what ordinary people thought but also of what they believed should occur, given that France's occupation of Algeria violated the moral order of things. This incident also reveals how distant events—war in the Crimea—were integrated into local information networks far from the scene of battle.

Yet a sense of moral righteousness did not suffice; even mahdis needed adequate military technology to win the battle with the forces of darkness. During his commercial operations in al-Awad, al-Hajj al-Lus had met with Sliman b. Jallab to plan for a new phase in the jihad. The Tunisian trader agreed to furnish Sliman with five cannons for Tuqqurt's defense in exchange for specified sums of money. Unaware of Jean Mattei's ties to the French consulate in Tunis, al-Hajj al-Lus contacted the Frenchman in Gabis regarding a collaborative venture. Mattei was asked to use his commercial ties to trading concerns in Marseille to import cannons from France to Sfax through the usual Maltese smuggling channels. In return, Mattei would receive a finder's fee of one thousand Tunisian piasters and Sliman b. Jallab would acquire the desired artillery; we can only speculate about al-Lus's return from the deal had it succeeded. In addition, the Algerian rebel leaders commissioned al-Hajj al-Lus to dispose of a large cache of defective firearms in Gabis, the product of an earlier contraband arms deal which proved a scam. (Many of the rifles bought previously by the sharif lacked working parts, and the Algerians hoped to recoup losses by reselling the firearms in the Tunisian port.) While al-Hajj al-Lus's negotiations with Mattei never progressed beyond this point, the merchants did unwittingly provide more evidence regarding the trans-Mediterranean arms traffic.[112]

Tunisia was, therefore, progressively drawn into Algerian upheavals, the outcome of transformations occurring on both sides of the turbulent frontiers which by now encompassed the beylik's southern reaches. Growing discontent with the bey's fiscal exactions, popular resentment of European meddling in the country's internal affairs, and antipathy toward the French in neighboring Algeria were all connected in the collective political consensus. Moreover, Shaykh Mustafa b. 'Azzuz had made this connection explicit for ordinary people in 1851 when he publicly declared that the extraordinary taxes levied that year were due to nefarious French influence upon Ahmad Bey.[113] In addition, the swelling numbers of Algerian refugees in the beylik, religious solidarity with the beleaguered Muslims of the colony, and long-standing commercial and cultural links between eastern Algeria and Tunisia momentarily created a local political environment favorable to the sharif.

The Saint, the Sharif, and the Sultan

From his zawiya in the Jarid, Sidi Mustafa b. 'Azzuz persevered in encouraging political action across the frontier. More than any other Saharan Rahmaniyya notable of his generation, Sidi Mustafa steadfastly, although cautiously, opposed the colonial regime, in large measure because he now resided in a region where opposition could be undertaken with relative impunity. As seen in the preceding chapter, Shaykh 'Azzuz extended the sheltering mantle of the zawiya's sacred space to political dissidents from his native land. Even as early as the fall of 1851, when the sharif's movement began to crystallize, Sidi Mustafa and his ally, Muhammad b. Ahmad b. al-Hajj, the former shaykh of Sidi 'Uqba, openly sanctioned the mahdi's mission.[114]

A glimpse of how sufi notables viewed the sharif's rebellion—or how these notables portrayed that rebellion to others—is provided by a letter Mustafa b. 'Azzuz composed in 1851 as Muhammad b. 'Abd Allah's forces were poised for the assault upon Tuqqurt. Intercepted by colonial officials in Algeria and later submitted to the Tunisian bey, 'Azzuz's missive was accompanied by official protests regarding the iniquitous intrigues of sufi exiles under Husaynid protection. Writing to another sufi leader, still residing in southeastern Algeria, Shaykh 'Azzuz sought to dissuade him from fleeing to the beylik:

> We, the 'Azzuz, have received your letter. You say that you will come and seek refuge with us, that you can no longer live in the country of the infidels. However, you should know that a military contingent of infidels has arrived near Tunis, and that the bey has gone out to meet them; the bey massacred a great number of French and they are now completely encircled. Turkish soldiers will arrive from Tripoli and the East; Tunis is full of these soldiers who will march against the French. The rule of France is over and now the rule of the descendants of the Prophet [shurafa'] is approaching.
>
> You serve us where you are because before long we will advance with power and force to you. Send us a letter by means of the [sufi] brothers of Gummar and keep us informed of all the news regarding the French infidels. A mahdi has arisen in the West and he will march upon Tuqqurt; the brother of the Amir 'Abd al-Qadir is near al-Kaf. Destroy this letter as soon as you receive it.[115]

What sorts of information can be teased from this letter, one of the few indigenous sources available from the period of the sharif's rebellion? First, it indicates that even those sufi leaders who had elected to remain in Algeria, for whatever reasons, were far from reconciled to colonial domination and were considering emigration to escape foreign rule. While the identity of the tariqa notable with whom Sidi 'Azzuz was corresponding is not clear, the mention of the village of Gummar in the Suf, the site of an important Tijaniyya zawiya, suggests that Shaykh Mustafa was writing to Sidi Muhammad b. al-'Id. As discussed above, in 1851 the Tijaniyya leadership of the Suf was uncertain about which stance to assume toward both the sharif's jihad and the colonial regime. Thus, Sidi 'Azzuz's letter may have been intended to persuade Shaykh Muhammad b. al-'Id (if indeed he was the intended recipient) to be patient—succor was on the way.

Second, the letter reveals that Sidi Mustafa b. 'Azzuz not only subscribed to popular mahdist expectations, then at their zenith in North Africa, but also that the sufi network served to reinforce those expectations by disseminating them among elites and the humble alike. At the same time, 'Azzuz requested that his sufi peer keep him informed of French activities in Algeria, another indication that the sufi zawaya functioned as information catchments as well as news distributors. The mention of 'Abd al-Qadir's brother suggests that many still looked to the amir's family for leadership, although at this time the amir was a prisoner in France; his brother was certainly not in al-Kaf. Related to this are the rumors regarding imminent deliverance by the Ottoman sultan and the bey of Tunis, which being contained in a missive from a powerful saint and sufi must have sustained hopes of outside assistance among the Algerian populace. This too is significant. The Algerians viewed the coming struggle against the Europeans as a confrontation necessitating military and ideological sustenance from other Muslim rulers to achieve the final victory.

Nevertheless, the letter raises an additional issue—did Shaykh 'Azzuz create "facts" or events as well as explain and interpret them? The year when the letter was written—1851—saw no infidel armies arriving in Tunis, even less so any military engagements between the Tunisian forces and the French. Quite the contrary, by then Ahmad Bey's modern army, forged largely with France's technological and organizational assistance, had peaked in strength, reaching nearly seventeen thousand men in 1852. Whether the increased military activity in northern Tunisia consequent to the building of the new army was construed by religious notables in the provinces as preparation for delivering the Algerians from colonial oppression is uncertain, but the question needs to be raised. On the other hand, this piece of improvised news may represent the kinds of ideal political behavior that religious notables expected from pious Muslims rulers after the true mahdi had made his appearance. Finally, the letter hints at the sort of social order which both ordinary people and elites anticipated after the redeemer's advent in time. His appearance would establish "rule by the Prophet's descendants"—the restoration of a religiopolitical golden age in which the "reign of God will commence."[116]

Sidi Mustafa b. 'Azzuz's involvement in the sharif's insurrection naturally did not go unnoticed by those at the pinnacle of the colonial regime. In November 1851, the governor-general of Algeria wrote to the French consul in Tunis concerning the intrigues of "certain individuals in the Jarid who attempt through the dissemination of false news spread about in the Ziban to exhort the people to rebellion. We have acquired proof of Shaykh 'Azzuz's political activities by means of his letters."[117] Subsequently Ahmad Bey came under heavy diplomatic fire from French officials in both Tunisia and Algeria to halt 'Azzuz's participation in across-the-border revolt. Accordingly in December 1851 the bey dispatched Ahmad Zarruq, the governor of the Jarid, to the Rahmaniyya zawiya in Nafta to inform (and perhaps warn) Sidi Mustafa of French accusations. Despite the immense pressures brought to bear upon the Tunisian ruler, the bey, out of deference for the sufi shaykh, refused to take action against him and, as seen in chapter 5, appears to have shielded 'Azzuz and other Algerian émigrés from French reprisals.[118]

In the 1851–1855 rebellion, therefore, Shaykh 'Azzuz's role was to undergird Muhammad b. 'Abd Allah's claims to mahdihood by allowing the sharif to tap into Sidi Mustafa's own large fund of spiritual legitimacy. Another part played by the Rahmaniyya shaykh was to goad ordinary people to action under the redeemer's banner. Yet the sufi leader preferred to work mainly from behind the scenes to mobilize and sustain collective protest. There is no indication that 'Azzuz returned to Algerian soil nor did he himself lead armed warrior bands, either in the colony or in Tunisia. But then leading a rebellion was something that few sufi shaykhs—Rahmaniyya or otherwise—actually did. That honor was left to the sharif and Sliman b. Jallab with whom Sidi Mustafa corresponded (as evidenced by seizures of letters) prior to their flight into the beylik. After their hijra to the Jarid late in 1854, the Rahmaniyya shaykh continued to lend his great moral and spiritual weight to the jihad.

Upon reaching Tunisia, Muhammad b. 'Abd Allah and Sliman b. Jallab set about rebuilding their shattered movement. One of the first things that the former sultan of Tuqqurt did was to contact the new bey of Tunis, Muhammad, who came to the throne in May 1855. Sliman's letters to the Husaynid ruler reveal how the exiles viewed their situation—or at least how they wanted the bey to see their plight.

> We have left our territory of Tuqqurt and we came to settle in the Nafzawa under God's protection and yours. We have always been under the tutelage of your throne. This country [Tunisia] is equally ours; we are your children and the father does not abandon his son. We beg you to take care of our interests; . . . the French have expelled the members of our family [from Algeria] without cause.[119]

Since the Jarid was deemed too close to the Suf, by then under French military occupation, the rebels selected as their Tunisian headquarters the Nafzawa, a no-man's-land of small oases lost in the protective arms of the shatt al-Jarid. From Nafta, directly linked to the Nafzawa by trails, Sidi Mustafa provided material and moral-ideological support, supplying the Algerians with badly needed armaments and provisions. Shaykh 'Azzuz had been involved in the trans-Mediterranean trade in firearms, and particularly in gunpowder, for several years. And the commerce in British gunpowder was brisk in the 1850s since general Algerian demand, the sharif's insurrection, and colonial efforts to impede the traffic had caused contraband prices to skyrocket. The black market price tag for one hundred kilograms of gunpowder had increased 100 percent, from 200 to 400 piasters in the Suf and southern Tunisia.[120] By 1855, Muhammad b.

Ahmad b. al-Hajj also acted as an arms dealer. He procured weapons and gunpowder from Malta via the port of Jirba, a favored haunt for smugglers since the town's customs officials were decidedly less than vigilant. The munitions were then transported by camel caravan to the Nafzawa, where the sharif was collecting military hardware for yet another attack upon Algeria.[121]

By June 1855, spies in the pay of France reported that the word-of-mouth news circuits were bristling with rumors about the insurgents. According to one version, the Jarid's people anticipated the arrival of the great shaykh of the Sanusiyya order from Cyrenaica, accompanied this time by a large contingent of Moroccan troops who were making their way to southern Tunisia. Another version held that the Tijaniyya shaykh of Tammasin had sent thousands of religious clients from the Suf across the borders into the Nafzawa to assist the sharif militarily. Yet another said that "the mahdi is now camped in Sahala, some thirty kilometers south of the Nafzawa along with Nasir b. Shuhra, his most devoted ally. The shaykh of Nafta, Mustafa b. 'Azzuz is of great utility to the sharif and his cause."[122]

While once again the rumors of outside help were collective expressions of wishful thinking—of how things ought to be—there was at least a grain of truth to the news. In preparing for the projected attack, Mustafa b. 'Azzuz chose to play an extensive part in popular mobilization. Addressing a large crowd of followers, he urged them to join the jihad, whose immediate objective was to amass sufficient manpower for a strike upon the Suf-Tuqqurt regions. Wielding redoubtable power over words, underwritten by immense religious prestige, Shaykh Mustafa convinced a number of Tunisian tribesmen to enroll at least temporarily under the sharif's banner.[123]

The attack planned for that year came to naught, however, for reasons that even a powerful saint and sufi like Sidi Mustafa was powerless to overcome. Due to the hardships of exile, and a nomadic existence devoid of the comforts of sedentary life, the Algerian rebel leaders' enthusiasm for rebellion was waning. Sliman b. Jallab, an aristocratic urban notable by birth and upbringing, soon wearied of camping in the Nafzawa and secretly contacted French officials to request an official pardon. His emissaries to Algiers and Constantine were rebuffed by colonial authorities, whose response was "you have followed the sharif, whatever you do we will not accept you." At the same time, Sliman wrote to the bey of Tunis begging him "to give us a small area in which to reside in tranquillity because we are city dwellers and can not move from place to place like bedouins."[124]

The shaykh of Sidi 'Uqba, Muhammad b. Ahmad b. al-Hajj, in theory allied with the sharif, also covertly negotiated with French diplomats in

Tunis for permission to travel to Syria and join the Amir 'Abd al-Qadir, by then residing in Damascus. In his letter to Léon Roches, the shaykh wrote: "We are like feathers torn from the wing of Sidi al-Hajj 'Abd al-Qadir." Before his request was granted, Muhammad b. Ahmad b. al-Hajj died of an unknown malady in Nafta at the zawiya of Shaykh 'Azzuz, where he and his family had sought asylum. The sharif himself was engaged in heavy bet hedging mainly because his ignorance of Tunisian tribal politics and saff alignments prevented him from putting together a solid coalition. As elite and popular enthusiasm for Algerian rebellion gradually waned, the mahdi himself made clandestine gestures to French officials; in exchange for being named qa'id of Warqala, Muhammad b. 'Abd Allah offered his public submission to France.[125]

While the rumors of impending revolt were much more enduring than collective protest itself, the disturbing hearsay from southern Tunisia and the border regions finally forced colonial officials into action. Now it was said that the sharif would join forces with the Sanusiyya shaykh heading for the Jarid or, in another variant, coming from Mecca to wage jihad in the beylik. Public opinion also believed that Algerian and Tunisian combatants were massed along the frontiers; once the reconquest had begun, tribal allies of France would defect to the mahdi, clearing the way for the march upon Tuqqurt. There the sharif would be hailed as a savior by the people: "It will be easy to plant the flag of Islam in Algeria, for the hour has come when the cross must bow down before the crescent."[126]

This more than anything caused General Desvaux, then in the Suf, to deploy mobile columns along the frontiers as a warning of France's resolve to maintain order. The presence of the troops terrorized the Jarid's population; letters were sent to the bey imploring his protection against the "Christian" invasion believed by many to be impending.[127] This perceived threat eroded popular sympathy for the sharif's movement in southern Tunisia as did generalized economic tribulations. These factors provoked a profound transformation within the sharif's movement. As conditions deteriorated on both sides of the borders, the redemptive banner of the mahdi gave way to tribal razzias and banditry directed against the very constituency which the mahdi hoped to coax into his jihad.

The End: From Mahdi to Bandit

Adverse socioeconomic conjunctures are frequently invoked as contributing or even key factors in the emergence of collective protest. Yet adversity can also act as a brake upon political action, particularly in the unforgiving desert. Deprived of Biskra's markets, the rebels had come to depend upon

Tunisia for arms, gunpowder, and grains. Indeed, the material assistance provided by the Jarid's oases prompted Governor-General Randon to demand that Ahmad Bey prohibit grain sales to Algerian dissidents in 1854 and to intern Muhammad b. 'Abd Allah away from the borders.[128] By then state restrictions on grain exports were largely unnecessary since the Tunisian harvest had failed once more and domestic demand went unmet. From 1854 on, oasis dwellers and pastoralists in the pre-Sahara were beset by calamities, including diseases that decimated herds and flocks, and torrential fall rains that totally destroyed the date harvest. This in turn upset the wool trade. Native merchants, who had unwisely sold advance promises of wool shipments to European dealers, were unable to meet their obligations and fell increasingly into debt. To compound commercial difficulties, attacks by bandits and tribes increased as conditions worsened, which in turn depressed the caravan trade; merchants, pilgrims,and travelers dared not venture into the south.[129]

The following years were scarcely more propitious for popular protest either in the beylik or the southern Constantine. In 1855, the sirocco destroyed cereals in the region from Batna to Biskra, and date yields in the Ziban and Wadi Righ proved exceptionally poor the next year. Cholera once again broke out along the borders. As drought and disease ravaged the pre-Sahara, bands of tribesmen from the Arba'a abandoned the sharif and retraced their steps to French-ruled territory.[130]

Thus, economic afflictions suffered in Tunisia caused the jihad to sputter to an inconclusive end. By 1855, many in southern Tunisia were too preoccupied with subsistence and survival to risk political ventures in Algeria. And any semblance of unity among the Algerian rebels had evaporated as they scrambled to eke out a precarious existence. Nasir b. Shuhra, along with his family and a few loyal tribal members deemed too compromised to return to Algeria, sought refuge with Shaykh Mustafa b. 'Azzuz in Nafta. The oasis's inhabitants, however, viewed them as troublemakers who might draw colonial forces or the bey's army into the Jarid and whose raids upon caravans had disrupted commerce. Hostilities between the exiles and Nafta's populace erupted in May 1856; fighting was averted only when Sidi Mustafa intervened to restore peace. The Rahmaniyya shaykh was called upon to induce the unwelcome guests to leave the Jarid, although Nasir b. Shuhra and his followers continued their raids, upsetting trade in the south for another decade until their capture by the bey's army.[131]

After taking refuge in Tuzar, where he owned date-palm gardens, the hapless Sliman b. Jallab was forced by the qa'id to travel to Tunis under armed escort in November 1856. Harassed by French officials beyond the limits of his endurance, Muhammad Bey ordered the former sultan's removal from the politically tempting borders. In a burst of hospitality, Sliman was at first accorded a generous subsidy by the Tunisian ruler. However, the Saharan prince fell upon evil days in the capital, drinking to excess, keeping dubious company, and squandering his beylical pension. Infuriated by his conduct, the bey withdrew financial support for Sliman, who ended his days in abject penury.[132]

Muhammad b. 'Abd Allah fared somewhat better than his compatriot in arms. In 1856, he too was finally persuaded by the bey to live under house arrest in Tunis. There the sharif remained for two years until he managed to escape from captivity by fleeing to Tripolitania. Disappointed by the lack of revolutionary fervor in that part of the Maghrib, the mahdi spent the next years in ceaseless peregrinations throughout the deep Sahara, the only area remaining outside of French colonial control. Near Ain Salah, he succeeded in building a tribal following among the Tuareg, who abetted him in raids and banditry directed against tribal groups allied with France. In 1861, Muhammad b. 'Abd Allah appeared once again in the Warqala region at the head of tribal contingencies drawn from the rebellious Sha'amba. Taken by the French army after a brief skirmish, the sharif was interned in Oran at first, then sent to France for measures of security. However, while confined to the fortress in Perpignan, his health deteriorated to the point that colonial authorities permitted him to return to Algeria to die in 1863.[133]

For two years (1855–1856), the sharif had proposed a Tunisian solution—men and supplies—for Algerian problems. At first some were willing to associate with his jihad, particularly due to Sidi Mustafa's urging, which coincided with deeply felt millenarian expectations. Nevertheless, unfavorable economic circumstances, the crumbling of the movement's core leadership, and the sharif's unfamiliarity with local political realities caused a steady erosion of popular identification with the jihad. And failure to score a victory worthy of the "Master of the Hour" inevitably raised questions about the mahdi himself. Had Muhammad b. 'Abd Allah's program included measures to alleviate distress among the beylik's southern peoples, mainly caused by intolerable state fiscal demands, then perhaps he might have created a stable, sustained popular base of support.

Ironically, the hijra to Tunisia, while providing a political haven, had placed the sharif in a contradictory situation. For if he needed to convince the bey's subjects to support the insurgency, Muhammad b. 'Abd Allah could not risk arousing the bey's ire. In turn the Husaynid prince could not affront his vastly more powerful European neighbor, who often served as Tunisia's patron in its dealings with the other Great Powers. As for ordinary people in Tunisia, most preferred to speculate and talk endlessly about this particular mahdi rather than fight with him. The redeemer as a legendary folk hero, whose calls to arms might be answered if the time was right, was ultimately overshadowed by the legend itself, or by the rumors constructed around that tradition.

However, the memory of the Sharif of Warqala, like that of Bu Ziyan, remained alive among the Sahara's populations and the people of southern Tunisia. In July 1865 the inhabitants of the recalcitrant port city of Sfax were much preoccupied with the news of a mahdist-led insurrection in Tuqqurt, a completely unfounded rumor connected to the great 1864 uprising in Tunisia and the ensuing central government repression. This suggests that the rebellion of a decade earlier still informed the popular collective memory. During the 1871 Muqrani revolt in the northern Constantine, another mahdist rebel arose in the Algerian Sahara and was accorded an enthusiastic reception in Warqala and Tuqqurt. Muhammad b. Tuni b. Ibrahim, or Bu Shusha (Bou Choucha) as he was called by his cohorts, purported to be the son of Muhammad b. 'Abd Allah. Such a claim indicates that in the popular mind at least, the social production of revolutionary mahdis, like saints and descendants of the prophets, was believed governed by the genealogical principle. For a brief period, Warqala's inhabitants proclaimed Bu Shusha their sultan in place of the French-appointed shaykh, which was tantamount to a declaration of revolt in the eyes of the colonial regime. General de Lacroix-Vaubois chased the would-be redeemer from the oasis in January 1872. As a punishment and an example to the rest of the desert's peoples, Warqala's residents were heavily fined and part of their city razed.[134]

Mustafa b. 'Azzuz continued to harbor dissidents from Algeria in his zawiya until the eve of his death in 1866. In 1861 a small-scale uprising erupted in al-Aghwat and moved northward into areas of European settler colonialism. The movement's leader, Tayyib b. Shanduqa, led a handful of rebels in a nighttime attack upon a pied-noir village near Djelfa. After killing several farmers, the group was beaten back by the French military. Shanduqa and his band subsequently fled over the border to seek refuge with Sidi Mustafa in the Jarid. A French-paid native emissary was dispatched to Nafta to search for Shanduqa and, discovering him at the Rahmaniyya center, requested that the saint hand the rebel over to French officials. Sidi 'Azzuz refused to violate the zawiya's traditional role as sanctuary and was upheld by a large throng of Rahmaniyya brothers who gathered in the courtyard to shield their sufi master from vexation. To protect Shanduqa from the French and spare the aging Sidi Mustafa, the Rahmaniyya disciples conducted the Algerian rebels to the camp of Nasir

b. Shuhra, still based in the Nafzawa, where they were accorded protection. In addition to Shanduqa and his band, also present at the Nafta zawiya were other Algerian political figures and an English spy, gathering sub rosa information on French taxation in Algeria for the British government.[135]

With the demise of the sharif's insurrection, Sidi Mustafa b. 'Azzuz appears to have eschewed active, direct involvement in revolt across the borders. In 1864 he would—paradoxically—work to quell popular discontent in the beylik to shore up the Husaynid regime's crumbling legitimacy. Nevertheless, so closely did 'Azzuz become associated with the sharif's rebellion that seventy-five years later some colonial authorities mistakenly transformed the Rahmaniyya leader into Muhammad b. 'Abd Allah himself. In a letter addressed to the resident-general of Tunisia in 1930, Algeria's governor-general wrote that "in 1851, Mustafa b. 'Azzuz left the Jarid and set about conquering the southern Constantine; he took the name Muhammad ibn 'Abd Allah and proclaimed himself the mahdi; he exerted domination over the south [of Algeria] until 1854 at which time he returned to the Jarid."[136] Thus, even modern colonial bureaucracies were nourished by legends and improvised news in the same way that the political and military activities of these same authorities gave rise to interminable speculation and rumormongering.

Conclusion

Seeking to block the French advance and expel the Europeans, the sharif's movement pushed the turbulent frontier deeper into the Sahara and across the borders into Tunisia. If his early partisans believed they were defending their homeland from the indignities of foreign rule, participation in jihad enhanced French hegemony rather than alleviated it. Paradoxically, Muhammad b. 'Abd Allah's claims to be a pious stranger from the East had formed the bedrock of his early popular following. Yet the fact that he hailed from the urbanized western Tell, and was thus unfamiliar with desert politics, caused his movement to falter. And military ineptness caused many of his initial promoters to doubt the authenticity of his mahdist credentials and to defect from the rebellion. Once in Tunisia, Muhammad b. 'Abd Allah's ignorance of the beylik's complex political alignments impeded his ability to reconstruct a lasting tribal following.

Although unfavorable economic conjunctures worked to circumscribe the sharif's jihad, it also failed for lack of sustained support from Saharan sufi notables, who in any case could not overcome the ecological constraints upon political action dictated by the unforgiving desert environment. The diffident, minimal role played by sufi notables, whether Rahmaniyya or Tijaniyya, in the sharif's jihad demonstrates that the political stance of many desert sufi leaders toward France was largely determined as early as the 1849 revolt. The terrible lessons of Za'atsha were sufficient to discourage large-scale violent confrontations with the colonial regime—at least in the Ziban. Pragmatism and realpolitik—not wild-eyed "fanaticism"—were the operative principles shaping the political behavior of most religious notables.

Even as insurrection gave way to various forms of avoidance protest, other modes of coping came to the foreground. As France's resolve to retain her African department became painfully clear and European settlers poured into Algeria, some Rahmaniyya leaders were parties to informal, implicit pacts. Gradually worked out between local colonial representatives and religious notables, these complex, subtle agreements constituted perhaps the most important consequence of Za'atsha and the sharif's failed jihad. This is seen in the cases of Shaykh 'Ali b. 'Uthman of Tulqa and, above all, the Rahmaniyya zawiya of al-Hamil, which by the century's end overshadowed all other Rahmaniyya establishments in Algeria and Tunisia. Sidi Muhammad b. Abi al-Qasim's chosen course of action combined a special kind of religious and social activism with political retreat and compromise. And apparent withdrawal more than anything shielded part of Algeria's cultural patrimony from the devastating force of triumphant settler colonialism.

7 The Shaykh and His Daughter

Implicit Pacts and Cultural Survival, c. 1827–1904

Drink deeply of science.[1]

Bu Ziyan's demise, the unraveling of the Sharif of Warqala's jihad, and the defeat of the Kabylia imposed other modes of political behavior upon religious notables in Algeria. After mid-century, sufi leaders and saintly lineages in areas under direct, or even indirect, colonial rule wavered between various forms of submission, accommodation, evasion, and resistance; survival demanded such. While emigration in the pre-1881 era was one option, it carried both penalties and rewards. If those Algerians who migrated to Tunisia, Morocco, or the Levant enjoyed the moral-religious comfort of residing in Islamic states, they faced the social adversities that all immigrants perforce suffer. After the imposition of the French protectorate upon Tunisia in 1881, even those with the will or means to emigrate found physical evasion increasingly difficult as the frontiers between the Maghribi countries were more efficiently policed. Nevertheless, some religious notables, including members of the 'Azzuz clan, departed Tunisia after 1881 for Istanbul or the Mashriq, where they frequently engaged in anti-French activities from afar.[2] And if hijra from Algeria to Tunisia proved riskier by the century's end, the beylik provided other sorts of refuge—intellectual and spiritual—for Algerian literati. In Tunis they were relatively freer to publish religious works and pursue Islamic studies. Of course, the Moroccan borders were still porous enough to permit some migration, whether clandestine or otherwise, although long before 1912, parts of Morocco were gradually absorbed into France's expanding empire. The years 1910–1911 witnessed several waves of mass departures from Tilimsan, much to the dismay of colonial authorities.[3]

The slow hemorrhaging of human resources, which migration represented, eroded Algeria's core of learned activists, great families, and religious notables. This imposed a heavier burden upon religious leaders

214

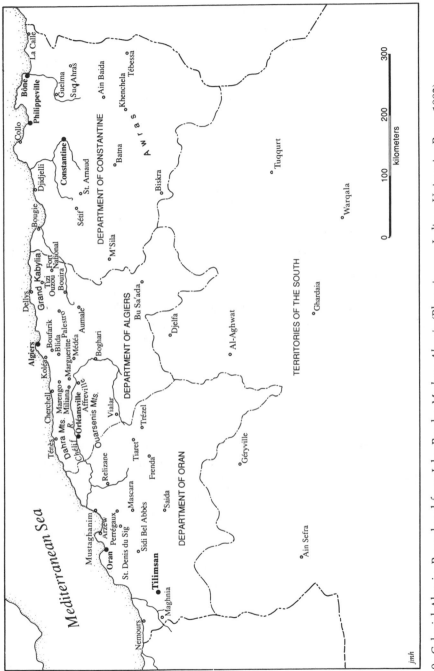

9. Colonial Algeria. Reproduced from John Ruedy, *Modern Algeria* (Bloomington: Indiana University Press, 1992), by permission of Indiana University Press.

electing to remain, for the sociospiritual services they provided were greatly oversubscribed. Nevertheless, the passing of the conquest era opened new avenues for some religious notables, including women, to engage in low-level political maneuvering to achieve limited cultural autonomy. For those who stayed in the colony, internal evasion or interior hijra represented a means of coping and therefore of endurance—*sauve-garde*, to use Jacques Berque's felicitous term.[4] And while safeguarding and preserving North African society demanded a measure of *inkimash* (withdrawal, retreat), this did not mean political passivity or social lassitude, far from it.

If a special type of salvation had earlier been expected from the mahdi, cultural salvation came to be the life's work of a few highly visible religious figures. Nothing proves this more than the biographies of the shaykh of al-Hamil and his daughter, Zaynab, whose lives span seventy-five years of Algeria's most turbulent history, from the twilight of Turkish rule to the eve of the nationalist movement.

Shaykh Muhammad b. Abi al-Qasim's (1823–1897) strategies for survival, and those of his successor, Lalla Zaynab (c. 1850–1904), did not constitute a total rupture with the past. Rather their mode of political adjustment resulted from a pragmatic assessment of the prospects for certain kinds of social action, based upon a reading of how and why earlier stratagems had failed. In this sense, they forged a new path. In a war of cultures, cultural weapons—and not militant opposition—proved the most formidable defense. And one of the most intrepid warriors in this bloodless battle was a woman, precisely because the colonial edifice was conceived of as an imperial man's world. While the colonial order had evolved a formidable arsenal of methods for containing unsubmissive Algerian men, it had few, if any, to repress rebellious females. Indeed, contrary to what is frequently asserted—that colonized women lost power and status—it can be argued that the contradictions of the French regime offered opportunities, under certain conditions, for women to offer nonviolent resistance.[5] Thus, Zaynab's confrontation with French authorities indicates that women could be political agents as well as social actors even in a system of dual patriarchy. "But it is principally her audacity that renders this woman remarkable," observed Zaynab's main opponent within French officialdom.[6]

The Zawiya of al-Hamil: Upon a Great Rose-Brown Mountain

The oasis of al-Hamil is located some twelve kilometers to the southwest of the market town of Bu Sa'ada, which, for colonial strategists, represented little else than a military station used to defend the Tell. Aside from Bu Sa'ada's garrison, few French civilians resided permanently there since the lack of cultivable land and the indigenous system of land tenure excluded settler colonialism.[7] If Bu Sa'ada was on the margins of the colonial state, al-Hamil was even more so; no Europeans inhabited the oasis, and foreign travelers through the region were infrequent before 1897. Thus al-Hamil offered the advantage of relative isolation, a space where Muslim society, then under cultural siege, could protect itself against the noxious effects of *Algérie Française.*[8]

Those few Europeans who visited the Rahmaniyya zawiya in al-Hamil before 1897 were inevitably surprised by its appearance. The village, constructed of dun-shaded mud brick, sat upon "a great rose-brown mountain" in the barren foothills of the Saharan Atlas. The square white minaret of the mosque adjacent to the zawiya formed the town's highest point. Not far away the wadi, which funneled water to the date-palm groves below, snaked down the side of the mountain. The sufi center was of recent construction, having been founded only in 1863; like other desert zawaya, it resembled a fortress.[9] By the close of the nineteenth century, thousands of pilgrims, scholars, students, and the needy flocked to the zawiya from all over Algeria and the Maghrib for it provided religious, cultural, and socioeconomic services not readily available elsewhere. Moreover, the life-giving waters of the wadi permitted agrarian development to feed the oasis's expanding population.

Al-Hamil's popularity as a pilgrimage site and educational center was due to the Rahmaniyya zawiya, which boasted a prestigious madrasa and a fine library, whose rich manuscript collection represented a significant portion of North Africa's cultural patrimony.[10] The Rahmaniyya complex was the work of Sidi Muhammad b. Abi al-Qasim, one of the most powerful saints, mystics, and scholars to emerge from the Rahmaniyya movement. Because of Shaykh Muhammad's piety, baraka, erudition, and unstinting generosity, the zawiya commanded a huge popular and elite following.[11] Moreover, the oasis attracted not only the living but also those nearing the end of their days. The village's relatively small size was accentuated by the vast burial grounds encircling it. From far away, Muslim families came to bury their dead and fulfill the deceased's last wish. Al-Hamil's cemeteries betrayed its moral importance. And the desire to retreat in death to a space untainted by the humiliations of foreign conquest produced the mass of tombs, qubbas, and simple graves, sheltering North Africans of all social ranks and ages.[12]

By the late nineteenth century, Sidi Muhammad claimed the single largest number of Rahmaniyya sufi clients in Algeria, which made him a spiritual power to be reckoned with by colonial authorities ever mindful of the threat of revolt. His equally pious and saintly daughter, Lalla Zaynab, inherited her father's clientele and control of the zawiya but only after a determined struggle with military officials to assert her rights to spiritual succession.

Shaykh Muhammad b. Abi al-Qasim: Cultural Survival and Implicit Pacts

Sidi Muhammad was from the Awlad Laghwini of the Jabal Tastara in the Bu Sa'ada region. His was a minor clan of ashraf, and sharifian descent could be a potent source of socioreligious authority if parlayed in the right manner. Another source of prestige was his lineage's reputed creation of al-Hamil through the performance of a miracle. According to popular lore, Sidi Muhammad's saintly ancestors arrived in the region many centuries earlier from Morocco as wandering holy men, thus the oasis's name "al-Hamil," or "errant." Sidi 'Abd al-Rahman b. 'Ayub thrust his walking stick into the arid soil and, upon extracting it, discovered to his amazement that verdant mulberry leaves tree covered the staff. This miraculous event was taken both as a sign of al-Hamil's sacredness and of the family's supernatural powers.[13] However, the translocal spiritual influence wielded by Shaykh Muhammad b. Abi al-Qasim in later centuries was the product of religious knowledge, good works, the miracles attributed to him by his disciples, and his leadership position within the Saharan Rahmaniyya hierarchy.

The future Rahmaniyya leader's early education was typical for local saintly lineages in the period. He began his religious studies under his father's direction and was "beginning to learn the Quran by heart" as a very small child when the French army landed in July 1830.[14] Since the Kabylia was one of the last areas subjugated, Sidi Muhammad was subsequently sent to northern Algeria for more advanced learning at the zawiya of the Awlad Sidi b. Da'ud near Akbou; there he mastered Muslim law, theology, and Arabic grammar.[15] In addition, the Kabyle Mountains constituted the religious hub for the Rahmaniyya tariqa, whose founder-saint had died only a half century earlier. It is uncertain whether Shaykh Muhammad was initiated into the Rahmaniyya order while in the Kabylia or later. However, his father had performed the ziyara to the zawiya of Sidi 'Ali b. 'Umar in Tulqa sometime before 1842. Thus, the shaykh's clan had ties to Rahmaniyya centers and lineages in the Ziban, including the 'Azzuz family of al-Burj.[16]

Sometime before the fateful 1848–1849 period and Bu Ziyan's uprising, Sidi Muhammad returned to al-Hamil, long regarded as a holy place.[17] The

fact that the small oasis was spared from colonial interference rendered it
all the more appealing. At the same time, its location on routes connecting
Bu Sa'ada with both the Tell and Sahara linked al-Hamil to vital markets
as well as providing pilgrims and students from the Kabylia, Constantine,
and the desert easy access to the oasis. In al-Hamil, Sidi Muhammad
founded a madrasa, began family life, and was endowed with the ability
to work miracles.

Supernatural gifts operated both to create and confirm piety and holiness; thus the saintly personage was at once the cause and consequence of
the divine marvel. Three miracles from this period in Muhammad b. Abi
al-Qasim's adult life are particularly revealing of the primary values of his
society and of the virtues ascribed to him by his followers. On one occasion,
the saint succeeded in warding off the devil, who had vainly attempted to
enter his chamber to tempt him with the glamour of evil. On another, the
oil reading lamp in the saint's study defied the laws of gravity, levitating
in the air. Finally, and most significantly, the holy man was visited by the
Prophet Muhammad one night in the course of a dream-vision.[18] Moral
probity, sacred knowledge, and personal piety—virtues that were ratified
by the Prophet's appearance—were qualities demanded of the holy person,
who thereby became the object of collective popular veneration and sup-
plication. By the middle of the past century, Sidi Muhammad's saintly
reputation attracted disciples from Bu Sa'ada's environs as well as more
distant regions.

The years 1849–1850 witnessed major political transformations in the
upper reaches of the Sahara which deeply affected local religious notables
and their disciples. Bu Ziyan's uprising provoked a small-scale revolt within
the oasis of Bu Sa'ada and among the surrounding Awlad Na'il. Terrorized
by the bloody repression of Za'atsha, Bu Sa'ada's inhabitants sued for peace
late in 1849; soon thereafter a fort and a Bureau Arabe, with all the
administrative paraphernalia of a military headquarters, were constructed
in the town. Several years later, despite the concerted attempts made by
Muhammad b. 'Abd Allah to lure Bu Sa'ada into his insurrection, its people
assumed a wait-and-see stance, largely due to the formidable military
presence there.[19] In this tumultuous period, Shaykh Muhammad b. Abi
al-Qasim remained largely unscathed by the larger, more ominous forces
around him, although he drew some important lessons from the experiences of his religious peers elsewhere in Algeria, including 'Abd al-Qadir.[20]

In 1857, he left al-Hamil for the Rahmaniyya zawiya of Awlad Jallal in
the Ziban, where he studied under the spiritual direction of Shaykh al-
Mukhtar b. 'Abd al-Rahman b. Khalifa, then nearing the end of his days.[21]
Also present at the zawiya was Sidi Mabruk b. Muhammad b. 'Azzuz,

Mustafa's brother with whom Muhammad b. Abi al-Qasim established a lasting friendship.[22] Shaykh al-Mukhtar initiated Muhammad b. Abi al-Qasim into the Rahmaniyya way; by the time of the master's death in 1862, he had become his closest sufi intimate, even inheriting Sidi al-Mukhtar's baraka. In addition, Sidi Muhammad was entrusted by his spiritual preceptor with the zawiya's administration and the education of Sidi al-Mukhtar's young sons. His stewardship of this zawiya lasted for only a year since some disgruntled family members looked askance at the succession passing to an individual from outside the lineage.[23] Apparently unfazed by the ill-will shown him, Shaykh Muhammad left the Ziban in 1862–1863 to return to al-Hamil, where he founded an independent Rahmaniyya center, using the older madrasa as its nucleus. He also claimed possession of Sidi al-Mukhtar's baraka, an enormous source of social legitimacy and spiritual authority. Soon the Rahmaniyya zawiya of al-Hamil rivaled the older establishments in the Ziban.[24]

Significantly, Sidi Muhammad created the earlier madrasa in al-Hamil in the wake of the region's first large-scale anticolonial uprisings. After the 1854 defeat of the Sharif of Warqala's jihad, a decade of uneasy calm descended upon much of the Sahara until the great Awlad Sidi al-Shaykh movement of 1864. Nevertheless, in the nearby Awras, the shaykh of Sidi Masmudi, Sadiq b. al-Hajj, led the tribesmen in the millenarian revolt of 1858–1859 which brought the Rahmaniyya zawiya's destruction at the hands of General Desvaux and the shaykh's exile and imprisonment in France.[25]

A similar fate awaited the great zawiya attached to the shrine of Sidi 'Abd al-Rahman in the Kabylia. After the Kabyles were crushed in the late 1850s, the zawiya's lands were sequestered by the colonial regime, resulting in the sufi center's ruin as its educational, religious, and social functions were circumscribed. No sooner had the 1864 Awlad Sidi al-Shaykh movement been suppressed than the Muqrani elite and the octogenarian Rahmaniyya leader, Shaykh al-Haddad, raised the banner of revolt in the Constantine. During the turmoil of 1871, the tomb of the Rahmaniyya's founder in the village of the Ait Isma'il was even bombarded by General Cerez. The leveling of Rahmaniyya zawaya located elsewhere in Algeria after each insurrection increased the al-Hamil's attraction as a religious and educational refuge.[26] Encircled by nearly continuous populist unrest, Shaykh Muhammad b. Abi al-Qasim opted for prudent yet active neutrality, which meant that the colonial regime left the zawiya alone for the most part.

Before long a collection of buildings—a family residence, library, mosque, guest house for travelers, an elementary school, meeting rooms for sufi ceremonials, and student lodgings—came to grace al-Hamil.[27]

These attested to the founder-saint's charismatic appeal to a large and diverse following; this in turn brought in funds, largely in the form of pious offerings, needed to finance a multitude of socioreligious services.[28] In addition, the zawiya functioned as a large storage depot for grains and other foodstuffs which, when penury threatened, were distributed to the unfortunate.[29] Shaykh Muhammad expanded the range of services available to include financial operations for the good of the local Muslim community. Individuals were able to deposit money at the zawiya for safekeeping, receipts of deposit were issued, and account books kept. This suggests the existence of a rudimentary savings bank, perhaps inspired by the *sociétés indigènes de prévoyance* then being organized in Algerian communities under direct French colonial control.[30] However, in contrast to some sufi elites elsewhere in Algeria and later in Tunisia, particularly the Tijaniyya shaykhs, there is no evidence that Sidi Muhammad b. Abi al-Qasim ever solicited or received financial subsidies from colonial authorities.[31] Until his death, he maintained his ascetic lifestyle and simple manners, a mode of behavior followed scrupulously by his daughter, Zaynab.

For Shaykh Muhammad and his followers, one symbolically charged method of survival was social redemption through agrarian development. In the Bu Sa'ada region alone, some nine hundred hectares of land were farmed for the benefit of the al-Hamil zawiya; outside the immediate area, hundreds of hectares were placed under the zawiya's protection in the form of religious endowments or hubus.[32] Yet, Shaykh Muhammad's involvement in the rural economy exceeded the cultivation of existing arable land. Zawiya revenues and pious offerings were employed to open up new areas for exploitation by peasant-clients. This contrasts with rural conditions in other areas after 1850 where indigenous cultivators suffered cruelly from the progressive loss of lands to settler colonialism, resulting in the peasantry's social marginalization and economic ruin. Naturally, the key elements permitting this form of rural redemption were the zawiya's distance from the main nodes of colonial agriculture and the region's aridity, which rendered it unsuitable for pied-noir settlement.[33]

The establishment and expansion of a Rahmaniyya center in this period represents a radical departure from the situation elsewhere in Algeria under the Second Empire. Due to Rahmaniyya participation in revolts, this sufi tariqa in particular was targeted by the colonial regime as prone to rebellion; sufi centers were closed or their activities closely surveyed to dampen future revolutionary ardor. After the great 1871 insurrection in the Kabylia, repression became even more draconian.[34] While the shaykh of al-Hamil apparently played no role in the massive Kabyle revolt, he did agree to shelter some of the rebellion's defeated leaders, above all, members of the Muqrani clan at his zawiya, which later brought him into muted conflict with French authorities.

By the last decades of the century, hundreds of students and scholars were involved in al-Hamil's educational endeavors on a yearly basis. Between seven and eight thousand people visited the zawiya annually, making it one of the largest pilgrimage sites in Algeria. The influx of pilgrims performing the ziyara to capture the shaykh's baraka was part and parcel of the educational process since donations were used to provide material support for students. Surprisingly rich in comparison with the Islamic education offered elsewhere in Algeria at the time, the curriculum blended "traditional" Maghribi religious education with what might be termed the "classical." In addition to standard courses devoted to the Quran, hadith, fiqh, Arabic, and tasawwuf, students mastered chemistry, mathematics, astrology, astronomy, and rhetoric, subjects which—outside of the large, urban madrasas—were no longer offered by provincial educational establishments.[35] Sidi Muhammad's intellectual prowess in the important discipline of 'ilm al-nahw (grammar) won him the sobriquet "imam of the grammarians." Yet his greatest contribution was to remind the community that the pursuit of knowledge and science was a duty incumbent upon all good Muslims, an attitude that hearkened back to the medieval Islamic era of Ibn Khaldun, while anticipating the modern reformist Islamic movements of the twentieth century. Moreover, one of his most enduring gifts to the Rahmaniyya tariqa was to have the saint-founder's spiritual lessons, al-Rahmaniyya, accompanied by Mustafa Bash Tarzi's commentary (sharh), published in Tunis in 1889 by the Imprimerie Officielle Tunisienne.[36]

Among the shaykh's numerous writings was a treatise which constituted a remarkable critique of some of the abuses associated with the cult of saints as then practiced in Algeria and the Maghrib. In it, the shaykh scrutinized one of the pillars undergirding his own immense authority and social prestige. Reproaching some of the saintly lineages for immoral behavior, Sidi Muhammad accused them of "spending their lives in the pursuit of the things of this world and lavish lifestyles."[37] Thus, his vision extended far beyond the mere maintenance of the cultural status quo to the more daunting task of social regeneration through the acquisition of knowledge and spiritual renewal, including the reform of the sufi-saintly idiom from which he himself issued. In fact, the shaykh had a fairly advanced pedagogical sense, for the education dispensed at the zawiya was organized into three clearly differentiated cycles, arranged according to the level of the students and the difficulty of the material. Certificates attesting to scholarly achievement were issued by the zawiya's school until 1962. In the sufi center's heyday at the end of the past century, between seven and eight hundred students sought instruction there annually.[38]

Among those studying at the zawiya was Abu al-Qasim al-Hafnawi (c. 1852–1942), a noted teacher, journalist, and "proto-historian."[39] Born at roughly the same time as Lalla Zaynab, al-Hafnawi's early years resemble those of the Rahmaniyya shaykh. Originally from Bilad al-Dis in the vicinity of Bu Sa'ada, al-Hafnawi studied first in a zawiya in the northern Constantine. He then resided in Tulqa and al-Hamil for more advanced studies in theology, law, and literature. Unlike his former teacher in al-Hamil, however, al-Hafnawi was eventually attracted to the sophisticated milieu of the ulama and literati of Algiers. There al-Hafnawi sought to deepen his knowledge of the North African past by delving into the classical works of Maghribi literature and history, including Ibn Khaldun's *al-Muqaddima*. At the same time he joined the association of young, mainly Francophone Muslim intellectuals known as the "Rashidiyya," created in 1894, a reform-minded group like the educational society "al-Khalduniyya" established in Tunis in 1896.[40] Al-Hafnawi's intellectual curiosity and his sound grounding in Arabic language and literature and in fiqh resulted from his residence in al-Hamil, providing evidence for the high quality of education offered in the small oasis.

As part of the officially sponsored Algerian renaissance, the governor-general of Algeria, Charles Jonnart, encouraged al-Hafnawi to compose *Ta'rif al-khalaf bi rijal al-salaf*, a sort of biographical dictionary. Published in Algiers in two volumes between 1906 and 1907, al-Hafnawi's work was part of a conscious attempt by Algerian Muslim intellectuals to use the past, in this case the lives of especially pious and virtuous religious figures, to reawaken a sense of pride in Algerian history. Al-Hafnawi's admiration for the shaykh of al-Hamil is reflected in the biographical notice devoted to Muhammad b. Abi Al-Qasim, one of the lengthiest in the work.[41]

Significantly, the author of *Ta'rif* excised any mention of the seventy-five-year French presence in the country, although he was the editor of the official bilingual government newspaper, *Mobacher*, from 1884 to 1926.[42] This strange, complicit silence—willed forgetfulness—about France's hegemony may have been in part an expression of cultural-cognitive dissidence within al-Hafnawi himself. Christelow has pointed out the book's curious juxtaposition of old-time sufis and saints with ardent proponents of religious reform—the former are as prominent in al-Hafnawi's work as "the most staunchly puritanical of reformists."[43] Yet, it might be argued that the space devoted to the al-Hamil zawiya was not necessarily a tacit statement that Islamic reformism belonged to the city, while in the countryside "sufism remained appropriate for the masses."[44] It could also be interpreted as an acknowledgment that without the work of cultural preservation carried out by zawaya like al-Hamil, the reform-minded leaders in Algeria would have faced more adversity than they did. And willed forgetfulness about Muhammad b. Abi al-Qasim's dealings with the French may be read as a subtle statement about the sociospiritual, intellectual, and ultimately political importance of those who coped successfully with European domination. Whatever interpretation is attached to al-Hafnawi's *Ta'rif*, his work is credited with inspiring Muslim Algerian literati to reexamine their own past, distant and near, to contend with the tribulations of the present.

The steady influx of visitors to al-Hamil from all over Algeria and the Maghrib required a large, permanent staff to oversee the day-to-day affairs—charity, education, hospitality—of the Rahmaniyya complex. Those in temporary duress, the poor or sick, the disinherited, and even fugitives from French justice found shelter in the zawiya, whose prosperity enabled it to dispense social services lacking elsewhere in the colony. The supervision of the zawiya's extensive hubus properties, mainly devoted to agricultural or pastoral production, also demanded administrative and managerial skills as well as bookkeeping to monitor incoming revenues and funds deposited for safekeeping. By the eve of the shaykh's death, the monetary worth of the zawiya's diverse holdings in gardens, land, flocks, mills, cash, etc., was evaluated at some Fr 2.5 million, a huge sum for the period, particularly in view of the general impoverishment of the Muslim Algerians.[45] Al-Hamil's monetary worth would be one important element in the struggle unleashed in 1897.

Once again general socioeconomic conditions outside al-Hamil diverged considerably from those in the oasis, while also explaining the popularity of the sufi center. From the 1860s on, the rural Muslim population was afflicted by drought, famine, and epidemics which rendered all the more precarious a subsistence level seriously compromised by massive land expropriations. One observer of the terrible 1867–1868 famine characterized those regions hit by starvation as "an open tomb."[46] At the same time, after the Muqrani uprising of 1871–1872, the colonial bureaucracy in the north passed fully into the hands of civilian administrators who were notoriously parsimonious about extending financial or other assistance to the beleaguered Muslim populace. Thus, the relatively thriving state of the oasis of al-Hamil and its environs stands in stark contrast to areas like the Kabylia after 1871, where, according to popular poets, "taxes rain upon us like repeated blows, the people have sold their fruit trees and even their clothes, the most fertile land goes for lowly sums."[47]

Much of the credit for al-Hamil's success was due to the postures and strategies adopted by Shaykh Muhammad toward the unpleasant reality of foreign occupation. In addition, the Rahmaniyya leader was blessed with a temperament that enabled him to deal skillfully with Europeans of whatever background. This too explains his adeptness in navigating the treacherous political waters of fin de siècle Algeria.

The Shaykh and the French: The Politics of Cultural Redemption

North Africans were not the only visitors to the zawiya in the latter part of the century, although aside from the permanent military administration in Bu Sa'ada, the region did not interest Europeans before 1897. This was naturally a critical factor in Sidi Muhammad's relative freedom to construct a social and religious space where the impact of asymmetrical power relations was attenuated. Officers stationed in Bu Sa'ada, however, periodically called upon the Rahmaniyya shaykh as part of the politics of supervised amity.[48] On one occasion sometime in the 1880s, the commandant arrived in the oasis, accompanied by a group of French women "with sun umbrellas unfurled," who evinced a mild curiosity in things Muslim and Saharan. Also present was the well-known French orientalist painter, Gustave Guillaumet, who by then had made numerous trips to Algeria to paint.

During this particular visit, Sidi Muhammad proved a cordial host, displaying an extraordinary equanimity in the face of European eccentricities. Not only did he open the doors of the very private women's quarters in his personal family residence to the French female guests but he also agreed to partake in a formal sit-down luncheon *à la française* at the zawiya. One can only wonder at his thoughts as he was seated for two hours with French women on either side for dinner companions, before a table set with the curious culinary implements of Western civilization which the delegation had thoughtfully furnished. For the first time in his life, Sidi Muhammad grappled with silverware, sat down with his guests while eating, and engaged in polite dinner conversation through an interpreter. Guillaumet left this account of the luncheon in the shaykh's residence:

> A long table is set for the guests, contrary to the traditional custom of eating seated on the floor. For two hours all the refinements of Arab cuisine are brought out. Out of respect for such a venerable host, we refrained from bringing wine or other forbidden items. . . . for drinks, there was water or milk smelling of tar and of the skin of a goat, and curiously served in bottles and flowered bowls, coming from French manufacturers. As the master of the house, the marabout [the shaykh] sat down to the feast

only upon the express invitation of the French commandant, who placed him between two ladies. For him, what an overturning of custom! Between two ladies! This is certainly not the way in which the Arab honors the gentle sex. In addition, the commandant's cook brought out a complete table service. And the marabout, whose beard was grey, learned for the first time to serve himself with a fork, eat upon a table cloth and with porcelain plates, a crystal glass in front of him. To every expression of attention given him by his table companions, the marabout always responded with a smile full of finesse and goodwill. His mien is light and sweet, and his face that of a scholar rather than a man of war.[49]

Guillaumet also observed that "Sidi Muhammad does not speak a word of our language; we appreciate his eloquence with the aid of interpreters."[50] This fact is significant and contrasts once again with other religious notables, some of whom by this period had acquired at least limited facility in French. Whether the shaykh consciously refused to learn the occupiers' tongue is uncertain; Zaynab was unversed in French as well. A lack of proficiency in the foreigners' language, however, preserved a subtle cultural distance between the holy man and those officials who strove to work with him or through him to govern the local populace. Maintaining a balance between rapprochement with, and detachment from, the conqueror was absolutely critical for highly visible social intermediaries like Sidi Muhammad. An overly cozy relationship with the French might erode popular indigenous support; while remoteness from those in power could undermine the shaykh's ability to negotiate concessions for his community from colonial authorities.

The saint prudently refused to accept any formal office, honoraria, or even decorations from the regime, which left his reputation for piety untarnished, assuring him of the continued support of his constituency.[51] This too contrasts with some other religious notables, who, seduced by the temptation of minor positions within the colonial order, saw their clients transfer loyalties to others less compromised by overt ties to the oppressors.[52]

At the same time, the shaykh welcomed Europeans to his zawiya, including the French painter E. Dinet, who did a large portrait of Shaykh Muhammad which until recently hung in the zawiya's reception room for visitors. More significant than an Algerian sufi shaykh posing for his portrait was the fact that Dinet converted to Islam under Sidi Muhammad's spiritual guidance. The shaykh also discreetly arranged for Dinet to be circumcised at the Hospital Mustapha in Algiers. However, fearing reprisals from colonial officials, who would have been scandalized at a Frenchman's conversion, Dinet and the shaykh kept the matter secret for years.[53] Sometime toward the end of his life, Sidi Muhammad even posed for a photograph obviously taken by a European visitor to the zawiya.[54]

Sidi Muhammad's hospitality earned him kudos from military officials, thus reinforcing the benevolence of the local commandant, who was a powerful figure in the region's affairs and those of the zawiya. Of this, Shaykh Muhammad was painfully aware. In an age when the *régime du sabre* had ceded to the more corrosive system of civilian bureaucratic domination, a consummate diplomat like Shaykh Muhammad could claim victory in wars waged far from conventional battlefields. Proof of this is furnished by the lengthy evaluations of him written by colonial officialdom. French authorities rarely indulged in gratuitous praise of Algerian Muslim leaders. Yet Sidi Muhammad was characterized more than once as being "of great intelligence, vast knowledge, and irreproachable morals; his authority stretches from Bou Saada, Djelfa, Boghar, and Biskra to the region of Aumale, Médéa, Tiaret, and Sétif."[55]

Shaykh Muhammad could not have undertaken extensive travels to visit his numerous affiliated zawaya and followers—the sine qua non of maintaining a religious network—without the blessings of the colonial regime. By this period many officials were frantic about the twin threats to France's African empire posed by Pan-Islam and by those sufi brotherhoods perceived as politically active. These apprehensions led them to monitor obsessively the physical displacements of North African religious figures. Written permits had to be obtained in advance of travel, a privilege which officials selectively conferred and more frequently refused. Denial of travel permits to uncooperative shaykhs loosened the highly personal bonds between sufi masters and distant clients, thus undermining spiritual loyalties, which in any case were deemed inherently subversive to France's hegemony.[56] As far as can be ascertained from the sources available, Sidi Muhammad enjoyed unrestricted travel, which helped to sustain the translocal nature of his sociospiritual clientele.

One of the saint's last journeys on this earth brought him to Maison Carrée, outside of Algiers, in April 1896. In the course of a single day, Shaykh Muhammad was greeted by some five thousand Muslim Algerians eager to capture some of his baraka by touching him or kissing the hem of his robes.[57] During this particular trip, the shaykh performed one of his most widely publicized miracles—a public demonstration of divinely conferred powers superior to those claimed by the French masters of Algeria. Since the scheduled departure for the train in which he rode conflicted with the afternoon prayer, the saint employed his supernatural gifts to stall the train so that he might perform his devotions undisturbed. His followers swore that the European mechanics were powerless to move the train forward until Sidi Muhammad had completed the prescribed prayers.[58] And here and there, in all the places where the shaykh had stopped to preach or rest, his disciples constructed small shrines (maqams) to commemorate his holy presence.

The positive attitude of colonial officials toward the director of the al-Hamil zawiya—indeed the very prosperity of the sufi center—was directly tied to Sidi Muhammad's decision not to oppose the French, at least not head on. Outwardly he maintained an amiable, if reserved, stance toward the regime, eschewed direct involvement in either profane politics or saintly squabbles, and even attempted to defuse movements of violent protest, for example, during the revolts of 1864 and 1871. Yet the shaykh was scarcely a pliant instrument in the hands of forces ostensibly more powerful than himself. His piety and erudition were infused by a large dose of realpolitik. Rather than being manipulated by the colonial order, he was quite adept at manipulating that same order to wring tangible concessions, material or otherwise, from his French mentors. The benefits from this quid pro quo arrangement were used solely for preserving the Muslim community under the less than favorable circumstances of the age. In short, the authorities needed the Rahmaniyya shaykh as much as he depended upon their goodwill to carry on the work of cultural survival. These then were the unspoken terms of the pact patiently worked out between religious notables, such as Sidi Muhammad, and local colonial authorities in places where pied-noir settlement was largely absent.

While steering clear of violent clashes pitting Muslim against European (or Muslim against Muslim), the shaykh openly risked the opprobrium of those in power. The most serious case of moderate, yet determined, insubordination had to do with the fact that he was "charitable, his house and purse are wide open to all."[59] Sidi Muhammad provided asylum to political figures deemed dangerous to colonial security, among them rebels involved in the Muqrani insurrection and Ibrahim b. 'Abd Allah, implicated in the 1864 revolt. With the defeat of the Muqrani family and of the Rahmaniyya shaykh, al-Haddad, the survivors fled to al-Hamil, where they were given special quarters near the zawiya. Forty families received shelter from French justice there, and even today the northwest wing of the sufi complex still bears the designation of "quarter of the Muqranis."[60] The presence of the once powerful Muqrani elite of the Majana in the oasis also led to matrimonial alliances between Shaykh Muhammad's lineage and his refugee guests.

As discussed above, asylum was traditionally expected of sufi-saintly lineages, whose centers were neutral havens of protection and hospitality.

To refuse sanctuary to fellow Muslims would have diminished Sidi Muhammad's prestige in the eyes of the faithful and compromised his ability to exercise moral persuasion and thereby shape collective political behavior. Local military officers preferred not to interfere with the shaykh's duty to welcome political "undesirables" to his zawiya—"people of disorder and intrigue," as one French officer described them—out of fear of alienating him.[61] Of this dilemma the saint was well aware, exploiting it to advantage. And colonial pleas that he furnish officials with a list of the names of those under his protective mantle were ignored; the shaykh felt no compulsion to answer these demands since the will to employ coercive means to effect compliance was lacking among local military officials.[62] In effect, the shaykh and his colonial masters were signatories to an unstated, yet mutually binding, pact whose implicit terms guaranteed political order in return for religious autonomy.

Nevertheless, the contentious issue of asylum and protection went deeper than this; at the heart of the matter were divergent cultural understandings of what constituted the proper domain of politics. Granting refuge to fellow Muslims was for Sidi Muhammad a religious duty; in French eyes, asylum was a political act. This incomprehension was expressed by a military officer in Bu Sa'ada who observed, in a long, favorable report devoted to the shaykh, that the saint "has a tendency to get involved in affairs whose solution depends entirely upon the authorities—criminal matters, political conflicts, and private concerns."[63] All of these affairs were also squarely within the rightful realm of sufi leaders in the countryside. As a guarantor of social order, the shaykh's duty was to define and uphold religious and spiritual principles. Since Sidi Muhammad's interpretation of those principles was generous, it poached upon territory deemed political by secular-minded authorities.

By the eve of his death, Muhammad b. Abi al-Qasim was clearly one of the most influential Rahmaniyya figures in North Africa. His disciples were estimated in the thousands; the educational prestige of his zawiya was rivaled only by the Rahmaniyya establishment in Tulqa, then under the directorship of Sidi 'Ali b. 'Uthman, who remained head shaykh until 1898. As was the case with al-Hamil, Tulqa's prosperity and its ability to meet its clientele's needs were a direct consequence of Sidi 'Ali's apolitical stance which earned for the zawiya the benign neglect of local officials. And benign neglect meant that the zawiya's various collective activities—religious, cultural, and social—could be carried on without interference from overly zealous or fearful administrators.[64]

As Shaykh Muhammad advanced in years, unease regarding the critical matter of his spiritual successor steadily mounted in colonial circles. These apprehensions were due to the internal affairs of al-Hamil itself and to the nature of moral-religious authority; nevertheless, France's larger African interests were also at stake. The saint appeared to be grooming his nephew Muhammad b. al-Hajj Muhammad (c. 1861–1912) for a future leadership role. This Sidi Muhammad did by presenting his nephew on several occasions to local French officers in Bu Sa'ada as well as to officials in Algiers.[65] Yet, the aging shaykh, who had suffered a serious heart attack years earlier, declined to publicly appoint a spiritual heir, despite increasing French insistence to do so. On the other hand, the individual most intimately involved in the zawiya's daily management was Sidi Muhammad's only surviving child, Zaynab, although no one in the colonial bureaucracy anticipated her audacious behavior or even considered her a likely candidate for leadership prior to 1897. In French eyes only a male could aspire to direct the zawiya; the burning question was—would Shaykh Muhammad's replacement be equally well disposed toward France? As the last decade of the century drew to a close, this unsettling question preoccupied not only the local military administration but also those at the top of the colonial hierarchy in the capital.[66] As Captain Fournier observed in his 1895 report:

> At the present time, in the region of Bu Sa'ada, the imposing personality of Shaykh Muhammad b. Abi al-Qasim guarantees upon all a form of behavior that is not politically suspect, but we can not assume that it will always be this way. It should be noted that, in effect, if the shaykh has acquired considerable authority, this influence is completely personal, and his successors will not necessarily inherit it.[67]

French worries about spiritual headship can be comprehended only in relation to a constellation of imperial anxieties reaching far beyond the Sahara or even Algeria. The specter of pan-Islamic "plots" haunted colonial administrators, both French and British, in Africa and Asia by the century's end. The publication of Octave Depont and Xavier Coppolani's study of the Islamic brotherhoods in 1897 did nothing to allay these phantasms but rather fed them. Predictably, older French phobias about inherently "dangerous" sufi orders resurfaced as Shaykh Muhammad's physical condition declined. According to colonial intelligence, families believed associated with the Sanusiyya and Darqawa brotherhoods—the bêtes noires of French Islamophobes—regularly sent their children to al-Hamil for education and even performed the ziyara to the Rahmaniyya shaykh; a weak successor might fall under the nefarious influence of "religious fanatics." In this way a friendly, or at least politically neutral, zawiya would be transformed into a hotbed of sedition—or so colonial reasoning had it.[68]

Connected to this was the unresolved problem of the Bu (Abu) 'Amama revolt along the Algerian-Moroccan borders, which threatened the security of the Sahara and western Algeria for decades after its inception in 1881.[69] Thus, by 1897 the issue of al-Hamil's future was a matter of no small consequence, not only for the zawiya, its personnel and clients, but also for those whose administrative careers depended upon the preservation of social tranquillity and political order in this remote corner of the Sahara. However, the expectation that Shaykh Muhammad's nephew would be accepted as head shaykh lulled some officers, particularly Captain Crochard, into a false serenity about what lay ahead. Two months prior to his death in June 1897, Sidi Muhammad, by then under intense pressure from local colonial authorities, had written a letter to Bu Sa'ada's military command stating that Muhammad b. al-Hajj Muhammad, his brother's son, was to succeed him.[70] However, it appears that only the French knew of the existence of this document. Zaynab was unaware of the letter designating her cousin as head shaykh; she later used it as one of the bases for her grievances against local military officials, asserting that the letter had been wrung from her ailing father when his faculties were waning.

This was the complex political legacy that Zaynab bint Shaykh Muhammad inherited, one which forced the shaykh's daughter to fight to succeed her father. While her father had deftly maneuvered and negotiated to avoid serious clashes, Zaynab chose, due to circumstances, to directly confront the colonial order. She contested the imperial system more vigorously than her father had deemed wise in order to sustain the zawiya's socioreligious functions so vital for the community's well-being, if not its very existence. In large measure, Zaynab's gender and femininity were at the root of the confrontation; yet conversely, it was precisely because she was a woman—an extraordinary woman—that she successfully defied those ostensibly monopolizing political power in a dispute over spiritual power. Zaynab did not seek out politics, but rather politics came to find her in the seclusion of al-Hamil.

The Shaykh's Daughter: Lalla Zaynab

Nineteenth-century Algerian historiography appears as an imperial male preserve, peopled almost exclusively by men, whether French military heroes like General Bugeaud, celebrated in colonial hagiography, or Muslim resistance figures, such as Amir Abd al-Qadir, venerated as an early nationalist leader.[71] One of the few exceptions was the "fille insoumise," the rebellious daughter of Muhammad b. Abi al-Qasim, although her story has remained untold until now.

In some ways, Zaynab is emblematic of the social situation of indigenous females in European settler-colonial societies of Africa or Asia. In addition to class or social ranking and gender distinctions, these societies were structured according to "racial" boundaries. For North Africans, the category of race was manipulated by eighteenth- and nineteenth-century European thinkers, writers, and colonial administrators to include cultural and ethnic attributes. By virtue of their Islamic religion and Arab-Semitic language, which had consequently "retarded" sociomoral development, most North Africans were deemed "racially inferior" to their colonial masters. Nevertheless, the Berbers were at times placed a bit higher on the "racial" scale than Arabic speakers.[72] In *Les femmes arabes en Algérie*, Hubertine Auclert stated quite bluntly the prevailing colonial estimation of the North Africans: "In Algeria, only a small minority of Frenchmen would place the Arab race in the category of humanity."[73] As for indigenous North African women, they were part of a social order that was doubly patriarchal—colonial, on the one hand, and indigenous, on the other.

Nevertheless, saintliness, sharifian descent, piety, and the miracles attributed to her by religious clients rendered Zaynab an extraordinary person, at least in the eyes of the Muslim faithful. Sainthood and special virtue placed her outside of the normal bounds defining female public behavior and sociolegal status in Muslim society. While colonial officials obviously did not subscribe to the same cultural norms, they were reluctant to take certain kinds of action against female religious notables, like Zaynab, out of fear of offending Muslim sensibilities and provoking unrest. Perhaps more than their male counterparts, some women were strategically situated to exploit the weaker points within the colonial system of control.

Information about Zaynab's early years is scanty; many things can only be posited from fragmentary evidence or deduced from her father's biography. While there is ample biographical, or more accurately hagiographical, material in published and unpublished Arabic sources devoted to the shaykh, Zaynab is conspicuous by her absence in the Arabic texts. (The rich oral traditions concerning Zaynab are still extant today and represent a potential, though underutilized, source.) In al-Hafnawi's *Ta'rif*, for example, she is referred to simply as the shaykh's "bint saliha" (virtuous daughter) with no further elaboration upon her life or works.[74] Al-Hafnawi was well acquainted with al-Hamil's history; when he composed his dictionary, Zaynab had just died and her first cousin, Muhammad b. al-Hajj Muhammad, had belatedly claimed spiritual directorship. European documentation devoted to Zaynab comes from two main sources. Foreign visitors, such as Guillaumet, who journeyed to the zawiya in search of the exotic (or in the case of Isabelle Eberhardt for personal salvation), have provided extremely sympathetic accounts of the female saint. More abundant are colonial archival sources, many of which, although not all, were written by hostile military officials during the period when al-Hamil's headship was hotly contested.

Although the exact date of her birth is unknown, Zaynab was born sometime in the 1850s, soon after Sidi Muhammad founded the religious establishment in al-Hamil which later grew into the Rahmaniyya center.[75] Zaynab spent most, if not all, of her life in the oasis, although she may have been with her father during his five years (1857–1862) in the oasis of Awlad Jallal in the Ziban. She was educated by Sidi Muhammad, who took his daughter's instruction very seriously. She attained an advanced stage of erudition, becoming well versed in the books and manuscripts housed in the zawiya's extensive library; she later helped to keep the accounts of the center's numerous properties. Her knowledge was viewed with admiration and respect by her father's followers and increased the "already great prestige she enjoyed in the community as the shaykh's daughter."[76] A later source claimed that Sidi Muhammad had "trained her from childhood to fill the role that awaited her."[77]

Zaynab was raised in the *harim* (harem) attached to the shaykh's private family residence. The harim housed some forty women—the shaykh's mother, sister, wives, and a large number of females who, deprived of male protectors, had been entrusted to Sidi Muhammad's care; even divorced wives continued to reside in the zawiya. After her father's death, Zaynab assumed the role of protector for the harim's women, shielding them on at least one occasion from harassment by local military officials. Many of these women led secluded lives devoted to spiritual exercises, not unlike cloistered nuns.[78] Following the custom of endogamy among North African saintly-sufi clans, Sidi Muhammad had wed spouses from other religious families of distinction and even from among the aristocratic Muqrani. While these liaisons brought a large measure of social notoriety and enlarged the clan's already extensive networks, they did not apparently produce any surviving male heirs.[79]

While she had many suitors as a young woman, Zaynab took a vow of celibacy, a somewhat unusual act since Islamic social values prize matrimony, family life, and progeny above all else.[80] Yet for the shaykh's daughter, virginity was a compelling source of spiritual authority and social empowerment. It permitted her to devote herself entirely to caring for the destitute, unencumbered by the burdens of domestic chores or child rearing. Zaynab's celibate state also conferred greater freedom of movement in the community, for as one colonial officer remarked, "She was not afraid to show herself to others."[81] Her frail appearance, the legacy of a lifetime of fasting, prayer vigils, and other forms of asceticism, enhanced her virtuous reputation. Another visitor described her during the early 1880s as a "saintly being whose face is marked by small pox and decorated with small tattoos" as was the custom among Saharan women.[82]

Shaykh Muhammad centralized the management of the sufi center's numerous properties and complex affairs within his own hands. Nevertheless, he apparently kept Zaynab informed of financial and other operations, viewing her as a confidant. After a massive heart attack in 1877, Sidi Muhammad directed the qadi in Bu Sa'ada to draw up a hubus document specifying the terms of inheritance under Maliki law. In this document, the shaykh's substantial possessions—land, houses, gardens, library manuscripts, valuable household items—were constituted as a family hubus "in favor of his daughter Zaynab and other children of either the male or female sex." In a departure from the usual inheritance practices, Zaynab was singled out to receive a "portion equal to male" descendants, although no sons were ever born (or survived to adulthood). All other female descendants would inherit only the customary one-half of a male share of property.[83] But the document was more than a legal blueprint for distributing material goods; it may have been an expression of the shaykh's desire that his daughter succeed him as head of the zawiya. Two decades later, Zaynab relied upon the 1877 hubus document as part of a campaign to advance her claims to spiritual succession over and against those of her male cousin.

The marked preference shown Zaynab can also be interpreted as a sign of the shaykh's deep attachment to her and his recognition of her very special piety. Nevertheless, the fact that she had renounced the pleasures of marriage meant that Zaynab would produce no offspring to complicate the matter of inheritance. Zaynab returned her father's affections, describing him with some passion in a letter dated 1899 as an exemplar whose life was motivated by a love for others, noting Shaykh Muhammad's "pity for the disinherited, his generosity, his great theological knowledge, disinterest in the things of this world, and his scrupulous observance of Muslim law in all matters."[84] Imagine Zaynab's profound distress when her beloved father passed away.

One 2 June 1897, Sidi Muhammad b. Abi al-Qasim suffered another heart attack while returning from a visit to the governor-general, Jules Cambon, in Algiers; he died among his religious clients, the Awlad Sahari in the hamlet of Buhaira Sakhiri; the qadi had his saintly remains transported back to al-Hamil.[85] According to Muslim tradition, he was quickly buried in the stately family mausoleum inside the zawiya's mosque. His tomb immediately became an enormously popular pilgrimage site for the multitude seeking the saint's blessings. The next month, on 16 July, a religious ceremony was held in his memory in Bu Sa'ada's principal mosque.

In addition to Rahmaniyya followers and members of the region's tribes, a number of colonial officials were present at the service. Speaking to the assembly was Major Crochard, soon to be Zaynab's nemesis in the succession struggle. In his speech, Crochard evoked Shaykh Muhammad's relationship with France, as he and all within the colonial hierarchy wanted to see it:

> Si Mohammed ben Belqacem [*sic*] was tied to the French cause, openly, loyally, and without ulterior motive. Due to his enlightened way of thinking, he offset the influence of those who were hostile to us, aiding us with all his means in the work of civilization which he so well understood. He struggled to see that civilization triumph, even risking his own prestige with many people to so do.[86]

Crochard's elegy in French was probably comprehensible to but a few of the assembled Muslim Algerians. After he had finished, the defunct shaykh's nephew and the qadi of Bu Sa'ada also addressed the crowd—the order of speaking reflected the arrangement of power. Here, of course, the language was Arabic, and while some of the military officers were versed in that tongue, the same can not be assumed for the rest of the Europeans. Moreover, the second elegy had nothing to do with France or her civilizing mission; far from it, the speakers recalled the saint's sharifian origins, his religious virtues, and his pious works.[87] Thus the two elegies in two different languages remembered two very different dimensions of the same man. Yet the mutual incomprehension went further than the merely linguistic domain; the lack of understanding was cultural and ideological and by extension political. It would seem, at least in this context, that the *mission civilisatrice* had thus far implicitly failed.

If the French could congratulate themselves momentarily for deftly managing an apparently willing ally like Shaykh Muhammad for years, and arranging a suitably docile heir, events in both the long- and short-term would cut short those felicitations. A generation later, Shaykh Muhammad's work of cultural survival produced individuals who would begin to aggressively reassert their authentic Algerian Muslim identity. As for the immediate future, Lalla Zaynab quickly ended comfortable illusions about smooth succession at the zawiya.

"Une Fille Insoumise": The Rebellious Daughter

No sooner had the shaykh been laid to rest and the funerary ceremonials concluded, than Zaynab's cousin belligerently affirmed his right to al-Hamil's headship. Accompanied by a band of followers, Muhammad b.

al-Hajj Muhammad went to the shaykh's residence and was immediately confronted by a resolute and hostile Zaynab, who refused to acknowledge his moral and spiritual authority. She forbade the students and zawiya personnel from obeying her cousin's orders, denied him entry to the center's library, books, and buildings, and imposed a sort of lockout by taking possession of the keys.[88] Zaynab's objections to her cousin were twofold. First, she and many others regarded him as impious and worldly, traits that rendered him undeserving to replace her father. And it was feared that his excessive attachment to the things of this life would endanger the zawiya's social services and its mission of cultural redemption. Second, Zaynab rejected the nomination letter, which she characterized as "apocryphal," extracted from the shaykh just before his death by Captain Crochard.[89]

The confrontation degenerated into a series of brawls between the two sides; some of Zaynab's partisans were beaten. Enraged, the cousin even went so far as to attempt to shut Zaynab up in the harim against her will. A desperate act by a desperate man, this stratagem for containing a willful female only brought disgrace upon the pretender and caused Zaynab to go on the offensive. Deprived of access to the zawiya's physical space and material assets, Muhammad b. al-Hajj Muhammad also forfeited the spiritual capital and social perquisites which accompanied that access. Of this, both Zaynab and her cousin were well aware. With al-Hamil's educational and devotional facilities off limits, Muhammad b. al-Hajj Muhammad created a counterfollowing by establishing a rival school on the outskirts of the village. A little less than a year after the schism erupted, the hapless cousin had enticed only a small group of thirty students to his side.[90]

The conflict soon widened. Zaynab sent letters to Rahmaniyya notables all over the region denouncing her cousin; she also contacted the nearby office of the Affaires Indigènes, demanding redress of her grievances. Accusing Muhammad b. al-Hajj Muhammad of advancing spurious claims to the post of head shaykh, she also informed French authorities of her cousin's untoward comportment toward her, insisting that they curb his "injustice and thievery" and reminding them pointedly of her father's "devotion to France and to [the maintenance] of public order."[91] In a war of words, Zaynab's arguments were a stroke of genius—her attack on French insistence upon her cousin as a fitting successor was based entirely upon the logic of keeping order.

The two-way struggle provoked divisions among al-Hamil's numerous religious clients, including various tribes in the Sahara. Most of the Awlad 'Alan, the Titteri, and the Sahari supported Zaynab's cause; several other tribal groups threw in their lot with her rival. While information is lacking about the motives of tribal support for either of the spiritual contestants, the split may have followed saff fault lines, which often occurred when the tribes were confronted with a politico-religious contest of this nature. In addition, the Rahmaniyya shaykhs of Tulqa seized upon the discord to woo some clients away from al-Hamil.[92] Zaynab's bold actions also presented Sidi Muhammad's closest spiritual intimates with a serious dilemma. She had declared that any Rahmaniyya brother who joined her cousin's side "could no longer hope to see the door of Lalla Zaynab's [zawiya] open to him."[93] Although some of her father's disciples believed that Muhammad b. al-Hajj Muhammad would be an acceptable successor, they recoiled from disavowing Zaynab due to their great respect for the shaykh's daughter. Moreover, Zaynab bore a striking physical resemblance to her father; her carriage and mannerisms recalled those of the deceased saint. Many believed that she had inherited her father's baraka. Finally, other Rahmaniyya notables questioned the claims of both Zaynab and her cousin, asserting that spiritual succession should return to the descendants of Shaykh al-Mukhtar in the oasis of Awlad Jallal.[94]

As far as can be ascertained from the available sources, the hesitation of some Muslim Algerians to endorse Zaynab's directorship did not necessarily revolve around the issue of gender and proper gender roles. The wellspring of legitimate succession was the matter of baraka and the worthiness of an individual to inherit the defunct shaykh's blessings and charisma. Moreover, within the Rahmaniyya tariqa, precedents existed for the assumption of spiritual authority by female saints, at least temporarily.[95] It was rather local colonial officials who argued most vehemently against Lalla Zaynab in 1897 solely because she was of the weaker sex. For French officers, Zaynab's femininity meant ipso facto that she would be a pliable instrument in the hands of anti-French forces; her very nature made her incapable of effective administration.[96] While Sidi Muhammad's political neutrality had kept colonial interference in the zawiya's spiritual affairs at bay, once Zaynab assumed control outside meddling escalated.

While massive French intervention was in large measure due to the prospect of a woman in charge, colonial authorities had been increasingly concerned about the zawiya's educational activities even before the shaykh's death. Astute officials perceived that Islamic education posed as much of a threat—perhaps more—to France's grand design for Algeria as did insurrection. Accordingly, decrees and laws regulating Muslim "private" schools were promulgated from the 1880s seeking to better supervise, and thus suppress, the taproot of North African culture and civilization— its religious schools.[97] Moreover, the great shaykh's death had come at a particularly inopportune moment for those whose military careers were

devoted to following maraboutic politics. One month before Sidi Muhammad's death, Tijaniyya factions from 'Ain Madi and Tammasin had become
embroiled in a macabre dispute over the recently defunct Tijani shaykh's
sacred remains and thus his baraka.[98] The tenuous peace in the Sahara
threatened to dissolve. This then was the subtext underlying Commandant
Crochard's alarm over Zaynab's daring bid for leadership.

Bu Sa'ada's military officers were stunned and infuriated since they had
anticipated that Muhammad b. al-Hajj Muhammad would take over al-
Hamil unopposed. Zaynab's public denunciations of her cousin placed them
on the defensive; striving to limit the damage done by an upstart woman,
they threw their full weight behind their chosen candidate. Captain Crochard naturally portrayed Zaynab's rival to his superiors in glowing
terms—as a faithful, upright individual, motivated solely by concerns for
the zawiya's welfare and the security of France. Nevertheless, others officials painted a somewhat different portrait of him, characterizing him as
"of average intelligence yet ambitious, haughty, and prone to excess."
Moreover, the zawiya's numerous clients regarded him as rapacious and
miserly, thus popular support was tepid at best.[99]

Predictably rumors spread among al-Hamil's inhabitants and its sufi
followers—Zaynab's cousin had gone to Algiers to enlist the assistance of
the authorities in seizing the zawiya's assets. Rumors such as this made
Muhammad al-Hajj Muhammad's claims to succession even less palatable
for most.[100] While Muslim Algerians revered sufi leaders marked by piety,
purity of morals, and closeness to God, the French privileged other be-
havioral attributes—above all, docility. Deprived of widespread communal
respect, Muhammad b. al-Hajj Muhammad would, therefore, be amenable
to manipulation, solely reliant upon his French allies to administer the sufi
center. In turn, the would-be shaykh expected the authorities to force
Zaynab to yield, something that they were unwilling or, more accurately,
unable to do. Political diffidence on the part of those ostensibly in power
increasingly alienated Zaynab's cousin from his colonial mentors, thus
complicating things.[101]

The rebellious daughter's unexpected behavior provoked a great deal of
bitter frustration among local military officers. Dealing with a defiant
Muslim woman was somewhat of a novelty for those long accustomed to
breaking the will of obstreperous Muslim males. At one point, the officers
of the Affaires Indigènes had indeed considered coercion to evict her from
the zawiya—an index of their sense of impotence. Yet Zaynab was a saint
and venerated mystic with her own popular following, which rendered the
matter all the more delicate. On the one hand, she had ensnared Crochard
in his own infernal trap: to drive her from office would rally the sufi

brothers and clients around her. They had already closed ranks to support their female leader, and rash actions would provoke the very unrest the officers sought to avoid. On the other hand, she defied French male authority—a double affront coming from a Muslim and a woman at that! The entire colonial edifice of control was in question.[102]

Evaluations of Zaynab contained in official correspondence translate the helpless rage felt by those in command, whose very careers were endangered by female recalcitrance. Not surprisingly, Captain Crochard felt compelled to characterize her as the passive, foolish victim of sinister, female intrigues within the zawiya. According to his reports, she was exploited by anti-French malcontents, who perceived Zaynab's cousin as inimical to their own political interests: "Among her associates, there are no good men; she is surrounded by untrustworthy people, capable of the worst excesses. . . . they know well that she can be manipulated."[103] Thus, her strength was interpreted as the product of inherent female weakness. In addition to revealing pervasive French male attitudes toward female nature in general, such explanations also unveil something much more profound: the absence of colonial mechanisms for containing small-scale, nonviolent rebellions, particularly by Muslim women.[104]

Zaynab was serenely conscious of the tactical edge that seeming powerlessness conferred and exploited this tiny breach in the prevailing system of domination. "She knows that a woman is always treated with circumspection and exploits this in order to embarrass and cause problems for local authorities whom she sees as favoring her cousin."[105] As he grew increasingly aware of his own political impotence, Crochard became more censorious of his feminine opponent: "Passionate to the point of hatred, bold to the point of insolence and impudence, very haughty and eager for deferential treatment, she displays in the worst ways her father's qualities; her charity is nothing but extravagance; she does not hesitate to deceive or make false accusations to pursue the plan of action she has in mind."[106] In concluding his vilification, Crochard gloomily predicted the ultimate ruin of the zawiya and its numerous social welfare functions—all because of a rebellious woman. Noteworthy here is that those very same qualities deemed laudable in Zaynab's father—philanthropy and largesse—were pernicious in a disobedient female. The captain also disclosed the true source of his resentment toward her, lamenting, "Lalla Zaynab's behavior has completely destroyed all that I have labored so hard to effect," that is, to arrange for a politically tranquil succession after Shaykh Muhammad's death. In late nineteenth-century Algeria, small defiant acts could be as menacing to the political order as large, militant gestures: "This affair demonstrates that Zaynab is a dangerous woman whose intrigues and activities should be closely surveyed.''[107] She had trespassed into political territory theoretically prohibited to the colonized.

The Riposte

Zaynab employed every means at her disposal to thwart the designs of the two men opposing her—Crochard and her cousin. The material stakes were considerable since control over the zawiya's substantial assets and properties was also at issue. With the French in Bu Sa'ada against her, Zaynab took a most unusual step—she cleverly petitioned those at the very top of the colonial hierarchy for assistance. In August 1897, she hired a French lawyer, Maurice l'Admiral, the general counsel for the circumscription of Aumale, and some of his associates, to represent her legally in Algiers.[108] L'Admiral, together with Bonnard, the general counsel for the prefecture of Algiers, and messieurs Pastoureau and Arene met with Zaynab at her residence in Bu Sa'ada on 13 September 1897. One of the four Frenchmen served as an interpreter for Zaynab during the long interview they had with her that day. L'Admiral subsequently brought her allegations regarding misconduct by Bu Sa'ada's Affaires Indigènes office to the attention of the head of the French judiciary, the *procureur-général*. The latter, alarmed by Zaynab's accusations and by the dimensions which the conflict was assuming, contacted the governor-general and the leading military officer for the province in October 1897.[109]

Once l'Admiral became embroiled in the conflict, the calculus of the succession dispute was utterly transformed. The mere threat of the semi-independent judiciary intervening in the matter caused considerable discomfiture in Algiers. Moreover, bad publicity about French treatment of Muslim dignitaries was also unwelcome. France in this period was engaged in an international public relations campaign to convince Muslims in Morocco, Tunisia, and elsewhere of the benefits of French rule; the al-Hamil affair might besmirch the desired image of benevolence and toleration for all things Islamic.[110]

In setting forth her grievances to those at the pinnacle of French Algeria, Zaynab displayed a remarkable knowledge of imperial and administrative structures and their potential soft spots. It was she who reminded French authorities of their duties under the terms of the colonial "pact" with the indigenous population rather than the reverse. Her familiarity with the ways of the infidels appears all the more extraordinary since as far as we know prior to 1897 she had remained largely within the environs of al-Hamil. However, Zaynab had access to three important sources of information: her father, who traveled widely, met with colonial officials, and treated her as a confidant; the Muqranis as well as the other political refugees who had long resided in the zawiya and who had previous experience with the colonial bureaucracy; and the thousands of pilgrims and students from Algeria and North Africa who had visited al-Hamil over the years, invariably bringing news of the world outside the oasis.

This information, combined with her own highly developed powers of persuasion and deep commitment to the zawiya's welfare, made Zaynab a formidable opponent. By involving French lawyers, the *procureur-général,* and the governor-general in the dispute, she managed to pit high-ranking officials against local officers—a shrewd appropriation of France's long-standing policy for governing the Algerians through "divide and rule" tactics. As General Meygret stated to his superior, Jules Cambon, Zaynab's complaint "contains allegations of a grave nature" against those heading the Bu Sa'ada command.[111]

Moreover, the appointment of Jules Cambon as the new, reform-minded governor-general in 1891 signaled a belated effort by Paris to rein in the European settlers and curb bureaucratic excesses vis-à-vis the indigenous Muslim community. No stranger to Algeria, Cambon attempted to soften the regime's hostile stance toward Islam and the sufi orders and to cultivate cordial relations with religious notables heading the great brotherhoods, the Qadiriyya, Tijaniyya, and Rahmaniyya.[112] The clumsy meddling by Crochard and others into the spiritual affairs of a friendly sufi center, such as al-Hamil, was viewed with displeasure in Algiers. Zaynab's actions had, therefore, thrown the colonial administration into a certain disarray. By the end of 1897, Meygret recommended to Cambon that the colonial regime refrain from further interference in the al-Hamil dispute. Convinced that she would never yield without recourse to force, the authorities in Algiers ordered Bu Sa'ada's officers to desist.[113] Muhammad b. al-Hajj Muhammad was relegated to the sidelines for the next seven years, although his gracious female cousin gave him managerial functions at the zawiya. Zaynab had defeated the combined forces of French officialdom and her cousin. More important, she had succeeded her father.

Feeling secure in her position as director, Zaynab had al-Hamil's mosque rebuilt in 1898, calling in Italian masons and artisans from Morocco and the East to construct a completely new structure, perhaps as a symbol of her hard-won spiritual authority.[114] While she was left more or less in peace, another assault upon her management of the center came in 1899 under the guise of financial claims against the zawiya's assets, an attack which Zaynab deftly repulsed. That year an Algerian named Sa'id b. Lakhdar requested that the military officers in Bu Sa'ada take action on his behalf against the Rahmaniyya establishment. Lakhdar, who as Zaynab observed in her letter was mentally deranged, maintained that Zaynab's father owed him the colossal sum of over two million francs. In addition, he asserted that Sidi Muhammad had designated him as the shaykh's spiritual khalifa or successor. Local officers, eager to push even patently fraudulent claims, subsequently contacted Zaynab, demanding an explanation.[115]

Drawing upon Islamic law, customary practice, French legal procedures, and her own highly developed powers of reasoning, Zaynab swiftly refuted all of Lakhdar's allegations. Among other arguments, she observed that "there is no native Algerian in all of our region who has ever possessed over two million francs in specie."[116] Moreover, the sum demanded by the plaintiff was not recorded in the zawiya's financial registers, nor did Lakhdar possess a written receipt of deposit from Shaykh Muhammad. Finally, Zaynab pointed out the irrational nature of the complaint and its true motives—to discredit the zawiya and its female director:

> Sa'id ibn Lakhdar says that he deposited this sum of money with my father. Assuming that the sum was in cash, [the plaintiff] would have been obliged to transport a heavy load of specie, requiring enormous numbers of donkeys to deliver it to the zawiya. . . . the claims of this individual have no foundation; . . . how ever, this affair is the work of someone other than Lakhdar, who is a tool for those who hate us and who are intent upon the ruin and loss of the zawiya.[117]

Zaynab's written rebuttals were a tour de force in terms of argumentation; her letters reveal not only a profound familiarity with the colonial regime—and with the mentality of Algeria's French masters—but also a singular sense of strategy. Once again, she pointedly reminds those in power of their obligations under the implicit colonial pact: "The French government, whose predominant qualities are those of justice and equity, will know how to foil the plans of evil people."[118] Finally, her intimate knowledge of all the details of Sa'id b. Lakhdar's past financial relations with her father demonstrates that Sidi Muhammad had kept his daughter informed of the zawiya's various banking activities.

In the course of this incident, she clearly emerged as the protector of the harim's secluded women, assuming a role previously fulfilled by her father. Still pressing his case several months later, Sa'id b. Lakhdar next sought to force the harim's women to travel to Algiers to one of the tomb-shrines of Sidi Muhammad b. 'Abd al-Rahman al-Azhari. There at the qubba of the Rahmaniyya tariqa's saint-founder, the women were to take an oath swearing they knew nothing of the money owed by their deceased spouse. Lakhdar's demands caused great distress among Sidi Muhammad's widows.

Once more, Zaynab adroitly discredited the legality of this ploy by appealing both to Islamic law regarding oaths and to French justice. If need be, she would take an oath upon the tomb of the great saint in Algiers—an extremely serious, morally binding act in the eyes of Muslims—but the harim's women were not parties to the dispute and thus should not be disturbed.[119] The matter ended there.

In part, Zaynab's victory sprang from her own determination and tactical skills as well as French powerlessness in the face of a refractory Muslim woman. The feckless, greedy nature of her cousin was another factor since popular enthusiasm for his cause was lacking. Paradoxically, the backing of local colonial authorities may have eroded the little respect Muhammad b. al-Hajj Muhammad enjoyed in the community. Nevertheless, Zaynab's father played a role in resolving the dispute—from the grave—by performing a posthumous miracle.

When the struggle over spiritual succession was in its most bitter stage, Lalla Zaynab took refuge one day at her father's tomb. There she wept and prayed for hours until nightfall. Alarmed by her distress, family and followers gathered at the tomb to implore her to return to the residence. As Zaynab refused to heed their pleas, the old imam raised his voice to heaven and cried out: "Oh Lord, come to our aid; who thus has inherited [Sidi Muhammad's] baraka?" Immediately all present heard Shaykh Muhammad's voice issue from the grave, saying: "It is my daughter, Zaynab, who has inherited my baraka." From that day forth, Zaynab's legitimate succession was confirmed; the ranks of her clientele swelled to include former skeptics.[120]

There was, however, one more significant, if less articulate, force determining the outcome of the succession conflict—public opinion and the collective consensus of the faithful. As much as colonial officials in the capital, Zaynab's clientele, drawn from the local community and wider sufi network, helped to resolve the issue. As stated earlier, Zaynab's father had bequeathed upon her a fund of sociospiritual capital which she then enlarged through her own piety, virtue, and erudition. Moreover, because baraka—which fused grace, blessings, supernatural powers, and charisma—was regarded as transmissible, the struggle between Zaynab and her cousin was in reality over the dead shaykh's baraka. Public recognition of Zaynab's worthiness to receive her father's baraka, together with overriding French concerns for maintaining public order, thus brought the succession quarrel to an end. Ordinary people, too, had a voice in electing saintly preceptors.

A rare eyewitness account of the forms that popular veneration for the female saint and sufi assumed is provided by the French artist, Charles de

Galland, who visited Lalla Zaynab in al-Hamil seven months after her father's death. De Galland noted that, anticipating Zaynab's appearance, a large crowd "of the faithful remaining completely immobile and silent" had gathered in a small square before the zawiya's immense doorway; the throng included both Rahmaniyya members and others not affiliated with the order. Zaynab's emergence from the residence dressed in flowing, white robes provoked a murmur that rippled throughout the throng, then a dead silence fell. When Zaynab reappeared later to wend her way through the people, they pressed around her, bending low to kiss the hem of her garments and capture some of her baraka as had earlier been done with her father.[121]

Contrary to Crochard's predictions that "the daughter of the marabout [would] be unable to administer alone the zawiya's vast fortune and properties, dispersed over three *départements*," Zaynab's seven-year stewardship was no less judicious than her father's. By 1899, local military officials reluctantly admitted that under her direction al-Hamil's fortune remained intact and "the gardens around al-Hamil [were] flourishing, the farmland cultivated, and the zawiya's numerous flocks [were] thriving."[122] As her father had done, Zaynab initiated sufi brothers and sisters into the Rahmaniyya tariqa with her own hands.[123] The number of annual pilgrims to the zawiya remained as high as in previous years, and students poured in seeking instruction. Thus, despite her deteriorating health and the taxing burden of caring for several hundred indigents per day, Zaynab directed the zawiya in vigorous fashion with, as one European remarked, "an incomparable authority."[124] The demands of running a complex sufi center with a widely dispersed following meant that Zaynab journeyed throughout the area, as her father before her. Wherever she paused to pray, the populace erected maqams—simple shrines or saint markers—to commemorate her presence, thereby designating the sacredness of the space.

After Sidi Muhammad's death, Zaynab emerged more fully into the public spaces largely reserved for males, whether French or Algerian. In part it was the very opposition of men like Crochard that compelled her to construct a more public persona. To wage the campaign against her cousin, she began to travel widely, visiting Rahmaniyya notables, Muslim dignitaries, and French officials, although she had always moved freely about in the local Muslim community due to her saintly status and celibate state. Yet it was not necessarily the dictates of gender roles, informed by Islamic custom, which had kept her in the old shaykh's shadow prior to 1897 but rather respect for his prestige, age, and authority. Similarly, deferential attitudes also determined the behavior of subordinate or junior males toward older sufi superiors. Finally, while European settler colonialism erected its own highly charged political spaces and boundaries in Algeria, Zaynab, as a female saint commanding a vast following, was able to challenge those boundaries to a degree that few Muslim males or ordinary women dared.[125]

By the century's close, the turbulent frontiers earlier created by populist protest and resistance had given way to sociocultural frontiers. Particularly in northern Algeria, the dividing lines between the two communities, European and Muslim, were becoming increasingly lithified and justified by reliance upon racial arguments. Nowhere was this more apparent than in the social place assigned to Western women in French Algeria, about which little has been written. Another woman who defied colonial cultural confines—in this case, the accepted norms of European female behavior in front of the "natives"—was Isabelle Eberhardt.

Zaynab and Isabelle, "The Passionate Nomad"

In 1902, an improbable relationship developed between the virgin saint and sufi and Isabelle Eberhardt (1877–1904), the "passionate nomad."[126] Eberhardt was the illegitimate daughter of a defrocked Armenian clergyman of nihilist persuasion and an aristocratic German woman. Her childhood and upbringing in Geneva were wildly eccentric, predisposing Eberhardt to unconventional behavior throughout her brief life. In 1897, the year of Sidi Muhammad's death, Eberhardt and her mother arrived in the city of Bône, hoping to escape the domestic unhappiness and social ostracism they had suffered in Europe. Instead the two women found themselves in Bône's bigoted, self-righteous pied-noir community, whose inhabitants suffered from acute "status anxiety" toward both the Muslim Algerians and expatriate foreigners.[127] There Eberhardt continued her study of Arabic and Islam, snubbing settler society and fraternizing instead with the colonized. Her marriage in 1902 to an Algerian Muslim soldier, Sliman Ehnni, one of the few Algerians to be granted citizenship, also ironically conferred French nationality upon Eberhardt, who carried a Russian passport, as well as provoking an uproar in colonial circles.

Eberhardt's evident sympathy for Islam and Arab culture aroused a great deal of overt hostility among officials and European settlers alike. In addition, Isabelle's disorderly conduct—a fondness for alcohol and drugs, illicit sexual liaisons, and cross-gender, cross-cultural dressing (she wore the garb of an Algerian male most of the time)—caused profound distress in colonial society. Since European women were the custodians of France's divinely ordained civilizing mission in Algeria (and elsewhere in Africa), white women defined social distance from, and political control over, the "natives." By mixing socially and sexually with Muslim Algerians, Eberhardt transgressed the culturally and legally defined "racial" barriers separating the two communities. Ironically, Eberhardt, a social marginal, posed the ultimate challenge to the colonial order.[128] It is uncertain how Lalla Zaynab and her zawiya first came to Eberhardt's attention, although when Isabelle and her mother rented their first house in Bône in 1897, they chose to live in the Arab quarter; a Rahmaniyya zawiya was located down the street from their home.[129] By this time, Zaynab's reputation for sanctity and miracles had spread far beyond the Sahara, and she was "spoken of with awe and reverence throughout every corner of Algeria where the disciples of the Rahmaniyya order were found."[130] Women, both European and Muslim, brought their ailing children to Zaynab, who was blessed with the ability to cure. Therefore, Eberhardt may have heard about the female saint either from Muslim friends or from the small circle of French "Arabophiles," or she may have read about her in travel accounts then being published by Frenchmen who had visited al-Hamil.[131] In addition, Eberhardt, as was true of many Europeans in this period, the heyday of European Orientalism, was fascinated by the desert. As Isabelle put it: "In the really Arab towns like the fortified oases of the south, the poignant and bewitching atmosphere of the land of Africa is quite tangible."[132] Thus, her unquiet soul and exoticist cravings drove Isabelle into the Sahara.

In the summer of 1902, Eberhardt made the arduous journey from Algiers to al-Hamil expressly to visit Lalla Zaynab, the first of several pilgrimages to the zawiya. By then the European woman was suffering from a host of physical and other afflictions—chronic malaria, syphilis, and drug addiction—and was bent upon pursuing some vague mystical vocation connected to her frantic search for inner tranquillity. Arriving in Bu Sa'ada during a violent summer rainstorm, Isabelle was forced to obtain written permission from local military authorities before proceeding on to al-Hamil. Clothed in Arab male garb and riding a horse, she set out for the oasis, noting:

> The route to al-Hamil goes through the hills, between the high mountains that surround Bou Sa'ada. The wadi follows this route, and near the zawiya of al-Hamil it flows into the gardens, whose date palms radiate with their peculiar color. The village of al-Hamil is made of very light *tub* (sun-dried bricks) and seems to be painted with whitewash. The village is rather large and situated half-way up the mountainside, dominating the gardens and the valley. The town's culminating point is formed by the zawiya.[133]

Zaynab had been absent from the oasis on some unspecified mission but returned the next day to greet her newly arrived guest. Overlooking the

European woman's dissolute ways, Zaynab welcomed Eberhardt to her residence and apparently consented to be her spiritual mentor and friend. The female saint made a huge impression upon Eberhardt, who described their first meeting at length in her diary. The troubled European woman bared her soul to Zaynab, who listened with evident sympathy to Eberhardt's story, although there is no way of knowing exactly how Isabelle portrayed herself. Zaynab sanctioned Isabelle's spiritual quest, even assuring her visitor of her undying friendship.[134] Isabelle left a moving account of the shaykh's daughter, whom she described as dressed in the simple, white costume of the women of Bu Sa'ada: "Her face, tanned by the sun because she travels frequently in the region, was wrinkled. She is nearly fifty years old. Her eyes are kindly and in them burns a flame of intelligence, though veiled by a great sadness. Everything—her voice, her mannerisms, and the welcome she accords to pilgrims—expresses a profound sincerity."[135]

According to Eberhardt, Shaykh Muhammad b. Abi al-Qasim had designated Zaynab to succeed him, educating her in the manner "of the best of his students." Al-Hamil "more so than any other sufi center is a refuge for the poor who come here from all over."[136] The European woman noted with alarm that Lalla Zaynab's health was declining; she appeared older than her years. By then Zaynab suffered from a painful throat disease that made talking arduous and rendered her voice hoarse. Their conversations were interrupted by a "harsh cough which shook [Zaynab's] frail body, fragile as that of a child under its burnus and veils."[137] A lifetime of fasting, asceticism, and illness had left its mark upon the saint; Isabelle was correct in foreseeing Zaynab's death before too long.

Despite the briefness of their first encounter, the two women took to one another, and Zaynab in turn confided in Isabelle. With tears in her eyes, she told her European visitor the following: "My daughter, . . . I have devoted my entire life to doing good for the love of God. Nevertheless, there are men who refuse to recognize the good that I have done for them. Many hate and envy me. And yet, I have renounced all in life; I never married, I have no children, no joy."[138] Isabelle's interview with Lalla Zaynab, as short as it was, brought her an inexplicable sense of joy and much needed inner peace. From the pilgrimage to al-Hamil, which passed as "as rapid as a dream," she returned to Algiers healed, momentarily, of the morbid languor which had so long afflicted her.[139] The next year while in the capital, Eberhardt happened upon one of al-Hamil's inhabitants, Sidi Abu Bakr, who greeted her, saying, "Won't you come see us again. . . . the trees are beginning to flower. . . . the marabuta [Zaynab] speaks often about you."[140] Isabelle, whose own health was declining, visited her spiritual mentor on several more occasions, writing in 1903 that "each time I see Lalla Zaynab, I experience a sort of rejuvenation. . . . I saw her yesterday twice in the morning. She was very kind and gentle toward me and expressed delight at seeing me again."[141] By this time, the friendship developing between the two women had come to the attention of the authorities.

The French military had been discreetly spying upon Zaynab's activities in al-Hamil since 1897 and monitoring Isabelle's movements since by then she was deemed an "undesirable." Despite the innocuous nature of their relationship, the police tracked Eberhardt's second visit to Zaynab in 1903, seeking to gather information about the meetings. The new governor-general, Charles Jonnart, urged the commanding general of the province to discover "the subjects of the two women's conversations."[142] In part high-level concern was a product of the succession dispute and colonial fears about the politicization of the Rahmaniyya zawiya. Moreover, on the eve of Lyautey's planned military sweep from Algeria into southwestern Morocco, calm in the Sahara was of paramount importance. Finally, some officials held the mistaken belief that Eberhardt exerted influence over the Algerian Muslims because of her sufi affiliation and Arabic fluency. Of course, it was quite the opposite, but the notion that a Muslim woman, like Zaynab, could have an enormous impact upon a European female did not occur to them.

This relationship between a colonized female saint, whose life was wholly devoted to self-abnegation, and a Western woman, whose manic personality impelled her to excess and self-destructive behavior, appears to be somewhat unusual in the annals of Maghribi history. However, both women flouted colonial male authority, although Isabelle's rebellion went much further than Zaynab's since Eberhardt violated the sexual and cultural norms of her own European society. Eberhardt's profession of Islam (she claimed to have converted while still in Europe sometime before 1897), her supposed membership in the Qadiriyya sufi order, and her fluent command of the classical and vernacular Arabic language probably gave her an entrée into Zaynab's circle, as did the North African custom of hospitality and courtesy toward guests. Yet as significant in the developing friendship was the fact that it took place on the physical and political margins of the colonial regime—in the Sahara, away from the centers of European settlement with its increasingly rigid lines of social demarcation.

The two women did not see one another again after 1903. The next year brought Isabelle's sensational death in October 1904 during a desert flash flood at 'Ain Sefra, where the French army, under Lyautey, was thrusting deep into Moroccan territory.[143] Flamboyant in death as in life, Eberhardt's story overshadowed that of her spiritual guide who also died the same year.

On 19 November 1904, Zaynab succumbed to the disease which had progressively undermined her health.[144] The next day she was buried alongside her father and her paternal uncle in the family mausoleum, in a "great tomb draped with green, yellow, and red coverings, surrounded by a spacious railed enclosure."[145] The crowd attending her funeral became so great and unruly in their grief that the zawiya's personnel buried her earlier than planned. Zaynab's tomb, like that of her father's, became a popular pilgrimage site; indeed it still is today. Now her cousin could at long last assume the long-coveted headship of al-Hamil—or so he thought. Yet Zaynab died intestate; whether she did this intentionally is impossible to ascertain. Without a valid will, and with several branches of the shaykh's family advancing claims to inheritance rights, the matter of succession was postponed for over a year while the complex judicial inquiry proceeded through the courts. Eventually the case ended up before the civil tribunal in Algiers for adjudication.[146]

Zaynab's Cousin: "Hard and Stony Is His Path"

When Muhammad b. al-Hajj Muhammad finally assumed full responsibility for the sufi establishment, the worst had happened. During the lengthy, at times bitter, court proceedings, the zawiya had forfeited its control over some of its lands, flocks, and other forms of wealth. Reduced material assets diminished the center's ability to provide social welfare services, which brought a corresponding decrease in moral and religious prestige. By 1910 al-Hamil's economic situation was so precarious that the new Rahmaniyya shaykh petitioned the French government to borrow money, thus falling into the very snare that Zaynab and her father had carefully avoided—financial dependence upon, and by extension political subjugation to, the colonial regime.[147] By the eve of the Great War, however, colonial officials were rather less concerned with sufi leaders on the Sahara's edge since other, more compelling, preoccupations confronted them: massive emigration from western Algeria, indigenous resistance to service in the French army, and increasing urban restiveness, where new political voices were being raised, if not heard, for the first time.[148] Therefore, Muhammad b. al-Hajj Muhammad's pleas for credit advances were regarded more as a minor irritation than an opportunity to shape the course of Muslim politics.

In 1912, another European woman, Helen C. Gordon, journeyed to al-Hamil, attracted to the oasis by its reputation as an "Arab university town." Over eight years had passed since Zaynab's death, yet her memory remained vivid among the villagers and zawiya's clients and would endure for decades thereafter.

> So beneficent had been her sway, so charitable was she that "her memory is still green in the hearts of her people," and by children her name is spoken as one would whisper that of a revered saint, with awe and to bear witness to the truth of some statement they have made which is open to suspicion.[149]

Gordon also noted that, while pilgrims continued to arrive in the oasis to offer alms to Zaynab's cousin and seek his baraka, Muhammad b. al-Hajj was "secretly considered to be avaricious and worldly" by the people.[150] Since his female cousin's pious reputation continued, even from the grave, to completely overshadow his in the eyes of the faithful, the Rahmaniyya shaykh looked elsewhere for gratification. When the sister of the English monarch visited al-Hamil in search of the exotic, Muhammad b. al-Hajj Muhammad expended lavish sums to honor her with an elegant luncheon. His efforts were inspired less by the dictates of customary hospitality than by the feverish expectation that he would be rewarded by some sort of magnificent medal or decoration. Bitter disappointment awaited him when the king's sister bestowed upon the shaykh no more than her photograph.[151] Under Muhammad b. al-Hajj's direction, the sufi zawiya was transformed into a "folkloric" center, a sort of ethnological museum where "Mauresque hospitality" entertained bored Europeans in search of colorful, authentic, yet domesticated native ambience. The cost of providing these distractions, complete with oriental food and drink, to demanding Western guests depleted the zawiya's coffers, at the expense of its social welfare services.[152] Thus, after 1904, al-Hamil experienced a fate similar to that of many other sufi centers in North Africa: localization, marginalization, and exoticization. These processes were frequently accompanied by an overly cozy relationship between religious notables and the colonial regime, which ultimately left sufi leaders open to charges of "collaboration" by Muslim reformist and nationalist forces after the Great War.[153]

Viewed in the short term, Zaynab's victory over her cousin and French officialdom was Pyrrhic. Fearing that her rival would squander the zawiya's resources, she fought successfully to retain management of al-Hamil's spiritual and mundane affairs. By dying intestate, she exposed the sufi establishment to a debilitating legal quarrel which ultimately led to direct French intervention in the zawiya's internal affairs, diminishing its ability to function as a cultural redoubt for a society under siege. Yet it could be argued that al-Hamil's socioeconomic importance would have dwindled anyway with the emergence of new, urban-based political forces and of the Reformist Ulama of Shaykh 'Abd al-Hamid b. Badis (Ben Badis), centered in Constantine. Nevertheless, the Algerian religious revival and nationalist movements were the cultural heirs of pious saints and sufis like the shaykh and his daughter.

This was not lost on one fervent reformer and nationalist, Ahmad Tawfiq al-Madani (1899–1954), an Algerian by origins but Tunisian by birth. The cofounder of the Tunisian Dustur (Old Destour) party and editor of the journal *Ifriqiya*, al-Madani was accused by Tunisian protectorate authorities of supporting 'Abd al-Karim's revolt (1921–1926) and the Moroccan rebel's drive to create an independent state in the Rif. In 1925, al-Madani was officially expelled from Tunisia and returned to the country of his forefathers, where he helped to launch the Association of the Reformist Ulama in 1931. In his memoirs, al-Madani devotes a section to the zawiya of al-Hamil, which the fiercely nationalist writer characterized as "ma'qil al-'uruba wa al-Islam," (the refuge of Arab culture and Islam). He also noted that "after the death of Shaykh Muhammad b. Bilqasim [*sic*] his daughter, al-sayyida Zaynab bint Muhammad, devout, chaste, and worthy, took over the direction of the zawiya, whose capacity [to provide] knowledge increased along with its prosperity."[154]

Even today, some three thousand pilgrims make the annual ziyara to al-Hamil from the distant Jurjura Mountains. Proceding as a cohort, they depart from the Kabylia in May after the olive harvest; a portion of the harvest is brought as gifts and offerings specifically dedicated to the zawiya. Again in autumn, two to three hundred Kabyle pilgrims come to al-Hamil to spent the night there in proximity to the very special dead. As late as 1985, the zawiya of al-Hamil still claimed five hundred sufi members; its educational activities persisted, although in a much attenuated form, even after independence from France.[155]

Postscripts

For Muhammad b. Abi al-Qasim, survival was more compelling than violent confrontations or armed struggle. More precisely, survival for Muslim Algerian culture represented in and of itself such an immense struggle that radical resistance gave way to subtler, perhaps more enduring forms of social action. Because he grasped and accepted some of the limitations imposed upon him, the saint was able to work all the more efficiently within a colonial system of domination that marginalized large numbers of people, while reinforcing the abusive powers of selected indigenous elites. In Sidi Muhammad's relationship with his colonial superiors can be detected the outlines of an tacit pact which imposed political restraints upon both parties to the agreement, the French and the Algerian Muslims. In return for cultural autonomy and the freedom to engage in socioreligious works, the shaykh refrained from politics, as narrowly defined by Algeria's European masters, and prudently avoided clashes with colonial forces wielding certain kinds of power. In large measure, withdrawal to al-Hamil spared him the types of painful, intractable choices faced by his peers in the Rahmaniyya tariqa during the conquest era. Compromising situations were skirted, although the zawiya was subject to the nervous scrutiny of nearby officials, especially after a woman came to power. Thus Shaykh Muhammad fits into none of the categories conventionally employed to identify the political behavior of religious notables during the colonial moment; for he was neither an "ignorer" of the West, nor a fence sitter or an accommodator, nor a last-ditch resistor, nor a collaborator.[156] He forged a novel course of action by combining all of these strategies to preserve Algerian culture. In this the shaykh of al-Hamil was a precursor of more militant leaders such as 'Abd al-Hamid b. Badis. Yet the political component inherent in Muslim education organized and funded outside of official channels would become glaringly apparent a generation after the shaykh's death only with the movement of reformed ulama in the interwar period.

During her lifetime and for decades after her death, Zaynab was revered as a god-fearing, learned woman and a saint by a her followers, both male and female. Her spiritual authority was constructed of a number of elements. Birth into a saintly lineage of sharifian descent furnished a threshold of inherited holiness; her own intensely personal spiritual itinerary rendered Zaynab the encapsulation of the virtuous woman. Communal recognition of her uncommon private virtue, as seen in public works of charity and in her chosen virginity, resulted in Zaynab's informal, popular election to the ranks of the uniquely pious. Indeed, the ritual transmission of baraka to Zaynab from her father's tomb may have merely endorsed what was already widely acknowledged.

Blessed with miraculous gifts, she was a healer of bodies and of unquiet spirits, as Isabelle Eberhardt learned. While part of her sociospiritual capital was clearly inherited from her father, Zaynab expanded that fund of popular veneration through her own actions, including an uncompromising stance against those ostensibly monopolizing political power. For the colonial pact still held in this period, and it was Zaynab who pointedly reminded officials of their contractual duties under the terms of the transaction worked out earlier with her father. She did so despite—or because of—opposition from officials and some members of indigenous society. By being both an obedient daughter and a rebellious woman, Zaynab transformed the terms of the colonial encounter, shifting the moral burden for the maintenance of order and implicit pacts upon imperial authorities.

Taken together, the stories of the shaykh and his daughter provide evidence for two historical processes whose significance has gone largely unrecognized: if resistance in the post-1871 era was mainly cultural and educational, it was no less deeply patriotic or politically subversive; and women as well as men, ordinary people as well as elites, were active agents in contests for power whose outcome assured the endurance of North Africa's cultural patrimony.

Conclusion

This has been a sort of archaeological dig to uncover the subterranean dimensions of rebellion against, as well as tacit agreements with, the colonial regime. Indeed the two—rebellion and uneasy accord—were intimately related, although they did not exhaust the range of political positions available to, indeed, created by indigenous actors. The flame, heat, and din of the numerous insurrections that jolted Algeria throughout the nineteenth century forged the very nature of the colonial order itself—not only in Algeria or North Africa but elsewhere. The uprisings, and the turbulent frontiers generated, drew France southward into the Sahara and toward the borders with Tunisia; they also defined the terms of numerous, subsequent colonial encounters enduring into the present century.

Yet the intensity of militant clashes has deflected attention away from other quieter, underground transformations that unfolded even as the banners of revolt were raised. As the stories of Sidi Muhammad b. Abi al-Qasim and Zaynab reveal, implicit pacts between religious notables and French officials may have ultimately proven as momentous to Algeria's historical trajectory as revolt.

The 1849 rebellion affords a rich, if fragmentary, police dossier for exploring a dense undergrowth of relationships whose existence was only partially suspected: relations between provincial sufi notables and populist protest, between migrant laborers and politics, between information and collective action, and between what political actors, both religious and secular, sought to do and what they in fact accomplished. Moreover, when placed against the backdrop of earlier and later protest movements, Bu Ziyan's jihad reconnects social and historical phenomena perceived as largely disconnected, spontaneous, and episodic.

So it seemed to the French conquerors, harassed in their imperial ambitions by seemingly endless unrest bursting out here and there across Algeria's unfamiliar landscape. However, by scrutinizing events from the vantage point of local religious notables, tribal leaders, and ordinary people, a continual thread of sociopolitical logic emerges, one that spans not only the decades making up the rebellious half-century but also the precolonial and colonial eras. Thus Za'atsha must first be considered in relation to the two decades immediately following the French invasion. The revolt was not only directly linked to but was also the product of two larger, transregional attempts to expel the intruders and resurrect different kinds of states. The failure of these two rather distinct styles of politics, together with Bugeaud's policy of total occupation and local conditions in the Sahara, cleared the way for mahdist solutions to the crises unleashed by the fall of Algiers.

The revolt centered in Za'atsha was in part a response to the colonial state's clumsy labors to subdue peoples long accustomed to a large degree of autonomy. The Ziban's villagers drew upon an ancient heritage of opposition to central governments. For centuries, they had repeatedly defied attackers from the safety of walled oases; in 1831 they spurned the advances of Ahmad Bey, which conferred a confidence born of victory. Previously, victory—or at least nondefeat—meant that the besiegers would pack up and depart, if only temporarily. In terms of organization and tactics, the Za'atsha rebellion resembled older forms of contention. These had worked well enough against the Turkish regime, which had marshaled means of violence roughly equal to those wielded by dissidents.

In a narrow sense, the rebellion failed due to the grave imbalance in material resources accessible to the two sides. By 1849 the colonial state mobilized limitless numbers of soldiers and new sorts of military technology, intervening more massively in the affairs of local communities than its Turkish predecessors had ever thought possible or desirable. However, the movement's ideology was utterly different from earlier contests. By its middle stages, the Za'atsha rebellion had been transformed into a mahdist crusade because alternative modes of political action had proven incapable of giving voice to shared grievances and righting a social order rendered topsy-turvy. Not only would the enemy retreat but also the infidels would be driven from North Africa by the mahdi's triumphant forces; Za'atsha constituted the antechamber to the long-awaited realm of justice, according to the oral information circuits. And the actions of the curious, if repellent, Europeans were continually "read," commented upon, and transcribed in a certain manner by North Africans, who either came into sustained contact with the occupiers or merely heard about them through the unremitting rumor mill. And the discursive field of power surrounding political actors shaped political decision and actions.

As the endless word-of-mouth tales about the mahdi and the letters from Shaykh Mustafa b. 'Azzuz indicate, both sufi leaders and followers believed in the eschatological lore concerning the "expected one." The mahdi's person embodied a bundle of symbols expressing religious aspirations and collective longings for social justice.[1] By first appropriating the paradigm of the holy person, Bu Ziyan subsequently went on to merge two political traditions—those of oasis and tribal society; and the Maghribi heritage of mass revivalist movements centered around charismatic prophets. Even as death awaited him, Bu Ziyan claimed two personae; to his reputation as a local warrior-hero were added messianic credentials.

Thus the Za'atsha revolt was not, as some colonial writers claimed, a localized, unrehearsed rebellion.[2] Its causation and dynamic were related to political dramas being played out in other parts of Algeria. And by countering colonial thrusts into the Sahara, Bu Ziyan's movement lured the Europeans into conflicts with other rebels, messianic and otherwise; the fallout from the uprising increasingly implicated adjacent North African states, particularly Tunisia, in Algerian struggles. While the 1849 debacle sent waves of refugees into the beylik, the rebellion remained a more or less Algerian affair. Nevertheless, it convinced some activist sufi leaders, such as Mustafa b. 'Azzuz, that continued resistance had to be an across-the-border enterprise, which conversely demanded remaining in the good graces of colonial authorities. Paradoxically, defeat did not dampen mahdist expectations but rather nourished them, providing sustenance for a successor movement—for a while at least.

Muhammad b. 'Abd Allah's revolt, at least initially, tapped deep into the bedrock of populist hopes fixed upon the mahdi. Powerful, fearsome legends regarding the redeemer's coming were manipulated both by the Sharif of Warqala and his backers to advance various causes. Muhammad b. 'Abd Allah was a complex individual—saint, sufi, mahdi, rebel, desert warrior, and eventually brigand. In its early gestation, his jihad demonstrated that large-scale uprisings against governments deemed illegitimate might emerge from factional infighting within a particular community. In its denouement after 1854, the rebellion's apocalyptic core metastasized once again to slide into banditry.

Had Muhammad b. 'Abd Allah been content with a purely defensive or quietist-scripturalist movement aspiring to renew Islam in a region removed from the Europeans' contaminating influence, he might have served as the cult figure for a new sufi tariqa. Sucked into the maelstrom of

Saharan politics—or perhaps shoved by his tribal backers—he became the rallying point for a wide-ranging, loosely knit coalition. Its failure, paradoxically, lay partially in successful mobilization. By attracting a diverse following from all over the Algerian and Tunisian Sahara, the rebellion lost its original meaning and impetus, adding new, often contradictory, aims to its platform.

If the rumors truly expressed collective expectations, some participants yearned for Algeria to return to her rightful master, the Ottoman sultan. For others, ending the humiliations of infidel rule signaled that the millennium was nigh. A few, mainly tribal, elites, aspired to carve out desert realms or reassert a long-cherished autonomy. For yet other followers and leaders, the objective was to restore the status quo ante invasion. As was true of 'Abd al-Qadir's movement, the sharif expended much energy attempting to eliminate native rivals, or rather the traditional enemies of his tribal supporters. The jihad, therefore, became embroiled in a myriad of local quarrels, saff realignments, and shifting political agendas. Buffeted by uncertainty and lacking an initial, resounding blow to the French to confirm divine favor, it too ended in defeat. Or more accurately, after a string of setbacks, the jihad's mobilized warriors gradually dispersed as their fervor was depleted and economic conditions deteriorated. In large measure, this dispersion was due to the desert's ecological imperatives; there were limits to the coercive power that religious notables or even mahdis could claim.

Like the Amir 'Abd al-Qadir, Muhammad b. 'Abd Allah was beset by the problem of adequately supplying his forces in the Sahara's unforgiving environment. This eventually made razzias imperative, which alienated real or potential allies. Precisely because of the transborder nature of commercial and other exchanges in the pre-1850 period, the sharif's movement endured as long as it did. Ironically, his jihad, which depended so heavily upon cross-border ties, ultimately undermined its own material bases. Constant turmoil along trade routes stretching from Warqala to the Jarid eventually weakened trade. This rendered patterned commercial exchanges riskier and rarer, as beylical and European records show.[3]

The sharif's movement demonstrates that collective protest in the Sahara depended as much upon wheat and markets as charismatic leadership, sufi networks, or a collective sense of grievances conflated with millenarian expectations. Unlike Za'atsha, the movement's demise was only partially due to the superiority of the French military machine. In the regions south of Biskra, Western technological might was attenuated by the ruthless nature of the terrain and, as important, its unfamiliarity. However, as the colonial state gradually learned to control strategic markets, trade routes, and passages, relatively small numbers of soldiers—aided by co-opted indigenous elites—could reduce the desperate or drive the recalcitrant farther into the Sahara or across the borders. There rebellions lost their urgency and constituencies, as partisans defected from practical considerations of subsistence.[4]

The jihad's displacement over the borders into the Jarid was ominous for future rebels, religious émigrés, and ultimately for Tunisia itself. Since the beylik was employed as a base of opposition to, or a retreat from, the colonial regime, Tunisia's political fate was sealed long before 1881. Collective protest that spilled over into both Tunisia and Morocco convinced colonial strategists that France's African *département* would never be secure without additional territorial acquisitions. From as early as 1849, the French pursued schemes and dreams of a transdesert empire, a path inadvertently carved out by figures such as Bu Ziyan, Mustafa b. 'Azzuz, and Muhammad b. 'Abd Allah. The challenges thus posed drove the colonial state inexorably to the far reaches of the desert—into the 1864 Awlad Sidi Shaykh rebellion, the 1881 Bu 'Amama revolt, and into Morocco by the turn of the century.[5]

Finally, the movement inspired by a pious stranger from the East reveals that the nation-state as a historical unit of analysis fails to accommodate the dynamics of popular protest in nineteenth-century North Africa. The French raj in Africa was built piecemeal and haphazardly rather than out of some grand master plan to subjugate an entire continent.[6] In the *longue durée*, Algerian rebellions were instrumental in convincing colonial adventurers that the whole of the Sahara must be subdued. Indigenous peoples, both leaders and clienteles, through efforts to oppose, as well as come to grips with, the European presence participated unwittingly yet forcefully in the construction of France's empire. The supreme irony is that activist saints and sufis, like Mustafa b. 'Azzuz, undermined the very sociopolitical and religious order they strove so mightily to defend.

Rebel and Saint, Rebel or Saint?

When evaluating the Rahmaniyya's part in populist protest, colonial writers erred in treating the tariqa as a monolithic organization whose leaders and followers sang the same political tune or perceived events through a similar lens. The proper unit of sociological analysis for the Rahmaniyya order—or any complex translocal movement—is not necessarily the overarching movement itself. Rather the inquiry should commence at the level of local histories and micropolitics. Privileged holy lineages, commanding diverse clienteles, were thoroughly enmeshed in shifting relationships of cooperation and conflict—with other saintly clans, tribal big men, and with state-level powers, both traditional and colonial. Moreover, desert Rahmaniyya clans, and the humble folk who constituted their followings, belonged to a highly specific ecological environment. Indeed, the nature of Saharan economy defined to no small degree the social niches occupied by sufis and saints and by extension the surrounding field of collective action. And if this field offered both opportunities for, and constraints upon, collective struggles to repel the invaders, it also dictated what the invaders themselves could or could not do. Finally, peoples of the Saharan rim did not merely offer day-to-day knee-jerk responses to the crises wrought by the French conquest. Rather, they shared a common vision of the kind of society that ought to result from the struggle. This vision was continually revised and adjusted in accordance with the ebb and flow of information, the counsel given by venerated religious figures, the conduct of the colonizer, and the arrival of rebellious prophets.

It has been argued that the 1849 movement represented a sea change in the customary political behavior of many religious notables, who until then preferred to avoid head-on contests.[7] Moreover, Za'atsha's terrible defeat molded the future course of action embraced by many sufi leaders residing in this part of the Sahara. Those who survived the disaster either resorted to various forms of avoidance protest or—once again—opted for apparent accommodation with the victors, often combining both strategies into a larger *realpolitik* of bet hedging.

The diffident Rahmaniyya and Tijaniyya support accorded the successor movement inspired by the Sharif of Warqala is proof of the devastating lessons learned at Za'atsha. After 1849, sufi notables, such as Mustafa b. 'Azzuz, preferred lending sub rosa support to apocalyptic and other militant rebels from political havens in Tunisia. Others, such as Sidi 'Umar b. 'Ali b. 'Uthman of Tulqa and Shaykh Muhammad b. Abi al-Qasim of al-Hamil, retreated into cultural resistance by providing crucial social welfare services for their followers. They neither fled contacts with the colonizers nor actively sought untoward relations with them. Rather, they effected subtle compromises with more powerful forces in the hope of leaving uncompromised their status as privileged holy lineages—a political act in itself which demanded infinite wisdom and consummate diplomacy. Only the Rahmaniyya center located in the oasis of Sidi Masmudi in the Awras later opted for violent political action, again in the form of a small mahdist uprising. And only Zaynab chose to engage meddlesome military officials in a fierce showdown after 1897 because the colonial regime had reneged on the terms of the pact so patiently worked out by her father, one which guaranteed the cultural survival of the community.

By interpreting 1849 rather than the 1870s as the point of rupture, the conventional periodization for nineteenth-century Algerian history, based on the interplay between politics and religion, is thereby challenged. The years 1849 to 1854 were as decisive as the early conquest era or the 1870–1871 insurrection led by Shaykh al-Haddad in the Kabylia. Until 1849, most desert Rahmaniyya notables preferred the safer, pragmatic stance of fence-sitting and temporizing. It was the destabilizing advent of the mahdi and pressures from clienteles to take action that forced many religious figures out into the uncertainties of the political arena. After the 1849 repression, these notables either withdrew from rebellious activity, concluding implicit pacts with the colonial regime—the case of al-Hamil—or emigrated—the avenue pursued not only by Shaykh Mustafa b. 'Azzuz and his followers but also by countless other Algerians. Nevertheless, withdrawal, hijra, and retreat were, in and of themselves, politically charged actions which ultimately bore cultural fruits with immense ramifications after the turn of the century.

Saints, Redeemers, and Ordinary People

Both the hero of Za'atsha and the Sharif of Warqala entreated prominent Saharan sufi notables to confirm their prophetic missions, thereby legitimizing them. The mahdi's long-awaited arrival appeared imminent, the appointed hour at hand. Nevertheless, there were hidden, culturally constructed norms that governed the political behavior of those same notables—despite, or perhaps because of, the redeemer's advent. Evidence of divine election had to be furnished before privileged saintly-sufi leaders would openly sanction the one sent from Heaven. And the most compelling proof of such—a decisive triumph over the forces of evil—eluded Muhammad b. 'Abd Allah in his 1852 campaigns around Biskra. Even though all of the religious notables examined here judged the European presence in Algeria as a calamity, endorsing a false prophet, even one whose purpose was to exterminate the infidels, was equally calamitous.

Thus, the sharif's jihad in the Ziban failed due to the lukewarm reaction elicited from revered religious notables who had long acted as patrons, educators, and mediators for village and tribal peoples and as spiritual exemplars for sufi disciples dispersed far and wide. Most studies of the great brotherhoods that consider the turuq as networks of zawaya and followers emphasize the political opportunities created by the translocal nature of sociospiritual ties and allegiances. Nevertheless, these same ties could, under certain circumstances, restrict militant activities. The most striking example of this is the "warrior-marabout" Sidi Hasan b. 'Azzuz. His ephemeral bid for profane power between 1837 and 1841 was undercut in large measure by those very religiocultural norms undergirding the sufi network. Attacking unsubmissive tribal groups made good political sense; dealing harshly with fellow tariqa members was unacceptable and brought collective moral censure.

Saints and sufis had long acted as peace brokers in local quarrels or as intermediaries between the community and the political center. Yet no religious leader in the Sahara could surmount the murderous play of the saffs. In the traditional order of things, the saffs represented "routinized conflict," which privileged saintly clans managed but never overcame.[8] The ultimately fatal attempts by Tulqa's Rahmaniyya shaykh, Sidi 'Ali b. 'Umar, to defuse saff struggles through saintly arbitration in the Ziban in 1842 offered proof of this. In addition, the entry of a third unpredictable force into the war of the saffs transformed the calculus of the leagues. After the French army established its desert headquarters in Biskra in 1844, mediation became incumbent upon Saharan religious figures but more complex. Even as General Herbillon's forces besieged the rebels in Za'atsha, the Rahmaniyya shaykh of Tulqa continually offered his good offices to negotiate a settlement. Progressively, however, the terms of mediation were fundamentally transformed.[9] During the 1881 military campaign against Tunisia, colonial authorities successfully pressured the Rahmaniyya shaykh of Tulqa to preach calm and submission to village and tribal followers—not to effect a compromise agreeable to both sides.[10] Mediation and brokerage, based upon spiritual and moral authority over religious clienteles, were gradually eroded and diverted to other purposes, much to the benefit of the colonial regime.

Ordinary people exercised no ordinary influence upon the political behavior of saintly patrons and the flow of events in nineteenth-century North Africa. In 1851, Muhammad b. 'Abd Allah drew upon the wellsprings of popular messianic expectations which had earlier coalesced around Bu Ziyan. Demands for action from tribal followers in the Awras coaxed the timorous sufi of Khanqa Sidi Naji to embark on rebellious adventures in 1849. Later in the century, popular recognition of Zaynab's uncommon piety and virtue forced French officials, ever fearful of mass unrest, to cease behind-the-scenes efforts to dislodge her from the zawiya's headship. Moreover, a whole constellation of people of modest substance forged the intricate networks making up the contraband trade between Europe, Malta, the Tunisian coast and Algeria. As these people helped to furnish the material wherewithal for resistance, they also acted as bearers of word-of-mouth news.

If baraka was a commodity eagerly sought by people of modest substance from those blessed with special grace and piety, information also represented a precious commodity fought over and fought for. Both religious notables and clients were dependent upon myriad informed channels which fed news about events transpiring elsewhere, about the Europeans' intentions, about what had happened, and perhaps about what lay ahead. The democracy of rumor meant that all members of indigenous society had a hand in constructing the discursive field that determined not only what people talked about but also what they chose to do or not to do.

Whispers of impending deliverance from mahdis or Muslim rulers, together with rumors of French weakness, were circulated round and about by the barranis, pilgrims, traders, colporteurs, and sufi notables. Taken in the aggregate, quiet whispers were transmuted into deafening rumors, a form of communication that flourishes when extraordinary upheaval becomes the commonplace. In his study of the 1857 Sepoy rebellion in India, Ranajit Guha located "the mobilizing power of rumor in the ambiguity of its signification; as an anonymous, verbal message whose source is unknown, it can be rearticulated at any point along its line of transmission."[11] And people of whatever social rank acted upon rumors since they represented virtually the only news available to many, and because they betrayed individual and collective hopes and aspirations.

But from the view of world history there is another significant element to consider. The informational circuits upon which North Africans drew for news and rumors were pushed outward in space during the course of the nineteenth century. It no longer sufficed to transmit news, whether oral or written in source, from village to tribe, from region to region, or from the Maghrib to the Mashriq and back again. Rather Europe and the activities of Europeans perforce entered into the sinuous information networks linking desert with Tell, countryside with city, Tunis to Algiers. Nevertheless, as the century drew to a close, politically inflammatory rumors about North Africa's French masters appear to have subsided for the most part—or at least were recorded with less care by the authorities.

In part this was due to shifts in the relative importance between the oral and written as Arabic publishing and printing, particularly in Tunis, came of age. Then too the extraordinary tumult of decades of conquest had ceased along with the uncertain certainty of deliverance by some divinely sent redeemer. However, there is another explanation for the waning of rumors; it is tied to the fact that implicit pacts and unwritten understandings between highly visible religious notables and colonial officials had at last been concluded. Both sides engaged, at least tentatively, in a series of uneasy truces and thought that they knew what the other expected.

Implicit Pacts and Cultural Survival

Out of these distressing adjustments and disquieting accommodations was born the last great flowering of the Rahmaniyya movement whose origins lay in the late eighteenth century; that this efflorescence transpired in the oasis of al-Hamil was no accident. Indeed, Shaykh Muhammad b. Abi al-Qasim prudently worked out his own brand of coping—as battles raged around him—precisely because his zawiya was located in "the lost town."

Like their oasis havens, which were situated on the periphery of, but not peripheral to, Maghribi states, religious notables such as Sidi Muhammad b. Abi al-Qasim and Zaynab were marginal yet central. From their places of refuge on the limits of *Algérie Française*, they attended to the salvation of Algerian Muslim culture. Between the two poles of political behavior represented by militant struggle and retreat (inkimash) from the world lay possibilities for significant, if circumspect, maneuvers. When parlayed in the right manner, these possibilities could empower those in theory subjugated. Thus it was Zaynab who pointedly reminded her foreign masters of their duties under the terms of the implicit pact:

> My deceased father never engaged in intrigues against France, yet in return I am subjected to endless vexations by the *commandant supérieur*. I know that father always acted vis-à-vis France with honesty and loyalty. This is why I have just demanded that you, in memory of my father, accord me benevolence and shield me from persecution and injustice.[12]

Zaynab's words represented a formidable dare to the colonial administration then caught in the infernal logic of its proclaimed civilizing mission—abide by the tacit agreement or suffer the consequences, not the least of which might be popular unrest.

The power that extraordinary persons wielded over words raises a final issue—that of the double discourse. Ordinary people turned to sufi masters or local saints for counsel in times of crisis. As the French army approached Biskra in 1844, the followers of Tammasin's Tijaniyya shaykh begged him for guidance about alternative courses of action to pursue. Shaykh Mustafa b. 'Azzuz was described in 1851 as a "dangerous" saint because, when publicly addressing assembled crowds, he was "extremely influential in speaking."[13] Extraordinary men and women in nineteenth-century North African society wielded rhetorical power in the form of imperialism over words.[14] And the imperialism of saintly discourse—pious words—was also used against the colonial regime.

Even as Sidi 'Abd al-Hafiz of Khanqa Sidi Naji reluctantly marched into battle in 1849, the saint wrote to French officials, explaining away his participation in rebellion. Shaykh 'Abd al-Hafiz's attempts to hedge his bets in an era marked by turmoil were not unusual. His words directed to colonial authorities can be translated as an artful attempt to cope with the unstable political environment. Both secular and religious elites, such as the Banu Ghana, the Bu 'Ukkaz, the Tijaniyya shaykhs of Tammasin, and Sidi Mustafa b. 'Azzuz deliberately employed two sets of discourse—one for European consumption, the other for their followers.[15] The double discourse served an eminently political purpose—it kept the French off balance and sowed doubt in the colonial mind about the true intentions, sentiments, and objectives of indigenous allies as well as declared enemies. This type of behavior, condemned by officials as devious and later by Algerian nationalists as evidence of "collaboration," was pragmatic and flexible, and above all it ensured survival in a world turned upside down.

In North Africa and elsewhere in Asia and Africa during the colonial moment, state-making encountered various kinds of responses—from large-scale rebellion or retreat, to rumors of revolt or to heroic folk ballads in praise of saints, rebels, and mahdis. Collective cultural discourses on revered saints and sufis, on the long-awaited redeemer, and on local heroes and resisters had much in common. The commonality of these narratives during the past century may have ultimately furnished the basis for a shared sense of identity and political community in the present century.

Postscripts

What traces does today's historian find of the great sufi orders, such as the 'Azzuziya, Qadiriyya, or Tijaniyya? In the Jarid, many sufi establishments are literally crumbling. The torrential rains and inundations of 1989 pummeled the Jarid's religious buildings just as desert flash floods destroyed the Rahmaniyya zawiya in Tulqa several decades ago. In both Tuzar and Nafta, the Qadiriyya zawaya are still functioning, albeit on a much reduced scale since they serve only as meeting places for the daily prayers. The *riwaq* (small cells or rooms) circling the central courtyard of Tuzar's Qadiriyya zawiya provides shelter for poor families rather than for visiting students or scholars. Nafta's Qadiriyya zawiya sits on a hill overlooking the palm trees down below gradually dying for lack of water; the nearby four-star tourist complex pitilessly depletes the underground sources as it brings in much needed foreign currency.

Nafta's 'Azzuziyya zawiya has apparently been abandoned in recent times, like the equally dilapidated Dar 'Azzuz, now boarded up and empty, in Tuzar's old quarter. Despite the buildings' present disrepair, the saints and sufis remain alive for the Jarid's inhabitants and for the pilgrims who still arrive annually from other parts of Tunisia or neighboring Algeria. The oldest shrine and its saint—Sidi Bu 'Ali—seem to have weathered the centuries the best. In Nafta every evening, the faithful gather at the shrine lost in the luxuriant palm grove to recite prayers in unison from the Quran. And Sidi Bu 'Ali's zawaya in Tuzar and, particularly, in Nafta are both currently the object of restoration efforts. On the third day of al-'Aid al-Kabir, the mawsim in the saint's honor still takes place in Nafta. A huge procession, swelled by visitors from near and far, the pious and curious alike, assembles at the doors to the city. Known as the *dakhla* (or *kharja*), the ceremonial cortege is composed of men, women, and children as well as dancers and singers who procede from the outskirts of Nafta to the heart of the palm gardens where the saint's tomb is found. Baraka and abundance are thereby assured.

As for Sidi Mustafa b. 'Azzuz, his memory lives on in many ways and many places—among the inhabitants of Tala, for example, who, when affirming the veracity of a statement, swear ''bi-ra's Sidi 'Azzuz'' (literally, ''by the head of Sidi 'Azzuz''). And if Bu Ziyan's story furnished the plot for a recent teledrama in Algeria, Zaynab's life continues to inspire the populace of al-Hamil. Even in postcolonial Algeria, Zaynab endures as the stuff of pious legends and lore.

Abbreviations

ACCM	Archives de la Chambre de Commerce de Marseille
AESC	*Annales: Économies, Sociétés, Civilisations* (Paris)
AG	*Annales de Géographie*
AGGA	Archives du Gouvernement Général de l'Algérie (Archives d'Outre-Mer, Aix-en-Provence)
AGT	Archives du Gouvernement Tunisien (Dar al-Bey, Tunis)
AHR	*American Historical Review*
AHS	*African Historical Studies*
AMAE	Archives du Ministère des Affaires Étrangères (Paris)
AMG	Archives du Ministère de la Guerre (Service Historique de l'Armée, Vincennes)
AN	Archives Nationales (Paris)
BSGAO	*Bulletin de la Société Géographique et Archéologique d'Oran*
c.c.	correspondance commerciale (AMAE)
CHEAM	Centre des Hautes Études Administratives sur l'Afrique et l'Asie Modernes (Paris)
CIS	*Cahiers Internationaux de Sociologie*
CNRS	Centre National de la Recherche Scientifique (Paris)
c.p.	correspondance politique (AMAE)
CSSH	*Comparative Studies in Society and History*
CT	*Cahiers de Tunisie*
EI	*Encyclopedia of Islam*
ES	*Economy and Society*
ESA	*Exploration Scientifique de l'Algérie*
IBLA	*Revue de l'Institut des Belles Lettres Arabes* (Tunis)
IJMES	*International Journal of Middle East Studies*
JA	*Journal Asiatique* (Paris)

JAAS	*Journal of Asian and African Studies*
JAH	*Journal of African History*
JSH	*Journal of Social History*
mém./doc.	mémoires et documents (AMAE)
MES	*Middle Eastern Studies*
MR	*Maghreb Review* (London)
MW	*Muslim World*
n.s.	nouvelle série (AMAE)
PRO/FO	Public Record Office/Foreign Office Correspondence (Kew)
PUF	Presses Universitaires de France (Paris)
RA	*Revue Africaine*
RAC	*Revue Algérienne et Coloniale* (Paris)
RASJEP	*Revue Algérienne des Sciences Juridiques, Économiques et Politiques*
RDM	*Revue des Deux Mondes* (Paris)
RH	*Revue Historique*
RHM	*Revue d'Histoire Maghrébine* (Tunis)
RNMSAPC	*Recueil des Notices et Mémoires de la Société Archéologique de la Province de Constantine*
ROAC	*Revue de l'Orient, de l'Algérie et des Colonies*
ROMM	*Revue de l'Occident Musulman et de la Méditerranée*
RT	*Revue Tunisienne*
RTSS	*Revue Tunisienne des Sciences Sociales*
SNED	Société Nationale d'Édition et de la Diffusion (Algiers)
TIRS	*Travaux de l'Institut de Recherches Sahariens*

Notes

INTRODUCTION

1. Zaynab bint Muhammad b. Abi al-Qasim, zawiya of al-Hamil, to commanding officer, Bu Sa'ada, December 1899, AGGA 16 H 61.

2. More than two decades have passed since Edmund Burke III in "Recent Books on Colonial Algerian History," *MES* 7, 2 (1971): 241–50, urged historians to "begin the task of reassembling, out of the rubble of the colonialist tradition of historiography on Algeria, a history which focuses upon the Muslim inhabitants rather than the colonial regime as the prime object of study" (243). Several recent works on the nineteenth century that respond to Burke's intellectual call to arms are Colette Establet's *Etre caid dans l'Algérie coloniale* (Paris: Éditions du CNRS, 1991), and Allan Christelow's *Muslim Law Courts and the French Colonial State in Algeria* (Princeton: Princeton University Press, 1985).

3. Eric R. Wolf, *Europe and the People without History* (Berkeley and Los Angeles: University of California Press, 1982).

4. These religious figures are characterized as notables rather than elites in order to distinguish between various kinds of power and authority, which, however, could be intertwined. In both Ottoman and colonial North Africa, nonreligious elites, such as the shaykh al-'arab or the Muqrani clan of the northern Constantine, drew some, although not all, of their political authority from relationships with the state—either contesting it or supporting it—or both. State-derived authority would remain significant even after 1830 since opposition to the colonial order or political "mutualism" with it still defined, in large part, elite status. Religious notables on the other hand, tapped deep into other sources—sharifian descent, special piety, erudition, charity—the attributes demanded of the holy person. The most powerful belonged to a cosmopolitan republic of letters and learning, underwritten by an intensely sustained literacy. They thus wielded so-

ciospiritual and moral authority; their popular followings were evidence of communal recognition of their uncommon virtue. This did not mean that the state—whether the late Turkish or colonial—was unimportant to religious notables. It was, as will be seen.

5. The term "populist" was deliberately chosen to avoid the "high-low" polarities suggested by popular protest; the ordinary folk of the oasis and the learned shaykhs of Saharan zawaya shared to a great extent the same cultural assumptions. Moreover, there was considerable traffic between the domains of the written and oral traditions. On the current debate on popular culture, see Natalie Zemon Davis, "Toward Mixtures and Margins," *AHR* 97, 5 (December 1992): 1409–16.

6. Edmund Burke III, ed., *Struggle and Survival in the Modern Middle East* (Berkeley and Los Angeles: University of California Press, 1993), 3.

7. In studying various kinds of militant action, the historian confronts a dilemma—how to investigate a wide range of social and political phenomena whose very nature entailed the destruction of indigenous written sources. The village of Za'atsha was completely razed by the French army in December 1849 as were a number of Rahmaniyya sufi centers after seditious activities, for example, the zawiya of Sidi Masmudi in the Awras after a small mahdist rebellion in 1858. While some written materials were salvaged by the French regime, so much more was destroyed—and with it Algeria's own history.

8. For a reconsideration of the concept of moral economy, see Robert P. Weller and Scott E. Guggenheim, eds., *Power and Protest in the Countryside: Studies of Rural Unrest in Asia, Europe, and Latin America* (Durham, N.C.: Duke University Press, 1982). One flaw in James C. Scott's "strong version of moral economy" is that the implicit sociocultural constraints upon the political behavior of notables and elites are ignored. And when Muslim leaders are considered, they are invariably relegated to a category apart, defined solely by Islam's assumed inherent propensity toward militant political action. This interpretation is seen in Michael Adas's "Market Demand versus Imperial Control: Colonial Contradictions and the Origins of Agrarian Protest in South and Southeast Asia," in *Global Crises and Social Movements: Artisans, Peasants, Populists, and the World Economy*, Edmund Burke III, ed. (Boulder: Westview Press, 1988), 89–116, in which Adas seems to be arguing along lines not dissimilar to the colonial canon for North Africa—that Islam is somehow innately more prone to rebellion than other religious traditions.

9. Marcel Simian, *Les confréries islamiques en Algérie (Rahmanya-Tidjanya)* (Algiers: Jourdan, 1910), 44.

10. The historical and numerical importance of the "ignorers" of the West during the colonial assault in Africa has been itself ignored in much of the literature. R. S. O'Fahey points this out in his excellent study *Enigmatic Saint: Ahmad Ibn Idris and the Idrisi Tradition* (Evanston, Ill.:

Northwestern University Press, 1990), as does Louis Brenner in *West African Sufi: The Religious Heritage and Spiritual Search of Cerno Bokar Saalif Taal* (Berkeley and Los Angeles: University of California Press, 1984).

11. Clifford Geertz, *Islam Observed: Religious Development in Morocco and Indonesia* (Chicago: University of Chicago Press, 1971), 8–9.

12. Muhammad al-Hafnawi, *Ta'rif al-khalaf bi-rijal al-salaf*, 2d ed. (Tunis: al-Maktaba al-'Atiqa, 1982); and Ahmad ibn Abi al-Diyaf, *Ithaf ahl al-zaman bi-akhbar muluk tunis wa 'ahd al-aman*, 8 vols. (Tunis: al-Dar al-Tunisiyya lil-Nashr, 1963–1966).

13. On the nature and uses of hagiography, see Dale F. Eickelman, *Moroccan Islam: Tradition and Society in a Pilgrimage Center* (Austin: University of Texas Press, 1976), 35–43, and his "Traditional Islamic Learning and Ideas of the Person in the Twentieth Century," in *Middle Eastern Lives: The Practice of Biography and Self-Narrative*, Martin Kramer, ed. (Syracuse: Syracuse University Press, 1991), 35–59.

1. A DESERT CIVILIZATION

1. Muhammad ibn Salama, "al-'Iqd al-munaddad fi akhbar al-mushir al-basha Ahmad," MS. 18618, folio 82, Bibliothèque Nationale de Tunis. Salama was one of the few members of the elite *baldi* (old urban bourgeoisie) class from the Tunisian capital to travel in the south during the nineteenth century. Appointed to the post of *qadi al-mahalla* (jurisconsult of the beylical camp) in 1837, he participated in the expedition of 1838–1839, recording his impressions of the Jarid.

2. Eugène Fromentin (1820–1876), *Un été dans le Sahara*, new edition introduced and annotated by Anne-Marie Christine (Paris: Le Sycomore, 1981).

3. Much, though not all, of our information regarding the geography, history, and ecology of the pre-Sahara in the past century comes from European or colonial sources. In contrast to the medieval period, when the Sahara was written about by Arab savants (who were often merchants and missionaries), such as Ibn Hawqal, al-Bakri, al-Idrisi, Ibn Battuta, and Ibn Khaldun, indigenous Arabic sources for later centuries are less abundant. In large part, this is due to the cultural geography of the period; social mobility for ambitious provincial elites and notables dictated a movement from south to north—rarely the reverse. Nevertheless, the reports of the Tunisian *qa'id*s (provincial administrators) in the Jarid submitted to the central government in Tunis from the 1840s on are one valuable indigenous source, although these are mainly devoted to tax collection and political events. AGT, série historique, carton 20, dossiers (*dafatir*) 227–33.

4. Ibn Hawqal, the celebrated Arab geographer, visited the Sahara between 947–951 A.D. and remarked upon the flourishing state of oasis

agriculture in *kitab sura al-ard* (Beirut: Dar Maktaba al-Hayah, 1964), 92. Among numerous travel accounts from later periods is the 1710 description of Mulay Ahmad, a Moroccan pilgrim, in Adrien Berbrugger, trans., "Voyages dans le sud de l'Algérie," *ESA* 9 (Paris: Imprimerie Royale, 1846): 245; and L. R. Desfontaines, *Fragmens d'un voyage dans les régences de Tunis et d'Alger fait de 1783 à 1786* (Paris, 1838) 2: 72. The term "civilisation du désert" is Robert Capot-Rey's, *Le Sahara français* (Paris: PUF, 1953), 371–72. On the present problems of oasis agriculture, see among numerous works Bruno Sternberg-Sarel, "Les oasis du Djérid," *CIS* 25 (1961): 131–45.

5. André Martel's *Les confins saharo-tripolitains de la Tunisie (1881–1911)*, 2 vols. (Paris: PUF, 1965), is a noteworthy exception to this.

6. This part of the pre-Sahara, comprising both southern Tunisia and southeastern Algeria, is what Jean Despois calls the "bas-Sahara" in Jean Despois and Robert Raynal, *Géographie de l'Afrique du nord-ouest* (Paris: Payot, 1967).

Geological and geographical unity were underscored by commonly shared cultural traditions. Charles Monchicourt, "Fête de l'Achoura," *RT* 17 (1910): 278–301, observed that an ancient, popular (pre-Islamic) carnival—the *furja*—was celebrated by peoples of the Jarid, Suf, and Warqala. Also important is that many of the inhabitants of this region were Kharijite (Islamic schismatics) in religious persuasion until at least the thirteenth century. The Ziban and much of the province of Constantine had been incorporated into the Hafsid state centered in Tunis from the thirteenth to fifteenth centuries; on this see Robert Brunschvig, *La Berbérie orientale sous les Hafsides des origines à la fin du XVe siècle*, 2 vols. (Paris: Adrien-Maisonneuve, 1940–1947).

7. Georges Yver, "Biskra," *EI* (Leiden: Brill, 1928), 1: 732–33; Jean Despois, "Biskra," *EI*, 2d ed. (Leiden: Brill, 1960), 1: 1246–47; and Jean Ghisolfi, "L'oasis d'al-Kantara, sud Constantinois," *CHEAM* 4, 294 (1938).

8. André Nouschi, *Enquête sur le niveau de vie des populations rurales constantinoises de la conquête jusqu'en 1919* (Paris: PUF, 1961), 15; Jean Despois, *L'Afrique du Nord* (Paris: PUF, 1958), 56–70; and Robert Mantran, "Algérie turque et Sahara," *Sahara, rapports et contacts humains* (Aix-en-Provence: La Pensée Universitaire, 1967), 61–72.

9. Raoul de Lartigue, *Monographie de l'Aurès* (Constantine: Marle-Audrino, 1904).

10. Youssef Nacib, *Cultures oasiennes: Essai d'histoire sociale de l'oasis de Bou-Saada* (Paris: Publisud, 1986); and idem, *Chants religieux de Djurdjura* (Paris: Sindbad, 1988).

11. Mohamed-Hédi Cherif, *Pouvoir et société dans la Tunisie de Husayn bin 'Ali (1705–1740)*, vol. 1 (Tunis: Publications de l'Université de Tunis, 1984); and Jocelyne Dakhlia, *L'oubli de la cité: La mémoire collective*

à l'épreuve du lignage dans le Jérid tunisien (Paris: Éditions la Découverte, 1990).

12. Anonymous, "Étude sur le Sahara," 1839, AMG, Algérie, H 227; "Étude sur les oasis du Ziban," n.d., AMG, Algérie, H 230; and "Notice détaillé sur les zaouias, shuyukh, et mokkadem du cercle de Biskra," 1895, AGGA, 16 H 10.

Marcel Emerit, "Les liaisons terrestres entre le Soudan et l'Afrique du Nord au XVIIIe et au début du XIXe siècle," *TIRS* 11 (1954): 29–47; and C. W. Newbury, "North African and Western Sudan Trade in the Nineteenth Century: A Re-Evaluation," *JAH* 7, 2 (1966): 233–46.

13. Capot-Rey, *Le Sahara*, 356–65; Jean Despois, "Le Sahara et l'ecologie humaine," *AG* 70, 382 (1961): 577–84; and H. T. Norris, "Indigenous Peoples of the Sahara," in *Key Environments, Sahara Desert*, J. L. Cloudsley-Thompson, ed. (Oxford: Pergamon Press, 1984), 311–24.

14. Lucette Valensi, *Fellahs tunisiens: L'économie rurale et la vie des campagnes aux 18e et 19e siècles* (Paris: Mouton, 1977); Abraham L. Udovitch and Lucette Valensi, *The Last Arab Jews: The Communities of Jerba, Tunisia* (New York: Harwood Academic Publishers, 1984); Elizabeth D. Friedman, "The Jews of Batna, Algeria: A Study of Identity and Colonialism" (Ph.D. diss., City University of New York, 1977); Donald C. Holsinger, "Migration, Commerce, and Community: The Mizabis in Nineteenth-Century Algeria (Ph.D. diss., Northwestern University, 1979); and A. Sainte-Marie, "Aspects du colportage à partir de la Kabylie du Djurdjura à l'époque contemporaine," *Commerce de Gros, Commerce de Détail dans les Pays Méditerranéens (XVI-XIX Siècles)* (Nice: Université de Nice, 1976), 103–19.

15. The term *peasant* is employed as a rough equivalent for *fallah*, or tiller of the soil, farmer, cultivator, etc. In the indigenous Arabic sources from the nineteenth century, however, the term *fallah* is rarely used in state documents or letters to the bey expressing grievances from the oasis communities; rather the vaguer *ahl al-Jarid* (people of the Jarid) or *sukkan* (inhabitants) is employed as well as identity based upon membership in a specific lineage or kinship group.

The scholarly debate over what constitutes a peasant has produced an enormous literature; see Dale F. Eickelman, *The Middle East: An Anthropological Approach*, 2d ed. (Englewood Cliffs, N.J.: Prentice-Hall, 1989).

16. The Ziban and the Jarid enjoy unusually rich hydraulic resources which supported high population densities—twelve hundred inhabitants per square kilometer in the oases and near zero in the surrounding desert. Together Biskra's springs flow at a rate of five hundred liters per second; Tuzar has ten springs with similar flow capacities permitting the cultivation of some four hundred thousand date palms, supplemented by artesian wells. R. Arrus, *L'eau en Algérie: De l'impérialisme au développement*

(1830–1962) (Algiers: Office des Publications Universitaires, 1985); and Pierre-Robert Baduel, "Le pouvoir de l'eau dans le sud-Tunisien," *ROMM* 30 (1980): 101–34.

17. Le Comte d'Escayrac, *Le désert et le Soudan* (Paris, 1853), 10–11; and Vincent Guerin, *Voyage archéologique dans la régence de Tunis*, 2 vols. (Paris: Plon, 1862), 1: 250–65.

18. Henri Duveyrier, "Notice sur le commerce du Souf," *RAC* 3 (1860): 637–48.

19. Edmond Pellissier de Reynaud, *Description de la régence de Tunis*, vol. 16 of *ESA* (Paris: Imprimerie Royale, 1853).

20. James Richardson, 1845, "An Account of the Present State of Tunis," PRO/FO 102 (29).

21. Gapelin, 1844, "Rapport," AMG, Algérie, H 235; Warnier, n.d. (c. 1856), "Rapport sur l'Oued Souf et ses relations commerciales," AGGA, 22 H 26; chef de service des douanes, 1857, "Considérations sur le commerce et l'industrie des tissus de laine du Sahara," AGGA, 1 H 14; and de Fleurac, 1885, AMG, Tunisie, 36 H 29, no. 8.

22. Abdelhamid Henia, *Le Grid, ses rapports avec le Beylik de Tunis, 1676–1840* (Tunis: Publications de l'Université de Tunis, 1980), 47–50.

23. A proverb from the pre-Sahara recorded by a Bureaux Arabes officer, 1868, AMG, Algérie, H 230 bis. The literature on pastoral nomadism is extensive; Jacques Berque's "Qu'est-ce qu'une 'tribu' nord-africaine?" in *Éventail de l'histoire vivante: Mélanges à Lucien Fèbvre* (Paris: Colin, 1953) 1: 261–71, remains the classic statement on the notion of tribe in North Africa; see also Philip S. Khoury and Joseph Kostiner, eds., *Tribes and State Formation in the Middle East* (Berkeley and Los Angeles: University of California Press, 1990).

24. Douglas L. Johnson, *The Nature of Nomadism: A Comparative Study of Pastoral Migrations in Southwestern Asia and Northern Africa* (Chicago: University of Chicago, Department of Geography, Research Paper No. 118, 1969), 98–99; and Rada and Neville Dyson-Hudson, "Nomadic Pastoralism," *Annual Review of Anthropology* 9 (1980): 15–61.

25. The khammas were sharecroppers enjoying the right to some portion, usually although not always a fifth, of the harvest for which they provided labor; Valensi, *Fellahs*, 142–44.

26. Alain Romey, *Les Sa'id 'Atba de N'Goussa: Histoire et état actuel de leur nomadisme* (Paris: L'Harmattan, 1983).

27. The semiannual migration from the Ziban to the north followed three geographical lines. In the Zab Sharqi, the nomads ascended the Awras to reach Khenchela, Guelma, and Suq Ahras. From Biskra, they moved to Batna via al-Qantara and then fanned out in the Sétif region. Finally the Awlad Jallal skirted the limits of the Hodna mountains. Johnson, *Nomadism*, 98–105; Capot-Rey, *Le Sahara*, 250–84; Despois, *L'Afrique*, 221–32; and M. Dou, "Nomades et sédentaires à Biskra," n.d., *CHEAM* 2, 31 bis.

28. Donald C. Holsinger, "Trade Routes of the Algerian Sahara in the Nineteenth Century," *ROMM* 30 (1980): 57–70; and Benjamin E. Thomas, *Trade Routes of Algeria and the Sahara* (Berkeley and Los Angeles: University of California Press, 1957).

29. This does not imply that borders between the two Turkish regencies were nonexistent as colonial authorities attempted to claim. The political frontiers between Algeria and Tunisia were more or less stabilized in the early eighteenth century in contrast to other parts of the Ottoman Empire. These were both physical—the presence of *burjs*, or forts, delimited the territory of the Tunisian beys or Algerian deys—and fiscal. Most pastoral-nomadic groups, apart from those in the deep Sahara, were well aware of the identity of their fiscal masters. Daniel Nordman, "La Notion de frontière en Afrique du Nord: Mythes et réalités, vers 1830–vers 1912" (Doctoral diss., Montpellier University, Montpellier, France, 1975).

30. A. Cauneille, *Les Chaanba, leur nomadisme* (Paris: Éditions du CNRS, 1968).

31. Duveyrier, "Notice," 637–48; and anonymous, "Les populations musulmans du Souf et leur évolution politique," 1938, AGGA, 10 H 88 (7).

32. Mohamed-Hédi Cherif, "Document relatif à des tribus tunisiennes des débuts du XVIIIe siècle: Enseignements démographiques et économiques," *ROMM* 33 (1982): 76–95.

33. C. Jest, "Note sur les Ouled Amor du Souf," *TIRS* 18 (1959): 169–78.

34. Gapelin, 1844, "Rapport," AMG, Algérie, H 235.

35. Baudot, 1876 report, AMG, Algérie, M 1317.

36. Duveyrier, "Notice," 637–48; and anonymous, "Étude sur le Sahara," 1839, AMG, Algérie, H 227.

37. The Bureaux Arabes files, particularly the F 80 1426 sous-série, AGGA, contain endless references to contraband, which, together with banditry, has always flourished in deserts and mountains.

38. Nikki R. Keddie, "Socioeconomic Change in the Middle East since 1800: A Comparative Analysis," in *The Islamic Middle East, 700–1900: Studies in Economic and Social History*, Abraham L. Udovitch, ed. (Princeton: Princeton University Press, 1981), 761–84.

39. Geneviève Bédoucha, *L'eau, l'amie du puissant: Une communauté oasienne du sud-tunisien* (Paris: Éditions des Archives Contemporaines, 1987).

40. Valensi, *Fellahs*, 112.

41. Capot-Rey, *Le Sahara*, 347–51; Habib Attia, "Modernisation agricole et structures sociales: Exemple des oasis du Djérid," in *RTSS* 2 (1965): 59–79; and idem, "Water-Sharing Rights in the Jerid Oases of Tunisia," in *Property, Social Structure, and Law in the Modern Middle East*, Elizabeth A. Mayer, ed. (New York: SUNY Press, 1985), 85–106.

42. The Sahara constituted more of a political problem for the colonial regime than a site of potential economic ventures; Europeans invested in only a few regions, such as the Wadi Righ and Biskra, where new sources of water were found to cultivate the daqala al-nur date for export. Elsewhere European investors were discouraged by the labor-intensive nature of oasis agriculture, the intricate system of water/land rights, and low returns. The lack of interest in the Sahara—until the discovery of petrol and natural gas in the late colonial period—is attested to by the sparse number of Europeans residing there; Arrus, *L'eau en Algérie*, 160–73, and 212, note 87.

43. Anonymous, "Étude sur le Sahara," 1839, AMG, Algérie, H 227; and "Étude sur les oasis du Ziban," n.d., AMG, Algérie, H 230.

44. Bédoucha, *L'eau*; and Dakhlia, *L'oubli*.

45. In Biskra, Tuqqurt, and Warqala, the predominant system of water distribution was that of open canals linked to artesian wells or other sources of water. Jean Lethielleux, *Ouargla, cité saharienne des origines au début du XXe siècle* (Paris: Paul Geuthner, 1983); and Madeleine Rouvillois-Brigol, *Le pays de Ouargla (Sahara algérien): Variations et organisation d'un espace rural en milieu désertique* (Paris: Publications du Département de Géographie de l'Université de Paris–Sorbonne, 1975). In the Suf, a somewhat different system obtained; Claude Bataillon, *Le Souf: Étude de géographie humaine* (Algiers: Institut de Recherches Sahariennes, 1955); and Ahmed Najah, *Le Souf des oasis* (Algiers: Éditions de la Maison des Livres, 1971). Water distribution in the Jarid at the turn of the century was studied by P. Penet, *L'hydraulique agricole dans la Tunisie méridionale* (Tunis: La Rapide, 1913); for present-day Tunisia, Jean Duvignaud, *Chebika, suivi de retour à Chebika 1990* (Paris: Plon, 1991).

46. Cf. to Morocco, Gilbert Grandguillaume, "Régime économique et structure du pouvoir: Le système des foggara du Touat," *ROMM* 13–14 (1973): 437–56.

47. De Fleurac, 1885, AMG, Tunisie, 36 H 29, no. 8; and Attia, "Modernisation," 69–76.

48. When French officials inventoried property owners in Biskra after 1844, they found that the religious clan headed by Sidi 'Abd al-Malik held property and water rights second only to the bey of the Constantine; anonymous, "Renseignements sur Biskra," 1844, AGGA, 10 H 18.

49. Augustin Berque, "Essai d'une bibliographie critique des confréries musulmanes algériennes," *BSGAO* 39 (1919): 135–74, 193–233; Jacques Berque, *De l'Euphrate à l'Atlas* (Paris: Sindbad, 1978) 1: 20; and Latifa Lakhdar, *Al-Islam al-Turuqi (l'Islam confrérique)* (Tunis: Cérès, 1993).

50. Anonymous, "Considerations politiques sur les sédentaires et nomades d'Ouargla," n.d., AGGA, 10 H 52; and anonymous, "Itinéraire de Biskra à Tuggurth," 1851, AMG, Algérie, M 1317.

51. Lucette Valensi, "Calamités démographiques en Tunisie et en Méditerranée orientale aux XVIIIe et XIXe siècles," *AESC* 24, 6 (1969): 1540–62.

52. Anonymous, "Étude sur le Sahara," 1839, AMG, Algérie, H 227.

53. Charles Tissot, 1857, AMAE, Tunisie, mém./docs., vol. 8, no. 32; and de Fleurac, 1885, AMG, Tunisie, 36 H 29, no. 8.

54. Pierre Bourdieu, *The Algerians* (Boston: Beacon Press, 1962), 13. Here *saff* is employed in a more general sense for systems of political alliance making and breaking rather than the specific connotation attached to *leff* by Robert Montagne for Moroccan Berber political organization; Ernest Gellner, "Leff," *EI*, 2d ed. (Leiden: E. J. Brill, 1986), 5: 715.

55. Charles Tissot, 1857, report, AMAE, mém./docs., vol. 8, no. 32; Mustapha Kraiem, *La Tunisie précoloniale*, 2 vols. (Tunis: Société Tunisienne de Diffusion, 1973) 1: 145–53; and Cherif, *Pouvoir et société*, vol. 2.

56. Anonymous, 1924, "Renseignements concernant les soffs du Mzab et du sud Constantinois," AGGA, Algérie, 10 H 38.

57. James C. Scott, *The Moral Economy of the Peasant: Rebellion and Subsistence in Southeast Asia* (New Haven: Yale University Press, 1976), 2.

58. Gapelin, 1844, "Rapport," AMG, Algérie, H 235; "Notice sur les relations commerciales que Tougourt entretient avec Tunis," 1845, AMAE, Tunisie, c.c., vol. 54; 1856, "Rapport sur l'Oued Souf et ses relations commerciales," AGGA, Algérie, 22 H 26; and Henri Duveyrier, "Excursions dans le Djérid ou pays de dattes," *RAC* 2 (1860): 542–59.

59. Anonymous, "Étude sur le Sahara," 1839, AMG, Algérie, H 227; Antoine-Eugène Carette, *Recherches sur la géographie et le commerce de l'Algérie mériodionale*, vol. 2 of *ESA* (Paris: Imprimerie Royale, 1844); and E. Pellissier de Reynaud, *Description*.

60. Barbara K. Larson, "The Rural Marketing System of Egypt over the Last Three Hundred Years," *CSSH* 27, 3 (1985): 494–530; and F. Benet, "Explosive Markets: The Berber Highlands," in *Trade and Market in the Early Empires*, K. Polanyi, ed. (Glencoe, Ill.: Free Press, 1957), 188–217.

61. Laurence O. Michalak, "The Changing Weekly Markets of Tunisia: A Regional Analysis," (Ph.D. diss., University of California, Berkeley, 1983).

62. Anonymous, "Étude sur le Sahara," 1839, AMG, Algérie, H 227; Gapelin, 1844, "Rapport," AMG, Algérie, H 235; anonymous, "Renseignements sur le cercle de Biskra," 1845, AGGA, 10 H 18; and anonymous, "Rapport," 1856, AGGA, 22 H 26.

63. A. J. Wensinck, "Mawsim," in *EI*, 2d ed. (Leiden: E. J. Brill, 1990), 6: 903; and Sophie Ferchiou, "Les fêtes maraboutiques en Tunisie— 'Zarda' " in *Actes du 1er Congrès d'Études des Cultures Méditerranéennes d'Influence Arabo-Berbère* (Algiers: SNED, 1973), 532–37.

64. Anonymous, "Itinéraire de Biskra à Tuggurth," 1851, AMG, Algérie, M 1317; and the reports of the Tunisian qa'ids in AGT, carton 20, dossiers 227–33, armoire 1. Not all exchanges took place within the context of markets. Nor were these exchanges, whatever their venue, purely eco-

nomic in nature—many had a cultural or symbolic dimension whose social importance exceeded material value. And specie was chronically in short supply in many parts of Algeria and Tunisia, particularly the pre-Sahara. Many transactions, whether concluded in market centers or not, were effected through barter.

65. Michalak, "Weekly Markets," 72–73.

66. Gapelin, 1844, "Rapport," AMG, Algérie, H 235; the storyteller's political importance in North African society was alluded to by numerous writers; Auguste Cour, "Constantine en 1802 d'après une chanson populaire de Cheikh Belqasem er-Rahmouni El-Haddad," RA 60 (1919): 224–40; and idem, "La poésie populaire politique du temps de l'Emir Abdelqader," RA 59 (1918): 458–84.

67. Anonymous, 1839, "Étude sur le Sahara," AMG, Algérie, H 227; and "Itinéraire de Biskra à Tuggurth," 1851, AMG, Algérie, M 1317. Colportage represents another form of subsistence migration; the Kabyles dominated colportage in the nineteenth century, serving as bearers of information and rumors as well as goods.

68. Georges Marty, "A Tunis: Éléments allogènes et activités professionelles, djerbiens, gabesiens, gens du sud, et autres tunisiens," IBLA 11, 42 (1948): 159–87; and idem, "Les algériens à Tunis," IBLA 11, 43–44 (1948): 301–34; and AGT, A-1–14 to 20; A-2–21 and 22.

69. Anonymous, 14 March 1852, AGGA, 1 H 9.

70. Thiriet, 1938, AGGA, 10 H 88 (7).

71. The term murabit had different meanings depending upon the time and place. In the medieval period, it designated religious reformers issuing from frontier redoubts, or ribats. In the nineteenth-century lexicon of eastern Algeria and Tunisia, it meant "men, devoted to God's adoration and linked to Him, who enjoyed a reputation of saintliness which conferred upon them the title of 'waliy', friend of God" (Marcel Beaussier, Dictionnaire pratique arabe-français, new ed. by Mohamed Ben Cheneb [Algiers: Jules Carbonel, 1931], 378). The French equivalent of this complex term—marabout—was used and misused throughout the colonial period, giving rise to considerable confusion regarding the precise social and religious identity of the marabout. The term was employed less frequently in indigenous Arabic written sources from eastern Algeria and Tunisia than waliy (roughly "saint," although with some important differences when compared with sainthood in Christianity). The term waliy also encompassed a multiplicity of subtle cultural meanings which shifted with social context, region, and period. Moreover, the terms sufi and waliy were not necessarily coterminous in meaning, although they were frequently confused in the literature and conflated in social practice.

While the rendering of waliy and murabit as equivalent to "saint" is problematic, there has not been much scholarly debate on this matter; see

Julian Baldick, *Mystical Islam: An Introduction to Sufism* (New York: New York University Press, 1989), 16–17.

72. Dakhlia, *L'oubli*, 208, reports that a "semiliterate" individual from Tuzar evoked the names of over one hundred saints. Nacib, *Chants religieux*, 12, noted that in the Jurjura's oral poetry the most frequent themes were the saint and death.

73. Even today, Nafta's inhabitants recount the legend of Sidi Bu 'Ali, who was born in Morocco during the thirteenth century and traveled to the Jarid to reintroduce orthodox Sunni Islam to its inhabitants, many of whom were Kharijites. According to local lore, the holy man visited Tuqqurt en route to Nafta, where he collected some date pits which he then had planted, thus assuring fertility as well as orthodoxy.

74. Fanny Colonna, "Saints furieux et saints studieux ou, dans l'Aurès, comment la religion vient aux tribus," *AESC* 35, 3–4 (1980) 642–62; and Francois Masselot, "Les dattiers des oasis du Djérid," *Bulletin de la Direction de l'Agriculture* (Tunis, 1901).

75. Nacib, *Chants religieux*, 110.

2. SAINT AND SUFI

1. Muhammad al-Sadiq Basha Bey, 1276 AH (1859/1860), to Mustafa b. 'Azzuz, AGT, H, carton 81 bis, dossier 987.

2. The colonial production on saints and sufis, while of uneven quality, is extensive; see the numerous entries in Pessah Shinar's *Bibliographie séléctive et annotée sur l'Islam maghrébin contemporain: Maroc, Algérie, Tunisie, Libye (1830–1978)* (Paris: CNRS, 1983). For the postcolonial period, Jacques Berque's enormous contributions, for example, *L'intèrieur du Maghreb, XVe–XIXe siècle* (Paris: Gallimard, 1978), deserve first mention. Other recent works are Hassan Elboudrari, "Quand les saints font les villes: Lecture anthropologique de la pratique sociale d'un saint marocain du XVIIe siècle," *AESC* 40, 3 (1985): 489–508; Houari Touati, "Approche sémiologique et historique d'un document hagiographique algérien," *AESC* 44, 5 (1989): 1205–28; and Mohamed El-Mansour, "Sharifian Sufism: The Religious and Social Practice of the Wazzani Zawiya," in *Essays in Honour of David Hart*, Ernest Gellner and G. Joffé, eds. (Cambridgeshire: Menas Press, 1992), 1–15.

3. Jacques Berque, *Structures sociales du Haut-Atlas*, 1st ed. (Paris: PUF, 1955), 239.

4. Dale F. Eickelman, *Moroccan Islam, Tradition and Society in a Pilgrimage Center* (Austin: University of Texas Press, 1976), 19–33.

5. A number of scholars have attempted to define the concept of (or rather a cluster of concepts associated with) baraka; Edward Westermarck's *Ritual and Belief in Morocco*, 2 vols. (London: Macmillan, 1926), remains

the classic study; see also Raymond Jamous, *Honneur et baraka: Les structures sociales traditionnelles dans le Rif* (Cambridge: Cambridge University Press, 1981). Piety, or *taqwa*, is a social construct with political implications since the collective recognition of an individual piety's conferred moral ascendancy over the community.

6. Mohamed Kerrou "Le temps maraboutique," *IBLA* 54, 167 (1991): 63–72.

7. Louis Gardet, "Karama," *EI*, 2d ed. (Leiden: E. J. Brill, 1978), 4: 615–16 (quote on 615); and John O. Voll, "Two Biographies of Ahmad ibn Idris al-Fasi," *IJAHS* 6 (1973): 633–46.

8. Gardet, "Karama," 615–16; and Muhammad b. al-Hajj Muhammad, "Kitab al-rawd al-basim fi tarjama al-imam sidi Muhammad ibn Abi al-Qasim," A 80 3165, al-Khizana al-'Amma, Rabat, Morocco, 23.

9. Donal B. Cruise O'Brien and Christian Coulon, eds., *Charisma and Brotherhood in African Islam* (Oxford: Clarendon Press, 1988).

10. Anonymous, "Étude sur le Sahara," 1839, AMG, H 227; and Gapelin, "Rapport," 1844, AMG, Algérie, H 235. Henri Brunschvig, *La Berbérie orientale sous les Hafsides des origines à la fin du XVe siècle*, 2 vols. (Paris: Adrien-Maisonneuve, 1940–1947), 1: 245.

11. Jocelyne Dakhlia, *L'oubli de la cité: La mémoire collective à l'épreuve du lignage dans le Jérid tunisien* (Paris: Éditions la Découverte, 1990), 95–96.

12. Danielle Provansal, "Le phénomène maraboutique au Maghreb," *Genève-Afrique* 14, 1 (1975): 59–77; and Taoufik Bachrouch, *Le saint et le prince en Tunisie: Les elites tunisiennes du pouvoir et de la devotion, contribution à l'étude des groupes sociaux dominants (1782–1881)* (Tunis: Publications de l'Université de Tunis, 1989).

13. Stephen Wilson, ed., *Saints and Their Cults: Studies in Religious Sociology, Folklore, and History* (Cambridge: Cambridge University Press, 1984), 27–28.

14. Wim M. J. van Binsbergen, "The Cult of Saints in North-Western Tunisia: An Analysis of Contemporary Pilgramage [sic] Structures," in *Islamic Dilemmas: Reformers, Nationalists, and Industrialization, the Southern Shore of the Mediterranean*, Ernest Gellner, ed. (New York: Mouton, 1985), 199–239.

Studies of female participation in saint veneration or of women saints in Islam are much less extensive than the literature devoted to women's religiosity in Christianity; for examples, see Renate Blumenfeld-Kosinski and Timea Szell, *Images of Sainthood in Medieval Europe* (Ithaca: Cornell University Press, 1991); and Lynda L. Coon, Katherine J. Haldane, and Elisabeth W. Sommer, *That Gentle Strength: Historical Perspectives on Women in Christianity* (Charlottesville: University of Virginia, 1990). Recently works on female religiosity in contemporary Islamic societies have appeared, among them, Nancy Tapper's "*Ziyaret*: Gender, Movement, and

Exchange in a Turkish Community," *Muslim Travellers: Pilgrimage, Migration, and the Religious Imagination,* Dale F. Eickelman and James Piscatori, eds. (Berkeley and Los Angeles: University of California Press, 1990), 236–55. The past experience of women has hardly been studied at all.

15. Wilson, *Saints,* 14. In addition to those of humble station, cult centers attracted supplicants from the ranks of the ulama or sufi shaykhs; Abu al-Qasim Sa'adallah, *Tarikh al-Jaza'ir al-thaqafi,* 2d ed. (Algiers: SNED, 1981), 1: 510.

16. Allan Christelow, *Muslim Law Courts and the French Colonial State in Algeria* (Princeton: Princeton University Press, 1985), 31; and AGGA, 10 H 72 and 10 H 18.

17. AGGA, 10 H 18 (census of 1844).

18. AGT, H, armoire 8, carton 81 bis, dossier 987 [Awamir, masha'ikh wa muqaddamin 'ala al-zawaya].

19. Mohamed-Hédi Cherif, *Pouvoir et société dans la Tunisie de Husayn bin 'Ali (1705–1740),* 2 vols. (Tunis: Publications de l'Université de Tunis, 1984–1986).

20. Lucette Valensi, *Fellahs tunisiens: L'économie rurale et la vie des campagnes aux 18e et 19e siècles* (Paris: Mouton, 1977); and Fanny Colonna, "Présence des ordres mystiques dans l'Aurès aux XIXe et XXe siècles: Contribution à une histoire sociale des forces religieuses en Algérie," in *Les ordres mystiques dans l'Islam: Cheminements et situation actuelle,* Alexandre Popovic and Gilles Veinstein, eds. (Paris: Éditions de l'École des Hautes Études en Sciences Sociales, 1986), 249.

21. Victor Turner, *Dramas, Fields, and Metaphors: Symbolic Action in Human Society* (Ithaca: Cornell University Press, 1974). Turner's work was inspired in large measure by Arnold Van Gennep's earlier ethnological studies of Kabyle society in colonial Algeria.

22. Alex Wiengrod, "Saints and Shrines, Politics and Culture: A Morocco-Israel Comparison," *Muslim Travellers,* 217–35.

23. AGT, armoire 14, carton 142, dossier 516, contains numerous letters of official protest from European consuls in Tunis addressed to the Tunisian rulers between 1831 and 1880. These frequently had to do with the fact that Tunisians, who had fallen into debt to European creditors, sought financial asylum in the zawaya's sacred space. The beys did not always feel compelled to observe the tradition of sacred asylum when the government's authority was at stake. In a letter dated 1831, the French consul, de Lesseps, noted that the bey had ordered the door of one zawiya near Tunis closed "so that those seeking refuge would be deprived of food, thus forcing the guilty party to be delivered to justice."

24. Ernest Gellner, *Saints of the Atlas* (London: Weidenfeld and Nicolson, 1969); and F. Benet's "Explosive Markets: The Berber Highlands," in *Trade and Market in the Early Empire,* ed. K. Polanyi (Glencoe, Ill.: Free Press, 1957), 188–217.

25. Ahmad ibn Abi al-Diyaf, *Ithaf ahl al-zaman bi-akhbar muluk Tunis wa 'ahd al-aman* (Tunis: al-Dar al-Tunisiyya lil-Nashr, 1963–1966), 7–8: 142.

26. Dj. Sari, "Nafta," *EI*, 2d ed. (Leiden: E. J. Brill, 1992), 7: 890–91.

27. Roy P. Mottahedeh, *Loyalty and Leadership in an Early Islamic Society* (Princeton: Princeton University Press, 1980), 135–48.

28. Jamil M. Abun-Nasr, *The Tijaniyya: A Sufi Order in the Modern World* (London: Oxford University Press, 1965); Ahmad al-Dajjani, *al-haraka al-Sanusiyya* (Beirut: Dar Lubnan, 1967), and Abdulmola El-Horeir, "Social and Economic Transformations in the Libyan Hinterland during the Second Half of the Nineteenth Century: The Role of Sayyid Ahmad al-Sharif al-Sanusi" (Ph.D. diss., University of California, Los Angeles, 1981).

29. Documentation for the Rahmaniyya and its founder is not as abundant as for the Tijaniyya or Sanusiyya; in part this is the product of the immense destruction wrought by the colonial conquest of the Kabylia and other areas in Algeria where the Rahmaniyya was dominant. There exists a corpus of unpublished letters or epistles (for the most part undated) by the founder-saint, Sidi Muhammad b. 'Abd al-Rahman al-Azhari, and his students, "Majmu' min risa'il al-shaykh 'Abd al-Rahman al-Zawawi al-Jaza'iri shaykh al-tariqa al-Rahmaniyya," MS. K 956, al-Khizana al-'Amma, Rabat, Morocco.

30. Muhammad al-Hafnawi, *Ta'rif al-khalaf bi rijal al-salaf*, reprint of 1907 ed. (Tunis: al-Maktaba al-'Atiqa, 1982), 457–74; Sa'adallah's *Tarikh* 1: 514–16; E. Bannerth, "La Khalwatiyya en Égypte, quelques aspects de la vie d'une confrérie," *Institut Dominicain d'Études Orientales du Caire* 8 (1964): 1–74; and Fred de Jong, "Khalwatiyya," *EI*, 2d ed. (Leiden: E. J. Brill, 1978), 4: 991–93.

31. Julia Clancy-Smith, "The Saharan Rahmaniyya: Popular Protest and Desert Society in Southeastern Algerian and the Tunisian Jarid, c. 1750–1881" (Ph.D. diss., University of California, Los Angeles, 1988).

32. Georges Yver, "Kustantina," *EI*, 2d ed. (Leiden: E. J. Brill, 1986), 5: 530–32.

33. André Raymond, "Les caractéristiques d'une ville arabe 'moyenne' au XVIIIe siècle: Le cas de Constantine," *ROMM* 44, 2 (1987): 134–47.

34. Anonymous, report, 1838, AMG, H 226; A. Dournon, trans., "Kitab Tarikh Qosantina," *RA* 57 (1913): 265–305; Adrien Berbrugger, *Algérie, historique, pittoresque, et monumentale* (Paris: J. Delahaye, 1843); André Nouschi, *Enquête sur le niveau de vie des populations rurales constanti-noises de la conquête jusqu'en 1919* (Paris: PUF, 1961), and "Constantine à la vielle de la conquête française," *CT* 3, 11 (1955): 371–87.

35. Muhammad al-Zubiri, *al-Tijara al-Kharajiyya lil-sharq al-Jaza'iri* (Algiers, 1972); and James M. Malarkey, "The Colonial Encounter in French

Algeria: A Study of the Development of Power Asymmetry and Symbolic Violence in the City of Constantine" (Ph.D. diss., University of Texas at Austin, 1980). The province's population is estimated at 1.2 million by Xavier Yacono, "Peut-on évaluer la population de l'Algérie vers 1830?" *RA* 98, 3–4 (1954): 277–307; other estimates run as high as 3 million.

36. Raymond, "Les caractéristiques," 143–45, notes that the Banu al-Fakkun allied themselves quite early with the pro-Ottoman faction and were responsible for the definitive occupation of Constantine by the Turks in 1647. The family was handsomely rewarded, eventually controlling the offices of shaykh al-Islam, *amir rakb al-muslimin* (leader of the Hijazi pilgrimage), and imam and *Khatibkhatib* of the Great Mosque; these included substantial material benefits. Thus, the great religious families traditionally favored accommodation with central governments.

37. Sharif, saint, sufi, and 'alim not only overlapped but also could be combined within the same individual; treating these sociospiritual attributes as distinct typologies of holy persons (as colonial writers tended to do) is inaccurate. The shurafa' were found all over the Maghrib and ranged in social circumstance from the most illustrious urban ulama to those of unpretentious rank and manner of living. One example of the latter was a small tribe found in the Zab Qibli; named the Shurafa', its members were sedentary peasants, pastoral nomads, and merchant-landlords. Because of the recognition (that is, by both the central government and the local community) of their descent from the Prophet's clan, this kinship group did not pay taxes to the Turkish state as long as they remained in the Sahara. AMG, Algérie, H 227.

38. Anonymous, report, 1838, AMG, H 226.

39. Berbrugger, *Algérie*; and Nouschi, *Enquête* and "Constantine"; al-Hafnawi, *Ta'rif*, 457–474; and Muhammad ibn 'Abd al-Rahman, *al-Rahmaniyya*, trans. by Antoine Giacobetti as *Livre de la Rah'maniya* and *Le livre des dons de Dieu—Glose de la Rah'maniya* (Algiers: Maison Carrée, 1946). *Al-Rahmaniyya* comprises some 1,400 lines of verse and has been retained in the original Arabic version. The accompanying commentary by Bash Tarzi exists only in French translation, however. The manuscript from which Giacobetti worked in the 1940s was printed in Tunis by the Imprimerie Officielle Tunisienne in 1889 through the auspices of Sidi Muhammad b. Abi al-Qasim, the Rahmaniyya shaykh of al-Hamil.

40. Al-Hafnawi, *Ta'rif*, 460; anonymous, "Notes sur les ordres religieux dans le cercle de Constantine," 15 January 1850, AGGA, 16 H 2; Octave Depont and Xavier Coppolani, *Les confréries religieuses musulmanes* (Algiers: Jourdan, 1897); and Auguste Cherbonneau, "Sur le catéchisme des rahmaniens," *JA* 20 (December 1852): 515–18.

41. Mustafa Bash Tarzi wrote a didactic treatise in verse on the Rahmaniyya entitled *al-Minha al-rubbaniyya fi bayan al-manzuma al-rah-*

maniyya (Cairo: Dar al-Hajar, 1287/1870); the only extant copy of this work is apparently in the library of al-Azhar; I have not been able to consult this work.

42. Anonymous, report, 1838, AMG, H 226; Ernest Vaysettes, *Histoire de Constantine sous les beys depuis l'invasion Turque jusqu'à l'occupation française* (Constantine, 1869); and Ernest Mercier, *Histoire de Constantine* (Constantine, 1903).

43. It is uncertain whether the shaykhs administering the Saharan Rahmaniyya zawaya remitted a part of their offerings cum revenues—or any revenues at all—to the tariqa's centers in the city of Constantine or in the Kabylia. The Bash Tarzi clan did not apparently exert direct administrative control—as opposed to moral influence—over the Saharan zawaya. What is certain is that Rahmaniyya notables in the Ziban and elsewhere corresponded with sufi peers in Constantine and that religious figures from the pre-Sahara resided at the order's zawaya when visiting the city. Joseph-Adrien Seroka, "Historique de Biskra," 1855, AGGA, 10 H 76.

44. Mohamed Brahim Salhi, "Étude d'une confrérie religieuse Algérienne: La Rahmaniya à la fin du XIXe siècle et dans la première moitié du XXe siècle" (Ph.D. diss., Paris, Sorbonne, 1979).

45. In the Kabylia, the Rahmaniyya encountered bitter opposition from the powerful saints of the Chellata zawiya near Akbou in the Jurjura whose religious clients were enjoined from becoming Rahmaniyya members. Here the nascent sufi order threatened to draw clients away from a local saintly clan, which would have compromised its prestige, sociospiritual authority, and material resources, all measured by popular followings. The clan's antipathy for their Rahmaniyya competitors endured into the nineteenth century and may explain the pro-French stance of the saints of Chellata from the 1840s on. Nil-Joseph Robin, *Insurrection de la Grande Kabylie en 1871* (Paris: Lavauzelle, 1901), 544–58; and Charles-André Julien, *La conquête et les débuts de la colonisation, (1827–1871),* vol. 1 of *Histoire de l'Algérie contemporaine,* 2d ed. (Paris: PUF, 1979), 481–97.

46. Salhi, "Étude," 54, 60.

47. Anonymous, 1865, ARGT, carton 415.

48. AGT, D-84–3 and D-119.

49. Sa'adallah, *Tarikh* 1: 514–16.

50. Dureau de la Malle, *Province de Constantine, recueil de renseignements pour l'expédition ou l'établissement des français dans cette partie de l'Afrique septentrionale* (Paris: Gide, 1837), 142–43.

51. Auguste Cour, "Constantine en 1802 d'après une chanson populaire du Cheikh Belqasem Er-Rahmouni El-Haddad," *RA* 60 (1919): 224–60; Sa'adallah, *Tarikh* 1: 516, and 2: 247–330; and Jean Déjeux, *La poésie algérienne de 1830 à nos jours (approches socio-historiques),* 2d ed. (Paris: Publisud, 1982). The veneration of Muslim saints and sufis through the

vehicle of ballads and other popular musical forms was widespread in the Maghrib; however, the musical traditions of sufi orders and saints have received little scholarly attention thus far. Lura Jafran Jones's, "The 'Isawiya of Tunisia and Their Music" (Ph.D. diss., University of Washington, 1977), is one of few such studies.

52. David Robinson, *The Holy War of Umar Tal: The Western Sudan in the Mid-Nineteenth Century* (Oxford: Clarendon Press, 1985), 95; and Muhammad al-Hajj, "The Thirteenth Century in Muslim Eschatology: Mahdist Expectations in the Sokoto Caliphate," *Research Bulletin of the University of Ibadan* 3, 2 (1967): 100–115.

53. Bradford G. Martin, *Muslim Brotherhoods in Nineteenth-Century Africa* (Cambridge: Cambridge University Press, 1976).

54. Al-Hafnawi, *Ta'rif*, 482–86; Muhammad ibn 'Ashur, *Tarajim al-a'lam* (Tunis: Maison Tunisienne de l'Édition, 1970), 187–93; Depont and Coppolani, *Confréries*, 395; and Louis Rinn, *Marabouts et khouan: Étude sur l'Islam en Algérie* (Algiers: Jourdan, 1884), 459. Rinn confuses Muhammad b. 'Azzuz with his son Mustafa.

55. La Croix, report, 1844, AMG, Algérie, H 227; and M 1317.

56. Anonymous, "Étude sur le Sahara," 1839, AMG, H 227; and Gapelin, "Rapport," 1844, AMG, Algérie, H 235.

57. AMG, Algérie, H 227, H 230, and M 1317.

58. Statistics gathered by the French occupation forces in southern Tunisia in 1885 estimated that in Nafta there were some 108 religious establishments—mosques, madrasas, zawaya, qubbas, and small shrines—for a population of 8,800, or one religious establishment for every 80 people; this count apparently does not include the numerous saints' shrines without qubbas that were scattered throughout the oasis's gardens; de Fleurac, "Étude," 1885, AMG, Tunisie, 36 H 29, no. 8.

59. AMG, Algérie, H 227, H 230, and M 1317. As was the case elsewhere, al-Burj's population was divided into factions—some eight different groups organized according to kinship. In 1839, the total male population was estimated at roughly 430 individuals; of these 50 belonged to the 'Azzuz clan. In addition to engaging in date-palm cultivation and textile production, the inhabitants raised barley, owned livestock (cared for by allied pastoralists), and traded in the Ziban's markets. Finally, the surplus male population of al-Burj migrated to Algiers to work as boatmen in the city's port which created ties of a potentially political nature with the northern littoral.

60. On Muhammad b. 'Azzuz, see al-Hafnawi, *Ta'rif*; al-Hajj Muhammad, *Kitab*; Berque, *L'intèrieur*, 421; and Marthe and Edmond Gouvian, *Kitab aayane al-marhariba* (Algiers: Imprimerie Orientale, 1920), 147.

61. Why these religious clans were attracted to the Ziban and Jarid is a question worth raising. One factor may have been the oases' location along one of the principal hajj routes from Morocco to the Mashriq. Another was that these oases have always straddled the limits between

central government control, inevitably based in the north, and desert autonomy. Finally, there may have been "push" factors in that Moroccan sultans periodically exiled politically active holy men to Ottoman-held lands, as in 1668 during the assault upon the rebellious Moroccan zawiya of al-Dila; Jacques Berque in *Ulemas, fondateurs, insurgés du Maghreb* (Paris: Sindbad, 1982).

62. AGGA, 16 H 3, 10 H 72; and AMG, Algérie, H 230.

63. Al-Hafnawi, *Ta'rif*, 482.

64. Ibid.

65. Ibid.; Gouvian, *Kitab*, 147–48.

66. Depont and Coppolani, *Confréries*, 395–411; and Gouvian, *Kitab*, 147–65.

67. Ibrahim b. Muhammad al-Sasi al-'Awamir, *al-Suruf fi tarikh al-Sahra' wa suf* (Algiers: SNED,1977); Jean Pigoreau, "Les confréries religieuses musulmanes dans l'annexe d'El Oued," CHEAM, vol. 107, no. 2, 503, 4–10; and anonymous, 22 April 1908, ARGT, carton 989.

68. Al-Hafnawi, *Ta'rif*, 482–83.

69. The murid-shaykh relationship within the Rahmaniyya order is discussed at length by the founder in verses 623–38 of *al-Rahmaniyya*, 245–66.

70. Al-Hafnawi, *Ta'rif*, 482–83.

71. La Croix, report, 1844, AMG, Algérie H 227 and M 1317.

72. Gouvian, *Kitab*, 147; al-Hafnawi, *Ta'rif*; and AGT, D-97–2. Jean Despois, *Le Djebel Amour* (Paris: PUF, 1957), 96–97, observed that local pilgrimages to the tombs of Rahmaniyya notables, like Sidi Muhammad 'Azzuz of al-Burj in Algeria, continued in the pre-Sahara into the interwar period.

73. Here the Rahmaniyya founder's doctrines regarding membership or affiliation with the order appear to have directly influenced popular recruitment, especially compared with their sufi competitors, the Tijaniyya, which were much more exclusive in recruitment; Abun-Nasr, *Tijaniyya*.

74. See Dakhlia, *L'oubli*, 110, for the participation of the pastoral peoples in the sufi orders; also al-Hafnawi, *Ta'rif*, and al-Diyaf, *Ithaf* 7–8: 142–43.

75. Al-Hafnawi, *Ta'rif*, 483.

76. Information on Sidi 'Ali b. 'Umar's clan is relatively more abundant for the colonial period than for other Rahmaniyya notables. This is due, in large part, to their accommodating posture toward the French regime and accessibility to Europeans, which generated documentation. Shaykh 'Ali b. 'Uthman of Tulqa worked with Louis Rinn in researching *Marabouts et khouan: Étude sur l'Islam en Algérie*; in his preface, Rinn notes Sidi 'Ali's assistance. Data—of a certain nature—exist for religious leaders engaging in militant resistance; rebellions were inevitably followed by painstaking

investigations, such as those subsequent to the 1871 Muqrani-Rahmaniyya uprising. Conversely, the activities of those sufi-saintly families who assumed a political stance of retreat or avoidance protest are the most difficult to document, for example, Sidi 'Abd al-Hafiz of Khanqa Sidi Naji.

77. AMG, Algérie, H 227, H 230, H 235, and M 1317.

78. Jean Lethielleux, *Ouargla, cité saharienne: Des origines au début du XXe siècle* (Paris: Paul Geuthner, 1983), 148, 154, 240; and Eugène Fromentin, *Un été dans le Sahara* (Paris: Éditions le Sycomore, 1981). Fromentin visited the Ziban and Tulqa in April of 1848; he subsequently exhibited several paintings of the oasis in the 1850 Salon in Paris.

79. According to Brunschvig in *La Berbérie* 1: 296, Tulqa (Taulaga) dates back to antiquity; al-Bakri in the eleventh century noted that the oasis was composed of three cities, each surrounded by ramparts to protect Tulqa's inhabitants during interminable disputes between tribal groups, struggling to control the Ziban.

80. Michael Brett, "Arabs, Berbers, and Holy Men in Southern Ifriqiya, 650–750 / 1250–1350," *CT* 29, 117–18 (1981): 533–59.

81. Ibid.; and Brunschvig, *La Berbérie* 2: 334–35.

82. Brett, "Arabs, Berbers, and Holy Men," 549–51.

83. AMG, Algérie, H 230; and Brunschvig, *La Berbérie* 2: 335.

84. Sidi 'Ali b. 'Umar's genealogy, noted by Gouvian, *Kitab*, 148, indicates that the family claimed membership in the Moroccan Hasanid ashraf tracing descent from Idris b. 'Abd Allah, a direct descendant of the Prophet through his son-in-law 'Ali, and the founder of the Idrisid dynasty of Fez. In Morocco, the Idrisis traditionally furnished leading holy men and scholars who not infrequently assumed political roles.

85. Information on 'Ali b. 'Umar's clan is found in the following published sources: al-Hafnawi, *Ta'rif*; Salhi, "Etude"; Gouvian, *Kitab*; Depont and Coppolani, *Confréries*; and in unpublished archival sources found in AMG, Algérie, H 230; AGGA, 10 H 72 and 16 H 3; and in AGT, D series.

86. AMG, Algérie, H 227, H 230, H 235, and M 1317.

87. Ibid.

88. Al-Hafnawi, *Ta'rif*, 460; Gouvian, *Kitab*, 149. The term *qutb* originally referred to the head of a hidden hierarchy of awliya'; it later was applied to sufis who had attained an advanced degree of mystical perfection. Sidi 'Ali b. 'Umar's clan later appropriated the paramount miracle attributed to the founder of the Rahmaniyya tariqa, whose saintly remains were miraculously reduplicated so that two tomb-shrines resulted in 1793–1794. In the early twentieth century, Tulqa's Rahmaniyya shaykhs attributed to one of their pious family members, Sidi 'Ali b. Ahmad b. 'Uthman, the coveted sobriquet of "Abu Qabrayn" ("the man with two tombs"); Gouvian, *Kitab*, 150.

89. Gouvian, *Kitab*; and anonymous, "Notice historique de la zawiya de Khangat Sidi Naji," 1895, AGGA, 16 H 10. At the end of the nineteenth

century, René Basset was permitted to partially catalogue the holdings of some Rahmaniyya and Tijaniyya libraries whose contents reveal the reformed sufi emphasis upon the law and orthodoxy; René Basset, "Les manuscripts arabes de la zaouyah d'el Hamel," *Giornale della Societa Asiatica Italiana* (Firenze) 10 (1896–1897): 43–97; and idem, "Les manuscripts arabes des bibliothèques et des zaouias de Ain Mahdi, Temacin, et de Ourgla," *Bulletin de Correspondance Africaine* (Algiers) 3 (1885): 211–65 and 465–92.

90. Al-Hafnawi, *Ta'rif*, 482–83; anonymous, "Etude sur les oasis du Ziban," n.d. (c. 1844 or 1845), AMG, Algérie, H 230; "Carnet de notes," 1885, AGGA, 10 H 72; and anonymous, "Notice sur Si Ali ben Otmane," December 1898, AGGA, 16 H 3.

91. AMG, Algérie, H 227, H 230, and H 235.

92. Émile Masqueray, "Le Djebel Cherchar," *RA* 20 (1878): 208–12 (quote on 210). Masqueray devoted much of his life and research to the history of the Awras and its inhabitants; his magnum opus was *Formation des cités chez les populations sédentaires de l'Algérie* (Paris: Leroux, 1886).

Fanny Colonna has done the most significant recent work on the religious sociology of the Awras: "Saints furieux et saints studieux ou, dans l'Aurès, comment la religion vient aux tribus," *AESC* 35 (1980): 642–62; idem, "The Transformation of a Saintly Lineage in the Northwest Aurès Mountains (Algeria): Nineteenth and Twentieth Centuries," in *Islam, Politics, and Social Movements*, Edmund Burke III and Ira M. Lapidus, eds. (Berkeley and Los Angeles: University of California Press, 1988), 81–96; and idem, "Présence des ordres mystiques dans l'Aurès aux XIXe et XXe siècles: Contribution à une histoire sociale des forces religieuses en Algérie," in *Les ordres mystiques dans l'Islam: Cheminements et situation actuelle*, Alexandre Popovic and Gilles Veinstein, eds. (Paris: Éditions de l'École des Hautes Études en Sciences Sociales, 1986), 245–65.

93. Masqueray, "Djebel," 208–12; Raoul de Lartigue, *Monographie de l'Aurès* (Constantine: Marle-Audrino, 1904), 370–74; and Gouvian, *Kitab*, 158–65. The oasis of Sidi 'Uqba is located in the Zab Sharqi (or eastern wing of the Ziban) immediately south of the Jabal Cherchar. One of the most important pilgrimage sites in the Maghrib, the oasis boasts the tomb of the great Arab-Muslim conqueror 'Uqba b. Nafi', who founded the holy city of al-Qayrawan in Tunisia in 670 and later led an expedition in the Biskra region; he was killed and buried there in c. 682. His tomb-mosque, still revered today, is the oldest monument in existence from this period in the Maghrib.

94. Gouvian, *Kitab*, 158–60; anonymous, "Notice historique de la zawiya de Khangat Sidi Naji," 25 May 1895, AGGA, 16 H 10; also AGGA, 1 H 9 and 10 H 72.

95. AGGA, 10 H 72 and 16 H 2; and AMG, Algérie, H 230 bis.

96. AGGA, 10 H 72 and 16 H 2; and AMG, Algérie, H 230 bis; and Rinn, *Marabouts*. Here the hostility of colonial officers toward the Catholic church in France played a significant part in their interpretation of Islam in North Africa; Julia Clancy-Smith, "In the Eye of the Beholder: Sufi and Saint in North Africa and the Colonial Production of Knowledge, 1830–1900," *Africana Journal* 15 (1990): 220–57.

97. Al-Hafnawi, *Ta'rif*, 482; Gouvian, *Kitab*, 160; de Lartigue, *Monographie*, 373–74; and Masqueray, "Djebel," 208–12.

98. AGGA, 10 H 72 and 16 H 10; report, 1883, AGT-D-172–3; Gouvian, *Kitab*, 164; and de Lartigue, *Monographie*, 209.

99. Al-Hafnawi, *Ta'rif*, 483, lists some of the disciples of Shaykh Muhammad b. 'Azzuz yet omits Sidi Sadiq.

100. AGGA, 1 H 15, 10 H 43, and 16 H 2; also Depont and Coppolani, *Confréries*, 410–11. On the revolts centered in Sidi Masmudi and later in Timermacin (or Tibermacine), see Peter von Sivers, "The Realm of Justice: Apocalyptic Revolts in Algeria (1849–1879)," *Humaniora Islamica* 1 (1973): 47–60.

101. Al-Hafnawi, *Ta'rif*, 576–77, devotes a short notice to Shaykh al-Mukhtar al-Jallali which says little of his life but rather lists his virtues and concludes with an elegy composed in Sidi al-Mukhtar's honor by Muhammad al-Makki b. 'Azzuz, one of Mustafa's four sons.

102. Gouvian, *Kitab*, 153–57.

103. AGGA, 10 H 72, 16 H 8, and 16 H 73.

104. Sa'id Ghrab, "al-Tariqa al-Rahmaniyya—ta'rif mujaz," *IBLA* 54, 167 (1991): 95–108.

105. For Algeria, Sa'adallah, *Tarikh*, vol. 1; and Pierre Boyer, "Contribution à l'étude de la politique religieuse des Turcs dans la Régence d'Alger," *ROMM* 1, 1 (1966): 11–49; for Tunisia, Mohamed-Hédi Cherif, "Hommes de religion et pouvoir dans la Tunisie de l'époque moderne," *AESC* 35 (1980): 580–97.

Unlike Morocco and Tunisia, where the reigning sultans and beys confirmed the heads of the turuq and members of the ashraf by conferring letters of recognition and tax-free status, the bey of the Constantine does not appear to have issued such letters for the notables considered here.

106. Al-Hafnawi, *Ta'rif*, 459, recounts how Sidi Muhammad repeatedly refused the pasha's offer of gold dinars in return for instructing the ruler's family in Khalwatiyya sufi doctrines. Finally the saint went to the roof of the palace and flung the gold pieces from on high, after reciting verses from the Quran. With this, the pasha begged forgiveness; after accepting the dey's apology, Sidi Muhammad departed from the city. The obvious moral lesson is that residing among the powerful and wealthy for the purposes of spiritual edification is a worthy endeavor; accepting remuneration is not. The implicit political message is that the holy person might disobey a sovereign.

107. Anonymous, letter, 18 May 1856, AGGA, 25 H 16; and de Fleurac, "Étude," 1885, AMG, Tunisie, 36 H 29, no. 8.

108. Al-Hafnawi, Ta'rif, 483.

109. Anonymous, report, 1898, AGGA, 16 H 3; Gouvian, Kitab, 149–51; and Henri Garrot, Histoire générale de l'Algérie (Algiers: Crescenzo, 1910), 944–45.

110. "Notice sur Si Ali ben Otmane," AGGA, 16 H 3; "Memoire sur les oasis des Zibans," AGGA, 10 H 72; AMG, Algérie, H 230 bis and H 131; and de Lartigue, Monographie, 370–71.

111. Joseph-Adrien Seroka, "Le sud Constantinois de 1830 à 1855," RA 56 (1912): 400–401.

112. John Voll, Islam: Continuity and Change in the Modern World (Boulder: Westview Press, 1982), 52; also idem, "Hadith Scholars and Tariqahs: An Ulama Group in the Eighteenth-Century Haramayn and Their Impact in the Islamic World," JAAS 15, 3–4 (1980): 264–73.

113. Dale F. Eickelman and James Piscatori, eds., "Social Theory in the Study of Muslim Societies," Muslim Travellers, 3–25.

3. HEDGING BETS IN A TIME OF TROUBLES

1. Alf A. Heggoy, The French Conquest of Algiers, 1830: An Algerian Oral Tradition (Athens: Center for International Studies, Ohio University, 1986), 6–7.

2. Jamil M. Abun-Nasr, A History of the Maghrib in the Islamic Period (Cambridge: Cambridge University Press, 1987); Lucette Valensi, Le Maghreb avant la prise d'Alger (Paris: Flammarion, 1969); Abdeljelil Temimi, Le beylik de Constantine et hadj Ahmed Bey (1830–1837), vol. 1 (Tunis: Publications de la Revue d'Histoire Maghrébine, 1978); and Charles-André Julien, La conquête et les débuts de la colonisation (1827–1871), vol. 1 of Histoire de l'Algérie contemporaine, 2d ed. (Paris: PUF, 1979), 1–20.

3. Pierre Boyer, "Introduction à une histoire intérieure de la régence d'Alger," RH 235, 2 (1966): 297–316.

4. The history of the Ottoman period still awaits its historian. On Algeria under the Turks, see Mouloud Gaid, L'Algérie sous les Turcs (Algiers: SNED, 1974); Pierre Boyer, La vie quotidienne à Alger à la veille de l'intervention française (Paris: Hachette, 1963); dated but useful is Henri-Delmas de Grammont's, Histoire d'Alger sous la domination turque, 1515–1830 (Paris: Leroux, 1887). The best recent study of the evolution of the state in Algeria is John Ruedy's Modern Algeria: The Origins and Development of a Nation (Bloomington: Indiana University Press, 1992).

5. Abu Al-Qasim Sa'adallah, Tarikh al-Jaza'ir al-thaqafi, 2d ed. (Algiers: SNED, 1981), 1: 524–26; Roger Le Tourneau, "Darkawa," EI, 2d ed. (Leiden: E. J. Brill, 1965), 2: 160; Adrien Delpech, "Resumé historique sur

le soulèvement des Dark'aoua de la province d'Oran," *RA* 18 (1874): 38–58; and Mehdi Bouabdelli, "Documents inédits sur la révolte des Derqawa en Oranie," in *Les Arabes par leurs archives (XVIe-XXe siècles)*, Jacques Berque and Dominique Chevallier, eds. (Paris: CNRS, 1976), 93–100.

6. L. Charles Féraud, "Les cherifs kabyles de 1804 à 1809 dans la province de Constantine," *RA* 13 (1868): 211–24; and Dominique Luciani, "Les Ouled-Athia de l'oued Zhour," *RA* 33 (1889): 294–311.

7. Michael Adas in his "Bandits, Monks, and Pretender Kings: Patterns of Peasant Resistance and Protest in Colonial Burma, 1826–1941," in *Power and Protest in the Countryside: Studies of Rural Unrest in Asia, Europe, and Latin America*, Robert P. Weller and Scott E. Guggenheim, eds. (Durham, North Carolina: Duke University Press, 1982), 75–105, argues along lines similar to mine regarding the continuities between the precolonial and colonial eras in institutions, traditions, and economic arrangements.

8. Peter von Sivers, "Les plaisirs du collectionneur: Capitalisme fiscal et chefs indigènes en Algérie (1840–1860)," *AESC* 33, 3–4 (1980): 679–99; quote 680–81.

9. Joseph-Adrien Seroka, "Historique de Biskra," 1855, AGGA, 10 H 76.

10. I. Urbain, *Tableau des etablissements français en Algérie* (Paris, 1844), 401.

11. Jean Lethielleux, *Ouargla, cité saharienne: Des origines au début du XXe siècle* (Paris: Paul Geuthner, 1983); and L. Charles Feraud, "Notes historiques sur la province de Constantine: Les Ben-Djellab, sultans de Touggourt," *RA* 23–31 (1879–1887).

12. Muslim b. 'Abd al-Qadir al-Wahrani, *Tarikh bayat wahran al-muta'akhkhir*, new ed. (Algiers: SNED, 1974); Jamil M. Abun-Nasr, *The Tijaniyya: A Sufi Order in the Modern World* (London: Oxford University Press, 1965), 59–62; and Ernest Mercier, *Histoire de Constantine* (Constantine: Marle, 1903), 272–82. After the death of the order's founder, Ahmad al-Tijani, in 1815, the Tijaniyya, like Rahmaniyya, followed a pattern of alternating succession for the honor of head shaykh. Two main Tijaniyya centers existed in Algeria during the nineteenth century; one was located in the founder's birth place at 'Ain Madi in western Algeria; the other was situated in the eastern Algerian Sahara in Tamalhat, a suburb of Tammasin near the larger rival oasis of Tuqqurt.

13. Seroka, "Historique de Biskra," 1855, AGGA, 10 H 76.

14. Anonymous, report, 1844, AGGA, 1 KK 470.

15. Ibid.; Seroka, "Historique de Biskra," 1855, AGGA, 10 H 76; Feraud, "Les Ben-Djellab," 26: 376–86; and Peter von Sivers, "Insurrection and Accommodation: Indigenous Leadership in Eastern Algeria, 1840–1900," *IJMES* 6, 3 (1975): 259–75. The struggles lasted into the twentieth century; only in 1938 were the two families reconciled. The quote is from Seroka.

16. Lieutenant Prax, "Mémoire sur les oasis du Souf," 4 November 1847, AMAE, Tunisie, c.p., vol. 10; and AGGA, 10 H 18.

17. Al-Hajj Ahmad Bey, "Mémoires d'Ahmed Bey," Marcel Emerit, trans., *RA* 93 (1949): 65–125.

18. It is useful to compare the political situation in the eastern pre-Sahara of Turkish Algeria with the Tunisian pre-Sahara in the same period. In Husaynid Tunisia, a relatively more centralized state apparatus did not permit the existence of either Saharan princes, such as the Banu Jallab of Tuqqurt, or of great warrior families, like the Bu 'Ukkaz. However, in places like the Jarid, political struggles were also expressed by the binary saff mechanism, and the state had to work through local clans of notables; on relations between the Jarid and Tunis, see Abdelhamid Henia, *Le Grid, ses rapports avec le beylik de Tunis, 1676–1840* (Tunis: Publications de l'Université de Tunis, 1980).

19. Ann Thomson, *Barbary and Enlightenment: European Attitudes towards the Maghreb in the Eighteenth Century* (Leiden: E. J. Brill, 1987).

20. M. E. Chamberlain, *Decolonization: The Fall of the European Empires* (Oxford: Basil Blackwell, 1985), 3.

21. C. M. Andrew and A. S. Kanya-Forstner, "Centre and Periphery in the Making of the Second French Colonial Empire, 1815–1920," *Journal of Imperial and Commonwealth History* 16, 3 (1988): 9–34.

22. Philip D. Curtin, *Death by Migration: Europe's Encounter with the Tropical World in the Nineteenth Century* (Cambridge: Cambridge University Press, 1989), 28–30; the casualty rate among French soldiers in Algeria was so high that it became a public issue in France.

23. Michael Adas, "From Avoidance to Confrontation: Peasant Protest in Precolonial and Colonial Southeast Asia," *CSSH* 23, (1981): 217–47; and idem, " 'Moral Economy' or 'Contest State'?: Elite Demands and the Origins of Peasant Protest in Southeast Asia," *JSH* 13, 4 (Summer 1980): 521–46.

24. Popular lamentations were given public voice by the *maddah*—more so than by the urban literati or ulama, who, according to Jean Déjeux in *La poésie algérienne de 1830 à nos jours*, 2d ed. (Paris: Publisud, 1982), 20, remained silent about the conquest since "they did not wish to record the humiliations and affronts suffered at the hands of the infidels." The maddahs, on the other hand, were minstrels who sang in markets and gathering places; their ballads transmitted public consensus and collective historical memory to future generations.

According to Julien, *Histoire*, 60–61, the conquest of the capital was portrayed in the following manner: "the queen of all cities has fallen in the hands of the Christians with their degraded religion because the Muslims were unable to defend her." Collective aspirations centered upon a "ruler who would have pity upon the capital [and who] would return to the country as a king to administer Algiers according to Islamic law."

25. Charles Richard in *Étude sur l'insurrection du Dahra (1845–1846)* (Algiers: Besancenez, 1846), 104, wrote that "the Arabs believe that we will be chased out . . . like the Spanish were." General Bourmont's 1830 proclamation (in both Arabic and French) to the capital's inhabitants in Adrien Berbrugger, "La première proclamation addressée par les français aux algériens, 1830," *RA* (1862) 6: 147–56, stated: "I assure you that no one among us desires to harm either your possessions or your families."

On France's uncertainty over the fate of Algeria during the first decade of conquest, see Alf A. Heggoy, "Looking Back: The Military and Colonial Policies in French Algeria," *MW* 73 (1983): 57–66.

26. The literature, colonial and recent, devoted to 'Abd al-Qadir is staggering; for a partial listing of the colonial production, see Robert Playfair's *A Bibliography of Algeria from the Expedition of Charles V in 1541 to 1887* (London: Murray, 1892) and *Bibliographie militaire des ouvrages français ou traduit en français et des articles des principales revues françaises relatifs à l'Algérie, Tunisie, et au Maroc de 1830 à 1926* (Paris: Imprimerie Nationale, 1930–1935) 2: 300–306. The most recent English study is Raphael Danziger's *Abd al-Qadir and the Algerians: Resistance to the French and Internal Consolidation* (New York: Holmes and Meier, 1977). The best Arabic source remains Muhammad b. 'Abd al-Qadir al-Jaza'iri, *Tuhfa al-za'ir fi tarikh al-Jaza'ir wa al-amir 'Abd al-Qadir*, Mamduh Haqi, ed. (Beirut, 1964).

27. Louis de Baudicour, *La guerre et le gouvernement de l'Algérie* (Paris: Sagnier et Bray, 1853), 508.

28. The amir's subtle, calculated blend of accommodation with opposition undermines "resistance" theory's binary approach to political movements, pigeonholing political actors into either resistors/opponents or collaborators. 'Abd al-Qadir's movement resembles West African jihads; see David Robinson, *The Holy War of Umar Tal: The Western Sudan in the Mid-Nineteenth Century* (Oxford: Clarendon Press, 1985).

29. André Raymond, "Caractéristiques d'une ville arabe 'moyenne' au XVIIIe siècle: Le cas de Constantine," *ROMM* 44, 2 (1987): 134–47.

30. Emile Herbillon, *Insurrection survenue dans le sud de la province de Constantine en 1849. Relation du siège de Zaatcha* (Paris: Librarie Militaire, 1863), 6.

31. Seroka, "Historique de Biskra," 1855, AGGA, 10 H 76; and idem, "Le sud Constantinois de 1830 à 1855," *RA* 56 (1912): 386–88.

32. La Croix, report of 1844, AMG, Algérie, M 1317, H 227, and H 230 bis; Robert Capot-Rey, *Le Sahara français* (Paris: PUF, 1953), 236.

33. Seroka, "Historique de Biskra," 1855, AGGA, 10 H 76; and idem, "Le sud," 388.

34. Herbillon, *Relation*, 27; and Charles Bocher, "Le siège de Zaatcha, souvenirs de l'expédition dans les Ziban en 1849," *RDM* 10 (1851): 70–100.

35. Seroka, an officer of Batna's Bureau Arabe, set forth this policy of close political surveillance of local notables during the Sharif of Warqala's revolt in 1855; this policy would remain in force among military officials until the early twentieth century; Seroka, "Historique de Biskra," 1855, AGGA, 10 H 76.

36. Seroka, "Le sud," 391–408.

37. James M. Malarkey, "The Colonial Encounter in French Algeria: A Study in the Development of Power Asymmetry and Symbolic Violence in the City of Constantine" (Ph.D. diss., University of Texas at Austin, 1980). On 'Abd al-Qadir's complicated relationships with religious and tribal leaders in the Constantine, see al-Jaza'iri, *Tuhfa*, 300; Seroka, "Le sud," 391–408; and Leon Roches, 1839–1840, "Biographie d'Abdel Kader," AMG, Algérie, H 235.

38. Raymond, "Caractéristiques," 134–47; and Temimi, *Le beylik*, 220–22.

39. Even after the catastrophes of 1837, Constantine continued to function as an important center of Islamic learning with an active, if much more circumscribed, role in the province's cultural life. Two decades later, a British traveler, Joseph William Blakesley, visited one of the great madrasas there. He observed that the professors lecturing on the Quran still attracted students from all over the Maghrib and even the Mashriq, although the city's religious establishments had not been treated kindly by the colonial administration; Joseph William Blakesley, *Four Months in Algeria* (Cambridge, 1859), 1–36.

40. Various Algerian officials, including Ahmad Bey, continued to correspond with the Porte after the 1830 invasion, submitting reports to the sultan on French activities; see the documents contained in Temimi, *Le beylik*, 220–88. Equally significant, Constantine's populace wrote to the Ottoman sultan, Mahmud II, detailing the disasters suffered by the country and begging for assistance. As Temimi (220) points out, this was the first time that a petition had been directly addressed to an Ottoman ruler.

41. Al-Jaza'iri, *Tuhfa*, 300.

42. Ibid., 306; and Seroka, "Le sud," 400–402. In his introduction to his translation of Muhammad b. 'Abd al-Rahman's *al-Rahmaniyya* [*Livre de la Rah'maniya*] (Maison-Carrée, 1946), 3, Antoine Giacobetti noted that 'Abd al-Qadir joined the Rahmaniyya "in the hope of enrolling the Kabyles in his cause."

43. 'Abd al-Qadir al-Jaza'iri, *Tuhfa*, 306; Seroka, "Le sud," 400–402 and 422–23; and AGGA, 1 H 8.

44. Allan Christelow, *Muslim Law Courts and the French Colonial State in Algeria* (Princeton: Princeton University Press, 1985), 46–54.

45. Seroka, "Historique de Biskra," 1855, AGGA, 10 H 76; and idem, "Le sud," 409–14. On Gen. Thomas Robert Bugeaud (1784–1849) and his

writings, see *Par l'epée et par la charrue, écrits et discours de Bugeaud,* introduction and notes by Gen. Paul Azan (Paris: PUF, 1948); an exercise in colonial hagiography and apologia, the work offers insights into the man who decreed total occupation and relentlessly promoted settler colonialism in Algeria.

46. Muhammad b. 'Abd al-Rahman, *al-Rahmaniyya,* 267.

47. Seroka, "Le sud," 402–4.

48. Ibid; and anonymous, report, 1840, AGGA, F 80 1673.

49. Anonymous, report, 1840, AGGA, F 80 1673; and Seroka, "Le sud," 402–4.

50. AMG, Algérie, H 230 bis; and Seroka, "Historique de Biskra," 1855, AGGA, 10 H 76.

51. AMG, Algérie, H 230 bis; and Seroka, "Le sud," 422–23.

52. AMG, Algérie, H 230 bis; Warnier's letter dated 1 August 1849, AGGA, 16 H 2; and Seroka, "Le sud," 422–23.

53. La Croix, report, 1844, AMG, Algérie, M 1317.

54. Anonymous, report, 1844, AGGA, 1 KK 470; and Seroka, "Le sud," 428–34. In reorganizing the Ziban, the French commander created a new post—that of qa'id, who was subordinate to the shaykh al-'arab but resided permanently in Biskra; a qadi was also named for the entire region. For each oasis, local qadis and heads of village councils were appointed to offset the shaykh al-'arab's power, whose authority was thereby diminished. The French-imposed administrative curbs on the shaykh's traditional political clout made the Banu Ghana less than faithful allies; this explains their ambiguous behavior during Bu Ziyan's revolt.

55. Anonymous, report, 1844, AGGA, 1 KK 470. Since the French-appointed khalifa in the Majana resided permanently in his administrative bailiwick, he was constantly aware of the "political state of mind" of those under him; this was critical for the isolated French troops and officers scattered about in garrisons. In the pre-Sahara, the shaykh al-'arab normally moved with the tribes and was frequently absent from Biskra. This meant that the small French military presence there relied wholly upon the good-will of the settled oasis population. As the 1844 report observed after the massacre: "The Biskris had no need for France's protection to market their products, a need of the greatest significance for the nomads; the political sympathies of Biskra's sedentary population are with the Amir 'Abd al-Qadir."

56. E. Pellissier de Reynaud to French consul, Tunis, 7 April 1846, ARGT, carton 416.

57. Claude Martins, *Tableau physique du Sahara oriental* (Paris: J. Claye, 1864), 21.

58. Bureau Arabe, Biskra, AGGA, 1 KK 5 and 1 KK 13; and Kenneth J. Perkins, *Qaids, Captains, and Colons: French Military Administration in the Colonial Maghrib, 1844–1934* (New York: Africana, 1981).

59. Von Sivers, "Insurrection," 259–75; and idem, "Les plaisirs," 679–99.

60. Warnier, letter, 1 August 1849, AGGA, 16 H 2.

61. La Croix, report, 1844, AMG, Algérie, M 1317; "Renseignements, Biskra," 1844, AGGA, 10 H 18; and Seroka, "Le sud," 431.

62. "Renseignements, Biskra," 1844, AGGA, 10 H 18.

63. Bureau Arabe, Biskra, 29 September 1846, AGGA, 1 KK 5.

64. Ahmed Nadir, "Les ordres religieux et la conquête française (1830–1851)," *RASJEP* 9, 4 (1972): 819–72; and Marthe and Edmond Gouvian, *Kitab aayane al-marhariba* (Algiers: Imprimerie Orientale, 1920), 147.

65. Emile Masqueray, "Le Djebel Cherchar," *RA* 20 (1878): 210–11.

66. Abun-Nasr, *The Tijaniyya*, 72–73; Edouard de Neveu, *Les khouans: Ordres religieux chez les musulmans de l'Algérie* (Paris: A. Guyot, 1846), 140–41. The struggles between the Tijaniyya of western Algeria and the Turkish regime earlier in the century may have convinced some sufi shaykhs that French rule was less pernicious than that of fellow Muslims. How the Tijani leader's advice was received by those seeking counsel in 1844 is less certain.

67. Anonymous, report, 1846, AGGA, 1 KK 470.

68. Seroka, "Le sud," 432. In al-Aghwat, for example, Ahmad b. Salim, the local leader and head of a prestigious saintly clan, opened direct negotiations with General Marey-Monge in 1844 to explore French aims in the Sahara and determine whether those aims were consonant with his own political objectives; Roger Le Tourneau, "Occupation de Laghouat par les français (1844–1852)" in *Études maghrébines: Mélanges Charles-André Julien* (Paris: PUF, 1964), 111–36.

69. Bureau Arabe, Biskra, September 1846, AGGA, 13 KK 5. French colonial interference in market exchanges and the distribution of wheat, particularly the interdiction upon the export of grains from Biskra, negatively affected the Suf and Tuqqurt regions.

70. AGGA, 10 H 18 and 10 H 76; and Prax, "Mémoire," 1847, AMAE, Tunisie, c.p., vol. 10.

71. Anonymous, report, 1844, AGGA, 1 KK 470: "prior to 1844, no attempt was made to impose administrative order [upon the Ziban]. French-named qa'ids collected taxes in a completely arbitrary manner; the quantity collected varied considerably. Tribal markets were neither uniformly governed nor taxed. The administration of justice was completely disorderly."

72. Correspondence, Bureau Arabe, Biskra, September 1846, AGGA, 13 KK 5; in 1845 tax exemptions were accorded to some religious notables for not opposing the French regime; the next year this policy was abruptly changed. The inconsistency and arbitrary nature of the exemptions were as much a source of grievance as the measures themselves.

73. AGGA, 10 H 76; and AMG, Algérie, H 131 and M 1317. Charles Bocher in "Le siège de Zaatcha," 76, dismissed taxation as a primary cause

of the revolt as does Seroka, "Le sud," 505. Herbillon in his 1850 report, AMG, Algérie, H 131, and in *Relation*, 12, concedes that the new taxes were a bit "exaggerated" and that subjecting religious notables to taxation for the first time was unwise. Yet Herbillon, who commanded the French forces during the 1849 siege, maintained that insurrection was already in the "minds and hearts of the Ziban's inhabitants." This interpretation naturally exonerates French military authorities. Peter von Sivers in "The Realm of Justice: Apocalyptic Revolts in Algeria (1849–1879)," *Humaniora Islamica* 1 (1973): 47–60, argues that while excessive taxation may have been a contributing factor, economic grievances alone do not suffice to explain why the movement assumed the form of a mahdist rebellion instead of a classic tax revolt.

74. Anonymous, "Historique de 1849," AGGA, 10 H 18.

75. Anonymous, report, 1844, AGGA, 1 KK 470.

76. Eugène Daumas, *Le Sahara Algérien* (Paris: Langlois et Leclercq, 1845), 108. Much of the information for economic changes in this region and this period is found only in archival sources in AMG, AGGA, AMAE, and ARGT.

77. AGGA, 10 H 76; La Croix, report, 1844, AMG, Algérie, M 1317; Herbillon, *Relation*, 5; and Bocher, "Le siège," 76.

78. Marcel Emerit, *L'Algérie à l'epoque d'Abd el-Kader* (Paris: Larose, 1951), 199–200, views the 1844 seizure of the hubus properties as instrumental in pushing local religious leaders toward collective militant protest.

79. Correspondence, Bureau Arabe, Biskra, 1847, AGGA, 13 KK 5; and John Ruedy, *Land Policy in Colonial Algeria: The Origins of the Rural Public Domain* (Berkeley and Los Angeles: University of California Press, 1967).

80. L. Carl Brown, *The Tunisia of Ahmad Bey, 1837–1855* (Princeton: Princeton University Press, 1974), 321–25.

81. Julien, *Histoire* 1: 347–49.

82. Von Sivers, "The Realm," 51.

83. AMG, Algérie, H 227 and M 1317. Ahmad Bey, "Mémoires," 87–88, describes in vivid terms the devastation wrought by the cholera epidemic—*al-rih al-asfar*—as the disease was known; the bey stated that in the city of Constantine alone seven hundred persons died in a single day.

84. Carette, report, 1839, AMG, Algérie, H 227; also M 1317.

85. Inconsistent colonial policies toward indigenous desert elites were mainly due to confusion over the nature of Saharan alignments and politics. French military officers more often than not acted without authorization from superiors when dealing with notables, also creating contradictory policies. Prior to 'Abd al-Qadir's surrender, the army frequently lacked adequate soldiers or supplies. Seroka sarcastically remarked in "Le sud,"

425, that "two battalions would have better served the interest of maintaining political order in the pre-Sahara than the mass of letters sent by the commanding general in Constantine exhorting desert peoples to obedience."

86. Bureau Arabe, Biskra, 29 September 1848, AGGA, 1 KK 5.

87. Both 'Abd al-Qadir and Ahmad Bey had surrendered with the understanding that they would be allowed to go into exile in Muslim states. In both cases, French colonial authorities failed to keep their promises; the amir was held in confinement in the Chateau d'Amboise until 1852, when he was permitted to go to Damascus. Ahmad Bey fared less well; he died in prison of poisoning in 1850 and was buried at the zawiya of Sidi 'Abd al-Rahman in Algiers.

88. James C. Scott, The Moral Economy of the Peasant: Rebellion and Subsistance in Southeast Asia (New Haven: Yale University Press, 1976), 193–98, argues that when the peasantry experience a sudden and similarly felt exploitation which threatens the very basis of the rural subsistence ethic and agrarian moral economy then collective action becomes an option, particularly in geographically peripheral regions characterized by an "unpromising ecology."

89. General Herbillon to governor-general, Algiers, November 1849, AMG, Algérie, H 131.

90. Scott, Moral Economy, 193–95.

91. Timothy Weiskel emphasized the importance of political uncertainty and what he terms a "pervasive sense of the unpredictable" in French Colonial Rule and the Baule People: Resistance and Collaboration, 1889–1911 (Oxford: Clarendon Press, 1980).

92. Bureau Arabe, Biskra, 1844 report, AGGA, 1 KK 470.

93. Von Sivers, "Insurrection," and "The Realm."

94. Bradford G. Martin, Muslim Brotherhoods in Nineteenth-Century Africa (London: Cambridge University Press, 1976); and Muhammad A. al-Hajj, "The Thirteenth Century in Muslim Eschatology: Mahdist Expectations in the Sokoto Caliphate," Research Bulletin, Center of Arabic Documentation, Ibadan University (Nigeria) 3, 2 (1967): 100–115.

95. W. Madelung, "al-Mahdi," EI, 2d ed. (Leiden: E. J. Brill, 1986), 5: 1230–38.

96. The last recorded mahdist movement in Morocco was led by M'bark ibn al-Husayn al-Tuzunini between 1914 and 1919; the last such uprising recorded for Tunisia occurred in 1906 in the region of Tala.

Studies of the mahdi, mahdism, and the Islamic apocalypse are: James Darmesteter, Le mahdi depuis les origines de l'Islam jusqu'à nos jours (Paris: Le Roux, 1885); D. S. Margoliouth, "On Mahdis and Mahdism," Proceedings of the British Academy 7 (1915–1916): 213–33; S. M. Hasan, al-Mahdiya fi al-Islam mundhu al-usul hatta al-yawm (Cairo, 1953); Abdulaziz Sachedina, Islamic Messianism, the Idea of the Mahdi in

Twelver Shi'ism (Albany: State University of New York Press, 1980); Thomas Hodgkin, "Mahdism, Messianism, and Marxism in the African setting," in *Religion and Rural Revolt,* Janos M. Bak and Gerhard Benecke, eds. (Manchester: Manchester University Press, 1984); and Michael Adas, *Prophets of Rebellion: Millenarian Protest Movements against the European Colonial Order* (Chapel Hill: University of North Carolina Press, 1979). The literature on apocalyptic movements in Christianity is too extensive to be cited here; two classic works on this topic remain Norman Cohn, *The Pursuit of the Millennium: Revolutionary Millenarians and Mystical Anarchists of the Middle Ages,* revised and enlarged ed. (Oxford: Oxford University Press, 1970); and Sylvia Thrupp, ed., *Millennial Dreams in Action* (The Hague: Mouton, 1962).

97. Popular lore regarding the mahdi, including the oral traditions of Sidi al-Aghwati, were recorded from native informants by the French military officer Richard in *Étude,* 86–98.

98. Théodore Pein, *Lettres familières sur l'Algérie, un petit royaume arabe* (Algiers: Jourdan, 1893), 51–52, says that a local holy man visited him while he was serving as an officer in Bu Sa'ada between 1850 and 1859. The saint, who bore the same name as the eighteenth-century holy man, offered to instruct Pein about the predictions contained in Sidi al-Aghwati's book; this indicates that a century later these prophecies were still read and talked about. On manuscript prophecy and issues of oral tradition in Algerian historiography, see Allan Christelow's "Oral, Manuscript, and Printed Expressions of Historical Consciousness in Colonial Algeria," *Africana Journal* 15 (1990): 258–75.

4. MAHDI AND SAINT

1. Ibn Khaldun, *The Muqaddimah: An Introduction to History,* 2d ed., Franz Rosenthal, trans. and ed. (Princeton: Princeton University Press, 1967), 2: 156.

2. Ibid. 2: 164. Peter von Sivers's "The Realm of Justice: Apocalyptic Revolts in Algeria (1849–1879)," *Humaniora Islamica* 1 (1973): 47–60, is the only recent study of the Za'atsha rebellion. On the mahdi as a socioreligious type in North African history, see Michael Brett, "Mufti, Murabit, Marabout, and Mahdi: Four Types in the Islamic History of North Africa," *ROMM* 29, 1 (1980): 5–16; and Mercedes Garcia-Arenal, "La conjunction du sufisme et sharifisme au Maroc: Le mahdi comme sauveur," *ROMM* 55–56 (1990–1991): 233–56.

3. Eugen Weber, "Comment la Politique Vint aux Paysans: A Second Look at Peasant Politicization," *AHR* 87, 2 (1982): 357–89 (quote on 357).

4. Emile Herbillon, *Insurrection survenue dans le sud de la province de Constantine en 1849. Relation du siège de Zaatcha* (Paris: Librarie Militaire, 1863), 26.

5. Charles-André Julien, *La conquête et les débuts de la colonisation (1827–1871)*, vol. 1 of *Histoire de l'Algérie contemporaine*, 2d ed. (Paris: PUF, 1979), 1: 201.

6. Charles-Robert Ageron, *Modern Algeria: A History from 1830 to the Present*, Michael Brett, trans. (London: Hurst and Co., 1991), 20.

7. Anonymous, report, 1847, AGGA, 1 KK 470. The participation in Bu Ma'za's movement of these two oases and the Awlad Na'il reveals how ecologically based relationships between pastoralists and agrarian communities influenced political behavior. The Awlad Na'il traditionally used these particular oases as storage places; the ties of patronage between the oases' inhabitants and fellow tribal combatants provided a framework for political cooperation. As important, most belonged to the same saff, the Banu Ghana.

8. Ibid.; and Charles Richard, *Étude sur l'insurrection du Dahra (1845–1846)* (Algiers: Besancenez, 1846); and Joseph-Adrien Seroka, "Le sud Constantinois de 1830 à 1855," *RA* 56 (1912): 442–44.

9. Pierre Bourdieu, "The Sentiment of Honour in Kabyle Society," in *Honour and Shame: The Values of Mediterranean Society*, J. G. Peristiany, ed. (Chicago: University of Chicago Press, 1966), 201–2, characterized tribal warfare as a set of rituals in which the aim was to avenge honor; "one did not seek to kill or crush one's opponent." Firearms were a last resort and the struggle was not necessarily to the death. Thus the function and operation of warfare in traditional North African society could differ substantially from the European context.

10. Richard, *Étude*; and Seroka, "Le sud," 442–44. Bu Ma'za's fate after his capture by the French resembled that of the Amir 'Abd al-Qadir. The ex-mahdi was imprisoned in Paris, where he became, as was true of the amir, an exotic object of curiosity on the part of the French. Finally, Emperor Louis Napoleon pardoned him; he was allowed to settle in the Ottoman Empire, where he was admitted to the Ottoman army as a colonel.

11. James C. Scott, *Weapons of the Weak: Everyday Forms of Peasant Resistance* (New Haven: Yale University Press, 1985), xv.

12. Von Sivers, "The Realm," 47–60, notes that millenarian movements tended to occur when alternative forms of militant protest had failed or were deemed inferior to the mahdi's self-proclaimed mission.

13. In anonymous, report, 1844, AGGA, 1 KK 470, an officer with the Bureau Arabe in Biskra observed that the administration of justice was completely in abeyance throughout the Ziban. This continued to be the case until the 1849 revolt. "The administration of justice was disorderly; qadis were appointed without official character, and the means to enforce their sentences were lacking. The qadis were no longer consulted in judicial matters by the tribes of the countryside and the *majlis*, or superior tribunal, no longer functioned either. Fines and punishments were inflicted upon the tribes without order or reason."

14. Charles Tilly, *From Mobilization to Revolution* (Reading, Mass.: Addison-Wesley, 1978); and idem, *The Contentious French* (Cambridge, Mass.: Belknap Press, 1986).

15. Julien, *Histoire*, 342–47.

16. La Croix, report, 1844, AMG, Algérie, M 1317; Adrien Berbrugger, *Algérie, historique, pittoresque, et monumentale* (Paris: Delahaye, 1843) 3: 19–20; and Allan Christelow, *Muslim Law Courts and the French Colonial State in Algeria* (Princeton: Princeton University Press, 1985), 87. The barranis had traditionally supplied information; under the Turkish regime, the Mzabis, due to constant comings and goings between the Sahara and the Mediterranean, were the main source of news for the central government in Algiers. Julien, *Histoire*, 13.

17. Thiriet, report, 1938, AGGA, 10 H 88 (7).

18. Estimates of the exact numbers of barranis in the precolonial and early colonial periods are impressionistic. In the 1870s, when statistics become more reliable, it was estimated that nearly half of the adult male population of the small oasis-village of al-Burj had at one time or another worked in Algiers or Constantine. AMG, Algérie, H 230, "Étude sur les oasis du Ziban" (n.d., c. 1876); M 1317 (1847); and H 227 (1839).

19. Carette, a Saint-Simonian army officer and later prefect of the Constantine, was a pioneer in colonial studies devoted to the Sahara, then believed to contain vast, unexplored riches. In 1839 Carette began to gather meticulous data on the desert from native informants who were Algerian or Tunisian merchants.

In 1844 Carette's study was published as "Recherches sur la géographie et le commerce de l'Algérie méridionale" in a multivolume compilation, *Exploration scientifique de l'Algérie*, vol. 1 (Paris: Imprimerie Royale, 1844), patterned after its Napoleonic precursor, *Description de l'Égypte*. While the interests of the French military naturally tended toward political and strategic concerns, commerce was regarded as a necessary adjunct to domination of the pastoral-nomadic and oasis peoples. Even though Carette, who published a number of studies, never visited many of the regions about which he wrote, his work was remarkably accurate due to his research methods. Two manuscripts by Carette are contained in AMG, Algérie, H 227 and H 229.

20. Anonymous, 14 March 1852, dispatch no. 58, AGGA, 10 H 9.

21. The Biskris or Saharan barranis were the North African version of the Auvergnats in France. By this period, some had a limited understanding of the French language; the professions monopolized by the Biskris in Algiers and elsewhere—messengers, porters, and water carriers—made them especially well placed to both gather and disseminate rumors and information.

22. Anonymous, "Historique de 1849," AGGA, 10 H 18. Evidence that the barranis were colporteurs of politically subversive rumors is also

found in Herbillon, *Relation*, 8–10; Bocher, "Le siège de Zaatcha: Souvenirs de l'expédition dans les Zibans en 1849," *RDM* 10 (1851): 70–100; and Seroka, "Le sud," 501–5. The fact that taxation was integrated into the rumor mills suggests that fiscal disorder played a role in focusing economic grievances prior to the Bu Ziyan uprising.

23. The National Assembly in Paris allocated considerable sums of money in 1848 for settling French families in Algeria; this act was followed by the arrival of large numbers of colons the next year, much to the distress of the indigenous population, who correctly foresaw the loss of their lands to the settlers.

24. Ahmad ibn Abi al-Diyaf, *Ithaf ahl al-zaman bi-akhbar muluk Tunis wa 'ahd al-aman*, annotated by Ahmed Abdesselem (Tunis: Publications de l'Université de Tunis, 1971), 121; and Leon Carl Brown, *The Tunisia of Ahmad Bey, 1837–1855* (Princeton: Princeton University Press, 1974), 325.

25. Anonymous, report, 1844, AGGA, 1 KK 470.

26. Anonymous, "Historique de 1848," AGGA, 10 H 18; and Herbillon, *Relation*, 8–9. In August 1846, E. Pellissier de Reynaud reported to the French consul de Lagau in Tunis in AMAE, Tunisie, c.p., vol. 10, that he had recently made a trip to southern Tunisia. Along the borders with Tripolitania were Tunisian tribes, many of whom had "never before laid eyes upon a European." Nevertheless, the tribespeople accurately reported to Pellissier de Reynaud events then occurring in the Constantine. Later he was able to ascertain the exactitude of what the tribes had told him through European newspapers. As in previous centuries, trade routes and traders functioned as a news wire service in the nineteenth century, and information regarding political changes in Algeria had been transported into southwestern Tunisia by merchants from the Constantine. The significant change is, however, the expansion of the information circuits in North Africa to include Europe and the Europeans. This global distribution of news was a product of imperialism, colonialism, and the Eurocentric world market system which made news an politically indispensable commodity of exchange.

27. As Jack Goody notes in *The Interface between the Written and the Oral* (Cambridge: Cambridge University Press, 1987), there exists a constant dialectic between the domains of the written and oral; North Africa had an ancient tradition of writing and written knowledge, whether devoted to the realms of the sacred or profane. Unfortunately, Goody does not address the issue of rumors and spontaneous news; see also Allan Christelow, "Oral, Manuscript, and Printed Expressions of Historical Consciousness in Colonial Algeria," *Africana Journal* 15 (1990): 258–75.

28. My conclusions regarding the significance of rumors in North Africa are confirmed by similar observations made by Anand A. Yang in

"A Conversation of Rumors: The Language of Popular Mentalites in Late Nineteenth-Century Colonial India," *JSH* 20 (1987): 485–505.

29. Anonymous, "Historique de 1848," AGGA, 10 H 18.

30. Richard, *Étude*, 105.

31. Augustin Cour, "Constantine en 1802 d'après un chanson du Cheikh Belgasem Er-Rahmouni El-Haddad," *RA* 60 (1919): 224–40; and Jean Déjeux, *La poésie algérienne de 1830 à nos jours (approches socio-historiques)* (Paris: Éditions Publisud, 1982). The belief in the mahdi's arrival remained in force in the Maghrib among both ordinary people and elites until the early twentieth century; the Kabyle scholar, al-Zawawi, still believed that the mahdi's appearance was possible at the turn of the century; Pessah Shinar, "A Controversial Exponent of the Algerian Salafiyya: The Kabyle 'Alim, Imam and Sharif Abu Ya'la Sa'id b. Muhammad al-Zawawi," in *Studies in Islamic History and Civilization in Honour of Professor David Ayalon*, Moshe Sharon, ed. (Leiden: E. J. Brill, 1986), 267–90.

Scott, *Weapons*, 22–27, points out that malicious tales, anecdotes, slander, and gossip about those wielding power were part of the arsenal of the weak in what he calls a "cold war" of class antagonisms.

32. Lloyd Cabot Briggs, *The Tribes of the Sahara* (Cambridge: Harvard University Press, 1967), 101.

33. During tax-collection forays into the Sahara, the Turkish regime employed paid spies to locate tribes for taxation purposes; Walsin Esterhazy, *De la domination turque dans l'ancienne Régence d'Alger* (Paris: Gosselin, 1840), 251–52.

34. Gapelin, report, 1844, AMG, Algérie, H 235, contains information on spies in the caravan trade; also Arnold van Gennep, *En Algérie* (Paris: Mercure, 1914): 105–7.

35. Jean Mattei, Sfax, to French consul-general, Tunis, 1856, ARGT, carton 414.

36. Anonymous, AGGA, 1 H 9; Eugène Perret, *Récits algériens* (Paris: Bloud et Barral, 1887) 2: 6; and Elisée Reclus, *L'Afrique septentrionale*, vol. 11 of *Nouvelle Géographie Universelle* (Paris: Hachette, 1886), 639; Mabruk b. 'Azzuz's instructions are found in AGT, 1850, 206-91-21.

37. Examples of these rumors are found in prefect of the Constantine to governor-general, Algiers, June 1852, AGGA, 1 H 9; the monthly and bimonthly reports of the Bureaux Arabes in the AGGA, 1 H sous-série, are particularly valuable sources of information on what Muslim Algerians were talking about; these contain numerous references to rumors regarding the Ottoman sultan, the mahdi, and the Tunisian bey, all of whom were regarded as potential saviors. In addition, the Public Record Office (Kew) and the French Ministry of Foreign Affairs (Paris, Quai d'Orsay) contain consular reports from nineteenth-century Tunisia which also mention

rumors and the rumor mill; for example, AMAE, Tunisie, c.p., vol. 7 (1843); and PRO, Tunisia, FO 102/10 (1841).

38. In a letter of 25 October 1846, a Bureau Arabe officer in Biskra reported to Algiers that a reconnaissance cavalry had arrested a Tunisian courier carrying a packet of letters from the Bey of Tunis to Hajj Ahmad Bey of the Constantine, then in hiding in eastern Algeria. According to the military officer who read the seized missives, they "contained the worst lies but these letters find much credence among the Arabs and the Kabyles. The arrested courier, named Muhammad b. 'Uthman, rendered a packet of 20 letters. His father is a servant of the bey in Tunis and for four years now his father has been in the [Tunisian] bey's household service."

39. Mustafa b. 'Azzuz to the Tijaniyya (?) shaykh of Gummar and Tammasin, November 1851, AGT, carton 206, dossier 91, armoire 21.

40. Yang, "A Conversation," 485. Perhaps the first social historian to study the relation between rumors and political action was Georges Lefebvre, *The Great Fear of 1789: Rural Panic in Revolutionary France*, J. White, trans. (New York: Vintage, 1973); see also Niels Kastfelt, "Rumours of Maitatsine: A Note on Political Culture in Northern Nigeria," *African Affairs, Journal of the Royal African Society* 88, 350 (1989): 83–90.

41. Ted W. Margadant, *French Peasants in Revolt: The Insurrection of 1851* (Princeton: Princeton University Press, 1979), 256–57, observed that "false rumors stimulated widespread popular participation in the revolt."

42. Anonymous, "Historique de Biskra," 1849, AGGA, 10 H 18; there were other outbreaks of insubordination toward French authorities in 1849 which are subtle indicators of the political climate. One such example is from the Awras region; an ordinary woman, who was also a female member of the Rahmaniyya tariqa, threatened French military officers in Batna; reported in AGGA, 16 H 2 (1849).

43. The traditions held that the mahdi would be a descendant of 'Ali and Fatima through their son, Husayn. One popular mahdist tradition recorded later in the century but representative of earlier such lore claimed that "a sharif will appear before you; he will be from the line of Husayn, son of 'Ali and Fatima. He will be recognized by the following signs: he will have white teeth, his banner will be green, his age 35 years; he will create a majlis composed of 40 faqihs." Octave Depont and Xavier Coppolani, *Les confréries religieuses musulmanes* (Algiers: Jourdan, 1897), 259. Whether Bu Ziyan attempted to fabricate a sharifian genealogy for himself prior to or during the construction of his mahdist persona is uncertain.

44. A similar pattern in recruitment is seen in Western Europe in the middle ages. Norman Cohn, *The Pursuit of the Millennium: Revolutionary Millenarians and Mystical Anarchists of the Middle Ages*, rev. ed. (Oxford: Oxford University Press, 1970), observed that former clerics, drawn from

the lower ranks of the clergy, were often self-proclaimed messiahs or prophets.

45. Georges Yver, "La conquête et la colonisation de l'Algérie," in *Histoire et historiens de l'Algérie*, Stéphane Gsell, ed. (Paris: Alcan, 1931), 277.

46. Maj. G. B. Laurie, *The French Conquest of Algeria* (London: Hugh Rees, 1909), 197, claims that Bu Ziyan had been a water carrier in Algiers; von Sivers in "The Realm," 50–51, also states that the leader of the Za'atsha uprising was of humble origins—as were most other mahdist figures in Algeria.

47. Perret, *Récits* 2:7–8.

48. Seroka, "Le sud," 507.

49. Audrey Wipper, *Rural Rebels: A Study of Two Protest Movements in Kenya* (Oxford: Oxford University Press, 1977); J. R. Goody, "Reform, Renewal and Resistance: A Mahdi in Northern Ghana," in *African Perspectives*, C. Allen and R. W. Johnson, eds. (Cambridge: Cambridge University Press, 1970), 143–56; and Michael Adas, *Prophets of Rebellion: Millenarian Protest Movements against the European Colonial Order* (Chapel Hill: University of North Carolina Press, 1979).

50. Perret, *Récits* 2: 8.

51. Anonymous, "Historique de 1849," AGGA, 10 H 18; and Seroka, "Le sud," 505.

52. Gilbert Delanoue, *Moralistes et politiques musulmans dans l'Égypte du XIXe siècle (1798–1882)* (Cairo: Institut Français d'Archéologie Orientale du Caire, 1982) 1: 221–27, discusses the importance of dreams and visions—not only in sufi circles but also among the learned and popular classes as well. Dreams had several functions: some permitted communication with pious persons long deceased; others provided insights and enlightenment into the correct course of action to follow; while others warned of future dangers or brought physical or spiritual healing. Moreover, the founder of the Rahmaniyya, Sidi 'Abd al-Rahman, himself, had been assured of the rightness of his "way" in the course of seven dreams in which the Prophet appeared to him.

53. Bocher, "Le siège," 78.

54. Anonymous, "Historique de Biskra," 1849, AGGA, 10 H 18.

55. Kenelm Burridge, "Millennialisms and the Recreation of History," in *Religion, Rebellion, and Revolution: An Interdisciplinary and Cross-Cultural Collection of Essays*, Bruce Lincoln, ed. (New York: Macmillan, 1985), 219–35, argues that millennial movements signal the suspension of ordinary time.

56. Herbillon, *Relation*, 12–19, 40.

57. Anonymous, "Historique de 1849," AGGA, 10 H 18.

58. Ibid.; anonymous, report, 1844, AGGA, 1 KK 470; and von Sivers, "The Realm," 51.

59. Herbillon, *Relation*, 15–19; and Perret, *Récits*, 2: 9–10.

60. Herbillon, *Relation*, 15–19; Perret, *Récits*, 2: 9–10; and Seroka, "Le sud," 505–6.

61. Anonymous, "Historique de 1849," AGGA, 10 H 18; Anonymous, "Journal de marche de la colonne de Zaatcha," 1849, AGGA, 10 H 76; Herbillon, *Relation*, 95; and Théodore Pein, *Lettres familières sur l'Algérie, un petit royaume arabe*, 2d ed. (Algiers: Jourdan, 1893), xxi.

62. L. Charles Féraud, *Histoire des villes de la province de Constantine* (Constantine: Arnolet, 1869), 356.

63. Ibid., 356–60.

64. Anonymous, 26 September 1846, correspondence, Bureau Arabe of Biskra, AGGA, 13 KK 5. In addition to importing gunpowder, mainly from Tunisia via the Jarid, the Ziban traditionally manufactured gunpowder, supplying it to the pastoral-nomadic and mountain populations. The oases of Sidi Khalid and Awlad Jallal were particularly active in the production of gunpowder, one of whose ingredients—saltpeter—was found in abundance in the desert; sulfur had to be imported clandestinely from Nafta.

65. "Journal de marche de la colonne de Zaatcha, 1849," AGGA, 10 H 76; Bocher, "Le siège," 80–81; and Perret, *Récits* 2: 8. Perret noted that the Sharif Jamina had persuaded his Kabyle followers that the walls of el-Arrouch would collapse magically due to the mahdi's divinely conferred powers.

66. "Journal de marche de la colonne de Zaatcha," 1849, AGGA, 10 H 76; and Perret, *Récits* 2: 8.

67. Jocelyne Dakhlia, *L'oubli de la cité: La mémoire collective à l'épreuve du lignage dans le Jérid tunisien* (Paris: Éditions la Découverte, 1990).

68. Von Sivers, "The Realm."

69. AGGA, 16 H 3 and 10 H 72; AMG, Algérie, H 230 bis; and Seroka, "Le sud," 375–446, 500–565.

70. AGGA, 10 H 76 and 10 H 18; Herbillon, *Relation*, 89; and Colonel Noëllat, *L'Algérie en 1882* (Paris: Librarie Militaire, 1882), who notes, 99, that the Shaykh 'Ali b. 'Uthman attempted to broker a peace during the siege, obviously without success. It is possible that Sidi 'Ali was playing a double game—extending his good offices to France while offering behind the scenes encouragement to the rebels.

71. AGGA, 1 H 9, 10 H 18, and 1 H 132; AMG, Algérie, H 131; AGT, D-172–3; Herbillon, *Relation*, 35, 39; and Seroka, "Le sud," 508–9.

72. AGGA, 10 H 18 and 10 H 76; Herbillon, *Relation*, 95.

73. AMG, Algérie, H 131 and H 230 bis.

74. AMG, Algérie, H 131 and H 230 bis; Herbillon, *Relation*, 194; Seroka, "Le sud," 513; and Perret, *Récits* 2: 13.

75. AGGA, 10 H 18; Seroka, "Le sud," 509–10; and Herbillon, *Relation*, 43–47. The oasis of Sariana, a small hamlet some twenty kilometers

to the east of Biskra, was situated near a strategic pass, the Wadi Biraz, leading from the southern Awras into the Sahara.

76. Anonymous, report, 22 January 1850, AGGA, 10 H 18; AGGA, dispatch no. 26, 1 H 7; and AGGA, 10 H 56; AMG, Algérie, H 131; and Seroka, "Le sud," 513.

77. Herbillon, *Relation*, 43.

78. A biographical notice devoted to General Herbillon is found in Raymond Peyronnet, *Livre d'or des affaires indigènes, 1830–1930* (Algiers: Soubiron, 1930) 2: 142–44.

79. Anonymous, report, 1853, AMG, Algérie, M 1317; and Perret, *Récits* 2: 14–21. The cholera outbreak among colonial troops was part of a pandemic which may have begun as early as 1847 in the Hijaz, although its exact origins are still unknown; see Nancy E. Gallager, *Medicine and Power in Tunisia, 1780–1900* (Cambridge: Cambridge University Press, 1983), 44–49; and Philip D. Curtin, *Death by Migration: Europe's Encounter with the Tropical World in the Nineteenth Century* (Cambridge: Cambridge University Press, 1989), 72, where he notes that the third pandemic of 1849–1850 "attacked all of Algeria and Tunisia" and was as mortal for the Europeans as for the indigenous populations.

80. AGGA, 10 H 76; Saint Arnaud, "Histoire des Oulad Nail," *RA* 17 (1873): 379–80; Perret, *Récits* 2: 20–21; and Seroka, "Le sud," 515–17.

81. Daniel R. Headrick, *The Tools of Empire: Technology and European Imperialism in the Nineteenth Century* (New York: Oxford University Press, 1981).

82. AMG, Algérie, H 131; Herbillon, *Relation*, 89; Perret, *Récits* 2: 21–22; and Bocher, "Le siège," 87–92.

83. Bocher, "Le siège," 22–28; and AMG, Algérie, H 131. Julien, *Histoire* 1: 320, cites some of the horrors visited upon Za'atsha's inhabitants by the soldiers—rapes, murders of children and women, etc.

84. AGGA, 10 H 76; and AMG, Algérie, H 131. One example is a study of oasis warfare completed by Lt. C. Cholleton in 1853 and entitled "Plan et projet d'attaque de l'oasis de Sidi Oqba," found in AMG, Algérie, 1317.

85. Julien, *Histoire*, 384–85, notes that General Herbillon's scorched earth policy and inability to control his troops drew criticism from some French officials; Herbillon's account of the siege—*Insurrection*—was intended in part to exonerate himself. While I have used this work as one source of information, I relied on only those parts that could be corroborated with other documentation.

86. This is clearly seen in the report written by General Marey-Monge in 1849 entitled "Au sujet des sectes religieux en Algérie," found in AGGA, 1 EE 17; see Julia Clancy-Smith, "In the Eye of the Beholder: Sufi and Saint in North Africa and the Colonial Production of Knowledge, 1830–1900," *Africana Journal* 15 (1990): 220–57.

87. AMG, Algérie, H 131; anonymous, "Mémoire de 1855," AGGA, 10 H 76; Thomas Reade, British consul, Tunis, 17 August 1850, PRO, Tunisia, FO 102/38; the quote is from Perret, *Récits* 2: 21.

88. One example of passive resistance occurred in 1851 in Guelma, where the Rahmaniyya shaykh, 'Ali b. Mahjub, advised the tariqa's members to cease working for the infidels as laborers on agricultural estates; AGGA, 16 H 1.

89. Charles-Robert Ageron, "L'émigration des musulmans algériens et l'éxode de Tlemcen (1830–1911)," *AESC* 22, 2 (1967): 1047–66.

90. Governor-general, Algiers, to the minister of foreign affairs, Paris, December 1849, AMG, Algérie, H 131.

91. Colonel Bissuel, "Histoire de Biskra," 1856–1879, AGGA, 10 H 43. The letter written by Muhammad al-Sadiq b. al-Hajj of Masmudi to Rahmaniyya followers in Batna on the eve of the 1858 uprising contains clues regarding how the Za'atsha participants viewed their struggle in 1849. Sidi Muhammad stated that "the Christian (Rumi) acts against our religion, our prayers, our zakkat, and our pilgrimage. He demands that we follow his religion; this we were not ordered to do neither by God nor by His Prophet. If the Christian only demanded of us the corvée, taxes, and requisitions, there would be nothing to say; but our religion, which is the most important thing, must not be abandoned." AGGA, 1 H 15.

92. Shaykh 'Abd al-Hafiz's official pardon is found in 22 January 1850, AGGA, 10 H 18; see also 1850, dispatch no. 26, AGGA, 1 H 7; AGGA, 10 H 56; and AMG, Algérie, H 131.

93. Emile Masqueray, "Le Djebel Cherchar," *RA* 22 (1878): 210–11.

94. Charles de Galland, *Excursions à Bou-Saada et M'Sila* (Paris: Ollendorff, 1899), 32–33; and Pein, *Lettres*, xxi–xxiii.

95. Anonymous, "Historique du cercle de Biskra, 1853," AGGA, 10 H 18; anonymous, "Résumé de la situation du cercle de Biskra, 1853," 1 H 10; and Herbillon, *Relation*, 195. The Kabyle rebel Bu Dali was also believed to have miraculously survived death; several rebellious leaders after him claimed to be the still-living hero; L. Charles Féraud, "Les chérifs kabyles de 1804 à 1809 dans la province de Constantine," *RA* 13 (1868): 211–24.

The American traveler and writer, Frederick Arthur Bridgman, *Winters in Algeria* (New York: Harper, 1890), noted that the memory of Za'atsha remained vivid among the Ziban's inhabitants even thirty years later.

96. AMG, Algérie, H 131 and H 230 bis; whether Bu Ziyan himself was literate is open to question.

97. L. Charles Féraud in "Notes historiques sur la province de Constantine: Les Ben-Djellab, sultans de Touggourt," *RA* 29 (1885): 398–423; and 'Abd Allah Rakibi, *al-Shi'ir al-dini al-Jaza'iri al-hadith* (Algiers: SNED, 1981), 378.

98. Déjeux, *Poésie*, 9–18; Mervyn Hiskett, *The Development of Islam in West Africa* (London: Longman, 1984), points out that the mahdi was a popular folk hero in Africa south of the Sahara and was often made the protagonist of village tales and stories.

99. Marcelin Beaussier, *Dictionnaire pratique arabe-française*, 2d ed., Mohamed Ben Cheneb, ed. (Algiers: Jules Carbonel, 1931), 924; compare his definition with that of N. Boratav, "Maddah," *EI*, 2d ed. (Leiden: E. J. Brill, 1984), 5: 951–53.

100. Steven C. Caton, "Power, Persuasion, and Language: A Critique of the Segmentary Model in the Middle East," *IJMES* 19 (1987): 77–102.

101. Gabriel de Margon, *Insurrection dans la province de Constantine de 1870 à 1880* (Paris: Berger-Levrault, 1883).

102. Augustin Cour, "La poésie populaire politique au temps de l'emir Abdelqader," *RA* 59 (1919): 458–84.

103. Anonymous, "Historique de 1853," AGGA, 10 H 18; L. Charles Féraud, "Ferdjioua et Zouar'a, notes historiques sur la province de Constantine," *RA* 22 (1878): 345, mentions not only that the maddahs extolled the virtues of local political autonomy but also that poets were viewed by ordinary people as endowed with the ability to foresee the future.

On poetry in sub-Saharan Africa as a vehicle for expressions of political discontents, see Leroy Vail and Landeg White, "Forms of Resistance: Songs and Perceptions of Power in Colonial Mozambique," *AHR* 88, 4 (1983): 883–919.

104. Féraud, "Les Ben-Djellab," 29: 410–13.

105. A local maddah, describing Bu Baghla's revolt in the Jurjura mountains between 1849 and 1856, employed similar imagery: "I will speak of the Christian; when he embarks upon a campaign, [his soldiers] are more numerous than the locusts when they swarm over our fields"; Déjeux, *Poésie*, 29.

106. Féraud, "Les Ben-Djellab," 29: 416–20; a similar appeal for assistance from Muslim rulers is found in the verses inspired by the fall of Constantine in 1837; the poet called upon the bey of Tunis, the sultan of Fez, the Egyptian "bey" (Muhammad 'Ali Pasha), the sultan of Istanbul, and the bey of Tripoli for succor; Déjeux, *Poésie*, 25–26.

107. Féraud, "Les Ben-Djellab," 29: 410–20.

108. L. Veuillot, *Les français en Algérie en 1841* (Tours: Mane, 1845), also recorded ballads sung by popular poets during the 1830 French invasion and the 1837 siege of Constantine appealing to reigning Muslim rulers for assistance in delivering the country from the infidels.

109. Gen. Ahmad Zarruq to the Khaznadar, Tunis, 1849, letter no. 6, AGT, 20-227–1.

110. AMG, Algérie, H 131 and H 230 bis; Féraud, "Les Ben-Djellab," 29: 398, 423, claimed the Ottomans in Tripoli were implicated in the

Za'atsha revolt. This claim should not be dismissed entirely since there appears to have been support from the governor of Tripolitania for the Sharif of Warqala's movement in 1851. Nevertheless, it seems unlikely that top Ottoman officials in Istanbul could have taken much interest in Bu Ziyan's rebellion given the more pressing matters in the period demanding attention—political turbulence in Egypt, Palestine, and the Danubian principalities. On the other hand, the Porte never officially recognized the French occupation of Algeria and Tunisia. According to Julien, *Histoire*, 1, as late as the early twentieth century, maps of the Ottoman Empire displayed in the offices of high court dignitaries in Istanbul still showed the North African provinces as Ottoman domains.

111. The *Times* (London), Saturday, 17 November 1849 and Wednesday, 21 November 1849, are among numerous articles devoted to Za'atsha.

112. Anonymous, "Mémoire de Biskra," 1855, AGGA, 10 H 76; also AGGA, 10 H 18; Herbillon, *Relation*, 194; and Seroka, "Le sud," 518–19.

113. Anonymous, "Historique de 1853," AGGA, 10 H 18.

114. Yvonne Turin, *Affrontements culturels dans l'Algérie coloniale: Écoles, médecines, religion, 1830–1880* (Paris: Maspéro, 1971), 315, notes that in the oasis of Sidi 'Uqba alone 385 out of 1,500 people died of cholera in one month.

115. Anonymous, "Historique de 1853," AGGA, 10 H 18; the officer also noted the following about the moral and political climate: "as for details of a purely administrative nature, the situation in the Ziban is satisfactory; orders are easily carried out; but we can entertain no illusions [about the natives]; we have not made the least conquest as regards Muslim fanaticism."

116. Governor-general, Cavaignac, to minister of war, Paris, 23 November 1849, AMG, Algérie, H 131; new administrative policies for Biskra, Tuqqurt, and Warqala are outlined in AGGA, 8 H 4, 8 H 5, and 8 H 6.

117. André Martel, *Les confins saharo-tripolitains de la Tunisie (1881–1911)*, 2 vols. (Paris: PUF, 1965); and Abdurrahman Cayci, *Buyuk Sahra'da Türk-Fransiz Rekabeti (1858–1911)* (Erzurum: Publications of the Atatürk University, 1970).

5. BARAKA AND BARUD

1. Governor-general of Algeria to minister of foreign affairs, Paris, December 1849, AMG, Algérie, H 131.

2. Muhammad Masud, "The Obligation to Migrate: The Doctrine of *Hijra* in Islamic Law," in *Muslim Travellers: Pilgrimage, Migration, and the Religious Imagination*, Dale F. Eickelman and James Piscatori, eds. (Berkeley and Los Angeles: University of California Press, 1990), 29–49; and Humphrey J. Fisher, "Liminality, *Hijra*, and the City," in *Rural and*

Urban Islam in West Africa, Nehemia Levtzion and Humphrey Fisher, eds. (Boulder: Lynne Rienner, 1987), 147–71.

3. In West Africa, the hijra-jihad complex ultimately created the matrix for state formation based upon new social classes; see David Robinson, *The Holy War of Umar Tal: The Western Sudan in the Mid-Nineteenth Century* (Oxford: Clarendon Press, 1985); and Bradford G. Martin, *Muslim Brotherhoods in Nineteenth-Century Africa* (Cambridge: Cambridge University Press, 1976).

4. In 1852 the governor-general of Algeria, Jacques Randon, reported that hundreds of Algerian Muslim families from the Constantine were leaving for Tunis; Randon, Algiers, February 1852, AGGA, 1 H 9. See also Fanny Colonna, "The Transformation of a Saintly Lineage in the Northwest Aurès Mountains (Algeria): Nineteenth and Twentieth Centuries," in *Islam, Politics, and Social Movements,* Edmund Burke III and Ira M. Lapidus, eds. (Berkeley and Los Angeles: University of California Press, 1988), 81–96. Colonna studied the career of a local religious notable from the Awras, Si Lhachemi, who spent the years 1845 to 1870 in the Jarid, which attracted "many Algerian students of the religious sciences" (87).

5. AGT, D-97-3. Louis Rinn, *Marabouts et khouan: Étude sur l'Islam en Algérie* (Algiers: Jourdan, 1884), 459, incorrectly asserted that Muhammad b. 'Azzuz emigrated from Biskra to the Jarid in 1844 when in fact he had died in 1819 of the plague. This error is repeated by several other authors.

6. Abdelhamid Henia, *Le Grid, ses rapports avec le beylik de Tunis, 1676–1840,* (Tunis: Publications de l'Université de Tunis, 1980), 132 and 153–54, discusses a lineage named 'Azzuz in Nafta which monopolized the post of local tribal shaykh in the eighteenth century. It is uncertain whether there were any kinship ties between the 'Azzuz of the Jarid and those from al-Burj in the Ziban; none of the sources thus far consulted mention any such ties.

7. The issue of hijra became politically charged in Algeria after 1830 with 'Abd al-Qadir's jihad; the amir wrote a treatise on the duty of removal from French-held lands. It is contained in the biography of the amir by his eldest son, Muhammad b. 'Abd al-Qadir al-Jaza'iri, *Tuhfa al-za'ir fi ta'rikh al-Jaza'ir wa al-amir 'Abd al-Qadir,* Mamduh Haqqi, ed., 2d ed. (Beirut, 1964).

8. Hasan b. 'Azzuz's capture by the French army in 1841 was facilitated by the powerful al-Muqrani family of secular warrior notables based in the Majana; the Muqrani had first thrown in their lot with 'Abd al-Qadir. Subsequently seeing the political and military advantage shifting to the French, they concluded an agreement with colonial authorities. 'Azzuz was at first exiled to Sainte-Marguerite in France and finally interned in Bône, where he died in 1843.

9. Even after 1881, the Jarid retained a measure of autonomy not found in northern Tunisia. Lieutenant de Fleurac, "Étude sur le Djérid Tunisien," September 1885, AMG, Tunisie, 36 H 29, no. 8, described the region as "a center for the exchange of ideas in the middle of the Sahara where people can without danger trade news and information." See also F. Gendre, "De Gabès à Nefta (le Nefzaoua et le Djerid)," *R.T.* 15 (1908): 381–421, 499–520.

10. Daniel Nordman, "La notion de frontière en Afrique du Nord: Mythes et réalités, 1830–1912" (doctoral diss., Montpellier University, France, 1975), 187, noted a purification ritual practiced by Algerian emigrant tribes. Once they had reached the Tunisian Dar al-Islam, a religious ceremony was held to cleanse the tribesmen of the polluting influence of the infidels.

11. Arnold H. Green, *The Tunisian Ulama, 1873–1915: Social Structure and Response to Ideological Currents* (Leiden: E. J. Brill, 1978); Muhammad Ibn 'Ashur, *Tarajim al-a'lam* (Tunis: Maison Tunisienne de l'Édition, 1970), 187–93; and Muhammad 'Ali Dabbuz, *Nahda al-Jaza'ir al-haditha wa thawratuha al-mubaraka* (Algiers: Imprimerie Cooperative, 1965), 144–47.

12. On the Jarid, see Henia's *Le Grid*; Moncef Rouissi, "Une oasis du sud Tunisien: Le Jarid, essai d'histoire sociale," 2 vols. (doctoral diss., École des Hautes Études en Sciences Sociales, Paris, 1973); and 'Umar al-Shabbi, *Wahat al-Jarid wa hayat sukkanha* (Brussels, 1979).

13. Lucette Valensi, *Fellahs tunisiens: L'économie rurale et la vie des compagnes aux 18e et 19e siècles* (Paris: Mouton, 1977), 17, estimates the population of Tuzar and Nafta at eight thousand each in 1860; only Tunis, al-Qayrawan, Sfax, and Sousse had larger populations.

14. Muhammad ibn Salama, "al-'Iqd al-munaddad fi akhbar al-mushir al-basha Ahmad," Ms. 18618, folio 82, Bibliothèque Nationale de Tunis.

15. Salama, ibid., noted that the finished textiles produced in the Jarid were eagerly sought by the upper classes of Egypt and Istanbul.

16. Valensi, *Fellahs*, 170–71.

17. Le Comte d'Escayrac, *Le désert et le Soudan* (Paris, 1853), 4–11; Ernest Carette, "Recherches sur la géographie et le commerce de l'Algérie méridionale," *ESA* (Paris: Imprimerie Royale, 1844) 2: 208; and de Fleurac, report, 1885, AMG, Tunisie, 36 H 29, no. 8.

18. Edmond Pellissier de Reynaud, *Déscription de la régence de Tunis*, vol. 16 of *ESA* (Paris: Imprimerie Royale, 1853); and Charles Tissot, May 1857, AMAE, mém./doc., vol. 8, no. 32.

19. Carette, "L'Algérie méridionale," 202–5.

20. Donald C. Holsinger, "Trade Routes of the Algerian Sahara in the Nineteenth Century," *ROMM* 30 (1980): 57–70; and idem, "Migration, Commerce, and Community: The Mizabis in Nineteenth-Century Alge-

ria" (Ph.D. diss., Northwestern University, 1979). There is no recent work on nineteenth-century trade between Algeria and Tunisia; information can be found in Carette's reports in AMG, Algérie, H 227 and H 229; E. Pellissier de Reynaud, *Description*; and Charles Tissot, May 1857, AMAE, mém./doc., vol. 8, no. 32, among numerous archival sources.

21. AMG, Algérie, M 1317 and H 229; and Ernest Carette, *Études des routes suivis par les Arabes dans la partie méridionale de l'Algérie et de la Régence de Tunis*, vol. 1 of *ESA* (Paris: Imprimerie Royale, 1842).

22. Ducouret, "Rapport général sur la régence de Tunis, l'Ouad Sus, et l'Oued Rir par Hadji Abd el-Hamid Bey en mission en Afrique," 1850, AN, F 17 2957 [2]; A. Goguyer, "Gabès, port du Touat, de l'arrière-terre algérienne et du Soudan," *RT* 2 (1895): 112–23; and Marcel Emerit, "Les liaisons terrestres entre le Soudan et l'Afrique du Nord au XVIIIe et au début du XIXe siècle," *TIRS* 11 (1954): 29–47.

23. André Martel, *Les confins saharo-tripolitains de la Tunisie (1881–1911)*, 2 vols. (Paris: PUF, 1965).

24. Henri Duveyrier, *Sahara algérien et tunisien: Journal de route* (Paris: Challamel, 1905); and idem, "Excursions dans le Djérid ou pays de dattes," *RAC* 2 (1860): 542–59.

25. Anonymous, report, January 1854, AGGA, 1 H 8.

26. M. Prax, "Commerce de l'Algérie avec La Mecque et le Soudan," *ROAC* 5 (1849): 1–32; H. T. Norris, trans. and ed., *The Pilgrimage of Ahmad* (Warminster, England: Aris and Phillips, 1977); and Abdeljelil Temimi, *Les affinités culturelles entre la Tunisie, la Libye, et le Centre et l'Ouest de l'Afrique à l'époque moderne* (Tunis: Publications de la Revue d'Histoire Maghrébine, 1981).

27. Ministère de la Guerre, État-Major Général, Service Historique, *Notice descriptive et itinéraires de la Tunisie, région du sud, 1884–1885* (Paris: Imprimerie Nationale, 1885), 72. In 1881 an incident occurred in Tuzar that provoked an uproar in colonial circles in Tunisia and proved that the Jarid was far from resigned to French rule. The imam of the oasis's principal mosque publicly offered prayers in the name of the Ottoman sultan, 'Abd al-Hamid, during an audaciously seditious *khutba* (sermon) for the Friday service. This resulted in the imam's immediate dismissal but his khutba probably echoed collective, popular sentiments in favor of Ottoman rule; 23 October 1891, AMAE, Tunisie, n.s., vol. 128.

28. Sir Grenville Temple, *Excursions in the Mediterranean, Algiers and Tunis*, 2 vols. (London: Saunders and Otley, 1835), 2: 181–82.

29. A. Marcescheau, "Voyage de Marcescheau dans le sud de la régence de Tunis en 1826," *RT* 8 (1901): 149–55.

30. Valensi, *Fellahs*, 353. A Moroccan pilgrim passed through the Jarid while performing the hajj in 1710. He was horrified by the system of taxation, which he considered not only in violation of Quranic principles but also unjust by reason of the heaviness of state fiscal impositions; Adrien

Berbrugger, "Voyages dans le sud de l'Algérie," vol. 9 of *ESA* (Paris: Imprimerie Royale, 1846): 245–46.

31. Mohamed-Hédi Cherif, *Pouvoir et société dans la Tunisie de H'usayn bin 'Ali (1705–1740)*, 2 vols. (Tunis: Publications de l'Université de Tunis, 1984–1986); idem, "Documents relatifs à des tribus tunisiennes des débuts du XVIIIe siècle," *ROMM* 33 (1982): 67–95; and anonymous, "Notes sur les tribus de la régence," *RT* 9 (1902): 185–94.

32. When present in the south, the bey al-mahalla acted as a sort of magistrate, hearing complaints from local notables and ordinary people; J. Clark Kennedy, *Algeria and Tunisia* (London: Henry Colburn, 1846) 2: 20. In addition, the qa'ids' correspondence, Dar al-Bey, Tunis, from Ahmad Bey's reign until the eve of the protectorate contain numerous letters laying forth grievances against local officials; for examples, the letters signed by the "ahl Tuzar," 1846, carton 20, dossier 227, armoire 1, no. 49, and by the "ahl Nafta," 1855–1856, carton 20, dossier 227, armoire 1, no. 122.

33. Jocelyne Dakhlia, *L'oubli de la cité: La mémoire collective à l'épreuve du lignage dans le Jérid tunisien* (Paris: Éditions la Découverte, 1990), points out that the great family of the Awlad al-Hadif served as Tuzar's shaykhs and qadis from the sixteenth through nineteenth centuries; their power was so immense in the prereform era that the bey himself dared not enter the city when they were absent.

34. Ibrahim ibn 'Un, Tuzar, to the Khaznadar, Tunis, 2 Safar 1260 AH (1844–1845), AGT, carton 20, dossier 227, armoire 1, no. 13.

35. AGT, 206–91–21.

36. Dakhlia, *L'oubli*.

37. Ibid.; AGT, D series; and de Fleurac, "Étude," 1885, AMG, Tunisie, 36 H 29, no. 8.

38. Dakhlia, *L'oubli*; and Rinn, *Marabouts*.

39. Green, *Tunisian Ulama*, 62, points out that sufism in Tunisia was largely spared from attacks by the reformed ulama until the 1920s.

40. Anonymous, report, 1933, AGT D-97–3; and Jamil M. Abun-Nasr, *The Tijaniyya: A Sufi Order in the Modern World* (London: Oxford University Press, 1965), 83–85.

41. Edouard de Neveu, *Les khouans: Ordres religieux chez les musulmans de l'Algérie* (Paris: Guyot, 1845), 107; and Abun-Nasr, *Tijaniyya*, 85.

42. De Fleurac, "Étude," 1885, AMG, Tunisie, 36 H 29, no. 8. Dakhlia, *L'oubli*, 192, provides statistics for Tunisia's Quranic schools in 1913; the Jarid had by far the greatest concentration of schools in the south—116 as opposed to 107 in the A'radh, 32 in Gafsa, and 35 for the Nafzawa.

43. Rinn, *Marabouts*, 120–21; and AGT, D-97–3 and D-182–2.

44. De Fleurac, "Étude," 1885, AMG, Tunisie, 36 H 29, no. 8; and AGT, D-97–3 and D-182–2.

45. Dakhlia, *L'oubli*, 219–20.

46. Ibid., 121.

47. Cherif, *Pouvoir et société*, and Taoufik Bachrouch, *Le saint et le prince en Tunisie: Les élites tunisiennes du pouvoir et de la dévotion., contribution à l'étude des groupes sociaux dominants (1782–1881)* (Tunis: Publications de l'Université de Tunis I, 1989).

48. The use of local saints' shrines and sufi zawaya as places of political and fiscal refuge is repeatedly mentioned in beylical and European archival sources; for examples, E. Pellissier de Reynaud to de Lagau, 10 August 1846, AMAE, Tunisie, c.p., vol. 10, and in AGT, dossier 516, carton 142, armoire 14, which contains protests of European consuls to the beys concerning the right of asylum in religious establishments. Asylum was frequently manipulated by some Tunisians who fallen in debt to European moneylenders.

49. Mustafa b. 'Azzuz had four sons—al-Makki, al-Hafnawi, Muhammad, and al-Azhari—and eight or nine daughters. On the family, see Ibn 'Ashur, *Tarajim*; AGT, D-172–3; ARGT, cartons 989 and 1218; and Green, *Tunisian Ulama*. Al-Makki b. 'Azzuz (died 1916) was the mufti of Nafta and muqaddam of the Rahmaniyya zawiya there; he later married the daughter of Mustafa Bu Kharis, a middling religious family from Tunis. Sometime before 1900, al-Makki emigrated to Istanbul, going to Medina in 1912.

50. April 1885, AMG, Tunisie, carton 28 bis, no. 53. For comparative statistics on sufi membership in Tunisia, see Bachrouch, *Le saint*, 193–208; a colonial census of 1933 showed the Rahmaniyya as having some fifty zawaya with one of the largest sufi followings in the country.

51. Fred de Jong, "Khalwatiyya," *EI*, 2d ed. (Leiden: E. J. Brill, 1978), 4: 991–93. Octave Depont and Xavier Coppolani, *Les confréries religieuses musulmanes* (Algiers: Jourdan, 1897), 398, mention Rahmaniyya members of the 'Azzuziyya in Medina.

52. AGT, D-97–3 and D-182–2.

53. Duveyrier, *Sahara algérien*, 41–42.

54. Ibid. Saintly protection was not, however, limited to the Muslim faithful. After the establishment of colonial control over the Sahara's northern rim after 1850, some of the region's sufi orders, notably the Tijaniyya, supplied French explorers with guides and letters of safe conduct. This may have facilitated European advances into the desert; Abun-Nasr, *Tijaniyya*, 73–77.

55. Duveyrier, *Sahara algérien*, 41–42.

56. Jean Mattei to Duchesne de Bellecourt, 5 February 1865, ARGT, carton 415; AGT, D-97–3 and D-182–2; Lieutenant Becheval, 1887, "Etude sur le Nefzaoua," AMG, Tunisie, carton 30 bis, no. 18; and Charles Monchicourt, *La région du Haut Tell en Tunisie* (Paris: Colin, 1913), 314–18.

57. Jean Mattei to Duchesne de Bellecourt, 5 February 1865, ARGT, carton 415.

58. Henia, *Le Grid*, 37–39.

59. AGT, dossier 987, carton 81 bis, armoire 8, nos. 18, 67, and 131; for example, 'Ali Bey's 1882 decree characterizes the 'Azzuz's zawiya as one whose "dignity and sacredness are such that its resources should not be wasted nor its revenues decreased nor its assets liquidated."

60. Muhammad al-Sadiq Bey to Mustafa ibn 'Azzuz, 1859–1860, AGT, dossier 987, carton 81 bis, armoire 8, no. 67.

61. James Richardson, "An Account of the Present State of Tunis," 1845, PRO/FO 102/29.

62. Ahmad ibn Abi al-Diyaf, *Ithaf ahl al-zaman bi-akhbar muluk Tunis wa 'ahd al-aman* (Tunis: al-Dar al-Tunisiyya lil-Nashr, 1963–1966), 8: 143.

63. Ibid., 222.

64. AGT, D-112–10.

65. Jean Mattei, Sfax, to Duchesne de Bellecourt, 5 February 1865, ARGT, carton 415.

66. Rinn, *Marabouts*, 458.

67. Léon Roches, Tunis, to governor-general, Algiers, 18 May 1856, AGGA, 25 H 16.

68. Abundant archival documentation for the issue of Algerian refugees exists, for example, Prax, report, 1847, AN, Tunisie, F 80 1697; and in ARGT. Georges Marty, "Les algériens à Tunis," *IBLA* 11, 43–44 (1948): 301–34; idem, "A Tunis: Éléments allogènes et activités professionnelles, djerbiens, gabesiens, gens du sud, et autres tunisiens," *IBLA* 11, 42 (1948): 159–87; and Pierre Bardin's *Algériens et tunisiens dans l'Empire Ottoman de 1848 à 1914* (Paris: Éditions du CNRS, 1979). For Morocco, Charles-Robert Ageron, "L'émigration des musulmans algériens et l'éxode de Tlemcen (1830–1911)," *AESC* 22, 2 (1967): 1047–66.

69. Bureau Arabe, Biskra, report, 1849, AGGA, 16 H 2, dossier 1.

70. Decrees, 14 March 1852, AGGA, 1 H 9, no. 58; and AGGA, 8 H.

71. Anonymous, "Notice sur Si Ali Ben Otmane," AGGA, 16 H 3, dossier 2; and Marthe and Edmond Gouvian, *Kitab aayane al-marhariba* (Algiers: Imprimerie Orientale, 1920), 148–51.

72. Anonymous, "Histoire de la zawiya de Khanqat Sidi Naji," 1895, AGGA, 16 H 10; and AGT, D-172–3. Raoul de Lartigue, *Monographie de l'Aurès* (Constantine: Marle, 1904), 373.

73. E. Pellissier de Reynaud, Sousse, to French consul, Tunis, 7 April 1846, ARGT, carton 416.

74. Ministry of War, Paris, 22 April 1847, AMAE, Tunisie, c.p., vol. 10; Prax, report, 4 November 1847, AMAE, Tunisie, c.p., vol. 10.

75. Bissuel, "Histoire de Biskra," AGGA, 10 H 43; and Jean Mattei to Léon Roches, 1855, AMAE, Tunisie, c.p., vol. 15.

76. Martel, *Les confins* 1: 144; Louis Rinn, *Histoire de l'insurrection de 1871 en Algérie* (Algiers: Jourdan, 1891); and AGT, D-172–3.

77. Bissuel, "Histoire de Biskra," 1861, AGGA, 10 H 43.

78. AGT, carton 141, dossier 512, armoire 14.

79. ARGT, carton 423.

80. 8 July 1851, PRO, Tunisia, FO 102/40; and 14 March 1851, AMAE, Tunisie, c.p., vol. 12; the outbreak of cholera in the Jarid may also have added to the inhabitants' woes.

81. AGT, carton 20, dossier 227, armoire 1, doc. no. 21.

82. For example, anonymous, report, 17 August 1858, AGGA, 1 H 15. French consular correspondence for al-Kaf, ARGT, carton 423, contains abundant documentation on cross-border manipulations.

83. AMAE, Tunisie, c.p., vol. 12 (1851); and PRO, Tunisia, FO 102/40 (1851).

84. AGT, carton 20, dossier 227, armoire 1, nos. 64–69.

85. Ibid.; 8 July 1851, PRO, Tunisia, FO 102/40; and 30 March 1851, ARGT, carton 414.

86. 8 July 1851, PRO, Tunisia, FO 102/40.

87. Augustin Espina, Gabis, to French consul, Tunis, March 1851, ARGT, carton 414.

88. French consul, Tunis to Ahmad Bey, November 1851, AGT, 206–91–21.

89. Ibid.

90. Al-Diyaf, *Ithaf* 8: 142.

91. Leon Carl Brown, *The Tunisia of Ahmad Bey 1837–1855* (Princeton: Princeton University Press, 1974); Jean Ganiage, *Les origines du protectorat français en Tunisie (1861–1881)* (Paris: PUF, 1959); and Khelifa Chater, *Dépendance et mutations précoloniales: La régence de Tunis de 1815 à 1857* (Tunis: Publications de l'Université de Tunis, 1984).

92. Growing British strategic interest in Tunisia, influenced by Great Britain's acquisition of Malta and France's occupation of Algeria, is reflected in the diplomatic correspondence, particularly after 1855, when Richard Wood was appointed as British consul to Tunis; see PRO, Tunisia, FO 102, vols. 1–90 (1838–1871). Arthur Marsden, *British Diplomacy and Tunis, 1875–1902* (Edinburgh: Scottish Academic Press, 1971).

93. James Richardson, "An Account of the Present State of Tunis," 1845, PRO/FO 102/29.

94. Ducouret, "Rapport," 1850, AN, F 17 2957 [2]; and Robert Mantran, "Une relation inédite d'un voyage en Tunisie au milieu du 19e siècle," *CT* 3, 11 (1951): 474–80; and Marcel Emerit, "Un collaborateur d'Alexandre Dumas: Ducouret Abd al-Hamid," *CT* 4, 14 (1956): 243–47.

95. Charles Tissot, "Rapport sur une expédition dans le sud de la régence de Tunis, adressé au chargé d'affaires de France," October 1857, AMAE, Tunisie, mém./doc., vol. 8, no. 28.

96. Ibid.

97. Ibid.

98. Duveyrier, *Sahara algérien*, 49; Duveyrier's laudatory evaluation of the Rahmaniyya shaykh contrasts with his later vilification of the Sanusiyya and other sufi orders. This may perhaps be explained by the fact that the meeting with 'Azzuz occurred during Duveyrier's first excursions into the Sahara before the colonial canon regarding the sufi menace had taken shape—a canon that the explorer himself helped to create in subsequent writings.

99. Daniel R. Headrick, *The Tools of Empire: Technology and European Imperialism in the Nineteenth Century* (Oxford: Oxford University Press, 1981). During his state trip to France in 1846, Ahmad Bey visited shipyards, arsenals, and factories as recorded in al-Diyaf, *Ithaf*. Presumably rural religious figures, such as 'Azzuz, were aware of the technological bases of European power through the reports of Tunisians accompanying the bey on his voyage to Europe or in the course of their own travels to the mashriq and to the Hijaz.

100. Anonymous, "Frontières de Tunisie, 1844–58," AGGA, F 80 956; anonymous, "Confins de la Tunisie et du sud algérien," and "Contraband terrestre et maritime," AGGA, F 80 1695–97.

101. 'Abd al-Qadir al-Jaza'iri, *Tuhfa*, 313–15; AGGA, F 80 1426; and Georges Yver, "Abd el-Kader et le maroc en 1838," *RA* 60 (1919): 93–111. Abdulmola S. El-Horeir mentions Sanusiyya involvement in the arms traffic in "Social and Economic Transformations in the Libyan Hinterland during the Second Half of the Nineteenth Century: The Role of Sayyid Ahmad al-Sharif al-Sanusi" (Ph.D. diss., University of California, Los Angeles, 1981).

102. Commanding general, province of Algiers, to minister of war, Paris, 8 June 1841, AGGA, F 80 1426. The Tunisian ruler was also accused of sending munitions to Ahmad Bey of the Constantine in a British report dated 10 December 1839, PRO, Tunisia, FO 102/5.

103. Even in today's Tunisia, contraband is a flourishing concern in the south, where daring entrepreneurs make an "honest" living smuggling illicit goods such as whiskey, sugar, or coffee between Libya, southern Tunisia, and Algeria. This information was kindly furnished to me by Monsieur Belqacem al-Chabbi during the course of interviews in 1982–1983.

104. Research on the cultural meanings ascribed to firearms in sub-Saharan Africa reveals similar associations; Gavin White, ed., "Introduction," *JAH* 12, 2 (1971): 173–254; and Gerald M. Berg, "The Sacred Musket: Tactics, Technology, and Power in Eighteenth-Century Madagascar," *CSSH* 27, 2 (1985): 261–79.

105. For example, the mahdist leader Bu Baghla claimed invulnerability during the Kabyle uprising of 1850–1854; Nil-Jospeh Robin, "Histoire du Chérif Bou Bar'la," *RA* 24–28 (1880–84). Both Bu Ziyan, and the last Tunisian Mahdi of Tala in 1906, convinced supporters that they were

immune to firepower as did numerous Moroccan mahdis. Corneille Trumelet, *L'Algérie légendaire en pélérinage çà et là aux tombeaux des principaux thaumaturges de l'Islam (Tell et Sahara)* (Algiers: Jourdan, 1892); Adolphe Hanoteau and A. Letourneux, *La kabylie et les coutumes kabyles*, 2 vols. (Paris: Challamel, 1872–1873), 1: 467–68.

106. Abun-Nasr, *Tijaniyya*, 60.

107. C. Pinon, "Le Mzab," CHEAM 3, 8 (1937), 3, stated that "the mosque in the Mzabi cities is at once a storage place, an arms depot, and a fortress." De Neveu, *Les khouan*, 153 and 177, reports that Darqawi centers contained arms depots. The Sanusiyya arsenals are repeatedly mentioned in various diplomatic sources, among them, AGGA, 1 I 95 (1874) and 16 H 38 (1906). Information on Algerian hajjis is contained in AGGA, F 80 1426 (1850).

108. L. S. Stavrianos, *A Global History*, 3d ed. (Englewood Cliffs, N.J.: Prentice-Hall, 1983), 320.

109. The documents in AMAE, Tunisie, c.p., vols. 5–66 (1841–1881), ARGT, cartons 414–423, and AGT, H series, cartons 205, 206, and 208, contain numerous references to the borders. Taoufik Bachrouch, "Pouvoir et souveraineté territoriale: La question de la frontière tuniso-algérienne sous Ahmed Bey," in *Actes du Premier Congrès d'Histoire et de la Civilisation du Maghreb*, 2 vols. (Tunis: Université de Tunis, 1979), 2: 195–208; and Denis Camisoli, "La frontière algéro-tunisienne (1844–1851)," *Revue Historique de l'Armée* 11 (1955): 72.

110. Lieutenant Prax, 1847, AGGA, F 80 1697.

111. AGT, carton 94, dossier 116, armoire 9.

112. Ross E. Dunn, "Bu Himara's European Connexion: The Commercial Relations of a Moroccan Warlord," *JAH* 21, 2 (1980): 235–53.

113. Michael Adas, *Machines as the Measure of Men: Science, Technology, and Ideologies of Western Dominance* (Ithaca: Cornell University Press, 1989).

114. Maj. G. B. Laurie, *The French Conquest of Algeria* (London: Hugh Rees, 1901), 162, observed that when the French army disarmed the tribes, hundreds of muskets would be delivered at a single time. Headrick, *Tools*, 91, claims that the Algerians had "guns as good as the Europeans." This needs to be qualified since diplomatic and military correspondence from the period indicates that obtaining parts or the right ammunition for imported weaponry posed enormous problems for North Africans; for example, Mattei to Béclard, 24 June 1854, ARGT, carton 423.

115. 'Abd al-Qadir al-Jaza'iri, *Tuhfa*; and Dr. Warnier, "Biographie d'Abdel Kader," n.d., AMG, Algérie, H 235.

116. AGGA, F 80 442 (1847); A. Sainte-Marie, "Aspects du colportage à partir de la Kabylie du Djurdjura à l'époque contemporaine," in *Commerce de gros, commerce de détail dans les pays méditerranéens (XVI–XIXe siècles)* (Nice: Université de Nice, 1976), 104–6, noted that some

Kabyles traveled about repairing arms; others distributed or bartered arms, swords, and gunpowder, which had traditionally been produced in their mountains. Much of the sulfur, lead, and gunflints were imported clandestinely from Tunisia prior to 1881. For the Mzab, see Eugène Daumas, *Le Sahara Algérien* (Paris: Langlois et Leclercq, 1845), 61–70; one of the reasons the colonial regime moved against the Mzabi cities in 1882 was to stop the traffic in arms and gunpowder.

117. M. Subtil's two reports dated 1844, AMG, Algérie, H 229, no. 7, and E. Pellissier de Reynaud's account of 1846, AMAE, Tunisie, c.p., vol. 10, both mention that the caravan trade was declining due to increased customs duties levied by the Tunisian state and the ban on slavery. Henri Duveyrier, *La Tunisie* (Paris: Hachette, 1881), 24, observed that the traffic in humans in southern Tunisia and other parts of the Maghrib continued, despite the prohibition, although on a much reduced scale. In commanding general, Oran, to governor-general, Algiers, 2 August 1856, AGGA, 1 H 27, it was noted that traders dealing in contraband armaments in the Oran also trafficked in black slaves.

118. F. Robert Hunter, "Observations on the Comparative Political Evolution of Tunisia and Egypt under Ahmad Bey and Muhammad Ali," *RHM* 13 (1986): 43–48; much of the material in this section was kindly furnished by F. Robert Hunter from a work currently in progress.

119. Martel, *Les confins*; and *Actes du 1er Séminaire sur l'Histoire du Mouvement National: Réactions à l'occupation française de la Tunisie en 1881* (Tunis: Publications Scientifiques Tunisiennes, 1983).

120. Subtil, 1844, AMG, Algérie, H 229, no. 7; E. Pellissier de Reynaud, 1846, AMAE, c.p., vol. 10; and Francois Arnoulet, "Les relations de commerce entre la France et la Tunisie de 1815 à 1896" (doctoral diss., Université de Lille, 1968).

121. Henia, *Le Grid*.

122. James C. Scott, *Weapons of the Weak: Everyday Forms of Peasant Resistance* (New Haven: Yale University Press, 1985); and idem, *Domination and the Arts of Resistance: Hidden Transcripts* (New Haven: Yale University Press, 1990).

123. A 3 percent ad valorem duty was levied upon French and British goods imported into Tunisian seaports; other nations paid higher duties, which were regulated by treaty; Franco-Algerian products imported overland into the beylik also paid a 3 percent ad valorem duty; Ganiage, *Les origines*; and Chater, *Dépendance*.

124. Bureau Arabe, report, 12 April 1853, AGGA, 1 H 10; and E. Pellissier de Reynaud to minister of foreign affairs, 2 September 1843, AMAE, Tunisie, c.p., vol. 7.

125. J. B. Vilar, "Le commerce espagnol avec l'Algérie au début de la période coloniale," *RHM* 2 (1978): 286–92.

126. French representatives in Tunisia naturally opposed any unregulated commerce since they regarded the traffic in contraband munitions as a grave threat to Algeria. The political correspondence in AMAE, Tunisie, vols. 8–59 (1840–1881), contains endless complaints regarding the arms trade and the illegal activities of the Maltese. Smuggling prompted the French government to name consular agents to Gabis, Jirba, al-Kaf, and the Jarid (ARGT, cartons 400, 414–423). The imposition of the protectorate did not end arms smuggling, as indicated by the reports in AGT, E-547–3; for example, chef du bureau des affaires indigènes, Matmata, to the resident general, Tunis, 22 July 1920, details the arms trade between southern Tunisia and the Italian province of Tripoli.

Britain's position toward the contraband trade was more equivocal since many of the items were of British manufacture. Moreover, through the Maltese, British representatives to the Bardo could counter France's influence in Tunisia. While British officials regarded the unruly Maltese, who were often a nuisance, with barely concealed disdain, they did very little to discourage their activities. With Richard Wood's arrival in Tunis in 1855, pledges were made to the bey and the French to rein in the lawless Maltese but without much effect; Richard Wood to Muhammad Bey, 14 November 1856, AGT, carton 227, dossier 411, no. 59.

127. Jean Ganiage, "Les européens en Tunisie au milieu du XIXe siècle (1840–1870)," *CT* 3, 11 (1955): 388–421; and Ganiage, *Les origines,* 41.

128. 2 February 1852, PRO, Tunisia, FO 102/43, for Sousse; 24 June 1858, PRO, Tunisia, FO 102/56, for Mahdiyya; 4 July 1849, AGT, carton 26, dossier 89, mentions smuggling in Tabarka; and for the Tunis region, reports dated 1841–1843, AGGA, F 80 1426.

129. Donald Quataert, *Social Disintegration and Popular Resistance in the Ottoman Empire, 1881–1908: Reactions to European Economic Penetration* (New York: New York University Press, 1983).

130. French consular agent, al-Kaf, to French consul, Tunis, 1873, ARGT, carton 423; and anonymous, report, 1887, AGGA, 16 H 2, dossier 4.

131. Espina, Gabis, to de Beauval, Tunis, 23 June 1864, ARGT, carton 417; and Botmiliau to minister of foreign affairs, Paris, 28 October 1867, AMAE, c.p., vol. 29: "the tribes rarely use money to pay for foreign goods, the exception being arms." Also May 1834, AGGA, F 80 1426; January 1844, AMAE, Tunisie, c.c., vol. 54, and April 1853, vol. 56.

132. Ganiage, *Les origines,* 57–58; and Department of State, Despatch Book, vol. 7, January 1858–1864, National Archives, Washington, D.C.

133. Perry to Secretary of State Seward, 21 April 1864, Department of State, Despatch Book, vol. 7, National Archives, Washington, D.C.

134. 22 September 1842, PRO, Tunisia, FO 102/15.

135. British vice-consul, Sfax, to London, June 1845, PRO, Tunisia, FO 102/24; Tissot, "Rapport"; Carette, "Recherches"; and Daumas, *Le Sahara*, 196–300.

136. AMAE, Tunisie, c.c., vols. 55–60 (1848–1877); ACCM, Algérie, MQ 52; and Claude Bataillon, *Le Souf, étude de géographie humaine* (Algiers: Université d'Alger, 1955).

137. AMAE, Maroc, c.p. and c.c., n.s., vols. 168–179 (1905–1916).

138. ARGT, cartons 414–42; and anonymous, report, October 1851, AGGA, F 80 956.

139. AGT, "Correspondance au sujet de la contrebande en tabac," 1850–1881, carton 96, dossier 141, armoire 10; AMAE, Tunisie, c.c., vol. 54 (October 1843); and "Rapport sur l'Oued Souf et ses relations commerciales," 1856, AGGA, 22 H 26.

140. ARGT, carton 423; AMAE, Tunisie, c.c., vol. 56 (1854); and "Histoire de Biskra," AGGA, 10 H 43.

141. Richard Wood to London, 10 September 1863, PRO, Tunisia, FO 102/68; AMAE, Malte, c.c., vols. 21–23 (1843–68); and report, 24 August 1852, AGGA, F 80 1426. E. Fallot, "Malte et ses rapports économiques avec la Tunisie," *RT* 3 (1896): 17–38; and Lucette Valensi, "Les relations commerciales entre la régence de Tunis et Malte au XVIIIe siècle," *CT* 11, 43, 3 (1963): 71–83.

142. AMAE, Tunisie, c.p., vol. 7 (1843); ARGT, carton 423 (1866–1874); AGT, carton 207, dossier 102, no. 101 (1870); Richard Wood, Tunis, 10 September 1863, PRO, Tunisia, FO 102/68; and Botmiliau to Paris, 25 August 1868, AMAE, Tunisie, c.c., vol. 59.

143. "Rapport sur l'Oued Souf," 1856, AGGA, 22 H 26. Another branch of the contraband trade that became important in the 1860s was the route linking Sousse with al-Kaf; from al-Kaf, situated on the frontiers, large quantities of rifles and gunpowder were distributed to Tunisian and Algerian tribes as well as to Suq Ahras, Guelma, and Constantine. In 1868, ARGT, carton 417, the French consul in Sousse noted that Mzabi merchants had come to the port to purchase from Maltese suppliers contraband gunpowder intended for transport back to Algeria.

144. Report, 16 October 1851, AGGA, 1 H 8, no. 146; and 20 January 1852, AGGA, F 80 1426, no. 589.

145. E. Pellissier de Reynaud to minister of foreign affairs, Paris, 2 September 1843, AMAE, Tunisie, c.p., vol. 7; and anonymous, report, 12 April 1853, AGGA, 1 H 10.

146. ARGT, cartons 415 and 423; AMAE, Tunisie, c.p., vol. 14 (1853); and Tissot, report, 1853, AMAE, Tunisie, mém./doc., vol. 8, no. 28; the imposition of the French protectorate did not end the contraband arms trade, Lieutenant Becheval, report, 1887, AMG, Tunisie, 36 H 30, no. 18 bis.

147. Tissot, report, 1853, AMAE, Tunisie, mém./doc., vol. 8, no. 28. Abun-Nasr, *Tijaniyya*, 68–71, notes that by 1844 the Tijaniyya leaders of 'Ain Madi had publicly recognized the French colonial regime.

148. AMAE, Tunisie, c.p., vol. 14 (1853); and Tissot, report, 1853, AMAE, Tunisie, mém./doc., vol. 8, no. 28. Seizures of contraband munitions are constantly reported in the Bureaux Arabes documents; for example, the report of 23 December 1852, AGGA, 1 H 9, no. 373, stated that colonial military officials confiscated fifty-five kilograms in the market of Sidi 'Uqba on a single day.

149. Warnier, 1856, AGGA, 22 H 26. Even after the imposition of indirect French rule over the Suf in December 1854, the contraband trade continued, although with more circumspection. When Duveyrier visited the Suf in 1860, he noted the following items for sale in al-Awad: Maltese cotton goods (in the early 1860s, Malta experienced a boom in its local cotton industry due to the American Civil War), handkerchiefs of Indian cotton, finished silk textiles, raw silk, fine calico, gunflints, and rifles. The textiles all carried the stamps of various Anglo-Indian or English manufacturers; other items were marked by British commercial houses; Duveyrier, *Journal*, 15–17.

150. ARGT, cartons 415 and 423; report, 12 April 1853, AGGA, 1 H 15; and Béclard to minister of foreign affairs, Paris, October 1854, AMAE, Tunisie, c.c., vol. 56. The village of Tala developed around the nucleus of the Rahmaniyya zawiya; AGT, série A, dossier 28, carton 72; and A. Winkler, "Notice sur Thala," *RT* 3 (1896): 523–27.

6. THE SHARIF OF WARQALA'S JIHAD

1. Lieutenant Marguerite, Bureau Arabe, Miliana to Beauchamp, 11 July 1851, AGGA, 1 H 7; also 1 H 8. Marguerite's observations were based on reports furnished by indigenous spies, who alerted colonial authorities about three Algerians with information about seditious political and religious activities. Arrested and later interrogated, the three men agreed to exchange information for clemency. The long testimony of al-Hajj Muhammad ibn Ibrahim revealed the existence of an informal association of religious leaders, mainly sufi shaykhs from all parts of Algeria. Called the "association of the forty sharifs" by the colonial regime, knowledge of the group's existence sparked a sufi scare in French circles.

If al-Hajj Muhammad b. Ibrahim's testimony is credible, it seems that by 1848 prominent sufi notables from the Tayyibiyya, Qadiriyya, Darqawa, Awlad Sidi al-Shaykh, and the Rahmaniyya orders had joined forces to achieve several goals. One was to maintain a system of sustained communication to monitor events in Algeria and particularly the activities of the colonial regime. Another was to foment rebellion in communities throughout the colony.

During his lengthy interrogation, al-Hajj Muhammad b. Ibrahim claimed that the sufi association had decided to "exchange news and information regarding the French, their situation, and their intentions." It was part of a larger plan to drive the infidels from North Africa; when the time was right, the sufi shaykhs would declare a general jihad. As a prelude to large-scale revolt, local dissidents, often with mahdist pretensions, were to be encouraged to provoke disturbances in the countryside and ordinary folk persuaded to support chiliastic rebels. When the French army was sufficiently distracted by numerous, simultaneous uprisings, the sufi leaders would give the signal for massive rebellion. In his statement, the informant named Mustafa b. 'Azzuz, who had been residing in the Tunisian Jarid for nearly a decade, as representing the Rahmaniyya order along with his brothers, Muhammad and Mabruk. See also, Ahmed Nadir, "Les ordres religieux et la conquête française (1830–1851)," *RAS-JEP* 9, 4 (1972): 819–72.

2. Madeleine Rouvillois-Brigol, *Le pays de Ouargla (Sahara Algérien): Variations et organisation d'un espace rural en milieu désertique* (Paris: Publications du Département de Géographie de l'Université de Paris–Sorbonne, 1975); Jean Lethielleux, *Ouargla, cité saharienne des origines au début du XXe siècle* (Paris: Paul Geuthner, 1983); Georges Rolland, *L'Oued Rir et la colonisation française au Sahara* (Paris, 1887); Georges Yver, "Tuqqurt," *EI* (Leiden: E. J. Brill, 1934) 4: 250–51; and L. Charles Féraud, "Notes historiques sur la province de Constantine: Les Ben-Djellab, sultans de Touggourt," in *RA* 23–31 (1879–1887).

I arrived at these population estimates by using demographic data from AMG, Algérie, H 230 bis and M 1317; Féraud, "Ben-Djellab," 23 (1879): 59; and Henri Jus, *Les oasis de l'Oued Rir' en 1856 et 1879* (Constantine: Marle, 1879), 8.

3. Théodore Pein, *Lettres familières sur L'Algérie, un petit royaume arabe*, 2d ed. (Algiers: Jourdan, 1893), 6–7.

4. Féraud, "Ben-Djellab," 23 (1879): 49–60.

5. Ibid.; Eugène Cherbonneau, *Précis historique de la dynastie des Benou-Djellab, princes de Touggourt* (Paris, 1851); and AMG, Algérie, M 1317.

6. Cherbonneau, *Précis*; and Lethielleux, *Ouargla*, 180.

7. Yver, "Tuggurt," 251.

8. E. Pellissier de Reynaud, *Annales algériennes*, 2d ed. (Paris: Librarie Militaire, 1854), 1: 325, noted that while the Banu Jallab's official title under the Turks was "shaykh" of Tuqqurt, Saharan peoples referred to them as "sultan" out of deference for their power.

9. Rouvillois-Brigol, *Ouargla*, 27; and Féraud, "Ben-Djellab," 23 (1879): 217.

10. AMG, Algérie, M 1317; Vincent Largeau, *Le pays de Rirha, Ouargla et Ghadames* (Paris: Hachette, 1879); and idem, *Le Sahara Algérien* (Paris: Hachette, 1881); also Pein, *Lettres*, 43–45.

11. AMG, Algérie, M 1317; Rouvillois-Brigol, *Ouargla*, 25–31; and Lethielleux, *Ouargla*, 185–200.

12. AMG, Algérie M 1317; Eugène Daumas, *Le Sahara Algérien* (Paris: Langlois et Leclercq, 1845), 137; and Elisée Reclus, *L'Afrique septentrionale*, vol. 11 of *Nouvelle géographie universelle: La terre et les hommes* (Paris: Hachette, 1886), 561–65.

13. AMG, Algérie, H 235; and de la Porte, Tunis, to minister of foreign affairs, Paris, "Notice sur les relations commerciales que Tougourt entretient avec Tunis," 8 April 1845, AMAE, Tunisie, c.c., vol. 54; and Daumas, *Sahara*, 137.

14. L. Charles Féraud, *Kitab el-Adouani ou le Sahara de Constantine et de Tunis* (Constantine: Arnoulet, 1868), 185–86; and Pein, *Lettres*, 7–9.

15. AMG, Algérie, M 1317.

16. Pellissier de Reynaud, *Annales* 1: 325, noted that the sultan of Tuqqurt even sent forces to battle the bey of the Constantine in 1833, but the bey's use of artillery brought defeat. The humiliation suffered by the Banu Jallab caused them to contact the French military concerning an alliance. In exchange for overthrowing Ahmad Bey and rendering tribute to France, 'Ali b. Jallab requested that the French nominate him as the bey of the Constantine.

17. Lieutenant Prax, "L'Algérie méridionale ou Sahara Algérien, Tougourt, le Souf," in *ROAC* 4 (1848): 129–204; and E. Watbled, "Cirta-Constantine," *RA* 14 (1870): 208.

18. AMG, Algérie, M 1317.

19. Joseph-Adrien Seroka, "Le sud Constantinois de 1830 à 1855," *RA* 56 (1912): 415, 500–503.

20. Ibid., 521–24; and "Historique de 1851," AGGA, 10 H 18.

21. Cherbonneau, *Précis*; and Prax, "L'Algérie mériodinale."

22. Anonymous, May 1850, AMG, Algérie, 1 H 133; and Seroka, "Le sud," 524–28.

23. Rouvillois-Brigol, *Ouargla*, 1–5; Féraud, *Kitab el-Adouani*, 202–7; and Reclus, *L'Afrique*, 607.

24. Rouvillois-Brigol, *Ouargla*, 27–32.

25. "Considerations politiques sur les sédentaires et nomades d'Ouargla," n.d., AGGA, 10 H 52; and Colonel Noix, *Algérie et Tunisie*, vol. 6 of *Géographie militaire*, 2d ed. (Paris: Librarie Militaire, 1890), 152–55.

26. C. W. Newbury, "North African and Western Sudan Trade in the Nineteenth Century: A Re-Evaluation," *JAH* 7, 2 (1966): 233–46; and Jean-Louis Miège, "La Libye et le commerce transsaharien au XIXe siècle," *ROMM* 19 (1975): 135–68.

27. "Considerations politiques sur les sédentaires et nomades d'Ouargla," n.d., AGGA, 10 H 52; Ismael Bouderhab, "Relation d'un voyage à R'at en août 1858," AGGA, F 80 1677; and Rouvillois-Brigol, *Ouargla,* 27–32.

28. Lethielleux, *Ouargla,* 223–48; and Alain Romey, *Les Sa'id 'Atba de N'Goussa* (Paris: L'Harmattan, 1983), 55–69.

29. Le Capitaine Bou Said, *Lalla Mouina* (Paris: Librarie Militaire, 1886), 91–96.

30. Georges Yver, "Wargla," *EI* (Leiden: E. J. Brill, 1934) 4: 1123–24; and idem, "Notes pour servir à l'historique de Ouargla," *RA* 64 (1923): 381–442.

31. Féraud, "Ben-Djellab," 25 (1881): 121–26.

32. Pein, *Lettres,* 215.

33. Sidi al-Aghwati's prophecies and those of other saints were recorded from oral traditions by Charles Richard, *Étude sur l'insurrection du Dahra (1845–1846)* (Algiers: Besancenez, 1846). Sidi al-Aghwati's written and oral prophecies were passed around in the nineteenth century. Pein, *Lettres,* 51–52, mentions a local holy man residing in Bu Sa'ada, where Pein was the commanding officer from 1850 until 1859. The holy man read the predictions of Sidi al-Aghwati to Pein and, in the French officer's words, "explained to me" the meaning of the defunct saint's words. This reveals the extraordinary power over words which holy persons wielded in North Africa; the uncertainties unleashed by the French conquest would have increased the social demand for those who could foretell the future and thus bring assurance to communities gripped by anxieties regarding what lay ahead.

Jean Mattei also noted that Sidi al-Aghwati's predictions were passed around by word of mouth in the cities of southern Tunisia in 1854; Mattei to Béclard, 24 June 1854, ARGT, carton 423. This indicates that Tunisia participated in the information and rumor circuits centered in Algeria.

34. Clifford Geertz, "Centers, Kings, and Charisma: Reflections on the Symbolics of Power," in *Culture and Its Creators: Essays in Honor of Edward Shils,* Joseph-Ben David and Terry N. Clark, eds. (Chicago: University of Chicago Press, 1977), 150–71. Michael Adas, *Prophets of Rebellion: Millenarian Protest Movements against the European Colonial Order* (Chapel Hill: University of North Carolina Press, 1979), 92–93, observed that the prophetic figure "molded millennial tendencies into a persuasive ideology."

35. Corneille Trumelet, *Les français dans le désert: Journal historique, militaire, et descriptif d'une expédition aux limites du Sahara Algérien* (Paris: Challamel, 1885), 43.

36. Annie Rey, "Mohammed b. 'Abdallah, ou le combat du chérif de Ouargla," in *Les Africains,* Charles-André Julien, ed. (Paris: Éditions Jeune Afrique, 1978), 12: 201, states that his name was either Ibrahim Ibn Abi

Faris or Ibrahim Ibn 'Abd Allah; Seroka, "Le sud," 530, claims that his name was Ahmad b. Husayn.

37. Seroka, "Le sud," 530. Emile Dermenghem's *Le culte des saints dans l'Islam maghrébin* (Paris: Gallimard, 1954), 71–86, contains a description of Sidi Abu Madiyan's shrine and the devotional practices associated with it. Peter von Sivers in "The Realm of Justice: Apocalyptic Revolts in Algeria (1849–1879)," *Humaniora Islamica* 1 (1973): 47–60, discusses the social construction of the messianic personality.

38. Rey, "Mohammed b. 'Abdallah," 201–3; Seroka, "Le sud," 530–31; and Trumelet, *Français*, 44–52.

39. On the Sanusiyya and its founder, see Ahmad S. al-Dajani's *al-Haraka al-Sanusiyya* (Beirut: Dar Lubnan, 1967); Bradford G. Martin, *Muslim Brotherhoods in Nineteenth-Century Africa* (London: Cambridge University Press, 1976), 99–124; and Abdulmola S. El-Horeir, "Social and Economic Transformations in the Libyan Hinterland during the Second Half of the Nineteenth Century: The Role of Sayyid Ahmad al-Sharif al-Sanusi" (Ph.D. diss., University of California, Los Angeles, 1981).

40. E. Mangin, "Notes sur l'histoire de Laghouat," *RA* 39 (1895): 148–54.

41. Charles-André Julien, *Histoire de l'Algérie contemporaine*, 2d ed. (Paris: PUF, 1979), 1: 391–92. Martin, *Brotherhoods*, 109, states that Muhammad b. 'Ali al-Sanusi left Cyrenaica in eastern Tripolitania for Mecca in 1846, remaining there until 1853.

42. Dajani, *al-Haraka*, 295–96, contains the letter from the sharif to the governor, Sidi al-Hajj Musa Agha, dated 8 April 1851. In Muhammad b. 'Abd Allah's letter, he mentions receiving another missive from the mudir, which suggests that they were in correspondence.

43. Féraud, "Ben-Djellab," 25: 124–26; also anonymous, "Notice sur le Chérif Snoussi," 1856, AMG, Algérie, H 229; and "Historique du cercle de Biskra," 1851, AGGA, 10 H 18.

44. Rey, "Mohammad b. 'Abdallah," 208; and Trumelet, *Français*, 55–60.

45. Trumelet, *Français*, 57.

46. Ibid.; and Rey, "Mohammad b. 'Abdallah," 208.

47. Anonymous, "Ordres religieux, Ouargla," AGGA, 10 H 52; "Renseignements politiques, état des confréries," 1895, AGGA, 16 H 8.

48. AMG, Algérie, M 1317; and Féraud, "Ben-Djellab," 23: 54–55.

49. Lethielleux, *Ouargla*, 223–48.

50. Commandant of Oran to governor-general, Algiers, 10 January 1852, AGGA, 1 H 8; and Trumelet, *Français*, 60–61.

51. Rey, "Mohammad b. 'Abdallah," 207–8; and Trumelet, *Français*, 57–59.

52. Commandant of Oran to governor-general, Algiers, 10 January 1852, AGGA, 1 H 8; and Trumelet, *Français*, 60–61. For the Awlad Sidi

al-Shaykh's history and for the sharif's relationship with Sidi Hamza, see Peter von Sivers, "Alms and Arms: The Combative Saintliness of the Awlad Sidi Shaykh in the Algerian Sahara, Sixteenth–Nineteenth Centuries," *MR* 8, 5–6 (1983): 113–23.

53. Rey, "Mohammed b. 'Abdallah," 214–15. The new construction's architecture and spatial placement were symbolic of the political essence of the sharif's movement; it signaled a break with the past and the sharif's disassociation from the ancient quarrels dividing Warqala, quarrels which were not permitted within the palace confines.

54. Trumelet, *Français*, 61–62; and Dajani, *al-Haraka*, 295–96. In his letter to the mudir of Ghadamis, the sharif attributed his victory over the infidels to the baraka that he obtained directly from Sidi Muhammad b.'Ali al-Sanusi.

55. Dajani, *al-Haraka*, 295–96; and Mangin, "Notes," 148–54.

56. Dajani, *al-Haraka*, 295–96; and Mangin, "Notes," 148–54.

57. Pein, *Lettres*, 217–18.

58. Gianni Albergoni, "Variations italiennes sur un thème français: La Sanusiya," in *Connaissances du Maghreb: Sciences Sociales et Colonisation* (Paris: Éditions du CNRS, 1984), 111–34. Nevertheless, El-Horeir, "Transformations," 114, asserts that French suspicions of Sanusiyya and Ottoman involvement in Algerian politics should be given credence.

59. AMG, Algérie, 1 H 136; "Historique du cercle de Biskra," 1851, AGGA, 10 H 18; and Trumelet, *Français*, 63–64.

60. AMG, Algérie, 1 H 136; "Historique du cercle de Biskra," 1851, AGGA, 10 H 18; and general of Constantine to governor-general, Algiers, 22 January 1853, AGGA, 1 H 10.

61. Seroka, "Le sud," 532–33; Mattei to Béclard, Tunis, 24 June 1854, ARGT, carton 423; and AMG, Algérie, 1 H 133.

62. Franco-Tunisian negotiations over the borders were under way in 1850–1851, *Watha'iq* [Tunis] 15 (1991), 50–81.

63. Mattei to Béclard, Tunis, 24 June 1854, ARGT, carton 423; AMG, Algérie, 1 H 133 and 1 H 136; "Historique du cercle de Biskra," 1851, AGGA, 10 H 18; and general of Constantine to governor-general, Algiers, 22 January 1853, AGGA, 1 H 10.

64. Anonymous, "Apparition d'un chérif à Ouargla," 1851, AGGA, 1 H 8; Trumelet, *Français*, 64–66; and Seroka, "Le sud," 532–35.

65. Report, 22 August 1853, AGGA, 1 H 10; Seroka, "Le sud," 538; and Féraud, "Ben-Djellab," 25 (1881): 134–35.

66. Féraud, "Ben-Djellab," 25 (1881): 135, 198–201; Seroka, "Le sud," 533–35; Trumelet, *Français*, 65.

67. Trumelet, *Français*, 67–68; and Bael Hadj Merghoub, *Le développement politique en Algérie: Étude des populations de la région du Mzab* (Paris: Colin, 1972).

68. Seroka, "Le sud," 538, 541; report, 2 May 1852, AGGA, 1 H 9; 17 May 1853, AMAE, Tunisie, c.p., vol. 13, no. 42; and Féraud, "Ben-Djellab," 26 (1882): 109–11.

69. 2 May 1852, AGGA, 1 H 9; 17 May 1853, AMAE, Tunisie, c.p., vol. 13, no. 42; Seroka, "Le sud," 538, 541; and Féraud, "Ben-Djellab," 26: 109–11.

70. 17 May 1853, AMAE, Tunisie, c.p., vol. 13, no. 42; AGGA, 10 H 18; and Pein, *Lettres*, 225. The Banu Jallab traditionally maintained diplomatic relations with Tunisian rulers, as seen for example by the letter from 'Abd al-Rahman b. 'Umar b. Jallab to Ahmad Bey in 1841 in which the new sultan of Tuqqurt notified the bey of his accession to Tuqqurt's throne and expressed the desire to "confirm the existence of good relations." "Makatib Awlad ibn Jallab, Bay Tuqqurt," AGT, H series, dossier 930, carton 78, armoire 7.

71. Bureau Arabe, Biskra, to governor-general, Algiers, 11 May 1852, AGGA, 1 H 9; report, 26 October 1852, AMG, Algérie, 1 H 134; and Seroka, "Le sud," 540–44.

72. Bureau Arabe, Biskra, to governor-general, Algiers, 11 May 1852, AGGA, 1 H 9; report, 26 October 1852, AMG, Algérie, 1 H 134; and Seroka, "Le sud," 540–44.

73. Ali Merad, "Laghouat," *EI*, 2d ed. (Leiden: E. J. Brill, 1986), 5: 595–97; R. Zannettacci, "Laghouat," CHEAM (1937) 9, no. 210; and Odette Petit, "Laghouat: Essai d'histoire sociale" (doctoral diss., École des Hautes Études en Sciences Sociales, Paris, 1967).

74. Pein, *Lettres*, 393.

75. Eugène Fromentin, *Un été dans le Sahara*, new edition introduced and annotated by Anne-Marie Christine (Paris: Le Sycomore, 1981), 124–36; and Roger Le Tourneau, "L'occupation de Laghouat par les français (1844–1852)," in *Études maghrébines: Mélanges Charles-André Julien* (Paris: PUF, 1964), 111–36. Merad, "Laghouat," 596, cites the folk rituals. From 1927 on, the oasis became one of the principal centers of the Islamic Reform Movement under Shaykh 'Abd al-Hamid b. Badis's leadership.

76. Eugène Graulle, *Insurrection de Bou-Amama* (Paris: Lavauzelle, 1905); Peter von Sivers, "Secular Anxieties and Religious Righteousness: The Origins of the Insurrection of 1881 in the Nomadic and Sedentary Communities of the Algerian Southwest," *Peuples Méditerranéens* 18 (1982): 145–62; and Ross E. Dunn, "Bu Himara's European Connexion: The Commercial Relations of a Moroccan Warlord," *JAH* 21, 2 (1980): 235–53; and idem, "The Bu Himara Rebellion in Northeast Morocco: Phase I," *MES* 17, 1 (1981): 31–48.

77. Trumelet, *Français*, 67–79.

78. Report, 22 September 1853, AGGA, 1 H 10; and Seroka, "Le sud," 545–49.

79. Pein, *Lettres*, 215.

80. Trumelet, *Français*, chapter 5; and Rey, "Mohammad b. 'Abdallah," 208–20. Shaykh Hamza was probably playing a double game with his colonial mentors; he was rewarded for the capture of Warqala with a khalifalik stretching from Geryville to Djelfa.

81. Report, 26 October 1854, AGGA, 1 H 11.

82. Féraud, "Ben-Djellab," 26 (1882): 113–16; report, 23 January 1855, AGGA, 1 H 12; "Historique de 1854," AGGA, 10 H 18; and Seroka, "Le sud," 549–62.

83. "Historique de 1854," AGGA, 10 H 18; Féraud, "Ben-Djellab," 26 (1882): 113–16; and Seroka, "Le sud," 549–62.

84. Report, 23 January 1855, AGGA, 1 H 12.

85. Report, 23 January 1855, AGGA, 1 H 12; and Féraud, "Ben-Djellab," 26 (1882): 113–16.

86. Jamil M. Abun-Nasr, *The Tijaniyya: A Sufi Order in the Modern World* (London: Oxford University Press, 1965), 71–74; and the biographical notice devoted to 'Ali al-Tammasini in Muhammad al-Hafnawi, *Ta'rif al-khalaf bi rijal al-salaf*, 2d ed. (Tunis: al-Maktaba al-'Atiqa, 1982), 282–86.

87. "Historique du cercle de Biskra," 1851, AGGA, 10 H 18; and Seroka, "Le sud," 533–36.

88. AGGA, 1 H 8, 10 H 18, and 10 H 72; AGT, D-97–3; and Tissot, report, 1853, AMAE, Tunisie, mém./doc., vol. 8, no. 29.

89. Rey, "Mohammad b. 'Abdallah," 212.

90. AGGA, 25 H 16 (2), 1 H 8, and 10 H 18; and Abun-Nasr, *Tijaniyya*, 68–74.

91. Abun-Nasr, *Tijaniyya*, 85–88; and Bice Slama, *L'insurrection de 1864 en Tunisie* (Tunis: Maison Tunisienne de l'Édition, 1967).

92. AGGA, 16 H 2, 1 H 15, and 10 H 43; AMG, Algérie, 1 H 135. The 1858 revolt of Sidi Masmudi is discussed by von Sivers, "The Realm."

93. AGGA, 10 H 72 and 16 H 8; Marthe and Edmond Gouvian, *Kitab aayane al-marhariba* (Algiers: Imprimerie Orientale, 1920), 153–57; and Seroka, "Le sud," 524.

94. AGGA, 10 H 72, 16 H 2, and 16 H 3; Gouvian, *Kitab*, 148–53. Yvonne Turin's findings in *Affrontements culturels dans l'Algérie coloniale: Écoles, médecines, religion, 1830–1880* (Paris: Maspéro, 1971), 128–35, support my contention that the practice of Islam as locally lived moved into the pre-Sahara away from areas in proximity to settler colonization. Sufi centers, like Tulqa and al-Hamil, which had eschewed involvement in rebellious activities, were able to provide religious and educational services not available to Algerian Muslims in the northern Tell regions or in regions where revolts had occurred.

95. AGGA, 10 H 72 and 16 H 2; AGT, D-97–3 and D-172–3; Seroka, "Le Sud," 548; and Gouvian, *Kitab*, 158–64.

96. AGGA, 16 H 8; AGT, D-97–3; and letter, 15 November 1851, AGT, carton 206, dossier 91, armoire 21.

97. Report, 21 February 1852, AGGA, 1 H 9, no. 47.

98. Report, 23 January 1855, AGGA, 1 H 12.

99. Mattei to Béclard, 21 April 1853, AMAE, Tunisie, c.c., vol. 56; and Mattei to Béclard, 22 January 1854, ARGT, carton 423.

100. Ibrahim b. Muhammad al-Sasi al-'Awamir, *al-suruf fi tarikh al-Sahra' wa Suf* (Tunis: al-Dar al-Tunisiyya l'il-Nashr, 1977); and Claude Bataillon, *Le Souf: Étude de géographie humaine* (Algiers: Université d'Alger, 1955).

101. "Étude sur le Sahara", 1839, AMG, Algérie, H 227; Warnier, "Rapport sur l'Oued Souf et ses relations commerciales," c. 1856, AGGA, 22 H 26; and Féraud, "Ben-Djellab," 26 (1882): 46–47.

102. Lieutenant Baudot, 1876, "A travers le Souf," AMG, Algérie, M 1317; also H 229.

103. AMG, Algérie, M 1317; "Considerations sur le commerce et l'industrie des tissus de laine du Sahara," 1857, AGGA, 1 H 14; and report, 1856, AGGA, 22 H 26.

104. Captain Warnier, Bureau Arabe, Biskra, 1856, AGGA, 22 H 26.

105. AGGA, 10 H 18 and 1 H 10; AMG, Algérie, 1 H 134 and 1 H 135.

106. AGGA, 10 H 18 and 1 H 10; AMG, Algérie, 1 H 134 and 1 H 135.

107. "Historique de 1854," AGGA, 10 H 18; Féraud, "Ben-Djellab," 26: 113–16; and Seroka, "Le sud," 549–62.

108. AGGA, 1 H 11 and 1 H 8; and Rey, "Mohammed b. 'Abdallah," 214.

109. Tissot, 1853, AMAE, Tunisie, mém./doc., vol. 8, no. 28; Mattei to Roches, 5 June 1855, AMAE, Tunisie, c.p., vol. 15; and Mattei to Béclard, 20 January 1854, ARGT, carton 423.

110. Jean Mattei, Sfax, to French consul, Tunis, 1856, ARGT, carton 414.

111. Mattei to Béclard, 24 June 1854, ARGT, carton 423.

112. Ibid.

113. Augustin Espina, Gabis, to French consul, Tunis, 30 March 1851, ARGT, carton 414.

114. Report, "Apparition d'un chérif," October 1851, AGGA, 1 H 8; and report, June 1850, AMG, Algérie, 1 H 133.

115. November 1851, AGT, carton 206, dossier 91, armoire 21.

116. In *Lalla-Mouina*, 202–10, Bou-Said, a French spy and flawless speaker of Algerian Arabic, transcribed the words of a popular ballad recited in an Arab cafe in Tigdit (near Mustaghanam) in honor of the mahdi. As

the military officer observed, the ballad "to which the most incredulous are not indifferent describes the aspirations of the Arab people. The music augmented the effect of the song upon the audience. We give the song in its original version to show that the Arabes have in no way been disarmed":

> Beaten, pursued, the infidels will escape in their ships; and after besieging their cities, they will be taken by storm. . . . The reign of God will commence, because the whole earth adores Him and the end of the world is near; listen people, listen to the song of the last day; when the sun will fold upon itself; when the stars fall from the sky; when the mountains move; when the female camels and their offspring will be neglected; when the wild beasts will be mixed together; when the seas will boil; when the souls will be rejoined to their bodies.

Pessah Shinar, in his "A Controversial Exponent of the Algerian Salafiyya: The Kabyle 'Alim, Imam and Sharif Abu Ya'la Sa'id B. Muhammad Al-Zawawi," in *Studies in Islamic History and Civilization in Honour of Professor David Ayalon*, Moshe Sharon, ed. (Leiden: E. J. Brill, 1986), 267–90, noted that until late in the nineteenth century, the Berber scholar, Abu Ya'la, and many others viewed the mahdi as the only one capable of ridding Algeria of European rule.

117. Governor-general of Algeria to French consul general, Tunis, 6 November 1851, AGT, carton 206, dossier 91, armoire 21.

118. Report, December 1851, AGGA, 1 H 8, no. 239; and Mattei to French consul, Tunis, 1851, ARGT, carton 415.

119. Sliman b. Jallab to Muhammad Bey, Tunis, AGT, H series, dossier 930, carton 78, armoire 7, no. 10.

120. Mattei to Béclard, 24 June 1854, ARGT, carton 423.

121. Tissot, 1853, AMAE, Tunisie, mém./doc., vol. 8, no. 28; Mattei to Roches, 9 June 1855, AMAE, Tunisie, c.p., vol. 15; and ARGT, carton 423.

122. Tissot, 1853, AMAE, Tunisie, mém./doc., vol. 8, no. 28; Mattei to Roches, 9 June 1855, AMAE, Tunisie, c.p., vol. 15; and ARGT, carton 423.

123. Mattei to Roches, 9 June 1855, AMAE, Tunisie, c.p., vol. 15; and ARGT, carton 423.

124. Sliman b. Jallab to Muhammad Bey, Tunis, c. June 1855, AGT, H series, dossier 930, carton 78, armoire 7, no. 10; and Mattei to Roches, 9 June 1855, AMAE, Tunisie, c.p., vol. 15.

125. "Histoire de Biskra," AGGA, 10 H 43 and 1 H 8; and Mattei to Roches, 28 August 1855, Tunisie, c.p., vol. 15.

126. Mattei to Roches, 9 June 1855, AMAE, Tunisie, c.p., vol. 15; AGGA, 1 H 13; and AGT, 227–20–1.

127. Bissuel, "Histoire de Biskra," AGGA, 10 H 43.

128. Béclard, Tunis, to minister of foreign affairs, Paris, 28 February 1854, AMAE, Tunisie, c.p., vol. 14.

129. Mattei to Béclard, 23 January 1854, ARGT, carton 423; and AGGA, 1 H 12 and 1 H 13.

130. Mattei to Béclard, 23 January 1854, ARGT, carton 423; and AGGA, 1 H 12 and 1 H 13.

131. Bissuel, "Histoire de Biskra," AGGA, 10 H 43.

132. AGGA, 1 H 12 and 10 H 43; the numerous letters from Sliman and his descendants to Muhammad Bey and Muhammad al-Sadiq Bey attest to the growing financial embarrassment suffered by the émigrés in the Tunisian capital; AGT, H series, dossier 930, carton 78, armoire 7.

133. Rey, "Mohammed b. 'Abdallah," 220–21; Féraud, "Ben-Djellab," 30: 430–33; and Eugène Perret, *Récits algériennes* (Paris: Bloud et Barral, 1886–1887) 2: 84–85.

134. 5 July 1865, ARGT, carton 415; Rouvillois-Brigol, *Ouargla*, 32; and Louis Rinn, *Histoire de l'insurrection de 1871 en Algérie* (Algiers: Jourdan, 1891).

135. AGT, carton 207, dossier 97, armoire 21, number 40; and AGGA, 10 H 43.

136. Governor-general of Algeria to resident-general of Tunisia, 1 August 1930, AGT, D-172–3.

7. THE SHAYKH AND HIS DAUGHTER

1. Muhammad b. 'Abd al-Rahman, *Majmu' min risa'il al-shaykh 'Abd al-Rahman al-Zawawi al-Jaza'iri shaykh al-tariqa al-Rahmaniyya*, MS. K 956, al-Khizana al-'Amma, Rabat, Morocco.

2. According to Arnold H. Green, *The Tunisian Ulama, 1873–1915: Social Structure and Response to Ideological Currents* (Leiden: E. J. Brill, 1978), 223, one of Mustaf b. 'Azzuz's four sons, al-Makki, left Tunisia for Istanbul sometime prior to 1900. In 1912 he arrived in the Hijaz to teach at the Islamic university in Medina. There he also established an association, Jam'iya al-shurafa' or "The Society of the Descendants of the Prophet," one of whose objectives was to wage a moral campaign against the French in North Africa. Thus, one of Mustafa b. 'Azzuz's sons carried on his father's tradition of combining emigration and avoidance protest with political activism.

3. Charles-Robert Ageron, *Les algériens musulmans et la France (1871–1919)* (Paris: PUF, 1968) 2: 1079–92; and Ageron, "L'émigration des musulmans algériens et l'éxode de Tlemcen (1830–1911)," *AESC* 22, 2 (1967): 1047–66. The international dangers posed to France by emigration is reflected in voluminous dossiers in AGGA, 9 H 99–101 (1846–1911). Colonial authorities in the Maghrib were particularly alarmed by anti-

French propaganda disseminated by North African emigrants in the Levant, where France was attempting to portray its rule as beneficent.

4. Jacques Berque, *L'intérieur du Maghreb, XVe–XIXe siècle* (Paris: Gallimard, 1978), 419.

5. David C. Gordon, *Women of Algeria: An Essay on Change* (Cambridge: Harvard University Press, 1968), 47.

6. General Collet Meygret to governor-general of Algeria, 22 October 1897, AGGA, 16 H 61, quoting Captain Crochard, Affaires Indigènes, Bu Sa'ada.

7. As late as 1891, Bu Sa'ada had a military garrison of five hundred men and a resident European civilian population of only twelve individuals. Youssef Nacib, *Cultures oasiennes: Essai d'histoire sociale de l'oasis de Bou-Saada* (Paris: Publisud, 1986).

8. Allan Cristelow, "Intellectual History in a Culture under Siege: Algerian Thought in the Last Half of the Nineteenth Century," *MES* 18 (1982): 387–99; and Fanny Colonna, "Cultural Resistance and Religious Legitimacy in Colonial Algeria," *ES* 3 (1974): 233–63.

Gustave Guillaumet, *Tableaux* (Paris: Librarie Plon, 1891), 119, noted the moral importance of a space free from the colonial presence: "The people [of al-Hamil] are content to avoid the detested [Europeans] and only see the faces of their conquerors at rare intervals. The inhabitants evaluate the *moeurs* of their conquerors through stories told in the evenings, legends that inspire in the young a distrust of the Christians and in the old, a nostalgia for happier times."

9. Captain Fournier, "Notice sur l'ordre des Rahmanya" (hereafter "Notice"), 28 June 1895, AGGA, 16 H 8.

10. According to René Basset, "Les manuscrits arabes de la zaouyah d'el Hamel," *Giornale della Societa Asiatica Italiana* 10 (1896–1897), 43, General Meygret asked that the library's holdings be inventoried at Basset's request. The list of manuscripts and books reveals that published materials were being acquired from the Egyptian Press at Bulaq, probably through North African pilgrims visiting the Mashriq. Thus, the hajj continued to be one channel for private library acquisitions by the Maghrib's great families; indeed, one mark of notable status was possession of these libraries. The fact that French requests for information about al-Hamil's collection were granted is indicative of Shaykh Muhammad's amiable relations with the colonial regime.

11. Information on al-Hamil and its shaykh is found in Muhammad al-Hafnawi, *Ta'rif al-khalaf bi rijal al-salaf*, 2d ed. (Tunis: al-Maktaba al-'Atiqa, 1982), 345–52; Muhammad b. al-Hajj Muhammad, *Kitab al-zahr al-basim fi tarjama shaykh shuyukh al-tariqa*. This work was apparently privately printed in Tunis circa 1904, although the only copy I have come across is located in Rabat, al-Khizana al-'Amma, MS. A 80 3165.; Muhammad 'Ali Dabbuz, *Nahda al-Jaza'ir al-haditha wa thawratuha al-*

mubaraka (Algiers: Imprimerie Cooperative, 1965), 52–75; and Ahmed Nadir, "La fortune d'un ordre religieux algérien vers la fin du XIX siècle," *Le Mouvement Social* 89 (1974): 59–84. In addition, extensive documentation is found in archival form, for example, in the newly opened *sous-série* 2 U ("Fonds de la Préfecture, Département d'Alger, Culte Musulman"). Finally, the holdings of the zawiya itself constitute a rich, yet still unexploited source of documentation.

12. Guillaumet, *Tableaux*, 126; among the many notables buried in al-Hamil's graveyards was one of 'Abd al-Qadir's sons, al-Hashimi; Nacib, *Cultures*, 241.

13. Nacib, *Cultures*, 239.

14. Al-Hafnawi, *Ta'rif*, 348.

15. Ibid.

16. Al-Hajj Muhammad, *Kitab*, 7–8; and Marthe and Edmond Gouvian, *Kitab aayane el-marhariba* (Algiers: Imprimerie Orientale, 1920), 202.

17. Al-Hafnawi, *Ta'rif*, 348, gives A.H. 1265 (1847–1848) as the year when Sidi Muhammad began his public ministry in al-Hamil.

18. Al-Hajj Muhammad, *Kitab*, 23.

19. Charles de Galland, *Excursions à Bou-Saada et M'Sila* (Paris: Ollendorff, 1899), 32–33.

20. Nacib, *Cultures*, 240, notes that 'Abd al-Qadir maintained a correspondence with Shaykh Muhammad in the last years of the jihad; in letters to the shaykh of al-Hamil, the amir outlined his "ideas and plans," in an attempt to garner support from Sidi Muhammad. Moreover, 'Abd al-Qadir even sent a large shipment of arms to al-Hamil just before his final defeat, perhaps to safeguard them at the zawiya.

21. On Shaykh al-Mukhtar, see al-Hafnawi, *Ta'rif*, 576–77; and chapters 2, 4, and 5 above.

22. Al-Hajj Muhammad, *Kitab*, 7–8; and Gouvian, *Kitab*, 202.

23. Fournier, "Notice," 1895, AGGA, 16 H 8.

24. Ibid.; and governor-general to commanding general, 27 February 1907, AGGA, 2 U 22. Berque, *L'intérieur*, 421, states that he was initiated in the Rahmaniyya order by Sidi 'Ali b. 'Umar of Tulqa. The disagreement over succession at Awlad Jallal appears to have been smoothed over since Sidi al-Mukhtar's two sons were educated by Shaykh Muhammad himself at the al-Hamil zawiya.

25. Peter von Sivers, "The Realm of Justice: Apocalyptic Revolts in Algeria (1849–1879)," *Humaniora Islamica* 1 (1973): 47–60.

26. Insurrection followed inevitably by repression meant that the social demand for education and religious services was increasingly concentrated upon fewer Islamic establishments, particularly the pre-Sahara's zawaya, the least adversely affected by the elaboration of the colonial order due to location. After the 1852 insurrection near Guelma, for example,

educational activities at the Rahmaniyya center there ceased since the teaching staff fled to Tunis. Yvonne Turin, *Affrontements culturels dans l'Algérie coloniale: Écoles, médecines, religion, 1830–1880* (Paris: Maspéro, 1971), 134–35.

27. Fournier, "Notice," AGGA, 1895, 16 H 8.

28. According to Guillaumet, *Tableaux*, 125, Sidi Muhammad's moral clout was potent enough, and the popular fear of saintly retribution strong enough, to discourage highway bandits.

29. Major Monot to commanding general, 28 December 1904, AGGA, 2 U 22.

30. Ageron, *Algériens* 2: 861–71, characterizes the *sociétés de prévoyance* as "instruments of administrative intervention" in Muslim Algerian life. The simpler, but socially useful, financial services provided by the al-Hamil zawiya were completely outside of official bureaucratic control and fully in the hands of the local community, another expression of autonomy.

31. Gouvian, *Kitab*, 205; and Jamil M. Abun-Nasr, *The Tijaniyya: A Sufi Order in the Modern World* (London: Oxford University Press, 1965), 77–78.

32. Fournier, "Notice," 1895, AGGA, 16 H 8; also 2 U 20, 21, and 22. Guillaumet, *Tableaux*, 119–26, observed the relationship between popularly recognized piety and material prosperity. The shaykh of al-Hamil was "as venerated as the Tijanis in their zawiya of Ain Madhi, [and he] has acquired for himself the reputation in this region of a sage; his followers boast of his knowledge as much as they honor his piety. People travel great distances to come and consult him; from all over offerings pour in, . . . the natives make detours on their journeys to stop here, . . . one gives the best of his wheat; another the fattest of his lambs; another the best part of his date harvest. . . . gifts in nature, gifts in money. . . . Even the *'arsh* lands (tribal communal properties) are made available to the marabout as temporary tenure or rights of enjoyment."

33. John Ruedy, *Land Policy in Colonial Algeria: The Origins of the Rural Public Domain* (Berkeley and Los Angeles: University of California Press, 1967).

34. *Insurrection de 1871: Mémoire d'un accusé, Si Aziz Ben Mohammed Amzian ben Cheikh el Hadded, à ses juges et à ses défenseurs* (Constantine: Imprimerie Marle, 1873); Louis Rinn, *Histoire de l'insurrection de 1871 en Algérie* (Algiers: Jourdan, 1891); Yahya Bu 'Aziz, *Thawrat 1871 (dawr 'a'ilatay al-Muqrani wa-l-Haddad)* (Algiers: SNED, 1978); and Pierpaola C. d'Escamard, *L'insurrezione del 1871 in Cabilia e la confraternita Rahmaniyya* (Rome: Accademia Nazionale dei Lincei, 1977).

35. Fournier, "Notice," 1895, AGGA, 16 H 8; and Gouvian, *Kitab*, 203.

36. Muhammad b. 'Abd al-Rahman, *al-Rahmaniyya*, Antoine Giacobetti, trans. (Algiers: Maison-Carrée, 1946), 485.

37. Al-Hajj Muhammad, *Kitab*, 105–06; Berque in *L'intèrieur*, 422–23, first called attention to the significance of Sidi Muhammad's critique of maraboutism as then practiced in Algeria.

38. Nacib, *Cultures*, 246–47.

39. Rachid Bencheneb, "Le mouvement intellectuel et littéraire algérien à la fin du XIXe et au début du XXe siècle," *Revue Française d'Histoire d'Outre-Mer* 70, 258–59 (1983): 11–24; and Saadeddine Bencheneb, "Quelques historiens arabes modernes de l'Algérie," *RA* 100, 449 (1956): 475–99.

40. Abu al-Qasim Sa'adallah, *La montée du nationalisme algérien (1900–1930)*, 2d ed., trans. from the English by Nevine Fawzy-Hemiry (Algiers: Entreprise Nationale du Livre, 1985), 106–7.

41. I have relied upon the 1982 reprint edition published in Tunis by al-Maktaba al-'Atiqa in a single volume; Shaykh Muhammad's biography is found on 345–52.

42. The newspaper, first created in 1847, was bilingual from its inception; its editorial staff was largely composed of members of Algeria's tiny Francophone Muslim elite; Sa'adallah, *La montée*, 101.

43. Allan Christelow, *Muslim Law Courts and the French Colonial State in Algeria* (Princeton: Princeton University Press, 1985), 251–52.

44. Ibid.

45. Nadir, "La fortune," 59–84.

46. Guillaumet, *Tableaux*, 188–90.

47. Ageron, *Les algériens* 1: 33, note 3.

48. Conversely, the saint carefully paid official calls to authorities in Bu Sa'ada and Algiers when traveling outside al-Hamil to visit his followers. His willingness to maintain contacts with the conquerors in their political space might be read as a shrewd attempt to keep colonial officialdom out of the sacred space of al-Hamil.

49. Guillaumet, *Tableaux*, 120–21.

50. Ibid.

51. Gouvian, *Kitab*, 205.

52. There are numerous accounts in the colonial archives of religious figures whose moral authority in their communities was compromised by an overly friendly relationship with French officials. One such account concerned a Rahmaniyya muqaddam in northern Algeria whose three-year tenure (c. 1906–1909) in some minor office earned him little else than the opprobrium of his followers. Seeking to right the wrong, the muqaddam resigned from his post, performed the hajj to Mecca as an atonement, and, returning to his village, was able to recapture some of his lost socioreligious prestige as well as his popular support; anonymous, "Dossiers de renseignements," 1916, AGGA, 2 U 20.

53. Nacib, *Cultures*, 240, 261.

54. The photograph is inserted between pages 406 and 407 of Octave Depont and Xavier Coppolani's *Les confréries religieuses musulmanes* (Algiers: Jourdan, 1897); unfortunately no photographic credits nor dates are provided.

55. Fournier, "Notice," 1895, AGGA, 16 H 8.

56. The colonial archives in Aix-en-Provence (AGGA) and in Tunis (AGT) contain numerous written requests from religious notables, families, and others seeking permission to travel outside of their respective communities; in many cases, French authorities denied such requests.

57. Mathieu, commissioner in charge of security, Maison Carrée, 23–24 April 1896, AGGA, 16 H 61.

58. Cecily Mackworth, *The Destiny of Isabelle Eberhardt* (London: Quartet Books, 1977), 157.

59. Fournier, "Notice," 1895, AGGA, 16 H 8.

60. Ibid.; and Nacib, *Cultures*, 240.

61. Fournier, "Notice," 1895, AGGA, 16 H 8.

62. General de Mazieux to the commanding general, 10 October 1899, AGGA, 2 U 22.

63. Fournier, "Notice," 1895, AGGA, 16 H 8.

64. Ibid.; and Gouvian, *Kitab*, 148–51.

65. Fournier, "Notice," 1895, AGGA, 16 H 8.

66. Monot to commanding general, 29 November 1904, AGGA, 2 U 22; and governor-general to commanding general, 20 October 1896, AGGA, 2 U 22; also AGGA, 16 H 8 (1895) and 16 H 8 (1897).

67. Fournier, "Notice," 1895, AGGA, 16 H 8.

68. Fournier, "Notice," 1895, AGGA, 16 H 8; and governor-general to commanding general, 20 October 1896, AGGA, 2 U 22.

69. E. Graulle, *Insurrection de Bou-Amama (avril 1881)* (Paris: H. Charles-Lavauzelle, 1905); and Peter von Sivers, "Secular Anxieties and Religious Righteousness: The Origins of the Insurrection of 1881 in the Nomadic and Sedentary Communities of the Algerian Southwest," *Peuples Méditerranéens* 18 (1982): 145–62.

70. Muhammad b. Abi al-Qasim to Captain Crochard, 10 March 1897, AGGA, 16 H 61; as Nacib, *Cultures*, 255, observes, the language used by the shaykh strongly suggests he was under duress when designating his nephew to succeed him.

71. Women, whether European or indigenous, are notably absent from the enormous literature both colonial and recent on nineteenth-century Algeria. Aside from a few brief references in the literature to extraordinary females—holy, learned women like Zaynab or heroines such as Lalla Fatima, who led the 1854 Kabyle resistance—the history of women in colonial North Africa or in earlier periods constitutes a virtually blank page. There are two recent contributions to the historical literature on women in nineteenth-century Africa: Dalenda Largueche and Abdelhamid Largueche,

Marginales en terre d'Islam (Tunis: Cérès Productions, 1992), which examines, among a number of significant topics, the legends surrounding a female saint, Lalla Manoubia; and Jean Boyd's study of a female religious leader from the Sokoto Caliphate, *The Caliph's Sister, Nana Asma'u, 1793–1865: Teacher, Poet, and Islamic Leader* (London: Frank Cass, 1989).

72. Ann Thomson, *Barbary and Enlightenment: European Attitudes towards the Maghreb in the Eighteenth Century* (Leiden: E. J. Brill, 1987); and Marnia Lazreg, "The Reproduction of Colonial Ideology: The Case of the Kabyle Berbers," *Arab Studies Quarterly* 5, 4 (1983): 380–95.

73. Hubertine Auclert, *Les femmes arabes en Algérie* (Paris: Éditions Littéraires, 1900), 3.

74. Al-Hafnawi, *Ta'rif*, 352. Dabbuz in *Nahda* does not mention Zaynab, although her father and cousin are discussed at length. The lack of information on Zaynab is no mere coincidence. Zaynab's cousin and rival may have had his revenge by excising her from the written record since he composed the history of al-Hamil, *Kitab*.

75. Nacib, *Cultures*, 254, states that she was about forty years old at the time that Isabelle Eberhardt visited her in 1902, which would mean that her date of birth was closer to 1860; if we accept the later date, Zaynab may have been born while the shaykh was in the Ziban at the Rahmaniyya zawiya of the Awlad Jallal. Most French colonial officers from the period, however, estimated that she was about fifty years old at the time of her death in 1904.

76. Commanding general, "Rapport," 1897, AGGA, 16 H 8.

77. Mackworth, *The Destiny*, 157.

78. Guillaumet, *Tableaux*, 121. Seclusion should not, however, be equated necessarily with powerlessness or social marginalization. In 1903–1904, Isabelle Eberhardt resided in the zawiya of Kanadsa, located in the southwestern confines between Morocco and Algeria. There she observed that while the women of the zawiya formed "a little world apart," that world had its own hierarchy which was endowed with certain kinds of power. Moreover, the mother of the zawiya's head shaykh, Sidi Brahim (Ibrahim), "was entirely in charge of its internal administration: expenses, monetary funds, pious offerings. One never sees her but one feels everywhere her power, feared and venerated by all, this old Muslim queen-mother lives here almost cloistered and but rarely leaves (the zawiya), heavily veiled, to visit her spouses' tombs." Isabelle Eberhardt, *Écrits sur le sable*, vol. 1 of *Oeuvres complètes*, annotated and introduced by Marie-Odile Delacour and Jean-René Huleu, preface by Edmonde Charles-Roux (Paris: Bernard Grasset, 1988), 248.

79. Al-Hajj Muhammad, *Kitab*, 60; and Fournier, "Notice," 1895, AGGA, 16 H 8.

80. Helen C. Gordon, *A Woman in the Sahara* (New York: Stokes, 1914), 77.

81. Major Crochard to commanding general, 20 July 1897, AGGA, 2 U 22, says the following: "Those who see her, because she does not fear to show herself, recognize in [Zaynab] the physical traits of her father."

82. Guillaumet, *Tableaux*, 121.

83. The hubus document, dated 31 August 1877, is found in AGGA, 16 H 61, appended to the report dated 3 September 1897.

84. Zaynab to commander of Bu Sa'ada, 29 September 1899, AGGA, 16 H 61.

85. Gouvian, *Kitab*, 205.

86. Depont and Coppolani, *Les confréries*, note 1, 409–10.

87. Ibid.

88. Commanding general, "Rapport," 1897, AGGA, 16 H 8.

89. General Collet Meygret to governor-general, 22 October 1897, AGGA, 16 H 61.

90. General de Mazieux to commanding general, 10 October 1899, AGGA, 2 U 22.

91. Commanding general, "Rapport," 1897, AGGA 16 H 8.

92. Ibid.; and numerous dossiers contained in AGGA, 2 U 22.

93. Commanding general, "Rapport," 1897, AGGA, 16 H 8; and AGGA, 2 U 22.

94. Fournier, "Notice," 1895, AGGA, 16 H 8; Crochard to commanding general, 20 July 1897, AGGA, 2 U 22; and commanding general, appendix to the 1897 "Rapport," 1898, AGGA, 16 H 8. As mentioned above, Muhammad b. Abi al-Qasim had inherited his sufi master's baraka upon Sidi al-Mukhtar's death in 1862. With the passing of Sidi Muhammad in 1897, some argued that the spiritual succession and the baraka should return to the Rahmaniyya zawiya in Awlad Jallal. Indeed, one of Sidi al-Mukhtar's sons, Muhammad al-Saghir, had resided in al-Hamil for a long time. Other Rahmaniyya centers—as well as the Tijaniyya—often followed the practice of alternating succession between two prominent families and zawiyas. Rahmaniyya notables in the pre-Sahara invoked the precedent set by Shaykh Muhammad b. 'Azzuz, who at his death in 1819 passed over his own sons to designate Sidi 'Ali b. 'Umar of Tulqa as his spiritual successor.

95. Julia Clancy-Smith, "The House of Zainab: Female Authority and Saintly Succession in Colonial Algeria, 1850–1904," in *Women in Middle Eastern History: Shifting Boundaries in Sex and Gender*, Nikki R. Keddie and Beth Baron, eds. (New Haven: Yale University Press, 1992), 254–74.

96. Crochard to commandant, cercle of Bu Sa'ada, 20 July 1897, AGGA, 2 U 22.

97. The issue of moral-political "rapprochement" or "control" over Islam and indigenous educational institutions was of grave concern to colonial authorities at the century's end. This is illustrated by two works

published in the 1880s—Ernest Mercier's *L'Algérie et les questions al-gériennes* (Paris: Challamel, 1883) and Gustave Benoist's *De l'instruction et de l'éducation des indigènes dans la province de Constantine* (Paris: Hachette, 1886). Benoist, 3, laments the fact that the goals of "moral rapprochement" and "assimilation" between the "two races" had not been achieved even after half a century of French colonialism. The explanation for this singular failure lies in the works and educational activities of Muslim leaders, like Muhammad b. Abi al-Qasim, whose partial withdrawal into a neutral space permitted the semiautonomous zawaya schools to exist.

98. Commanding general, "Rapport," 1897, AGGA 16 H 8. The dispute was over the body of Sidi Ahmad al-Tijani, who had expired in Gummar, near Tammasin; Sidi Ahmad's brother and successor, Sidi Bashir, backed by the powerful Aurélie Picard, sought to exhume the corpse in the heat of summer and take it back to 'Ain Madi for burial, thereby assuring control over the popular pilgrimages connected with the dead saint.

99. Fournier, "Notice," 1895, AGGA, 16 H 8.

100. General de Mazieux to commanding general, 10 October 1899, AGGA, 2 U 22.

101. Commanding general, "Rapport," 1897, AGGA, 16 H 8.

102. Another element that placed colonial authorities in an awkward position was Zaynab's fragile health. According to local officers, she suffered from a "grave nervous condition" and from "chronic bronchitis." While the first disorder, "une maladie nerveuse," was frequently cited in European medical circles of the period as a typically female pyschosomatic complaint and is thus subject to skepticism, the second was probably due to tuberculosis, which grievously afflicted the Muslim population; Crochard to commander, cercle of Bu Sa'ada, 20 July 1897, AGGA, 2 U 22.

103. Ibid.

104. Abun-Nasr, *Tijaniyya*, 88–89, and AGT, D-156–1, note that colonial efforts to control sufi orders in Tunisia were less successful when females members were concerned. Significantly, the protectorate was able to interfere more massively in the selection of male muqaddams than of female shaykhs of the Rahmaniyya or Tijaniyya brotherhoods. Between 1891, when the first colonial sufi investigation was launched, and 1917— some twenty-seven years—French officials were completely ignorant of the existence of female sufis. Finally in 1917, an investigation revealed that in the Tunis region alone, some eighteen women held authentic *ijazas* (certificates attesting to sufis' worthiness to initiate members in an order) as muqaddamat (female sufi circle leaders) of the Tijaniyya order.

105. Crochard to commanding general, 22 October 1897, AGGA, 16 H 61.

106. Ibid.

107. Ibid.

108. General Moutz to commanding general, 18 September 1897, AGGA, 2 U 22.

109. General Meygret to governor-general, 22 October 1897, AGGA, 16 H 61.

110. Allan Christelow, "Algerian Islam in a Time of Transition, c. 1890–c. 1930," *MR* 8, 5–6 (1983): 124–30.

111. General Meygret to governor-general, 22 October 1897, AGGA, 16 H 61.

112. Ageron, *Les algériens* 1: 478–527; and David Prochaska, *Making Algeria French: Colonialism in Bône, 1870–1920* (Cambridge: Cambridge University Press, 1990), 198–205.

113. General de Mazieux, 10 October 1899, AGGA, 2 U 22.

114. Gouvian, *Kitab*, 207; and "Dossiers de Renseignements," 29 April 1916, AGGA, 2 U 22.

115. Zaynab to commandant, cercle of Bu Sa'ada, 29 September 1899, AGGA, 16 H 61; and AGGA, 2 U 22.

116. Zaynab to commandant, cercle of Bu Sa'ada, 29 September 1899, AGGA, 16 H 61; and AGGA, 2 U 22.

117. Zaynab to commandant, cercle of Bu Sa'ada, 29 September 1899, AGGA, 16 H 61; and AGGA, 2 U 22.

118. Zaynab to commandant, cercle of Bu Sa'ada, 29 September 1899, AGGA, 16 H 61; and AGGA, 2 U 22.

119. Zaynab to commandant, cercle of Bu Sa'ada, 29 September 1899, AGGA, 16 H 61; and AGGA, 2 U 22.

120. Gouvian, *Kitab*, 205–6.

121. De Galland, *Excursions*, 73–74; the Frenchman also noted in the course of his personal interview with Zaynab in her residence that he had time to "examine her face; her eyes were particularly beautiful."

122. General de Mazieux, 10 October 1899, AGGA, 2 U 22.

123. Ibid. One of the many lacunae in our information about Zaynab's spiritual life and activities is the matter of her daily relationship with female members of the Rahmaniyya.

124. Captain Lehureaux, *Bou-Saada, cité du bonheur*, 70, cited by Nacib, *Cultures*, 255.

125. In her provocative study "Rethinking Colonial Categories: European Communities and the Boundaries of Rule," *CSSH* 31, 1 (1989): 134–61, Laura Ann Stoler examines the crucial role of European women in shaping colonial rule. The part that indigenous females played in determining colonial boundaries has, for the most part, not been considered. See also the collection of essays in Nupur Chaudhuri and Margaret Strobel, eds., *Western Women and Imperialism: Complicity and Resistance* (Bloomington: Indiana University Press, 1992).

126. A fuller account of Eberhardt, as well as references to the numerous works devoted to her life and writings, is found in Julia Clancy-

Glossary

āfāqī: In Tunisia, literally those coming from the "horizons" or from the provinces; contrasts with the urbane inhabitants of the capital, Tunis.

ᶜālim: A religious scholar or savant (singular of ulama).

amān: An assurance of protection or clemency; a pardon.

amīn: Chief; head; master of a guild.

amīr/umarāᵓ: Prince, emir, or tribal chief; also governor of a province.

Awlād: Literally, "descendants," "sons." Employed in the plural with the meaning of "the tribe of"; the members of a tribe believed that they shared a common ancestor.

baraka: Supernatural blessings; quality of divine grace; abundance; holiness as an expression of spiritual power.

Bardo: Palace of the Tunisian ruler in the capital; seat of the Bey.

barrānī: Outside; foreign; by extension, the migrant or temporary laborers in Algerian and Tunisian cities.

bey: In Husaynid Tunisia, the reigning princes of the dynasty theoretically ruling in the name of the Ottoman sultan; in Algeria, the beys were provincial governors subordinate to the dey of Algiers.

burj: A fortress, tower, or fortified place.

burnus: A hooded wool cloak worn in the Maghrib.

daftar/dafātir: A notebook, roster, dossier, or file.

daqala al-nūr: A variety of dates prized for their high sugar content.

Dār al-Ḥarb: Land or territory of war; enemy territory.

Dār al-Islām: The abode of Islam; the Islamic world.

dey: In Ottoman Algeria, a title designating the ruler of Algiers, who was theoretically subordinate to the sultan.

dhikr: "Remembrance"; a sufi litany employed in spiritual exercises aimed at invoking God or the Prophet's remembrance.

dīwān: Council; administrative office; chancellery.

fallāḥ: Peasant or farmer.

faqīh: Expert of fiqh; a legist or jurisprudent.

fatwā: An authoritative legal opinion regarding Islamic law.

fiqh: Islamic jurisprudence.

ḥadīth: A Prophetic tradition; narrative relating the deeds and utterances of Muhammad and his Companions.

ḥaᵓik: An outer garment usually made of a long piece of white woolen material and
covering the head and body.

ḥajj: Pilgrimage to Mecca incumbent upon all able Muslims once in their lifetimes.

Haramayn: The two holy cities, Mecca and Medina.

Hijaz: The western region of the Arabian Peninsula where the holy cities of Mecca
and Medina are located.

hijra: Migration for religious purposes; based upon the Prophet's migration from
Mecca to Medina in A.D. 622.

ḥubus: A charitable or religious foundation; property of inalienable legal status
whose revenue serves pious purposes; in the Mashriq, a *waqf*.

ḥurma: holiness; sacred; sacrosanct.

Ibāḍiyya/Ibāḍites: Islamic schismatics of the Khārijite movement; in North Africa
today found mainly in the Algerian Mzab in the deep Sahara.

ibn/banū: Son/sons; in the plural can designate the members of a tribe recognizing
a common ancestor.

iḥsān: Blamelessness, virtue, integrity; by extension piety.

ijāza: A certificate or diploma; written authorization permitting local sufi figures to
initiate members into an order.

ᶜilm: Science; knowledge; learning.

imām: A leader in prayer; leader; master.

ᶜināya: "Providence" or "care"; a guarantee of safe conduct.

jihād: Religious or holy war.

karāma: Miracle worked by a saint.

kātib: A writer, scribe, or secretary.

khalīfa: Caliph; also a deputy of a ruler or a senior official.

khalwa: Retreat or seclusion; place or state of seclusion associated with sufi practices.

khammās: A sharecropper who receives a fifth or some portion of the harvest in
return for labor.

kharja: A ceremonial procession, often of a venerated sufi leader, accompanied by
music and special prayers.

khāṣṣa: The elite; notables; upper class.

khaznadār: State treasurer; keeper of the state's revenues.

khirqa: A ritual garment symbolizing a sufi disciple's obedience to the rule of his
order; the tattered woolen mantle of the sufis worn as a sign of renunciation and
asceticism.

khuṭba: The sermon delivered at the mosque during the Friday noon service.

kibār: Plural of great, old, powerful; by extension, village or tribal elders.

kuttāb: A Quranic school; lowest elementary school.

maddāḥ: A panegyrist or bard; storyteller.

madīḥ: In North Africa, a poem or versified panegyric often recited publicly by the maddāḥ in honor of religious figures or local heroes.

madrasa: A religious school or college, often attached to a mosque.

maḥalla: In Algeria and Tunisia, the annual military expedition by the central government to collect taxes, punish rebellious subjects, and render justice.

mahdī: "Rightly guided"; the mahdi or divinely inspired redeemer who will appear at the end of the world and usher in the millennium.

maḥshasha: A cafe or popular gathering place.

majba: In Tunisia during the Ottoman era, a poll tax.

majlis al-sharī ͨa: An Islamic court or tribunal.

makhzan: A storehouse; by extension the central government.

mamlūk: "Owned" or "possessed." Purchased in the Caucasus or Greece, mamluks in Husaynid Tunisia were employed in high governmental or military service.

maqām: A site; sacred place; tomb of a saint.

Mashriq: The eastern Arab world as opposed to the Maghrib.

mawsim: Season; in North Africa, a rural or tribal fair or celebration, often to honor holy persons.

milk (mulk): Private property.

misbaḥa: Muslim prayer beads or rosary.

muftī: An expert in Islamic law authorized to issue fatwas.

mu ͨjiza: Miraculous powers or miracles usually associated with a prophet or the mahdi.

muqaddam: Administrator or trustee; a sufi representative capable of formally initiating followers into an order.

murābiṭ: Often rendered in French as "marabout"; a holy person, living or dead, believed to enjoy a special relationship with God which enables him or her to transmit blessings or grace from God to the community; roughly, a saint.

murīd: An aspirant, disciple, or sufi novice.

nāʾib: A representative, agent, or deputy.

qabr: A tomb, grave, or sepulcher.

qāḍī: A Muslim judge or magistrate.

qāḍī al-maḥalla: The judge or jurisconsult accompanying the mahalla on its annual tax-collecting expedition.

qādūs: A water clock used to ascertain rights to water in the oases.

qāʾid: Chief or leader; tribal or provincial administrator; also governor.

qaṣba: Fortress or citadel; often the highest point in the city.

qubba: A dome; a domed building or shrine commemorating a saint.

ribāṭ: A fortified monastery.

sabkha: In the Sahara, a salt marsh or saline lake.

ṣaff: A league, alignment, or section; the system of binary political alliances grouping tribes and sometimes villages; in French, *soff*.

safsārī: A very fine white cloak or mantle often of wool and silk.

sharīᶜa: Literally, the "path to be followed"; the holy law of Islam.

sharīf/plural: shurafāᵓ/ashrāf: A descendant or descendants of the Prophet Muhammad or of his lineage; a noble person.

shaṭṭ: In the Sahara, a saline shallow lake or dried sea bed.

shaykh: An elder, chief, head of a tribe, master of a sufi order.

shaykh al-ᶜarab: In eastern Algeria, a government-appointed chieftain or administrator for the oases and tribes.

shaykh al-balad: Village chief; also town mayor.

shaykh al-shuyūkh: Literally, "shaykh of the shaykhs"; the head master of a sufi order.

silsila: A chain; in sufism, a spiritual chain or lineage.

Sūf: A collection of oases in southeastern Algeria near the Tunisian border; al-Awad is the capital of the Suf.

ṣūfī: An Islamic mystic; a member of a mystical order or brotherhood.

Suwāfa: Inhabitants of the region known as the Suf.

sūq: A market, bazaar, or fair.

tadhkira: Permit or license; in Tunisia, an export license.

tajdīd: Religious reform or renewal.

ṭālib: A student or scholar.

tanzimat: Reorganizations; used for Ottoman state-sponsored reforms of the nineteenth century.

taqwā: Piety, devoutness, God-fearing.

ṭarīqa/ṭuruq: Way, path, or method; the sufi way or path to spiritual perfection; a tariqa may be a method of spiritual discipline and mystical devotions or an order or brotherhood.

taṣawwuf: Islamic mysticism or sufism.

tell: In Arabic, tall; a hill or elevation; usually refers to the hills immediately beyond the coastal plain; when used in opposition to Sahara, the fertile rain-fed northern coast of the Maghrib.

ᶜurf: Customary law.

wādī: In North Africa, a valley or riverbed that remains dry except during the rainy season; a stream that flows through such a channel.

walīy/awliyāᵓ: A "friend (or protégé) of God"; a saint or holy person who is close to God.

zamāla: A tribal camp or settlement; also in Turkish North Africa, a tribal cavalry serving or allied with the state.

zāwiya/zawāyā: Literally, a "corner": a religious building enclosing a saint's tomb; a small mosque or prayer room; a sufi center often including a mosque, hospice, and educational facilities.

ziyāra: Visitation to a shrine or saint's tomb; a pious offering made to a saint, sufi, or member of the shurafā'.

Select Bibliography

ARCHIVES AND OTHER COLLECTIONS

Archives de la Chambre de Commerce de Marseille, France
Archives du Gouvernement Tunisien, Dar al-Bey, Tunis, Tunisia
Archives du Ministère de la Guerre, Vincennes, France
Archives du Ministère des Affaires Étrangères, Paris, France
Archives du Ministère des Affaires Étrangères, Archives de la Résidence Générale de France à Tunis, Nantes, Frances
Archives Nationales, Paris, France
Archives Nationales, Section d'Outre-Mer, Aix-en-Provence, France (Archives du Gouvernement Général de l'Algérie)
Bibliothèque Générale (al-Khizana al-'Amma), Rabat, Morocco
Centre des Hautes Études Administratives sur l'Afrique et l'Asie Moderne, Paris, France
National Archives, Washington, D.C.
Public Record Office, Foreign Office Correspondence, Kew, United Kingdom

UNPUBLISHED MANUSCRIPTS

'Abd al-Rahman, Muhammad ibn. "Majmu' min risa'il al-shaykh 'Abd al-Rahman al-Zawawi al-Jaza'iri shaykh al-tariqa al-Rahmaniyya." MS. K 956. al-Khizana al-'Amma, Rabat, Morocco.
Ibn al-Hajj Muhammad, Muhammad. "Kitab al-rawd al-basim fi tarjama al-imam sidi Muhammad ibn Abi al-Qasim." A 80 3165. al-Khizana al-'Amma, Rabat, Morocco.
Salama, Muhammad ibn. "al-'Iqd al-munaddad fi akhbar al-mushir al-basha Ahmad." MS. 18618, folio 82. Bibliothèque Nationale de Tunis, Tunis, Tunisia.

PUBLISHED WORKS

'Abd al-Qadir al Jaza'iri, Muhammad ibn. *Tuhfa al-za'ir fi tarikh al-Jaza'ir wa al-amir 'Abd al-Qadir.* 2d ed., Mamduh Haqqi, ed. Beirut, 1964.

351

'Abd al-Rahman, Muhammad ibn. *al-Rahmaniyya*, trans. by Antoine Giacobetti as *Livre de la Rah'maniya*. Maison-Carrée, 1946.

Abun-Nasr, Jamil M. *The Tijaniyya: A Sufi Order in the Modern World*. London: Oxford University Press, 1965.

———. *A History of the Maghrib in the Islamic Period*. Cambridge: Cambridge University Press, 1987.

Adas, Michael. *Prophets of Rebellion: Millenarian Protest Movements against the European Colonial Order*. Chapel Hill: University of North Carolina Press, 1979.

———. " 'Moral Economy' or 'Contest State'?: Elite Demands and the Origins of Peasant Protest in Southeast Asia." *Journal of Social History* 13, 4 (Summer 1980): 521–46.

———. "From Avoidance to Confrontation: Peasant Protest in Precolonial and Colonial Southeast Asia." *Comparative Studies in Society and History* 23, 2 (1981): 217–47.

———. "Bandits, Monks, and Pretender Kings: Patterns of Peasant Resistance and Protest in Colonial Burma, 1826–1941." In Robert P. Weller and Scott E. Guggenheim, eds., *Power and Protest in the Countryside: Studies of Rural Unrest in Asia, Europe, and Latin America*. Durham, N.C.: Duke University Press, 1982.

———. "Social History and the Revolution in African and Asian Historiography." *Journal of Social History* 19, 2 (Winter 1985): 334–48.

———. "Market Demand versus Imperial Control: Colonial Contradictions and the Origins of Agrarian Protest in South and Southeast Asia." In Edmund Burke III, ed., *Global Crises and Social Movements: Artisans, Peasants, Populists, and the World Economy*. Boulder, Colo.: Westview Press, 1988.

———. *Machines as the Measure of Men: Science, Technology, and Ideologies of Western Dominance*. Ithaca: Cornell University Press, 1989.

Ageron, Charles-Robert. "L'émigration des musulmans algériens et l'éxode de Tlemcen (1830–1911)." *Annales: Économies, Sociétés, Civilisations* 22, 2 (1967): 1047–66.

———. *Les algériens musulmans et la France (1871–1919)*. 2 vols. Paris: Presses Universitaires de France, 1968.

Alloula, Malek. *The Colonial Harem: Images of Subconscious Eroticism*. Myrna and Wlad Godzich, trans. Introduction by Barbara Harlow. Manchester: University of Manchester Press, 1986.

Arrus, René. *L'eau en Algérie, de l'impérialisme au développement (1830–1962)*. Algiers: Office des Publications Universitaires, 1985.

Baduel, Pierre-Robert, ed. *Les prédicateurs profanes: Poésie populaire et résistance au Maghreb. Revue du Monde Musulman et de la Méditerranée* 51 (1989).

Bachrouch, Taoufik. *Le saint et le prince en Tunisie: Les elites tunisiennes du pouvoir et de la devotion, contribution à l'étude des groupes sociaux dominants (1782–1881)*. Tunis: Publications de l'Université de Tunis, 1989.

Bak, Janos M., and Gerhard Benecke, eds. *Religion and Rural Revolt*. Manchester: Manchester University Press, 1984.

Bardin, Pierre. *Algériens et tunisiens dans l'Empire Ottoman de 1848 à 1914*. Paris: Éditions du CNRS, 1979.

Bédoucha, Geneviève. *L'eau, l'amie du puissant: Une communauté oasienne du sud-tunisien.* Paris: Éditions des Archives Contemporaines, 1987.

Berque, Jacques. "Qu'est-ce qu'une 'tribu' nord-africaine." Vol. 1 of *Éventail de l'histoire vivante: Mèlanges à Lucien Fèbvre.* Paris: Colin, 1953.

———. *L'intèrieur du Maghreb, XVe–XIX siècle.* Paris: Gallimard, 1978.

———. *Le Maghreb entre deux guerres.* 3d ed. Paris: Seuil, 1979.

Bourdieu, Pierre. *The Algerians.* Boston: Beacon Press, 1962.

Boyd, Jean. *The Caliph's Sister, Nana Asma'u, 1793–1865: Teacher, Poet and Islamic Leader.* London: Frank Cass, 1989.

Brenner, Louis. *West African Sufi: The Religious Heritage and Spiritual Search of Cerno Bokar Saalif Taal.* Berkeley and Los Angeles: University of California Press, 1984.

Brown, Leon Carl. *The Tunisia of Ahmad Bey, 1837–1855.* Princeton: Princeton University Press, 1974.

Brunschvig, Robert. *La Berbérie orientale sous les Hafsides des origines à la fin du XVe siècle.* 2 vols. Paris: Adrien-Maisonneuve, 1940–1947.

Burke, Edmund, III. *Prelude to Protectorate: Precolonial Protest and Resistance, 1860–1912.* Chicago: University of Chicago Press, 1976.

———. "Recent Books on Colonial Algerian History." In *Middle Eastern Studies* 7, 2 (1971): 241–50.

———, ed. *Global Crises and Social Movements: Artisans, Peasants, Populists, and the World Economy.* Boulder, Colo.: Westview Press, 1988.

———, ed. *Struggle and Survival in the Modern Middle East, 1750–1950.* Berkeley and Los Angeles: University of California Press, 1993.

Burke, Edmund, III, and Ira M. Lapidus, eds. *Islam, Politics, and Social Movements.* Berkeley and Los Angeles: University of California Press, 1988.

Capot-Rey, Robert. *Le Sahara Français.* Paris: Presses Universitaires de France, 1953.

Chater, Khelifa. *Dépendance et mutations précoloniales: La Régence de Tunis de 1815 à 1857.* Tunis: Publications de l'Université de Tunis, 1984.

Chaudhuri, Nupur, and Margaret Strobel, eds. *Western Women and Imperialism: Complicity and Resistance.* Bloomington: Indiana University Press, 1992.

Cherif, Mohamed-Hédi. *Pouvoir et société dans la Tunisie de Husayn bin 'Ali (1705–1740).* 2 vols. Tunis: Publications de l'Université de Tunis, 1984–1986.

Christelow, Allan. "Algerian Islam in a Time of Transition, c. 1890–c. 1930." *Maghreb Review* 8, 5–6 (1983): 124–30.

———. *Muslim Law Courts and the French Colonial State in Algeria.* Princeton: Princeton University Press, 1985.

———. "Oral, Manuscript, and Printed Expressions of Historical Consciousness in Colonial Algeria." *Africana Journal* 15 (1990): 258–75

Clancy-Smith, Julia. "Saints, Mahdis, and Arms: Religion and Resistance in Nineteenth-Century North Africa." In Edmund Burke III and Ira M. Lapidus, eds., *Islam, Politics, and Social Movements.* Berkeley and Los Angeles: University of California Press, 1988.

———. "In the Eye of the Beholder: Sufi and Saint in North Africa and the Colonial Production of Knowledge, 1830–1900." *Africana Journal* 15 (1990): 220–57.

———. "The House of Zainab: Female Authority and Saintly Succession in Colonial Algeria, 1850–1904." In Nikki R. Keddie and Beth Baron, eds., *Women in Middle Eastern History: Shifting Boundaries in Sex and Gender*. New Haven: Yale University Press, 1992.

———. "The 'Passionate Nomad' Reconsidered: A European Woman in *L'Algérie Française* (Isabelle Eberhardt, 1877–1904)." In Nupur Chaudhuri and Margaret Strobel, eds., *Western Women and Imperialism: Complicity and Resistance*. Bloomington: University of Indiana Press, 1992.

Cohn, Norman. *The Pursuit of the Millennium: Revolutionary Millenarians and Mystical Anarchists of the Middle Ages*. Rev. ed. New York: Oxford University Press, 1970.

Colonna, Fanny. "Saints furieux et saints studieux ou, dans l'Aurès, comment la religion vient aux tribus." *Annales, Économies, Sociétés, Civilisations* 35, 3–4 (1980): 642–62.

———. "Présence des ordres mystiques dans l'Aurès aux XIXe et XXe siècles: Contribution à une histoire sociale des forces religieuses en Algérie." In Alexandre Popovic and Gilles Veinstein, eds., *Les ordres mystiques dans l'Islam: Cheminements et situation actuelle*. Paris: Éditions de l'École des Hautes Études en Sciences Sociales, 1986.

———. "The Transformation of a Saintly Lineage in the Northwest Aurès Mountains (Algeria): Nineteenth and Twentieth Centuries." In Edmund Burke III and Ira M. Lapidus, eds., *Islam, Politics, and Social Movements*. Berkeley and Los Angeles: University of California Press, 1988.

Connaissances du Maghreb: Sciences sociales et colonisation. Paris: Éditions du CNRS, 1984.

Cruise O'Brien, Donal B., and Christian Coulon, eds. *Charisma and Brotherhood in African Islam*. Oxford: Clarendon Press, 1988.

Crummey, Donald, ed. *Banditry, Rebellion, and Social Protest in Africa*. Portsmouth, N.H.: Heinemann, 1986.

Curtin, Philip D. *Death by Migration: Europe's Encounter with the Tropical World in the Nineteenth Century*. Cambridge: Cambridge University Press, 1989.

Dabbuz, Muhammad 'Ali. *Nahda al-Jaza'ir al-haditha wa thawratuha al-mubaraka*. Algiers: Imprimerie Cooperative, 1965.

al-Dajani, Ahmad S. *al-Haraka al-Sanusiyya*. Beirut: Dar Lubnan, 1967.

Dakhlia, Jocelyne. *L'oubli de la cité: La mémoire collective à l'épreuve du lignage dans le Jérid tunisien*. Paris: Éditions la Découverte, 1990.

Danziger, Raphael. *Abd al-Qadir and the Algerians: Resistance to the French and Internal Consolidation*. New York: Holmes and Meier, 1977.

Déjeux, Jean. *La poésie algérienne de 1830 à nos jours (approches socio-historiques)*. 2d ed. Paris: Éditions Publisud, 1982.

Depont, Octave, and Xavier Coppolani. *Les confréries religieuses musulmanes*. Algiers: Jourdan, 1897.

Dirks, Nicholas, ed. *Colonialism and Culture*. Ann Arbor: University of Michigan Press, 1992.

al-Diyaf, Ahmad ibn Abi. *Ithaf ahl al-zaman bi-akhbar muluk Tunis wa 'ahd al-aman*. 8 vols. Tunis: al-Dar al-Tunisiyya lil-Nashr, 1963–1966.

Dunn, Ross E. *Resistance in the Desert: Moroccan Responses to French Imperialism, 1881–1912*. Madison: University of Wisconsin Press, 1977.

————. "Bu Himara's European Connexion: The Commercial Relations of a Moroccan Warlord." *Journal of African History* 21, 2 (1980): 235–53.

————. "The Bu Himara Rebellion in Northeast Morocco: Phase I." *Middle Eastern Studies* 17, 1 (1981): 31–48.

Duveyrier, Henri. *Sahara algérien et tunisien: Journal de route.* Paris: Challamel, 1905.

Duvignaud, Jean. *Chebika, suivi de retour à Chebika 1990.* Paris: Plon, 1991.

Eberhardt, Isabelle. *Écrits sur le sable.* Vol. 1 of *Oeuvres complètes.* Annotated and introduced by Marie-Odile Delacour and Jean-René Huleu. Preface by Edmonde Charles-Roux. Paris: Bernard Grasset, 1988.

Eickelman, Dale F. *Moroccan Islam: Tradition and Society in a Pilgrimage Center.* Austin: University of Texas Press, 1976.

————. *Knowledge and Power in Morocco: The Education of a Twentieth-Century Notable.* Princeton: Princeton University Press, 1985.

Eickelman, Dale F., and James Piscatori, eds. *Muslim Travellers: Pilgrimage, Migration, and the Religious Imagination.* Berkeley and Los Angeles: University of California Press, 1990.

Elboudrari, Hassan. "Quand les saints font les villes: Lecture anthropologique de la pratique sociale d'un saint marocain du XVIIe siècle." *Annales: Économies, Sociétés, Civilisations* 40, 3 (1985): 489–508.

Establet, Colette. *Etre caid dans l'Algérie coloniale.* Paris: Éditions du CNRS, 1991.

Féraud, L. Charles. "Notes historiques sur la province de Constantine: Les Ben-Djellab, sultans de Touggourt." *Revue Africaine* 23–31 (1879–1887).

Gallagher, Nancy E. *Medicine and Power in Tunisia, 1780–1900.* Cambridge: Cambridge University Press, 1983.

de Galland, Charles. *Excursions à Bou-Saada et M'Sila.* Paris: Ollendorff, 1899.

Ganiage, Jean. *Les origines du protectorat français en Tunisie (1861–1881).* Paris: Presses Universitaires de France, 1959.

Garcia-Arenal, Mercedes. "La conjunction du sufisme et sharifisme au Maroc: Le mahdi comme sauveur." *Revue du Monde Musulman et de la Méditerranée* 55–56 (1990): 233–56.

Geertz, Clifford. *Meaning and Order in Moroccan Society.* Cambridge: Cambridge University Press, 1979.

Gellner, Ernest. *Muslim Society.* Cambridge: Cambridge University Press, 1981.

Gellner, Ernest, and Jean-Claude Vatin, eds. *Islam et politique au Maghreb.* Paris: Éditions du CNRS, 1981.

Ghrab, Said. "al-Tariqa al-Rahmaniyya: ta'rif mujaz." *Revue de l'Institut des Belles Lettres Arabes* 54, 167 (1991): 95–108.

Goody, Jack. *The Interface between the Written and the Oral.* Cambridge: Cambridge University Press, 1987.

Gouvian, Marthe, and Edmond Gouvian. *Kitab aayane al-marhariba.* Algiers: Imprimerie Orientale, 1920.

Green, Arnold H. *The Tunisian Ulama, 1873–1915: Social Structure and Response to Ideological Currents.* Leiden: E. J. Brill, 1978.

al-Hafnawi, Muhammad. *Ta'rif al-khalaf bi-rijal al-saluf.* 2d ed. Tunis: al-Maktaba al-'Atiqa, 1982.

Hart, David M. *Banditry in Islam: Case Studies from Morocco, Algeria, and the Pakistan North West Frontier.* Wisbech, England: Menas Press, 1987.

Headrick, Daniel R. *The Tools of Empire: Technology and European Imperialism in the Nineteenth Century.* New York: Oxford University Press, 1981.

Heggoy, Alf A. *The French Conquest of Algiers, 1830: An Algerian Oral Tradition.* Athens: Center for International Studies, Ohio University, 1986.

Henia, Abdelhamid. *Le Grid, ses rapports avec le Beylik de Tunis (1676–1840).* Tunis: Publications de l'Université de Tunis, 1980.

Herbillon, Emile. *Insurrection survenue dans le sud de la province de Constantine en 1849. Relation du siège de Zaatcha.* Paris: Librarie Militaire, 1863.

Hobsbawm, Eric, and Terence Ranger, eds. *The Invention of Tradition.* Cambridge: Cambridge University Press, 1983.

Ibn 'Ashur, Muhammad. *Tarajim al-a'lam.* Tunis: Maison Tunisienne de l'Édition, 1970.

Ibn Khaldun. *The Muqaddimah: An Introduction to History.* Franz Rosenthal, trans. and ed. 2d ed. 3 vols. Princeton: Princeton University Press, 1967.

Julien, Charles-André. *La conquête et les débuts de la colonisation (1827–1871).* Vol. 1 of *Histoire de l'Algérie contemporaine.* 2d ed. Paris: Presses Universitaires de France, 1979.

Keddie, Nikki R., ed. *Scholars, Saints, and Sufis: Muslim Religious Institutions since 1500.* Berkeley and Los Angeles: University of California Press, 1972.

Khoury, Philip S., and Joseph Kostiner, eds. *Tribes and State Formation in the Middle East.* Berkeley and Los Angeles: University of California Press, 1990.

Lakhdhar, Latifa. *Al-Islam al-Turuqi (l'Islam confrérique).* Tunis: Cérès, 1993.

Largueche, Abdelhamid. *L'abolition de l'esclavage en Tunisie à travers les archives, 1841–1846.* Tunis: Alif, 1990.

Lethielleux, Jean. *Ouargla, cité saharienne: Des origines au début du XXe siècle.* Paris: Paul Geuthner, 1983.

Lifchez, Raymond, ed. *The Dervish Lodge: Architecture, Art, and Sufism in Ottoman Turkey.* Berkeley and Los Angeles: University of California Press, 1992.

Lincoln, Bruce, ed. *Religion, Rebellion, and Revolution: An Interdisciplinary and Cross-Cultural Collection of Essays.* New York: Macmillan, 1985.

Louis, William Roger, ed. *Imperialism: The Robinson and Gallagher Controversy.* New York: New Viewpoints, 1976.

al-Madani, Ahmad Tawfiq. *Hayah kifah (mudhakkirat).* 2 vols. Algiers: Société Nationale d'Edition et de la Diffusion, 1976–1977.

Martel, André. *Les confins saharo-tripolitains de la Tunisie (1811–1911).* 2 vols. Paris: Presses Universitaires de France, 1965.

Martin, Bradford G. *Muslim Brotherhoods in Nineteenth-Century Africa.* Cambridge: Cambridge University Press, 1976.

Nacib, Youssef. *Cultures oasiennes: Essai d'histoire sociale de l'oasis de Bou-Saada.* Paris: Éditions Publisud, 1986.

Nadir, Ahmed. "Les ordres religieux et la conquête française (1830–1851)." *Revue Algérienne des Sciences Juridiques, Économiques et Politiques* 9, 4 (1972): 819–72.

———. "La fortune d'un ordre religieux algérien vers la fin du XIXe siècle." *Le Mouvement Social* 89 (1974): 59–84.

Nouschi, André. *Enquête sur le niveau de vie des populations rurales constantinoises de la conquête jusqu'en 1919.* Paris: Presses Universitaires de France, 1961.

O'Fahey, R. S. *Enigmatic Saint: Ahmad ibn Idris and the Idrisi Tradition.* Evanston, Ill.: Northwestern University Press, 1990.

Perkins, Kenneth J. *Qaids, Captains, and Colons: French Military Administration in the Colonial Maghrib, 1844–1934.* New York: Africana, 1981.

Perret, Eugène. *Récits algériennes.* 2 vols. Paris: Bloud et Barral, 1886–1887.

Prochaska, David. *Making Algeria French: Colonialism in Bône, 1870–1920.* Cambridge: Cambridge University Press, 1990.

Raymond, André. "Les caractéristiques d'une ville arabe 'moyenne' au XVIIIe siècle: Le cas de Constantine." *Revue de l'Occident Musulman et de la Méditerranée* 44, 2 (1987): 134–47.

Richard, Charles. *Étude sur l'insurrection du Dahra (1845–1846).* Algiers: Besancenez, 1846.

Rinn, Louis. *Marabouts et khouan: Étude sur l'Islam en Algérie.* Algiers: Jourdan, 1884.

———. *Histoire de l'insurrection de 1871 en Algérie.* Algiers: Jourdan, 1891.

Robinson, David. *The Holy War of Umar Tal: The Western Sudan in the Mid-Nineteenth Century.* Oxford: Clarendon Press, 1985.

Ruedy, John. *Land Policy in Colonial Algeria: The Origins of the Rural Public Domain.* Berkeley and Los Angeles: University of California Press, 1967.

———. *Modern Algeria: The Origins and Development of a Nation.* Bloomington: Indiana University Press, 1992.

Rouvillois-Brigol, Madeleine. *Le pays de Ouargla (Sahara Algérien): Variations et organisation d'un espace rural en milieu désertique.* Paris: Publications du Département de Géographie de l'Université de Paris–Sorbonne, 1975.

Sa'adallah, Abu al-Qasim. *Tarikh al-Jaza'ir al-thaqafi.* 2d ed. Algiers: SNED, 1981.

———. *La montée du nationalisme algérien (1900–1930).* 2d ed., trans from the English by Nevine Fawzy-Hemiry. Algiers: Entreprise Nationale du Livre, 1985.

Sainte-Marie, A. "Aspects du colportage à partir de la Kabylie du Djurdjura à l'époque contemporaine." In *Commerce de gros, commerce de détail dans les pays méditerranéens (XVI–XIXe siècles).* André Nouschi and Maurice Aymard, eds. Nice: Université de Nice, 1976, 103–19.

Scott, James C. *The Moral Economy of the Peasant: Rebellion and Subsistence in Southeast Asia.* New Haven: Yale University Press, 1976.

———. *Weapons of the Weak: Everyday Forms of Peasant Resistance.* New Haven: Yale University Press, 1985.

———. *Domination and the Arts of Resistance: Hidden Transcripts.* New Haven: Yale University Press, 1990.

Sharpe, Jenny. *Allegories of Empire: The Figure of Woman in the Colonial Text.* Minneapolis: University of Minnesota Press, 1993.

Simian, Marcel. *Les confréries islamiques en Algérie (Rahmanya-Tidjanya).* Algiers: Jourdan, 1910.

von Sivers, Peter. "The Realm of Justice: Apocalyptic Revolts in Algeria (1849–1879)." *Humaniora Islamica* 1 (1973): 47–60.

———. "Insurrection and Accommodation: Indigenous Leadership in Eastern Algeria, 1840–1900." *International Journal of Middle East Studies* 6, 3 (1975): 259–75.

Stoler, Laura Ann. "Rethinking Colonial Categories: European Communities and the Boundaries of Rule." *Comparative Studies in Society and History* 31, 1 (1989): 134–61.

Temimi, Abdeljelil. *Le beylik de Constantine et hadj Ahmed Bey (1830–1837).* Vol. 1. Tunis: Publications de la Revue d'Histoire Maghrébine, 1978.

Thomson, Ann. *Barbary and Enlightenment: European Attitudes towards the Maghreb in the Eighteenth Century.* Leiden: E. J. Brill, 1987.

Tilly, Charles. *From Mobilization to Revolution.* Reading, Mass.: Addison-Wesley, 1978.

———. *The Contentious French.* Cambridge, Mass.: Belknap Press, 1986.

Tilly, Louise, and Charles Tilly, eds. *Class Conflict and Collective Action.* Beverly Hills: Sage Publications, 1981.

Touati, Houari. "Approche sémiologique et historique d'un document hagiographique algérien." *Annales: Économies, Sociétés, Civilisations* 44, 5 (1989): 1205–28.

Turin, Yvonne. *Affrontements culturels dans l'Algérie coloniale: Écoles, médecines, religion, 1830–1880.* Paris: Maspéro, 1971.

Turner, Victor. *Dramas, Fields, and Metaphors: Symbolic Action in Human Society.* Ithaca: Cornell University Press, 1974.

Valensi, Lucette. "Calamités démographiques en Tunisie et en Méditerranée orientale aux XVIIIe et XIXe siècles." *Annales: Économies, Sociétés, Civilisations* 24, 6 (1969): 1540–62.

———. *Le Maghreb avant la prise d'Alger.* Paris: Flammarion, 1969.

———. *Fellahs tunisiens: L'économie rurale et la vie des campagnes aux 18e et 19e siècles.* Paris: Mouton, 1977.

Weller, Robert P., and Scott E. Guggenheim, eds. *Power and Protest in the Countryside: Studies of Rural Unrest in Asia, Europe, and Latin America.* Durham, N.C.: Duke University Press, 1982.

Wilson, Stephen, ed. *Saints and Their Cults: Studies in Religious Sociology, Folklore, and History.* Cambridge: Cambridge University Press, 1984.

Wolf, Eric R. *Europe and the People without History.* Berkeley and Los Angeles: University of California Press, 1982.

Index

'Abd al-Hafiz, b. Muhammad:
joins the Rahmaniyya order, 55–
56; makes pilgrimage, 48; sup-
ports Bu Ziyan, 111–14; voluntary
exile and death of, 118; widening
influence of, 57; withdrawal by,
83–84

'Abd Allah, Muhammad b. (sharif of
Warqala): background and rise to
power, 177–80; betrayed by Sidi
Hamza, 190; capture and death of,
210; consolidates power, 183–85;
khalwa and declared jihad of, 181–
83; lasting memory as Sharif of
Warqala, 211; provisions for
forces of, 172–73; as rebellion
leader, 3, 95–96; rebuilds rebellion
movement, 206; surrenders to
French, 208; Tissot's report on
support for, 151–52; zawiya asylum during revolt of, 144. *See
also* Jihad (Sharif of Warqala's)

'Abd Allah Zabbushi, 67

'Abd al-Qadir, Amir: alliance against
French by, 76; influence of acquiescence by, 85; network of informants of, 8; rebellion movement
of, 71–72; surrenders to French,
88

'Abd al-Rahman, Muhammad b.: becomes heroic cult figure, 44; influence of, 7, 59; Rahmaniyya teachings spread, 42–43

Accommodation: asylum granted to
Major Pelisse as, 82–83; by desert
tribes, 84–85; to maintain cultural
survival, 262–64; by notables, 83–
84. *See also* Populist protest

L'Admiral, Maurice, 240

Al-Aghwati, Sidi, 90–91, 177

Agriculture: cash-crop oasis, 16–17;
connection between popular protest and, 162, 209; under protection of al-Hamil zawiya, 221; the
Suf's trading enterprises in, 199–
200. *See also* Date-palm gardens;
Economic structures

"Ahl Tulqa" league, 79–80

Ahmad Bey of the Constantine: capture of, 88–89; orders palm trees
cut, 74; territorial struggles of,
72–73, 75

Ahmad Bey of Tunisia: Bu Ziyan
appeals to, 112; French protests
to, 148–149; protects Algerian
émigrés from French, 205; reforms of, 157–59; relationship
with Sidi Mustafa, 141; rumored
supporter of sharif of Warqala,
184; strength of army of, 205;
symbolism of state visit by, 99

Ahmad Zarruq, 146–48

359

Compositor: Braun-Brumfield, Inc.
Text: 10/13 Aldus
Display: Aldus
Printer and binder: Braun-Brumfield, Inc.